Female and Male in West Africa

Female and Male in West Africa

Edited by

CHRISTINE OPPONG

*Sometime Senior Research Fellow, Institute of African Studies,
University of Ghana*

London
GEORGE ALLEN & UNWIN
Boston   Sydney

George Allen & Unwin (Publishers) Ltd,
40 Museum Street, London WC1A 1LU, UK

George Allen & Unwin (Publishers) Ltd,
Park Lane, Hemel Hempstead, Herts HP2 4TE, UK

Allen & Unwin, Inc.,
9 Winchester Terrace, Winchester, Mass. 01890, USA

George Allen & Unwin Australia Pty Ltd,
8 Napier Street, North Sydney, NSW 2060, Australia

First published in 1983.

British Library Cataloguing in Publication Data

Female and male in West Africa.
　1. Sex role
I. Oppong, Christine
305.3′0966　　GN479.65
ISBN 0-04-3011586
ISBN 0-04-3011594 Pbk

Library of Congress Cataloging in Publication Data

Main entry under title:
　Female and male in West Africa.
Bibliography: p
Includes index.
1. Interpersonal relations—Africa, West—Addresses,
essays, lectures. 2. Sex discrimination—Africa, West—
Addresses, essays, lectures. 3. Africa, West—Social
conditions—Addresses, essays, lectures. 4. Marriage—
Africa, West—Addresses, essays, lectures. I. Oppong,
Christine.
HM132.F45 1983　　305.3′0966　　82–20767
ISBN 0–04–301158–6
ISBN 0–04–301159–4 (pbk.)

Set in 10 on 11 point Times by Preface Ltd., Salisbury, Wilts.
and printed in Great Britain by Mackays of Chatham

For Meyer with respect and love

'it must not be forgotten that there is no known society in which the interdependence and complementarity of the sexes is not embodied in custom and sanctioned by law and morality. To consider the status of either sex without reference to the other, is to distort the reality we are trying to understand.'

(Fortes, 1980, p. 363)

Contents

List of Tables

List of Figures

Preface

There has been a growing interest in sex roles in recent literature in
the social sciences, especially in that focusing upon questions related
to employment and population issues and the relevance to these of
various facets of female–male relationships, especially within the
contexts of the home and workplace. There has also been an increasing recognition of the significance of cultural variation and differences in these spheres, even among social scientists from those disciplines which have not usually been noted for their cross-cultural
insights or comparative perspectives. Indeed, students and scholars in
a range of disciplines, as well as policy-makers and administrators
concerned with economic development, demographic change, family
welfare and planning, and political issues of poverty, inequality and
sexism, have increasingly begun to recognise the fact that an understanding of many current problems, and the ability to devise designs
for effective modes of solving them, require a firm grounding in the
comprehension of the relevant ethnographic facts and cultural processes, including those within the domestic domain – normally hidden
facts relating to everyday activities and concerning such mundane
processes as resource allocation, work-sharing and delegation on the
farm and in the home and office or factory, and modes of interaction
between spouses, sexual partners, colleagues, parents and children,
neighbours and kin, female and male.

Regrettably, in the recent deluge of writing about sex roles, in particular women's roles, more attention has been given to the legal,
political and formal dimensions of women's positions than to how
informal relationships between the sexes and their activities and
expectations are changing, partly, of course, because of the relative
lack of the required ethnographic facts. This volume is relevant to
these concerns, for a major goal is to document and increase the
understanding of the complexities and subtleties of the modes of
interaction between men and women in one region of the world and
some of the contrasts and differences in their behaviour and expectations. This is a region noted for its generally high fertility and the
energy and productivity and autonomy of many of its women as well
as men; a region in which there has been a considerable amount of
social anthropological and demographic research over the past fifty
years and in which the characteristic features of certain types of peasant modes of production and systems of kinship and marriage have
been documented with the greatest sophistication and detail. At the
same time it is a region with a rich variety of cultural contexts within

which female and male roles are played; with a range of traditional forms of kinship and marriage and of modes of parenting; and with a variety of traditional and modern economic contexts. It is also a region of contrasting historical experiences, subject over time to diverse political and economic influences, which have left their imprint upon educational, legal, political and economic institutions and in which the effects of urbanisation and industrialisation have begun to make their marks.

Thus the ethnographic data on which most of the chapters in this volume are based are richly varied. The contributions focus on the changing relationships between women and men in the domestic and wider social spheres; on marriage and refusal to marry; on sexuality, fertility and parenthood; on the relationships of female and male kin within their kin groupings and domestic settings, within lineage organisations, farms and factories, on the seashore in fishing villages, in the market place and in the community at large and the traditional and modern polities. Some also deal with the contrasts of life experiences of women and men – their different opportunities and resources, and susceptibility to migrate and seek and find employment outside the home; with their different childhood rearing experiences and, in later life, the different tasks they are trained to perform and their different rates of life expectancy.

Recurring themes of major concern are the two interlinked spheres of life within which women's and men's major activities are focused in the closest and frequently most enduring ways: in the begetting, bearing and rearing of children; and in the division of tasks and responsibilities, including domestic work and management, agricultural production and activities in the areas of formal and informal employment; that is, in the spheres of reproduction and production.

Several of the chapters portray some of the ways in which women of the twentieth-century world have had less access than men to important new resources, such as modern education and employment opportunities, thus leading to the tendency in some cases for women to depend to an increasing extent upon the men in their lives for financial and social support.

Conflict is a theme of some of the chapters – both latent and manifest – including conflicts between individuals, who because of their different sex roles have contrasting interests which are sometimes in conflict and in which jealousy may figure prominently in relationships of love and marriage, especially in cultural contexts in which polygyny and monandry continue to be the prevalent norms.

Section I gives the reader a comparative overview of the main economic and demographic features of the West African region, showing the relative mobility of the population and the different propensity of women and men to migrate from rural to rural or rural to urban areas, and to different countries. At the same time it demonstrates in profile the high levels of productive work of both women and men. Diversity and change are highlighted – geographical, cultural, religious and ethnic diversity and changing patterns of economic and demographic behaviour.

The map of the region on pp. xx–xxi shows the countries of the area, on which are identified the places described in the chapters that follow.

With the aim of interweaving certain sets of facts and themes, the volume has been divided into several interrelated parts. Thus, following the preliminary introductory section of comparative essays, which provide a statistical framework, the first set of case studies (Part Two) all in some sense are concerned with the theme of traditional separation and connectedness of female and male spheres of artistic expression, power, language, ideology, space and resources.

The next set of case studies (Part Three) all focus on aspects of daily productive and reproductive activities and show ways in which men and women co-operate and come into inevitable conflicts, as they act together in the processes of begetting, bearing and rearing children and earning a livelihood.

Part Four is concerned with relative resources and supports in modern urban and industrial contexts. Evidence is apparent of male biases which have been increased, if not caused, during recent social changes.

In Part Five the themes are individualism, autonomy and dependence. The increased individualism resulting from migration and the scattering of kin and breakdown of the co-operative work patterns of spouses and relatives is seen as leading to instances of increased dependence or growing autonomy for women, according to whether they have access to needed resources in the modern world.

Throughout the series of twenty-two case studies, all based upon recent ethnographic fieldwork in rural and urban contexts in West African countries, we see examples of the general points made in the introductory comparative chapters. We are, for instance, given diverse examples of mothers coping with the care and maintenance of large numbers of offspring, through their productive efforts in domestic and non-domestic settings. We see the effects of pervasive polygynous norms upon conjugal and kin relations and the effects of unequal access to resources for women and men upon their personal relationships.

Workers from many contexts are described: farmers, fishermen and fishmongers, traders, factory and office workers, rich and poor, from many different ethnic groups and several countries.

In putting together this volume we have sought to avoid a currently pervasive neo-sexist trap: the study of women, by women, for women! We have sought rather to assemble male and female accounts and observations of female and male relationships and activities, and to examine the processes of co-operation and complementarity, separation and conflict, communication and coercion – the sexual dynamic.

Christine Oppong
Legon

Acknowledgements

This volume of essays has involved a protracted and combined effort of patient and diligent authors, critical readers, editor and supportive and wise publisher. It was undertaken initially in the belief that these ethnographic facts and analyses of relationships and contrasts between women and men in different cultures of West Africa would be of great interest to people, both in the region and abroad, in many walks of life, including lay women and men, students, researchers, and administrators of several kinds.

The idea of producing this book would never have been conceived without the judicious interventions long ago of Kwame Wadie Oppong. The gestation period lasted many months and several friends, colleagues, former students and kin played an important role in its development and completion. These include especially Manga Bekombo Priso; Katie Abu, who together with Michael Houseman kindly assisted with translation; Amma Kyerewaa Oppong, who helped to compose the bibliography and other things; and last but by no means least, Kofi Wadie and Nana Yaa Pokuaa Afriyie, who provided some of the important incentives.

This work is dedicated with great respect and love to Meyer Fortes, who has had such a profound and reverberating effect upon ethnographic studies and social demography in the region, both through his own inspiring and monumental pioneering works among the Tallensi and Akan, and through his singular personal influence as a mentor and friend.

Finally, this volume would never have reached print without the clever and kind encouragement and sound advice of our publisher, Keith Ashfield, who helped to wield the painful but necessary editorial rapier.

List of Contributors

JEANNE BISILLIAT is an anthropologist who has worked extensively in Niger and Ivory Coast and other areas of the Sahel. She is currently working on a United Nations socio-demographic study in Upper Volta.

HELEN WARE is a sociologist/demographer who has for some time been based at the Demography Department of the Research School of Social Sciences of the Australian National University, Canberra. She has done considerable research in West Africa and has travelled extensively in the region.

KAMENE OKONJO is at the University of Nigeria, Nsukka. She has published several papers on the changing roles of Nigerian women.

KWAME ARHIN is Professor of African Studies at the University of Ghana, Legon. He has done extensive research in various aspects of Ghana's history, economy and culture.

WAMBUI WA KARANJA lectures at the University of Lagos in the Sociology Department. She has recently been a visiting scholar at Oxford University, where she has been writing up materials on the roles and status of Nigerian women.

DOROTHY DEE VELLENGA teaches in the Department of Sociology and Anthropology, Muskingen College, New Concord, Ohio. She has published a number of writings based on her Ghanaian fieldwork experiences.

LYNNE BRYDON teaches in the Sociology Department of the University of Liverpool. She has written a number of papers based on her ethnographic work among the Avatime of Ghana.

SJAAK VAN DER GEEST has carried out extensive ethnographic work in Ghana and Cameroun and has published a series of books and papers on a wide range of issues. He currently teaches anthropology in Amsterdam.

GEORGE PANYIN HAGAN is a senior research fellow at the Institute of African Studies, University of Ghana, Legon. He has carried out ethnographic research in Ghana on a wide range of topics, including Akan philosophy, the fishing industry, and domestic organisation in Winneba.

KATHARINE ABU has carried out fieldwork in Ghana and for some time worked as a research officer with the Ghana National Council on Women and Development. Much of her work to date has focused upon the changing roles of women.

CARMEL DINAN teaches sociology in Dublin. She has considerable ethnographic experience of Accra and has published several papers highlighting changes in women's roles.

MARGARET PEIL is Reader in Sociology in the University of Birmingham. She has long and wide experience of survey research in several countries of West Africa and has written various books and numerous articles on a range of issues including urbanisation, education and industrialisation.

ADERANTE ADEPOJU teaches and researches in demography at the University of Ife. He has published widely on migration and related topics.

ELEANOR R. FAPOHUNDA is in the Economics Department of the

University of Lagos. She has done fieldwork and published on a number of topics relating to change at the micro and macro level in Nigeria's economy.

SIMON OTTENBERG is Professor in the Department of Anthropology of the University of Washington, Seattle. He has long and varied fieldwork experience in several countries of West Africa and has published a number of well-known monographs and texts on a range of subjects.

ENID SCHILDKROUT is an assistant curator at the Museum of Natural History, New York. She has carried out fieldwork in several urban contexts in West Africa and has written a book and numerous papers on several topics, including Kumasi zongo, urban fostering and child labour in Kano.

The late EMILE VERCRUIJSSE was at the Institute of Social Studies, The Hague. He had several years of research experience in a variety of settings and for some time was a researcher with the Centre for Development Studies of the University of Cape Coast, Ghana.

CAROL MARTIN has recently been involved in policy-related research in education in Bauchi State, Nigeria. She is based at the Center for International Education at the University of Massachusetts, Amherst.

CHRISTINE OKALI worked at the University of Ghana, Legon, as a research fellow in the Cocoa Economics Research Unit (1970–6). Since 1976 she has continued her work in agriculture, in Nigeria, among food crop farmers and livestock producers. She is currently working for the International Livestock Centre for Africa in Ibadan, Nigeria.

EUGENIA DATE-BAH has undertaken surveys among several sectors of the Ghanaian population. She was a senior lecturer at the University of Ghana in the Sociology Department and is currently working as a programme officer with the International Labour Organisation.

CATHERINE M. DI DOMENICO teaches in the Sociology Department of the University of Ibadan. She has carried out a number of studies of industrial workers in the city and its environs and has published several papers on her findings.

CHRISTINE OPPONG has carried out research at the Institute of African Studies, University of Ghana, for a number of years mainly focusing on changes in family relations, and has written and edited several books and numerous papers. She is currently a research officer with the International Labour Organisation.

ROGER SANJEK teaches anthropology at Queens College, City University of New York. He has carried out ethnographic fieldwork in Accra and written numerous papers based upon his findings.

MONA ETIENNE has done fieldwork in Ivory Coast. She has published a number of works on a variety of themes including child fostering and women's changing roles.

LAWRENCE A. ADEOKUN is a senior lecturer in the Department of Demography and Social Statistics, University of Ife, Ile-Ife, Nigeria. His chapter was prepared whilst he was Cadbury Visiting Fellow at the Centre of West African Studies of the University of Birmingham, England.

NIMROD ASANTE-DARKO is employed in the Ghanaian Civil Service. He studied linguistics and public administration.

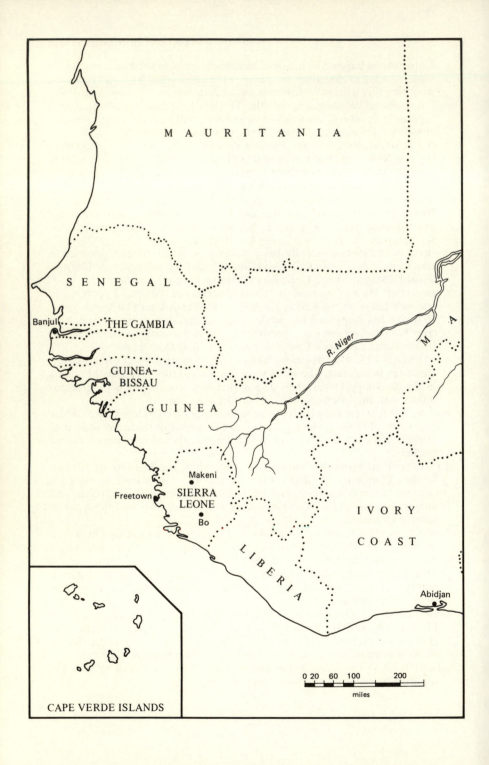

MAURITANIA

SENEGAL

Banjul   THE GAMBIA

GUINEA-
BISSAU

GUINEA

R. Niger

M A

Makeni

Freetown   SIERRA
LEONE

Bo

LIBERIA

IVORY

COAST

Abidjan

0 20 60 100   200
miles

CAPE VERDE ISLANDS

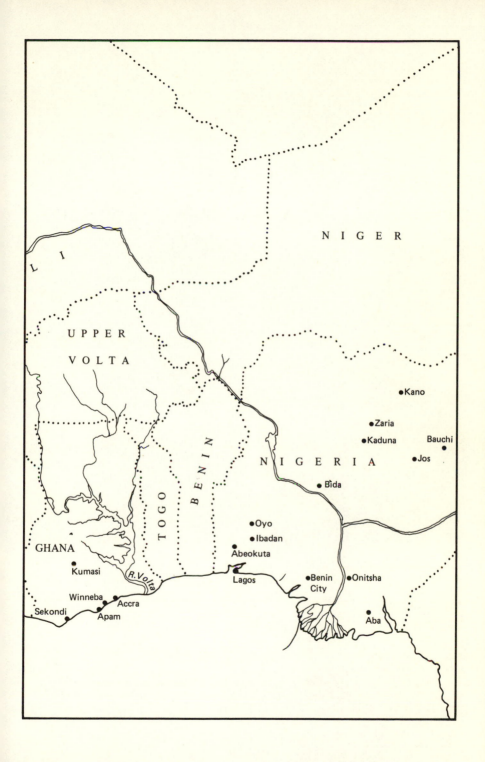

I Statistical Framework

Part One

Overviews: Comparative Perspectives

Introduction to Part One

This first part of the volume gives the regional framework for the subsequent detailed case studies, including fertility, mortality and migration, and for the educational and economic activities of the populations of the several countries of West Africa, showing the similarities and differences in economic and demographic behaviour of females and males.

Chapter I examines the divergent lives of men and women in West Africa as revealed by official statistics. From birth to death the life chances and experiences of males and females are seen to be very different. Although the figures cannot convey the full flavour of everyday experience, they provide a guide to the scope and extent of the differences revealed later by sociologists and anthropologists. It is within this framework that Helen Ware examines sex differences in births, infant mortality, educational experience, marriage, fertility, and mortality. Inevitably the emphasis is upon those countries for which adequate data are available: Senegal, Ivory Coast, Liberia, Ghana and Nigeria. However, the range of areas covered is sufficient to indicate those sex differences which are largely independent of culture (at least within West Africa) and those which are not. An examination of women's experiences as mothers, child-bearers and child-rearers is central; both in showing the biological experience of women, and in revealing the extent to which these alleged constraints fail to shape women's destinies. A salient fact emphasized, as in several of the later case studies, is that women of the region are both highly prolific – mothers of many children – and at the same time heavily engaged in productive work both inside and outside the home.

The second chapter, by Eleanor Fapohunda, examines work profiles of women and men in the region, again using available statistical sources, which tend to give the impression that women are less economically active than men and that the extent of female involvement in the labour force over the life cycle varies between the West African countries and within them.

The chapter develops the theme of the similarity of male work experience and the dissimilarity of the female work patterns, by looking at crude labour force participation rates, as well as by tracing the labour force participation rate patterns of the sexes in different countries. To illustrate the degree of dissimilarity of female work experience the case of Nigeria is examined in some detail; the country which supplies 52 per cent of West Africa's economically active female population. Within this context the female labour force participation patterns of several contrasting urban areas are compared and the shortcomings of the available statistics indicated.

The diverse female labour force participation patterns among and within West African countries are seen to reflect both the differing desire of women to seek employment outside the home and the extent of women's employment opportunities; themes which are taken up later in several case studies.

The concluding section of the chapter compares the occupational distribution of the sexes, noting that women tend to be concentrated in a more limited number of occupations than men, especially in the modern sector, in which men hold significantly more of the highly paid, high status jobs. Some of the factors causing the emergence of 'women's' occupations, as well as the implications in terms of income distribution, status etc. are mentioned.

In chapter 3 Aderanti Adepoju examines the major trends in migration patterns among males and females in countries of West Africa that have pertinent data. In doing so he explores the determinants of the migration patterns in the different countries and cultural and ecological settings. The diverse opportunity structures facing males and females are discussed within the context of the developmental framework and the constraints imposed upon women by marriage and kin ties. In addition so far as the data permit, recent changes in educational and employment opportunities are related to the apparent patterns of internal and international migration.

Chapter 1

Female and Male Life-Cycles

HELEN WARE

West Africa has a population of some 122 million. Probably 51 per cent of that population is female and 57 per cent is Nigerian (*United Nations Demographic Yearbook, 1977*). Even within the frontiers of the eighteen individual countries of the region there are great cultural, climatic and economic variations. Inevitably generalisations can have only a limited validity, when they have to cover the behaviour of Muslims, Christians and followers of traditional religious beliefs and to stretch from the pastoralists of the Sahel to the yam growers and fisherfolk of the coastal tropics. However, demographically the region is a relatively homogeneous zone of high mortality and high fertility levels, with a few distinctive pockets of low fertility scattered across Guinea, Upper Volta, northern Nigeria and the Cameroun (Retel-Laurentin, 1974).

The demographic similarities between countries make it easier to base generalisations about the differences between the lives of men and women upon their different life-cycle experiences than upon some alleged West African cultural core. The higher the level of fertility, the greater the strictly biologically determined differences in the experiences of the sexes. To claim this is not to adopt the simplistic view that biology is destiny and that the division of labour between the sexes is biologically determined and therefore immutable. Indeed, West Africa provides clear evidence that high fertility and both extensive and intensive labour force participation by women are not incompatible. The difference between the sexes results from direct biological experience, rather than from the social constraints associated with biology, which are almost entirely culturally determined.

For a total of less than two years in a life of seventy-five years' span, the European wife is likely to be biologically restricted by motherhood; all the rest of the burden is socially imposed. In contrast, the West African woman probably bears her first child in her early teens and continues to bear and breastfeed children until her mid-forties. Meanwhile, her life expectancy at birth seldom reaches 50 throughout the region. Society, in her case, defines many of the tasks of child-rearing as being the responsibility of the father, of older siblings and of relatives beyond the nuclear family, but biology ensures that at one level at least there will be a very great difference between the physical characteristics of her life and her husband's.

This chapter concentrates on the interaction between the organic experience of being a woman, moving from menstruation to pregnancy and lactation in a regular rhythm, and the culturally defined experience of living as a woman within a particular society. The emphasis is upon women's lives, both because these have often been ignored, and because demography is certainly one area where women's lives are of greater content and interest than men's.

Sex Ratios and Infant Mortality

All the available evidence for tropical Africa would suggest that the excess of males at birth is slighter than in most European populations and that the sex ratio at birth is close to 103 (Brass, 1968, pp. 38–43, 280–1).[1] Whatever the genetic or environmental cause of this, the result is that in most tropical African populations (in the absence of sex selective migration) there is an overall excess of females, since the slight excess of males at birth disappears as more boys than girls die in infancy. The extreme case is found in Gabon, where in 1960–1 there were only 85 males for every 100 females.[2]

Because women are biologically stronger than men, mortality is generally a little higher for males than for females among young and old alike. Thus, for example, in the Dakar region neo-natal mortality is 43 per 1,000 live births for boys but only 37 for girls. Meanwhile, the infant mortality rate is 90 for boys but only 76 for girls. Female mortality only exceeds male mortality, in high-mortality societies where males receive no preferential treatment in the way of better food or superior medical care, during the reproductive years from 15 to 45 when women are exposed to the uniquely female risk of mortality in childbirth and pregnancy. In urban Dakar maternity clinics are of a sufficiently high standard to ensure that male mortality is higher than female mortality at all ages. Overall the male mortality rate is 11·5 per 1,000 compared with 9·1 for females (Cantrelle, 1975, p. 114).

It is difficult to tell whether this favourable view of women's mortality experience would hold good for the whole of West Africa. In general, it is true that the higher level of mortality the less accurate the mortality data available and the greater the probability that males outlive females. To state the extreme case, those societies which prac-

Table 1.1   *Expectation of Life (in Years) at Selected Ages, Rural Nigeria, 1965–6*

Exact age	Southern Nigeria males	Southern Nigeria females	Northern Nigeria males	Northern Nigeria females	All Nigeria males	All Nigeria females
0	40·5	43·3	35·7	33·9	37·6*	37·3*
1	46·7	47·9	42·3	39·7	44·0	43·0
5	50·8	51·9	48·8	44·9	49·6	47·8
20	40·5	41·7	38·7	36·5	39·4	38·3
40	25·9	28·2	23·4	22·3	24·3	24·4
65	12·8	13·9	9·5	9·7	10·6	11·0

*Recalculated figures. The official figures were males 37·2, females 36·7.
Source: Demographic sample survey, 1965–6.

tise selective female infanticide do not have death registration systems. Equally, in societies where, if food is in short supply, male children are fed before female children, mothers are also more likely to 'forget' to mention the birth of girl children who died in infancy and thus to bias the mortality data available from retrospective surveys. The data from the intensive survey of Sakpe village in northern Nigeria show rates of child mortality (ages 1–4) of 148 for males and 142 for females, and infant mortality rates of 188 for males and 161 for females. The interesting contrast revealed by these figures is that the ratio of the child mortality rate to the infant mortality rate is higher for females (0·88) than for males (0·79). This suggests that girls fare less well than boys during the crucial weaning period (Katcha, 1978, p. 49).

Data from the 1965–6 Demographic Sample Survey of rural Nigeria showed Nigeria to be one of the few countries in the world where men live longer than women (*Population Index*, 1972, p. 515). Although these data are imperfect, they are unlikely to suffer from a systematic sex bias. In detail, the data show that it is only in northern Nigeria that men have the advantage in longevity (Table 1.1). This appears to be a reflection of the lower status of women in northern Nigeria. Most of the countries where men live longer than women are predominantly Muslim.

Maternal Mortality

There are very few data available for West Africa on the special female hazard of death in childbirth. A series of francophone multiround surveys which used comparable methodologies found that for every 1,000 deaths to men, women, and children, deaths related to complications of pregnancy and childbirth ranged from 10 to 24 in Senegal to 18 in Upper Volta and 19 in Benin (Cantrelle, 1965, p. 32). This compares with a rate of 1 per 1,000 in France as long ago as 1957. There were, in fact, more women who died in childbirth than there were persons who died from all forms of accident, from snake-bite to fires and traffic accidents. Some 20–32 per cent of all deaths of women aged 15 to 44 in West Africa are associated with pregnancy or childbirth (ibid., p. 21).

In areas where medical facilities are minimal, motherhood is a dangerous occupation. In Upper Volta in the late 1950s there was one maternal death for every hundred births, and approximately one mother in twenty could expect to die in childbirth. Yet these deaths were readily preventable, since for women whose children were born in the rudimentary maternity clinics with partially trained assistants the risk was reduced to one-quarter.

Life Expectancy

The life expectancy data in Table 1.2 have to be treated with considerable caution since many of the estimates are based upon models which incorporate the assumption that females live longer than males. The significant fact is that the estimates based more directly on real data, in three cases out of four, show men to live longer than women in Liberia, Nigeria and Upper Volta; the exception is Togo. In the absence of better data it is reasonable to accept that life expectancies for both men and women in West Africa are disturbingly low; and that there are certainly some areas where females are so disadvantaged that their lives are shorter than those of their brothers.

Sex Preference

One clear demographic indicator of the relative value placed upon males and females in a society is the extent to which parents show a marked preference for children of a particular sex. In many Asian and Muslim societies parents want sons not daughters and there is a very wide range of traditional formulae for ensuring the birth of sons and for determining the sex of the child before birth (Williamson, 1976). The position in West Africa is much less clear-cut even among Muslims.

Very few researchers in West Africa have systematically asked parents about their preference for sons or daughters. Almost all of the available data relate to Nigeria. In general, West African parents adopt the pragmatic attitude that both sons and daughters are

Table 1.2   *Infant Mortality Rates and Expectation of Life at Birth by Sex, Latest Available Year*

Country	Year	Infant Mortality Rate (%)		Expectation of Life at Birth	
		males	*females*	*males*	*females*
Benin	1970–5			39·4	42·6
Cape Verde	1970–5			48·3	51·7
Cameroun	1970–5			39.4	42.6
Gambia	1970–5			38·5	41·6
Ghana	1970–5	63·2	55·5	41·9	45·1
Guinea	1970–5			39·4	42·0
Guinea-Bissau	1970–5			37·0	40·1
Ivory Coast	1970–5			41·9	45·1
Liberia*	1971			45·8	44·0
Mali	1970–5			36·5	39·6
Mauritania	1970–5			37·0	40·1
Niger	1970–5			37·0	40·1
Nigeria*	1965–6			37·2	36·7
Senegal	1970–5			38·5	41·6
Sierra Leone	1970–5			41·9	45·1
Togo*	1961	140·7	113·8	31·6	38·5
Upper Volta*	1960–1			32·1	31·1

*Indicates countries whose life expectancy estimates are directly based upon census or survey data.
Source: United Nations Demographic Yearbook, 1977.

necessary to the continuance of the race, though many would prefer that their first-born be a son.

Education

Differential access to education is another factor distinguishing the life-course of females and males. The vital aspect of education is the extent to which it opens up new worlds. Where boys are educated and girls are not a vast gap opens up which is almost impossible to close again. In West Africa Western education teaches new life-styles, opens up economic opportunities, promotes religious change, creates new wants, sets new standards and cannot but bring radical change.

When the missionaries first introduced Christian schools to the coastal areas of West Africa the earliest classes contained approximately equal numbers of males and females. The missions were interested in both female and male souls and they also believed in the importance of educating the mothers of the next generation. The parents also appear to have been concerned to see both daughters and sons educated. However, a reaction against the education of girls soon set in. This was in part because, in so far as there was a colonial market for the employment of educated Africans, this demand was restricted to educated males. It was also because of the extremely disruptive effects of female education upon the marriage market. Educated girls learnt to regard marriage as a matter of individual choice and their insistence upon their individual rights constituted an attack upon the social system as a whole if marriages could no longer be used by the elders to regulate all social and political alliances (Dobkin, 1968).

In areas which were under strong Islamic influence very young girls might receive some basic Koranic education. However, there was, and still is, very strong resistance to a broader view of the education of girls. This is partly because of the restricted view of women's roles as being confined within the home. Education also runs contrary to the idea of marrying off all daughters at puberty before they can be dishonoured. (see Trevor, 1975a).

Looking at the data on literacy in West Africa in Table 1.3 the most striking feature is just how rare literacy has been until very recently. When talking of the effects of modernisation it should never be forgotten that the average West African, man or woman, is illiterate. Ghana is the only country coming close to the point where the literate will be in a majority. It is also the only country where more than a third of those who can read are female. The Muslim countries of Sahel are notable both for the very low proportions who are literate and for the very low proportions of individuals who can read who are female. In all cases where time-series data are available the proportion of females among the literate rises as the overall proportion literate rises. This is in cheering contrast to the Asian situation, where the percentage of women amongst the literate population fell as education spread from a small elite to a broader middle class, rising again only as literacy became much more widespread in the population as a whole.

Data on literacy rates amongst the adult population represent the educational situation as it was in the past (even when the data are less out of date than those currently available for much of West Africa). Data on children now in school represent the situation of the present and the future. Since the mid-1970s Nigeria has been making a sustained effort to provide universal primary education (UPE), and several other countries have similar goals. Yet in every West African country females are currently under-represented in the educational system (Table 1.4). In most countries there are two boys in school for every girl. However, Cameroun, Ghana, Nigeria, Senegal and Sierra Leone all share relatively high enrolment ratios and high proportions of girls in primary school. In looking at the percentages of girls at

Table 1.3   *Literacy by Sex*

Country	Year	Age Limit	*Percentage of Males Who Are Illiterate*	*Percentage of Females Who Are Illiterate*	*Percentage of Literate Who Are Female*
Benin	1962	15+	88	96	25
Cameroun	1962	15+	69	93	18
Chad	1963	15+	88	99	8
Gambia	1962	15+	91	97	25
Ghana	1960	6+	63	83	31
	1970	6+	47	66	39
Guinea	1965	15+	71	90	26
Guinea-Bissau	1962	15+	93	97	30
Ivory Coast	1962	15+	92	98	20
Liberia	1962	15+	86	96	22
Mali	1960	15+	96	99·5	11
Niger	1960	15+	98	99·7	20
Nigeria	1962	15+	75	94	19
Senegal	1961	15+	90	96	29
Togo (urban)	1962	15+	51	87	21
(rural)	1962	15+	88	98	14
	1970	15+	73	93	21
Upper Volta	1962	15+	98	99	32
(urban)	1975	5+	60	78	35
(semi-urban)	1975	5+	76	88	33
(rural)	1975	5+	91	98	20

Source: UNESCO Statistical Yearbook, 1976.

different educational levels it needs to be remembered that 50–1 per cent female would represent a situation where there was no discrimination against girls. Although this situation is not found in West Africa, there are parts of southern Africa, notably Botswana and Swaziland, where a clear majority of schoolchildren are girls. This is because the boys are kept out of school to tend the cattle. In West Africa it is generally girls who are likely to be kept home to act as child-minders, household helps and market assistants.

At each stage from primary to tertiary education the proportion of females falls. In part this is simply a sad reflection of previous experience at the lower levels. However, a more detailed examination of the time-series data shows that higher drop-out rates for female students are the principal cause of the lack of girls in secondary schools. At the tertiary level girls nowhere constitute more than one-fifth of the students. Separate figures for university enrolments show that the percentages of female students range from a maximum of 22 per cent in Liberia and Upper Volta to minimal shares of 5 per cent in Chad and 11 per cent in Niger. The data on the proportion of women

Table 1.4 Enrolment Ratios by Level and Sex, West Africa, 1960–75

Country	Year	Primary				Secondary				Tertiary			
		M Ratio	F Ratio	% Female (students)	% Female (staff)	M Ratio	F Ratio	% Female (students)	% Female (staff)	M Ratio	F Ratio	% Female (students)	% Female (staff)
Benin	1965	48	21	31	29	5	2	30	27	0·04	0·00	3	—
	1970	61	28	31	28	16	6	16	29	1·27	0·22	7	12
Cameroun	1960	87	43	36	—	4	1	21	—	—	—	—	—
	1970	124	91	43	12	13	5	29	23	0·98	0·08	12	—
	1973	125	97	44	—	16	8	32	21	1·84	0·23	14	—
Gambia	1970	36	16	31	33	12	4	24	26	—	—	—	—
	1975	43	21	33	33	13	5	27	22	—	—	—	—
Ghana	1960	80	39	30	27	4	1	20	17	0·42	0·05	11	—
	1970	69	54	43	33	16	6	28	22	1·51	0·20	12	—
	1974	68	53	44	—	42	28	39	—	1·74	0·44	20	11
Guinea	1960	45	16	26	—	3	0·36	11	—	—	—	—	—
	1970	45	21	32	—	21	5	19	—	1·07	0·09	8	—
Guinea–Bissau	1960	35	15	30	—	2	2	50	—	—	—	—	—
	1970	61	27	30	—	8	5	38	—	—	—	—	—
	1975	104	51	32	25	7	3	30	—	—	—	—	—
Ivory Coast	1960	68	24	26	—	4	1	20	—	0·19	0·02	10	—
	1970	97	55	36	13	17	5	21	—	2·01	0·33	14	—
	1974	108	64	37	12	26	8	24	—	2·74	0·54	17	—
Liberia	1960	45	18	29	—	3	1	25	—	0·71	0·18	20	—
	1975	80	44	36	30	24	8	25	—	2·59	0·72	22	—
Mali	1960	10	4	29	—	3	1	25	—	—	—	—	—
	1970	26	14	34	18	4	1	16	22	0·29	0·03	11	7
	1974	28	16	35	18	5	1	17	—	0·91	0·09	9	—
Mauritania	1960	13	3	19	—	1	0·04	3	—	—	—	—	—
	1970	23	9	28	5	4	0·47	11	—	—	—	—	—

Table 1.4 (continued)

Niger	1960	7	3	30	—	0.49	0.10	17	—	—	—	—	—
	1970	18	9	34	21	2	1	27	22	—	—	—	—
	1974	22	12	36	32	3	1	21	19	0.16	0.02	11	17
Nigeria	1960	46	27	37	—	4	1	18	18	0.13	0.01	7	—
	1970	43	25	37	24	6	3	32	20	0.52	0.08	15	—
	1974	59	39	40	—	14	7	33	—	0.81	0.15	15	—
Senegal	1960	36	17	32	—	4	2	32	—	0.83	0.18	17	—
	1970	53	33	39	—	16	6	28	—	2.43	0.49	17	—
Sierra Leone	1960	30	15	33	—	4	2	33	—	0.29	0.04	12	—
	1974	43	28	39	24	15	7	39	36	1.06	0.23	18	5
Togo	1960	63	24	28	—	4	1	20	25	—	—	—	—
	1970	100	45	31	19	11	3	22	16	0.93	0.12	11	—
	1975	129	68	35	—	29	9	23	—	2.11	0.33	14	—
Upper Volta	1960	12	5	29	—	1	0.25	17	—	—	—	—	—
	1970	16	9	36	16	2	1	28	—	0.07	0.01	15	—
	1974	18	11	37	17	2	1	31	—	0.22	0.07	22	19

Notes: In some cases definitions vary from country to country and year to year. The gross enrolment rates given here relate the total enrolments in primary or secondary school to the total population of primary or secondary school age. Tertiary enrolments are related to the population aged 20–24. Enrolment ratios of 100+ usually result from older children remaining in primary school. The enrolment ratios are expressed as percentages throughout.

Source: Data compiled from *UNESCO Statistical Yearbook, 1976.*

amongst schoolteachers and lecturers suggest that there is relatively little discrimination against women becoming teachers, once they have managed to secure an education. This is partly because of segregated education: most teachers in girls' schools are women.

Much of the differentiation between the sexes in education concerns the subjects studied. Women have been excluded from almost all agricultural courses, despite the fact that women in many areas are the agricultural labour force. To cite but one example: in an area of Cameroun where women are responsible for groundnut growing, out of the fifty-five farmers selected for a farmer training programme in improved techniques of groundnut production only one trainee was a woman, and she was a nurse (Lele, 1975, p. 167). There is a very great need to combat the Western-introduced beliefs that women are inherently incapable of understanding technical matters and that they have no natural grasp of economics. There will be little advantage in women securing equal access to secondary education if they continue to be sidetracked into the study of 'female' subjects with little market value, career prospects, or practical utility.

Marriage

The customary age at marriage for females varies considerably among the societies of West Africa. Such variations are closely related to the roles which women are expected to play and to their overall status relative to men. All West African societies attach great importance to age and seniority in status ranking. Thus the girl who, following the custom of her group, marries a much older man while still in her early teens experiences a very different relationship with her husband and status in society as a whole from that of the girl who, following the custom of another culture, marries at 20 a man who is of the same age-group.

As a result of the joint effects of polygny and the consequently delayed marriage of young males, in West African societies at any given point of time there are more married women than married men (although eventually more than 98 per cent of men and women alike will marry). Exceptions will only arise where widowers remarry but widows do not. In general, however, women spend a considerably greater proportion of their lives within marriage than do men. Almost by definition an adult woman is or has been a wife. In contrast, young men have to pass through an awkward transition stage of adulthood prior to marriage. On the other hand, again because of polygyny, women's experiences of marriage are at once of longer duration and of less intensity than those of men. The great majority of men, even of those who will ultimately become polygynists, have a prolonged experience of monogamy. In contrast, the woman who enters a polygynous marriage at menarche may never experience what it is to be an unmarried adult or to live in a one-to-one marital relationship.

Polygyny is not a dying tradition in West Africa: it is a flourishing institution. The number of married women per 100 married men may only range from 117 in Cameroun to 160 in Guinea, but it must be realised that even in the former case 29 per cent of wives are living in polygynous unions, while in the latter case 75 per cent share their husbands. To take the example of a single Nupe village, in Sakpe 62 per cent of all females but only 46 per cent of all males are currently married. There is no unmarried woman over the age of 20 but there are unmarried males up to the age of 33. Here the mean age at marriage for women is 15·5 and it appears to be declining in association with a declining age at menarche resulting from improved nutrition (Katcha, 1978, pp. 33–5). Elsewhere the spread of education for girls results in a rise in their age of marriage, but here there is a very strong local resistance to allowing post-pubertal girls to stay in school and run the risk of becoming pregnant before marriage (see Trevitt, 1973, p. 223). In terms of the intensity of their marital experience, the proportion of Sakpe wives in monogamous marriages falls from 82 per cent in the under-20 age-group to 57 per cent for those aged 20–24, 45 per cent for those aged 25–29 and 39 per cent for all older wives. Thus less than a fifth of young girls first marry into polygynous marriages, but three-fifths of women are ultimately to be found in

Table 1.5   *Age at First Marriage, Nigerian Rural Females*

Ethnic Group/ Survey Locations	Date	Number of Women	Mean Age at First Marriage
1 All rural Nigeria	1965–6	180,000	18·0
Nupe 2 Sakpe	1977	306	15·5
Yoruba 3 Rural west	1966	682	20·3
4 Imesi-Lasigidi	1974	1,526	19·5
5 Ekiti (rural)	1975	600	20·4
6 Ibadan (rural)	1975	497	20·0
Ibo 7 Rural east	1972	604	17·7
8 Ebendo	1973	395	16·4
Ibibio 9 Mbioto	1971	1,365	20·8

Source: Katcha, 1978, p. 34, where details of the individual surveys are given.

polygynous unions. In a broader sense, in a polygynous society all marriages are potentially polygynous, and women and men learn to structure their relationships on this basis (Clignet, 1970; Ware, 1979b.). Relationships with one's spouse or spouses are generally less close than those with one's mother, one's siblings, or one's own children. This theme of separation and distance in conjugal role relationships is taken up in several of the case studies which follow.

Work

The next chapter is devoted to contrasting patterns of employment so here I shall make only a limited reference to the importance of work in the life-cycles of women and men alike. Still, it is necessary to stress that all West African women work, and that most work longer hours and engage in more physical labour than men. Work, in the sense of playing an economically productive role, is central to the self-image of women, as many of the following chapters emphasise. Women do not expect to be, or want to be, dependent. Hence the terrible oversupply of petty traders in the urban areas. If no other opportunity is available, then a woman will endeavour to secure some measure of independence, some degree of identity, by setting up a streetside stall.

In the industrialised areas of the world the housewife's tasks may be monotonous and never-ending, but they are not comparable to the burdens of the village woman who has to carry all water, find and transport all wood and spend hours each day in basic food-processing. Yet in addition to this she also has the burdens associated with raising half-a-dozen children and, in many cultures, a basic responsibility for the agricultural production of food. It is necessary to emphasise this (1) because official labour force statistics as Eleanor Fapohunda notes, generally grossly underestimate the contribution of women, even in the area of agricultural production, and (2) because the West African experience destroys the claim that a strong female commitment to work is incompatible with high levels of fertility. There is a great need for more time-budget studies in West Africa to show the work undertaken by women and men. At present almost all agricultural development projects are vitiated by their false assumptions about the limited female contribution to agriculture.

Fertility and Parenthood

No one doubts that for most of West Africa fertility levels are high, and indeed among the highest in the world (Caldwell *et al.*, eds,

1975). National birth rates range from 39 births per 1,000 inhabitants in Sierra Leone and Guinea-Bissau to 54 in Nigeria and Benin (Adegbola, 1977). Total fertility rates, which in stable conditions are equivalent to the average number of children born to a woman in her lifetime, vary from just over 4·5 in Cameroun to something close to 7·0 in most countries of the region (Table 1.6). In the cultural conditions of the region such figures can never be exact, but they are certainly of the right order of magnitude. The available evidence also points to the possibility of a mild rise in fertility rather than to any incipient decline.

So much attention has been devoted to the population growth implications of these fertility levels that little thought has been spared for examining their significance at the level of the individual parent. Demographers have provided a wealth of data on the numerical dimensions of the phenomenon, but anthropologists have usually shown more interest in the formal structure of kinship than in the actual process of family-building. The general neglect of women's lives is reflected in accounts of reproduction which are restricted to a couple of pages on the taboos associated with childbirth. Even women anthropologists have been slow to study motherhood from the mother's point of view. In the literature more attention has been devoted to the plight of the childless wife than to the average experience of the mother who bears six children only to lose one, two, or even three in childhood. African mothers themselves have had little opportunity to be heard.[3]

One new approach to fertility studies is to examine the physical strains imposed upon women by repeated births and prolonged lactation. The index of physical and nutritional stress devised by Harrington (1978) measures the proportion of a woman's reproductive life spent either pregnant or breastfeeding. Harrington argues that this index

> represents an undeniable strain and a drain – an extra job that has no male equivalent. It gives muscle to the point that women are not only 'equal' in some philosophical/moral sense and therefore deserving and worthy of social services, but that they are in fact entitled to *more* in terms of program inputs because they do more than men – life is harder on them, especially if they have children.

Harrington's Nigerian data show that among those women who have ever been pregnant, the proportion of women who have spent more than 60 per cent of their adult lives either pregnant or breastfeeding ranges from 56 per cent in Ibadan to 52 per cent in Benin and 46 per cent in Kano. The proportions who have spent more than 80 per cent of their adult lives under this physical stress are as high as 27 per cent

Table 1.6 Fertility Rates in West Africa (Births per 1000)

Country	Date	Total Fertility Rate	15–19	20–24	25–29	30–34	35–39	40–44	45–49
Benin	1961	6·9	197	336	306	254	166	86	30
Cameroun	1960–2	4·6	157	221	199	157	113	51	22
Gambia	1973	5·0	156	237	226	167	128	58	32
Ghana	1968–9	7·1	163	308	314	275	211	100	56
Guinea	1954–5	7·0	240	335	311	246	171	69	28
Ivory Coast	1962–4	6·4	192	289	264	226	158	102	44
Liberia	1971	5·7	188	241	272	201	166	49	25
Mali	1963	7·0	156	375	298	245	195	90	45
Mauritania	1964–5	5·7	129	234	238	218	174	95	54
Niger	1959–60	6·9	171	333	299	253	186	97	46
Nigeria	1965–6	5·6	192	266	233	172	123	68	60
	1970–3	5·9	137	286	270	245	146	80	17
Senegal	1960–1	5·4	226	256	182	178	146	68	24
	1976	6·4	105	290	272	228	161	109	63
Sierra Leone	1973	6·4	212	279	259	244	174	86	13
Togo	1961	7·0	151	327	312	271	189	114	28
Upper Volta	1960–1	5·9	151	297	259	220	155	84	19
	1973–4	7·2	124	359	311	325	186	136	n.a.

Sources: These rates are selected from the wide range provided in US Bureau of the Census, A Compilation of Age-Specific Fertility Rates for Developing Countries (Washington, DC: Government Printer, 1979), which gives details of the individual surveys and adjustments involved.

in Benin, 26 per cent in Ibadan and 22 per cent in Kano. These are the proportions for adult women at all reproductive ages. However, owing to the gradual onset of sterility amongst the older mothers, the burden is greatest for mothers aged 15–24 where the proportions who have spent over 80 per cent of their adult lives in pregnancy and lactation attain 57 per cent in Benin, 42 per cent in Ibadan and 35 per cent in Kano (Harrington, 1978). The mothers of Kano experience lesser physical burdens associated with reproduction, because they suffer from higher levels of secondary sterility associated with the very early ages at which they first give birth and with the high incidence of venereal disease.

Unfortunately there are very few nutritional studies to measure the impact of child-bearing and prolonged lactation upon the health of the mother and her subsequent children (Fikry, 1977). One medical authority has claimed that 'maternal undernourishment is the rule rather than the exception in Africa' (Omolulu, 1974, p. 331). Certainly prolonged breastfeeding can create extreme anaemia in women who are already experiencing iron deficiency.[4] In a number of the cultures of the region the special diet prescribed for pregnant women might have been designed to ensure the maximum of malnourishment for mother and child.[5] It is very common to find that women are denied access to a wide range of local sources of protein when pregnant, for fear that the baby should develop some characteristic in common with the animal eaten.[6] Eggs are very widely taboo for women of reproductive age because 'one does not eat the children of others to feed one's own children' (N. Simmons, 1972, p. 410).

It is currently fashionable to stress the wisdom embodied in traditional medical and nutritional practices. However, it may be argued that these traditions are formed to maximise the welfare of the old men and not that of the women and children.

Age patterns of fertility also serve to reveal the extent to which women's lives are shaped by the biological experience of repeated child-bearing. Age-specific fertility rates show that even at ages 15–19, in any one year, 240 out of every 1,000 girls in Guinea, and 212 in Sierra Leone, give birth (Table 1.6). Indeed, the data from Sierra Leone show that 25 girls per 1,000 give birth each year in the age-group 10–14. Similarly, data from Niger suggest that at age 14 some 8 or 9 per cent of girls are already mothers (Niger demographic survey, 1962).

At the peak ages for child-bearing, in the early twenties, a third or more of all women will give birth in any one year. Rates decline gradually from then on, but it is only in the late thirties that the proportion of women giving birth falls below a fifth in most countries. Thus women can expect to spend twenty years of their lives bearing a child every third or fourth year, and more than half of all women who survive to 50 will bear a child in their early forties. The age data are imperfect (as the rates for women aged 45–49 might suggest) but the overall picture is clear and accurate enough. An average woman will give birth to six children.

In so far as there is clear evidence of change, births to women under the age of 20 are becoming somewhat less common than they were formerly. However, there is no consistent evidence that fertility is falling among older women and some evidence to suggest that it may actually be rising. The spread of education is certainly a vital factor in the declining number of births to teenagers. However, education for a significant proportion of rural women is so new (or, indeed, has yet to come) that it is impossible to tell what impact it will ultimately have on the number of children born to older women. However it seems reasonable to predict that education alone will not result in smaller families unless the roles played by adult women and by grown children are also transformed.

Women in West Africa undoubtedly spend their lives in child-bearing and child-rearing, and yet nowhere is child-rearing considered to be a full-time occupation which should exclude all other activities. It is the same women who become the mothers of six or seven children who also provide '60 to 80 per cent of the agricultural labour supplied on the continent of Africa' (Economic Commission for Africa, 1972). It is now commonplace to state that women's limited access to public roles results from the inevitable conflict with their all-important domestic and child-rearing roles. In the West African case it would be more reasonable to argue that the combination of child-rearing and economic roles leaves little time for public roles. Yet even that statement is an oversimplification which ignores the facts that some women do play important political roles (Hoffer, 1972), and that there are many traditional women's groups with political roles of their own (Van Allen, 1972), topics which are taken up below in Chapters 5 and 14.

It might well appear to be contradictory to stress both women's high fertility and their major contribution to the economy. Yet it is the combination of these two factors which is the distinctive feature of the lives of West African women. In the traditional context there was no question of women having to choose between motherhood and economic independence. They were secure in the ability to enjoy both. Too much emphasis upon formal status as viewed by males has served to obscure the advantages enjoyed by women as mothers rather than wives.

Sexual Intercourse and Abstinence

In most cultures there are considerable differences between the sexual experiences of women and men. In West Africa there are a number of interlocking features of traditional life which result in very different experiences and perceptions of sexual intercourse for the two sexes. Because of the very high levels of infant and child mortality in West Africa, it is necessary to make considerable efforts to maximise the survival chances of each baby born. One of the commonest strategies is to prolong breastfeeding and to strive for an interval of at least two or three years between births. Hence the widespread practice of prolonged post-natal sexual abstinence by the mother, as Lawrence Adeokun describes in Chapter 8. On the father's side the practice of polygyny, or extra-marital affairs, remove the need for prolonged abstinence. But for the wife there is no alternative, and the belief that semen in the vagina poisons the nursing mother's milk serves to strengthen her resolution and to reduce the incidence of closely spaced births. Amongst the Sahelian pastoralists children are given cow's milk, but in the forest zones cows cannot survive and children are apparently not given goat's milk.

In traditional society sexual experience for males begins whenever the youth is ready and has been initiated (where initiation is customary). For girls there is a clear division between those societies where considerable freedom is allowed to girls once they have been initiated, and those societies where all girls are expected to be virgins at marriage (see Table 1.7). Where virginity is required, and especially where girls are married at puberty to ensure that they will stain the wedding cloth, as is normal amongst many Muslim groups, girls have very little say in the timing of their first sexual experience which comes very early in life. Such a system creates a 'need' for women who will be accessible to men who have yet to get wives of their own, or whose wives are not currently available because they are pregnant or lactating. Hence institutions such as the Hausa *karuwai* described in Chapter 21 by Renée Pittin: women of child-bearing age who do not remarry after being widowed or divorced, and who in many cases exchange their sexual favours for gifts of money with a range of men (Hill, 1972, p. 275). They may also maintain traditional religious practices in staunchly Muslim areas (Smith, M. F., 1954, p. 25). Amongst the Hausa community Ibadan such 'prostitutes frequently marry and slip into the anonymity of wifehood, and wives frequently divorce and emerge into the freedom and independence of prostitution' (Cohen, A., 1969, p. 57). It should be remembered that in many West African cultures standards of sexual attractiveness 'center on more sexually mature women' (R. Cohen, 1967, p. 39). Men may wish to marry young girls who are sexually untouched and can easily be trained to fit in with the ways of the family, but they do not necessarily find them to be the most sexually attractive.

Little attention has been devoted to the question of what is sexually attractive to women, although it is generally accepted that they do not enjoy marriage to old men (Talbot, P., 1932, pp. 184ff. quotes complaints on this head dating back to 1914). In contrast to the strict Muslim areas, there are many ethnic groups where girls enjoy very considerable sexual freedom prior to marriage (e.g. Paulon, ed, 1963).

Marriage marks a dramatic transition both for the girl who has been chaste up until then and for the girl who is used to choosing her own sexual partners. For both women *and* men marriage is often more a matter of familial alliances than of individual choice as the chapter by Bisilliat illustrates. The birth of the first child marks another major transition. Both events are likely to come some ten years earlier in the life-cycle for women than for men. Once a woman has become a mother it would seem that much of the emotion which might otherwise transmute her relationship with the marital partner chosen by the lineage is transferred to her child. Among those groups which practise prolonged post-natal abstinence there will be some two and a half years of sexual abstinence associated with each birth (made up of the last three months of pregnancy, plus two years of lactation and three months of rest for the mother after weaning). Thus the woman who marries at 16, bears six children who are born alive and one stillbirth and becomes a widow at the age of 41 (which would be a typical life-cycle for much of the region) would spend more than fifteen of her twenty-five years of married life abstaining from sexual intercourse. Even for the wife who is not widowed before reaching the menopause (though this is a common occurrence where life expectancies are low and husbands are generally a decade or more older than their wives), many groups expect a woman to give up her sexual life once she becomes a grandmother, which is likely to happen in her late thirties (Ware, 1979). Some Yoruba, for example, believe that the mother who continues to bear children denies her daughters the opportunity to start child-bearing (Caldwell and Caldwell, 1977; see also Adeokun in Chapter 8). Even where prolonged post-natal abstinence is not customary, abstinence during pregnancy, and mourning, and in preparation for hunting and a range of rituals, considerably reduces the frequency of sexual intercourse. In most West African societies the only women who will experience a broad exposure to sexual intercourse throughout their reproductive lives are likely to be sub-fertile wives who are fortunate enough not to be divorced, or those who become prostitutes.

It is important to realise just how widespread the practice of

Table 1.7 *Sexual Prohibitions and Marital Customs*

Country	Ethnic Group	Sexual Intercourse before Marriage		Length of Post-Natal Abstinence		Interval between Widowhood and Widow Inheritance
		theory	*practice*	*theory*	*practice*	
Mauritania						
	Maure	No	No	40 days	40 days	4 months + 10 days
Senegal						
	Sérère	No	No	U.C.W.	U.C.W.	5 months
	Wolof	No	Yes	2 months	2 months	4 months + 10 days
	Toucouleur	No	Yes	3 months	3 months	4 months + 10 days
	Fulani	No	Yes	70 days	70 days	4 months + 10 days
Ivory Coast						
	Dida	No	Yes	2–3 years 3 years boy 2 years girl	U.C.W.	1 year
	Bété	No	Yes	U.C.W.	U.C.W.	5 days
	Godié	No	Yes	4 years boy 3 years girl	U.C.W.	1 year
	Guéré	Yes	Yes			2 years

	Yacouba	Yes	Yes	2–3 years	U.C.W.	6 months
	Malinké	Yes	Yes	3–4 years	U.C.W.	4 months + 10 days
	Tagouana	Yes	Yes	U.C.W.	U.C.W.	6 months–1 year
	Senoufo	Yes	Yes	U.C.W.	U.C.W.	6 months–1 year
	Baoulé	Yes	Yes	U.C.W.	U.C.W.	3 months
	Agni	Yes	Yes	3–6 months	U.C.W.	3 months
Upper Volta	Mossi	Yes	Yes	3 years boy 2 years girl	18 months	3 months
Niger	Hausa	Yes	Yes	3 months	40 days	No widow inheritance
	Gourmantché	No	Yes	3 years boy 4 years girl	U.C.W.	7 years
	Songhay	Yes	Yes	40 days	40 days	4 months + 10 days

Note: U.C.W. = Until the child can walk alone.
Source: Raulin, 1967.

prolonged post-natal abstinence is in this region. An uncritical use of the data on 102 West African societies in Murdock's (1967) *Ethnographic Atlas* shows sixty-five groups where there is no information on post-natal abstinence, eight societies where post-natal abstinence is traditionally less than one year, nine where it is one year but less than two years, and twenty where it is two years or more. In a survey devoted to this topic Lesthaeghe and colleagues (1979) found only four societies where abstinence was no longer than forty days (the period proscribed in the holy writings of Islam, although many West African Muslims will cite the Koran as their authority for abstaining for two years). They also found eight societies where it was traditional to abstain for more than forty days but less than one year; and twenty-six ethnic groups where abstinence lasted for more than one year, most commonly two years. Thus it is clear that the most common pattern for the majority of cultures in the region is to abstain until the child has a clear start in life.

Although in some cases the traditional proscriptions have been abrogated in length and extend only until the child can walk by herself or himself (Raulin, 1967), this is certainly not true everywhere. Data for the Yoruba of Ibadan show that even in this city with a population of close to a million souls prolonged abstinence is still the norm. At any given point in time 51 per cent of women aged 15–44 are abstaining from sexual relations, and the average duration of abstinence after the last birth ranges from twenty-four months for the illiterate to nineteen months for those who completed primary school and twelve months for the university educated (two-thirds of whom have supplemented abstinence with contraception) (Caldwell and Caldwell, 1977; Dow, 1977).

Old Age

There is very little systematic information available concerning the fate of old people in West Africa. The conventional wisdom states that they are well cared for in the bosoms of their extended families. Certainly this is the ideal to which all aspire in societies where there are no state pensions (except for certain state employees) and all savings and financial investments are extremely insecure in the long run. Thus educated children to care for one in old age are the best investment, as 98 per cent of Yoruba respondents agreed (CAF Nigeria 2 1974). However, for the childless, and for women who have had to leave their children behind after a divorce, the actual situation may be very different from the ideal. It is salutory to remember that the 1970 Ghana census found 1,664 old men over the age of 60 sleeping under market stalls and in lorry parks for want of another home to go to. Only 729 men of that age were in hospital. In contrast, only 140 old women slept out homeless, while 524 slept in hospital.

There are a number of reasons why West African societies should be expected to have more widows than widowers. Women generally marry men who are a decade or more older than themselves. Men can, and do, marry several wives of widely differing ages; when one of a polygynist's wives dies he does not become a widower. It is also the case that in a number of traditional societies, once a woman is past the menopause and incapable of bearing further children, there is no reason why she should remarry if she loses her husband. At the menopause Yoruba wives return to their families of origin if widowed, and sometimes even when the husband is still living. Other traditional societies assume that all adult women should be married, whether they are post-menopausal or not, and provide for widow inheritance, in which the widow becomes the wife of another male member of her husband's family, usually his brother or his son by another wife. If she is still young she will become a full wife and continue to bear children for her husband's line. But if she is older the marriage may be more a matter of social definition than of cohabitation. It is not clear how inherited widows are classified in national censuses. The 1954–5 Guinea survey was unique in providing a special category for inherited widows, although once the woman had borne a child by her inheritor she was reclassified as a wife. The results of the survey, which covered 300,000 people, showed that widows as a proportion of all women rose from 9 per cent at ages 40–44, to 17 per cent at ages 45–49, to 25 per cent at ages 50–54 and 52 per cent at 55+. The additional group of inherited widows was 10 per cent at 40–44, 11 per cent at 45–49 and 15 per cent at 50–54 and 55+. Thus in Guinea it would appear that widows are generally inherited only if still capable of bearing children.

More recent data from Togo and Liberia would seem to classify inherited widows as wives. In Liberia there are four widows for every widower, while in Togo there are six. In Togo at ages 65 and above 63 per cent of women are widowed while 30 per cent are still married (the remainder are single 2 per cent and divorced 5 per cent); however, 80 per cent of men are still married and only 13 per cent are widowed. The position is similar in Liberia, where for those aged 65 and above, 64 per cent of women are widowed and 25 per cent are still married, while among men the proportions are 78 per cent married and 14 per cent widowed. Thus, clearly, there are far more old women who have to face the world without the support of at least one spouse than there are men, even among the extremely elderly. The chapter by Sanjek on a district of Accra is an illustration of this pattern.

It is important to realise that at the high levels of mortality found in

West Africa many children never have elderly parents to care for. When the expectation of life at birth is 37 years, as in Niger or Mauritania (Table 1.1), out of 1,000 children aged 30, 478 will have lost both parents and 435 will have lost one, leaving only 86 children with both parents still surviving. No country in West Africa has mortality levels low enough to ensure that a third of all children have both their parents still alive as they reach their thirtieth birthdays (calculations from Locoh, 1978). This means that at the ages when most men are first becoming fathers their fathers will already be dead. Women fare better because they marry earlier and therefore the generations between mother and married daughter are shorter than the generations between father and married son. A man will probably be at least fifty before he becomes a grandfather, whilst a woman may well be a grandmother at thirty-five.

Evidently where mortality levels are high there is little chance that both parents will survive together to enjoy their grandparenthood. At the levels of mortality found in the Sahelian countries, out of a thousand couples who marry when the wife is 18 and the husband 26, by the time that the wife is 50 only 375 couples will still be together. In 310 cases the husband will be dead, in 172 cases the wife is dead and in 142 cases both husband and wife will be dead (Locoh, 1978).

Although there are no fully satisfactory data on the fate of the elderly in West Africa, the Ghanaian census of 1970 did tabulate the relationship of the individual to the head of the household by age, and this does make it possible to have some information. Among the elderly (aged 65 and above) 87 per cent of men are themselves household heads, 4 per cent are the father of the head, 3 per cent are brothers of the head, 1 per cent are husbands of the female head and 1 per cent are uncles of the head; the remainder are either guests or lodgers (1 per cent), or other relatives of the head (2 per cent)). In contrast, 46 per cent of the elderly women are heads of their own households, 26 per cent are the mother of the head, only 11 per cent are wives of the head, 6 per cent are sisters of the head and 2 per cent are aunts of the head; a further 3 per cent are guests or lodgers, and the remaining 6 per cent are other relatives of the head.

Certainly there are a number of problems associated with the use of these data to study differences between the experiences of the two sexes. The data do not show how many of the household heads among the elderly are at the head of one-person households (for household heads of all ages 24 per cent of males but only 15 per cent of females have no one else in the household). Again, where a father and son live together in one household, even an infirm father will usually be classified as the head of the household out of respect. However, when a widowed mother moves in to live with her adult son she will almost certainly be classified as the mother of the head. Still, it is notable that the proportion of males who are classified as the sons of the household head declines rapidly with increasing age, and is as low as 10 per cent by ages 30–34, suggesting that relatively few married sons stay in the households of their fathers. The census definitions of the terms 'household' and 'head of household' are given in Table 1.8, which shows the relationship to household head by sex and urban/rural residence for Ghanaians of all ages. Clearly there was some bias towards declaring men to be household heads, which makes it all the more remarkable that there are only three male household heads for every female household head. Some 29 per cent of all household heads in Ghana are women: among the elderly this

Table 1.8   *Relationship to Household Head by Sex and Urban/Rural Residence, Ghana, 1970 (%)*

	Total		Urban		Rural	
Relationship	*male*	*female*	*male*	*female*	*male*	*female*
Head	30·7	11·2	34·6	14·2	29·1	10·1
Temporary head	0·2	0·8	0·2	0·7	0·2	0·8
Husband/wife	0·4	21·5	0·4	18·5	0·3	22·7
Son/daughter	44·5	40·0	40·9	39·7	45·9	40·2
Son's wife/daughter's husband	0·0	1·1	0·0	0·5	0·1	1·4
Son's/daughter's child	8·2	8·6	7·4	8·2	8·5	8·7
Brother/sister	5·3	3·3	5·3	3·6	5·3	3·1
Sister's son/daughter	2·6	2·7	2·7	3·2	2·6	2·5
Brother's son/daughter	2·5	2·0	1·9	1·7	2·8	2·1
Father/mother	0·2	1·7	0·1	1·1	0·2	2·0
Parent's brother/sister	0·2	0·3	0·2	0·2	0·2	0·3
Parent's brother's/sister's child	0·6	0·4	0·8	0·6	0·5	0·3
Father's wife/mother's husband	0·0	0·3	0·0	0·1	0·0	0·4
Other relative of head	1·3	2·7	1·4	2·1	1·3	2·9
Other relative of head's spouse	1·0	2·1	1·2	2·9	0·9	1·7
Non-relative: guest/lodger, etc.	2·3	1·3	2·9	2·7	2·1	0·8
Total	100·0	100·0	100·0	100·0	100·0	100·0

Definitions: A Household 'consists of a person or a group of persons who live together in the same house or compound, share the same housekeeping arrangements and are catered for as one unit'. *The Head of Household* 'is generally the person responsible for the upkeep and maintenance of the household. In the nuclei [*sic*] family type of household, the head of household is usually the father'.

Source: 1970 Population Census of Ghana, Vol. 3, table B10 (Accra: Government Printer, 1975).

proportion only rises to 34 per cent largely because so many mothers live with their sons. In this volume Sanjek and Pittin have described urban households in some detail and given examples of different co-residential experiences for women and men. The anthropological evidence confirms that because of their special status as mothers, old women may be in a much better position than old men.[7]

Another factor which tends to give old women an added advantage is the casting-off of all of the restrictions associated with women of reproductive age. Where old men just grow older, gradually accumulating respect and losing physical strength, old women attain a new status as honoured and sexless beings. Discussions of the status of women in West Africa have little meaning unless they recognise that for women, to a much greater extent than for men, status varies with life-cycle stage. For the very young and for the old there is little difference between the respect shown to males and females. The greatest divergence usually comes at the point of marriage, when a young girl marries a considerably older man who adds the status associated with age to that associated with his sex. Daughter, wife and mother are roles with much more variation in status than son, husband and father. The anomalous position of the wife results from the practice of polygyny, the age-gap between the spouses and the implications of patrilineal descent (which is found over most of the region).

At another level West African women gain because their status is not entirely based upon their life-cycle stage. In many regions of the world a woman's status is defined by her life-cycle stage and the status of the man who has charge of her. However, in West Africa both women and men have independent economic roles to play and can gain in status through the skill with which they perform these roles. Hence the importance of self-sufficiency in the self-concepts of men and women alike, and the deleterious effects for women of the importation of European ideas concerning the dependent status of women.

> Is it the weaker breed who pounds the yam
> Or bends all day to plant the millet
> With a child strapped to her back?
> (Wole Soyinka, *The Lion and the Jewel*)

Notes: Chapter 1

1   In most European populations for every 100 girls that are born there are 105 or 106 boys. This masculine excess provides some compensation for the fact that male babies are exposed to a greater natural risk of mortality in infancy and early childhood. Sex ratios at birth in the United States show a similar differential with a white ratio of 106 and a black ratio of 103.

2   In 1938 the sex ratio was as low as 75: many men who had been drafted for forced labour in unhealthy areas had died; others had simply run away. Out of some 6,000 Gabonese births observed in 1970, 62 per cent of the stillbirths and 65 per cent of those who died within the first week of life were boys. Three-fifths of the total number of deaths registered in Libreville in 1970 were male but this may reflect differential reporting and migration as well as mortality. The male mortality rate in the 1960–1 survey, which was not subject to these biases, was 39 per 1,000 compared with only 22 for females. It is not clear why so many more male births were underweight and apparently premature, but the excess adult male mortality was certainly related to the startlingly high consumption of local and imported alcohol (François, 1975). The study of male and female access to alcohol and its social implications would indeed provide a fascinating insight into sex roles in this area.

3   Andreski's collection of *Old Wives' Tales* (1970) is patronising. M. F. Smith's (1954) biography of *Baba of Karo* is an invaluable account, but is devoted to the life of a woman beset by sterility.

4   As Sankale (1969, p. 107) has stressed in this context:

   It is far from superfluous to insist upon the needs of women and children in Africa for this is indeed a revolutionary idea. Tradition gave such a great priority to the man! Certainly children have a special place and are spoilt, but this is a matter of sentiment, their real needs remain unrecognised . . . To make the adults, and more especially the elders of the village, admit that women and children have priorities over them, particularly in matters of food and health, is truly to overturn an order of precedence which has stood for centuries. (Translated)

5   Thus among the Wodaabe Fulani of Niger pregnant women are forbidden to eat milk, goat meat, or sweets and are fed on a daily porridge of ashes of millet stalks which results in extreme anaemia. Babies with diarrhoea also die of dehydration because it is prohibited to give them water (Arnaldi, 1975).

6   Thus Ibibio women are forbidden to eat snails to prevent the child having too much saliva, to eat pigs lest the skin be blotchy, or to eat maggots in case the child's breathing should be affected (Talbot, 1915, pp. 20–1).

7   See Smedley, 1974, pp. 223–4, on the Birom of Nigeria. Tait (1961, p. 173) has described how ' "Old Women's Houses" are a delightful feature of Konkomba hamlet life', which they had need to be since Konkomba women are on average twenty-two years younger than their first husbands.

Chapter 2

Female and Male Work Profiles

ELEANOR R. FAPOHUNDA

Traditionally, work activities of some form both inside and outside the home have been an integral part of the life experiences of West African women and men from early childhood to later adult years. Although there exist similarities in the work experiences of the sexes among West African countries, diversity occurs between and within national boundaries, due to social and cultural factors as well as to the degree of economic development. Moreover, the characteristics of these work activities, differentiated by sex and age, have not remained static, but rather under the influence of exogenous and endogenous factors have been evolving gradually over time.

Ideally, with adequate quantitative data, a comparative work profile of men and women would consist of the following features:

(1) type(s) of work done and the degree of specialisation,
(2) type of technology used to do the work,
(3) the sector of the economy in which the work is done,
(4) worker status,
(5) the regularity of the work activity throughout the year and over the individual's lifetime,
(6) hours devoted to various work activities,
(7) the form of remuneration (if any),
(8) the physical location of work activities,
(9) migratory work patterns,
(10) retirement practices.

The scope of this chapter, however, will be more limited since the existing data are fragmentary, as well as being at times impossible to compare, because of definitional variations or different survey procedures. One major limitation of the data is that reports of women's labour force participation rates are affected by census or sample survey enumeration procedures. Specifically, the criterion used to determine whether a woman is economically active varies with the enumeration. For example, women who work within the confines of their homes, like the women described in northern Nigeria in Chapter 7 by Enid Schildkrout, and who do not receive any money wage, even though they may be making substantial monetary contributions to their households, are not likely to be counted as being economically active. Yet they are producing goods which are eventually sold or traded. Similarly, there may be undercounting of the activities of the fishmongers described by Vercruijsse and Hagan in Chapters 13 and 14. In view of the fact that there is probably serious under-enumeration of women's income-generating activities in some West African countries, the differences between women's labour force participation rates may not be as great as they seem from the published records.

As a prelude to the subsequent discussion, it is important to consider generally the factors which contour the work profiles of West African men and women. These include the region's geography, traditional social structures, colonial policies, evolving economic structures, urbanisation, migration, expanding education systems and post-independence government policies. Fundamentally, West Africa's physical geography shapes the content of male and female work activities. For example, the amount of rainfall and the length of the wet season decreases from the low-lying coastal plain to the central high plateaux to the low plains of the north, thereby affecting vegetation and the nature of agricultural activities. In the dry northern Sahel zone agriculture is limited to occasional areas of moisture and pastoral activities predominate. In contrast, in the moist rain forests of the coast, cattle raising and animal-powered agriculture are prohibited by the existence of the tsetse fly.

While nature delimits the general boundaries of work, traditional social structures define the division of labour by sex and age. Generally, in subsistence family production, each sex specialises in the production of particular types of goods and services. An adult is responsible for a particular activity and is assisted by younger persons of the same sex, or by children, as is illustrated by several of the case studies in this volume. Boserup has pointed out that a 'horizontal distribution of work between the sexes is combined with a "vertical" distribution of work between the adults and the young' (E. Boserup, 1970, p. 140).

Generally, West African women of both agricultural and pastoral traditions cannot expect to be completely supported by their husbands, especially in polygynous societies, and must find independent ways to support themselves and their children. This is a reality of life which several of the subsequent chapters emphasise. In addition, it is important for many women to solidify their ties with their own kin by giving gifts or rendering financial help. Among West African ethnic groups, women's work profiles are affected by their ability to control, use and dispose of the fruits of economic resources. This is in turn determined by the organisation of domestic groups, kinship practices, inheritance traditions and social customs. Among certain groups women can own land, hire labour and sell their products, while in others women cannot own land and need the permission of their spouses before they can dispose of their crops. In Chapter 11 Christine Okali has depicted a variety of such situations within one cultural area.

Over time, the traditional economic organisation with its sexual division of labour has been gradually undermined by both exogenous and endogenous forces in West Africa. The first major change occurred as European countries assumed territorial control of West Africa and penetrated the interior. The Europeans brought with them their own ideas about the social role of the sexes, which affected their administrative behaviour. For example, the British trained only African males for junior level administrative duties, and when British missionaries established schools for girls the curriculum emphasised the domestic arts. Meanwhile, because the British preferred to deal with males, British import-export trade became male-dominated, while internal trade in countries such as Ghana and Nigeria remained primarily a female occupation.

In addition, the colonial development strategy of introducing large-scale cash crops affected the nature and organisation of agricultural work. For example, the French colonial authorities in eastern Ivory Coast were eager to encourage commercial farming by local farmers who, lacking labour, especially during harvest season, began importing unskilled male labour from the northern region of the country and from neighbouring countries (Clignet, 1970, p. 65). These migrants usually left their women and children at home to take care of their farms, thereby changing the relative workload of the sexes. In the central and western parts of the Ivory Coast the colonial authorities encouraged the formation of large-scale European-owned plantations, forcing uncompetitive local farmers either to migrate or to become hired labour. The introduction of cash crops also caused a new distinction in male/female agricultural activities. The males were encouraged by their colonial rulers to produce cash crops and were given advice and agricultural extension assistance, while the women were relegated to less profitable subsistence farming. In Chapter 23 Mona Etienne takes up this theme and demonstrates the far-reaching effects such economic changes have had on relations between women and men among the Baule people of Ivory Coast.

The subsequent establishment of independent West African states affected male/female work experiences in several ways. First, the functions of government were enlarged in order to stimulate economic development and, consequently, government employment vastly increased. Secondly, some governments in the public and private sectors undertook a policy of Africanisation; that is, indigenous individuals were to replace expatriates, especially in administrative, managerial and clerical positions. Thirdly, governments embarked on massive educational programmes to stimulate economic development and to see that the benefits were more equally distributed. As government assumed more of education's financial cost, more boys, and especially more girls, went to school. Education affects an individual's employment potential and aspirations. Many rural youths who have gone to school expect to secure salaried 'white-collar' jobs in urban areas. However, the growth rate of such jobs has been low compared with the rapid increase of school leavers in many West African countries. This is a topic on which Carol Martin focuses in Chapter 15 with reference to the training and employment of young women in Bauchi State, Nigeria. Lacking suitable employment opportunities, young people of both sexes, especially young women, remain unemployed in urban centres, depending upon family and friends for subsistence. In Chapter 25 Dinan has described the situation and strategies of some of these young women in Accra, educated with rising expectations, who use links with lovers and kin to maintain themselves while they go about the sometimes fruitless task of looking for urban 'white-collar' employment.

In addition, the process of economic development itself also alters male and female work activities. During the process of economic development the population gradually moves from agricultural to non-agricultural occupations, and at the same time the population shifts from villages to town living (E. Boserup, 1970, p. 174). Fundamentally, economic development involves a movement from household subsistence production towards specialisation of activities outside the household. The process is accompanied by the growth of primary urban centres and an enlargement of the money exchange economy.

Accompanying the growth of the modern sector, a new system of occupational stratification develops. Modern sector occupational status is based on educational qualifications and is reflected in a widening of income differentials. As women tend to have lower educational opportunities than men, they become relegated to low-status, low-income occupations.

Furthermore, the work activities of women change as families migrate to urban areas in search of higher incomes. Often women find that many of the household subsistence activities which they perform in the rural areas cannot be carried on in urban settings (ibid., p. 172), leading to the new phenomenon of urban 'housewives' referred to by Peil in Chapter 20. Moreover, among some ethnic groups village women engage primarily in agricultural work and have few contacts with individuals outside the family. These women may find it difficult to adapt themselves to working in an urban environment with or under strangers (ibid., p. 175). Also, women find it harder to combine their activities as workers and mothers because of the increased separation of the home and workplace, the absence of supportive kin and the growing difficulty of hiring household help – themes which are taken up in Chapters 18 and 19 on factory workers in Accra and Ibadan by Date Bah and di Domenico.

These economic, political and social factors underlie the West African male/female work profiles constructed from existing quantitative information. As social and economic change is a rapid ongoing process in West Africa, the contours of these work profiles are evolving. This would be clearly revealed if more statistical information existed over time. Moreover, an important point to consider is that the direction and rate of evolution varies in terms of the different political and economic milieux of the several countries of the region, depending upon such factors as whether production is increasingly being modernised and mechanised, whether foreign trade is booming or declining, and so on. In this context, of critical importance is the speed, volume and character of migration from the rural areas described by Adepoju in the next chapter, as well as the extent to which peasant farmers are becoming landless labourers and unemployed urban dwellers.

Male and Female: Lifetime Work Commitments

The majority of West African men are recorded as economically active in one way or another. Some are self-employed or working for payment in cash or kind. Others are actively looking for work.

The common profile of male work experiences over the life-cycle within the West African countries is best revealed by looking at separate labour force participation rates for different male age-groupings. Generally, in all West African countries, by age 20–24, at least 80 per cent of the male population is economically active (Table 2.1). The peak male labour force participation occurs in all countries at age 25–44 when over 96 per cent of the males are in the labour force. Subsequently, the male labour force participation rates in all West African countries decline but significantly at age 65-plus 59–78 per cent of the male population is still working.

Graphs of male labour force participation rates for different age-groups by country follow a similar pattern. Figure 2.1 shows the labour force participation rate curves for two countries which have the highest male labour force participation rates, Mauritania and

Table 2.1 Estimated Female and Male Labour Force Participation Rates by Age-Group, Mid-Year 1975 (%)

Age-Group	Mali F	Mali M	Upper Volta F	Upper Volta M	Ivory Coast F	Ivory Coast M	Gambia F	Gambia M	Benin F	Benin M	Guinea F	Guinea M	Togo F	Togo M	Senegal F	Senegal M
−15	11·2	12·6	10·9	12·2	9·3	10·5	6·5	7·6	7·8	8·3	8·2	9·0	9·8	8·1	6·0	7·3
15–19	84·3	85·4	82·0	85·4	72·4	80·5	66·5	67·1	60·6	76·2	54·5	80·0	49·3	63·9	51·5	68·7
20–24	88·6	95·3	84·5	95·3	77·5	94·4	74·0	90·9	68·5	93·2	58·6	92·5	52·9	90·3	55·8	89·4
25–44	90·9	98·5	85·8	98·6	82·1	97·8	78·5	97·4	78·6	97·4	64·5	96·9	58·5	97·3	60·0	96·9
45–54	86·5	97·5	82·6	98·0	75·6	97·3	75·2	96·8	70·8	97·2	61·8	95·7	59·3	96·1	56·6	95·5
55–64	57·4	93·6	62·7	94·0	51·7	93·0	56·3	90·7	55·4	94·3	48·7	92·3	51·5	91·4	3·8	89·0
65+	30·7	74·5	35·5	78·2	26·5	74·4	30·1	68·1	41·6	76·6	23·2	72·3	32·2	73·1	1·4	66·1
Total	51·7	58·5	50·2	58·4	45·5	57·7	44·3	56·1	41·6	53·4	36·6	55·8	34·3	50·9	3·8	53·0

Age-Group	Nigeria F	Nigeria M	Ghana F	Ghana M	Sierra Leone F	Sierra Leone M	Liberia F	Liberia M	Niger F	Niger M	Mauritania F	Mauritania M	Guinea-Bissau F	Guinea-Bissau M
−15	3·5	4·6	2·0	3·3	4·4	5·8	4·0	5·9	1·3	13·4	0·9	12·4	0·3	7·9
15–19	40·4	51·2	39·0	45·3	34·2	56·6	29·7	61·0	8·9	89·8	3·8	87·5	3·5	79·6
20–24	49·5	83·0	54·5	84·1	44·3	85·8	37·4	84·9	10·9	97·1	2·8	96·5	3·4	96·6
25–44	58·1	96·5	61·9	96·5	47·8	97·0	44·0	97·5	11·3	99·4	3·8	98·5	3·8	97·9
45–54	66·9	96·3	72·1	96·1	49·4	96·0	45·4	96·1	11·1	98·7	5·3	97·9	4·7	98·2
55–64	58·5	88·6	67·1	89·1	38·8	86·6	34·9	87·3	10·2	94·9	4·9	94·2	2·9	93·8
65+	35·3	60·8	37·8	62·9	19·2	59·9	17·2	59·1	5·4	78·3	2·3	76·5	1·3	78·6
Total	31·0	47·4	31·0	44·3	26·5	51·0	24·4	52·6	6·3	57·5	2·6	59·9	2·3	61·3

Source: International Labour Organisation, Yearbook of Labour Statistics, 1978, pp. 18–24. As West African data on labour force participation are fragmentary, this table is based on ILO estimates.

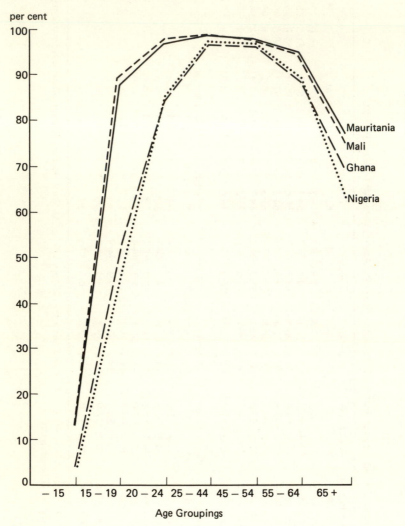

per cent

Mauritania
Mali
Ghana
Nigeria

Age Groupings

Figure 2.1 Men's labour force participation rates for selected countries.

Mali, and for two which have the lowest rates, Ghana and Nigeria.

The greatest variation in male labour force participation rates by age-group among West African countries occurs in the youngest and oldest age-categories. At the lower limit, important variations occur because of differences in the importance of unpaid family agricultural activities, as well as differences in the level of school enrolments by age. At the upper age-categories, the general availability of public or private pension provisions and the level of benefits cause significant differences in the male labour force participation rates.

In West Africa generally, women are recorded as being less economically active than men. However, among and within the countries of the region there are significant variations in the statistics on the extent of female economic activities. In 1975 estimated female labour force participation rates varied at the extremes from 51·7 per cent (Mali) to 2·3 per cent (Guinea-Bissau) (Table 2.1).

Another way of looking at the same phenomenon is to compare the distribution of the total West African female population and West African economically active female population by country (Table 2.2). In contrast to similar male statistics, the differences in these percentages by country are significant, suggesting a greater concentration of female economic activity within certain countries.

Furthermore, graphs of female labour force participation rates pictorially show the variation of female work experiences over the lifecycle among West African countries (Figure 2.2). In countries such as Upper Volta and Mali the general shape of the national women's labour force participation rate pattern, with its peak in the 45–54 age-group, closely resembles the male experiences. Most women by age 20 are in the labour force. They continue to remain economically active after marriage and the birth of children. In contrast, the peak in the Ghanaian and Nigerian patterns occurs not only at a substantially lower value but also at a later age-category. The patterns of recorded female labour force participation rates for Niger and Mauritania are quite different from the male patterns, for in each age-group only a small minority of women work.

Within West African countries women's labour force participation rate patterns vary widely. Nigeria, which constitutes over half of West Africa's economically active female population, provides a good example of the dissimilarity of female work experiences within West African countries. The charted 1963 census age-specific labour force participation rates for the Nigerian urban centres of Ibadan, Lagos, Zaria, Onitsha and Kaduna highlight the extent of these variations (Figure 2.3). These locations are defined as being urban centres based on a population size criterion. However, their respective economies and social fabrics are quite different. Some of the centres have many modern industries, while others are pre-industrial settlements. Geographically, these urban areas are located in different regions of the country – Ibadan and Lagos are in the west, Zaria and Kaduna are in the north, Onitsha is in the east.

In the city of Ibadan the women's labour force participation rate contour rises to 71·6 per cent for the age-category 25–34, peaks at 74·7 per cent in the 45–54 age-group and only begins to fall below the 70 per cent mark after 65 years of age. Both the Ibadan and the

Table 2.2 Distribution of Total West African Population and Economically Active Female and Male Population, Mid-Year 1975

	Population				Economically Active Population			
	number		per cent		number		per cent	
	F	M	F	M	F	M	F	M
West Africa	58,294	54,820	100·00	100·00	19,050	27,518	100·00	100·00
Benin	1,560	1,514	2·68	2·76	649	808	3·41	2·94
Gambia	253	256	0·43	0·47	112	144	0·59	0·52
Ghana	4,982	4,891	8·55	8·92+	1,545	2,165	8·11	7·87
Guinea	2,228	2,187	3·82	3·99	816	1,221	4·28	4·44
Guinea-Bissau	264	261	0·45	0·48	6	160	0·03	0·58
Ivory Coast	2,427	2,458	4·16	4·48	1,105	1,417	5·80	5·15
Liberia	866	842	1·49	1·54	211	443	1·12	1·61
Mali	2,863	2,834	4·91	5·17	1,481	1,659	7·77	6·03
Mauritania	649	634	1·11	1·16	17	380	0·07	1·38
Niger	2,334	2,266	4·00	4·13	146	1,303	0·77	4·74
Nigeria	31,950	31,099	54·81	56·73+	9,914	14,752	52·04	53·61
Sierra Leone	1,505	1,478	2·58	2·70	399	754	2·09	2·74
Togo	1,151	1,097	1·97	2·00	395	558	2·07	2·03
Upper Volta	3,029	3,003	5·20	5·48+	1,521	1,754	7·98	6·37

Note: Numbers are in thousands.
Source: As Table 2.1.

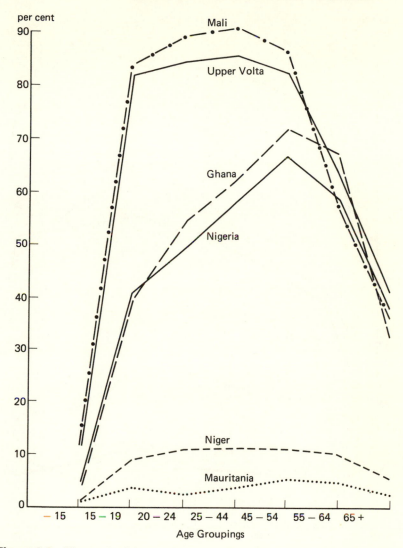

Figure 2.2 Women's labour force participation rates for selected countries.

all-Nigeria urban women's labour force participation rate patterns have similar shapes and peak in the 45–54 age-group. But Ibadan women show a higher commitment to working outside the home. The Ibadan women's participation rate profile shows substantially higher values at any given age than the Nigerian urban women's pattern. The Lagos women's labour force participation rate curve ascends

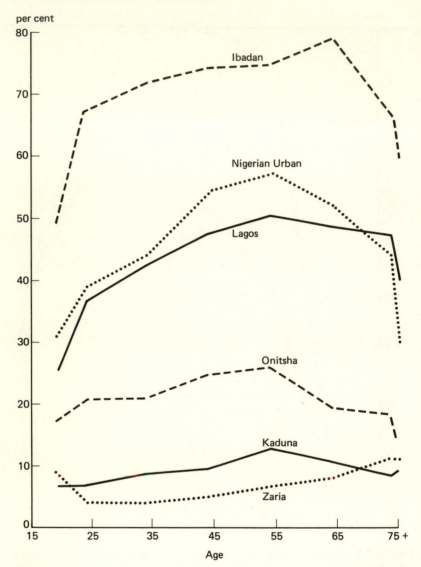

per cent

Figure 2.3 Women's labour force participation rates for selected Nigerian towns.

somewhat sharply to a 54 per cent mark in the 35–44 age-category and descends quickly to 44 per cent in the age-group 65–74. Although Lagos is the main industrial centre and at present the capital of the country, Ibadan women have appreciably higher age-specific participation rates. Chapter 18 by Catherine di Domenico describes aspects of the employment of women in factory contexts in Ibadan.

Since the demand for women's labour often influences the supply, women's labour force participation rate patterns are affected by the location and availability of women's jobs. In Nigeria, as in other parts of West Africa, most women are employed in the traditional sector rather than in the modern sector of the economy. This pattern results from limited educational opportunities, competition between the sexes for scarce job opportunities and problems of combining home and work responsibilities, all issues which are raised in more detail elsewhere in this volume. (See Chapters 1 and 15 by Ware and Martin regarding the relative access to educational opportunities of girls and boys; the situation of unemployed women in Accra by Dinan, Chapter 25; and di Domenico and Date Bah in Chapters 18 and 19 on women factory workers' problems of combining work outside the home and child care.)

Food processing and distribution has been an important female activity among many ethnic groups in Nigeria as well as in other West African countries. In Ibadan food distribution is a major activity of the local traditional economy and offers substantial employment opportunities for women. In urban areas such as Ibadan, with its large and growing traditional sector, many women find more job opportunities than in the capital, Lagos, with its larger modern sector. (Detailed studies of women engaged in food distribution are found in this volume in Chapters 12 and 13 by Vercruijsse and Hagan.)

In Zaria the women's labour force participation rate declines from 8·9 per cent for women in the 15–19 age-group, reaches a minimum of 3·9 per cent for those in the 35–44 age-category and gradually rises to a maximum value of 11·3 per cent in the 65–74 age-group. Not only are the age-specific participation rates extremely low, but the curve itself appears as the inverse of the Nigerian urban women's experience. However, as has already been noted, work which is done by women restricted to the confines of a compound is not recorded in official labour statistics. The higher labour force participation rates for the young and old women of Zaria reflect the fact that women in those age-groups move more freely outside the home.

Although Kaduna is only forty miles from Zaria, its official women's labour force participation rate pattern is quite different. The Kaduna women's labour force participation contour rises gradually from 6·6 per cent for women in the 15–19 age-group, reaches a maximum of 12·8 per cent for those in the 45–54 age-group and gradually declines in the older age-categories. However, this city has a considerable migrant population of people from ethnic groups which do not practise purdah for females, which makes the female work profile understandably different from those of neighbouring Hausa Muslim communities.

Again, compared with the two northern urban centres of Zaria and Kaduna, the eastern city of Onitsha has much higher women's labour force participation rates at all ages. The Onitsha women's labour force participation rate rises to 21·2 per cent for females in the 20–24 age-category, ascends to a maximum value of 25·7 per cent for those in the 55–64 age-category and does not fall below 20 per cent until after 74 years of age. Still, at every point the Onitsha rate lies substantially below the Nigerian urban women's labour force participation profile. However, in this area many women engage in farming as unpaid family workers and so may have been overlooked in official statistics. In addition, monogamy is more prevalent here than in western Nigeria and women are assumed to have more of their needs met by their husbands.

Industrial and Occupational Distribution of the Sexes

The nature of male and female work experiences varies with their distribution by industry, occupation and employment status. Sexual employment patterns can be described in terms of the economic activity of the establishment in which a person works (industry), or in terms of the nature of the work actually done by the individual (occupation). Employment status connotes whether an individual is an employer, self-employed, salaried employee, wage-earner, or family worker. Variations in the industrial distribution of the labour force between countries reflect different resource endowments as well as varying levels of economic development. As a country experiences a rise in its per capita income, the relative importance of the different economic sectors change responding to evolving patterns of consumer demand and technological improvements. Such a change is then reflected in the industrial distribution of the labour force.

Although the West African countries have basically agricultural economies, the percentage of the labour force in agriculture varies from 96 per cent (Niger) at one extreme to about 56 per cent (Ghana) at the other. The enumerated number of men employed in agriculture in each country is greater than the number of women, probably reflecting an undercounting of unpaid female family workers. But a larger proportion of the female labour force is employed in this sector in each country than is the case with the male labour force. Indeed, West African women workers are more highly concentrated in agriculture than are male workers. In fact, sub-Saharan agriculture has been characterised as being a 'female system of farming' (E. Boserup, 1970, p. 17).

Commerce is the second most important employment sector in many West African countries. The absolute and relative employment levels of the sexes in this sector vary by country, suggesting different cultural traditions as well as varying forms of business organisation. At one extreme Ghanaian women outnumber men in this sector by a ratio of over 2:1 and are more heavily concentrated in this sector than other groups of West African women (International Labour Organisation, 1973, pp. 46–7). In sharp contrast, seven times as many men in Niger as women are engaged in commerce, reflecting substantially higher general male labour force participation (ibid., pp. 50–1).

Since employment in the total service sector (commerce, transport, services, communication, utilities) generally increases with economic development, there is significant variation in the relative importance of employment generation within this total sector among West African countries. Compared with South Africa, the most industrialised country on the continent, service employment in any West African country is relatively small in terms of both total distribution and distribution by sex. Within the West African community the relative concentration of men and women in the total service sector varies by country. For example, in Liberia and Senegal men are more highly concentrated than women, while the reverse is true in Ghana. Although the percentage of women in each West African country's service sector is generally small, the region contributes significantly to the total proportion of African women employed in this sector.

As sectoral employment in agriculture declines with economic development, employment in the industrial sector (manufacturing, construction, mining) expands. By 1960 in Ghana 8·6 per cent of the labour force was employed in manufacturing compared with less than 0·6 per cent in Niger. Similarly 3·3 per cent of the Ghanaian labour force was employed in construction in contrast to less than 0·6 per cent in Niger. Generally, in terms of both absolute numbers and proportions, more men than women are employed in the industrial sector among West African countries.

In trying to draw work profiles of West African men and women, aggregate industrial categories provide limited information, since developing countries have dual economies; that is, within each sector a continuum of traditional enterprises coexists with modern forms. Therefore the nature of work, the conditions of employment, wage levels, the extent of worker organisation and the degree of worker protection under law varies within the traditional, intermediate and modern subsectors of each industrial category (E. R. Fapohunda, 1978). For example, focusing on manufacturing, modern sector workers are highly educated and are employed in capital-intensive enterprises using advanced technologies. These workers, often unionised and protected by labour legislation, are relatively highly paid.

Modern sector jobs and salaries are stratified by educational requirements.

In contrast, workers in the traditional manufacturing sector are generally handicraft workers who are usually self-employed, or unpaid family workers. Such workers use little capital, crude technologies and are not included under any labour legislation provisions. Their incomes are small and often irregular due to low productivity and substantial market competition.

Finally, workers in the intermediate manufacturing sector are generally employed in small non-unionised family enterprises that produce goods using labour-intensive technologies and local raw materials. Wages are generally low due to product competition and a large labour pool.

In agriculture, modern sector workers are either employed in large, fairly mechanised plantations, or are large cash crop farmers. In the intermediate sector, workers may be farmers who on their own account grow a combination of cash and subsistence crops, while the traditional agricultural sector includes subsistence farmers, share-croppers, unpaid family workers and seasonal migrants.

The combined traditional and intermediate sectors, the so-called 'informal sector', offers more employment opportunities than the modern sector because of its labour-intensive character. For example, in Abidjan, the capital of Ivory Coast, 63 per cent of the industrial workers, 97 per cent of the agricultural workers and 60 per cent of the construction workers were employed in 1970 in the informal sector (Joshi, Lubell and Mouly, 1976, p. 6). Moreover, available West African evidence suggests that the informal sector is growing at a faster rate than the modern sector. During 1965–70 in Abidjan, for example, employment in the modern sector grew by 7·5 per cent whereas in the informal sector employment increased 10·1 per cent (ibid., p. 2). Martin in Chapter 15 provides an indication of the importance of this sector for future female employment.

Although survey data on informal sector employment by sex are severely limited, indications are that West African women are heavily concentrated in the intermediate and traditional sectors. For example, based on 1970 Ghanaian census calculations, women constituted 43·2 per cent of the total workers employed in agriculture, but 44·0 per cent of those employed in the agricultural intermediate and traditional subsectors (Simms and Dumor, 1976–7, p. 48). Women were only 13·6 per cent of those employed in the modern agricultural sector. In manufacturing women were 56·1 per cent of the total workers, but only 7·2 per cent of the modern manufacturing sector workers. Ghanaian women were, however, 64·0 per cent of the workers in the manufacturing intermediate and traditional subsectors. Finally in commerce Ghanaian women constituted 83·7 per cent of all workers, but only 10·6 per cent of those in the modern commercial sector.

Although both men and women work within the general conditions of the informal sector, there are significant differences in their work characteristics. For example, in informal sector agriculture the extent of land ownership, opportunities for migratory activities, the type of crops grown, hours worked and size of income vary between the sexes within a particular country and ethnic group context. For instance, among the Abure of eastern Ivory Coast and other West African groups the men, on land they control, engage in commercial farming, leaving subsistence activities to their unpaid family workers – their wives and children (Clignet, 1970, p. 72). Although the Abure women are able to derive their own disposable income from the sale of subsistence crops, not all West African women have such rights, and male farming activities are often more productive as men derive larger cash flows from commercial crops and are more able to invest in fertilisers, pesticides, and so on.

Southern Ghanaian women, being part of matrilineal societies, are in large numbers farm-owners, rather than just being farm assistants. However, the characteristics of their farms differ significantly from male farms (Okali and Mabey, 1975, pp. 20–1). The women generally have smaller acreages, and are less likely to specialise in cocoa. Even women farm-owners assist on their husband's and other relatives' farms. Women start food farms at an earlier age than men and retire from production when their children are grown. As Okali describes in Chapter 11, women tend to acquire cocoa farms as gifts rather than by their own efforts, since the responsibilities of motherhood tend to limit their economic opportunities.

Within the informal agricultural sector women spend more hours at work activities than men, since they are engaged in field activities as well as in laborious domestic activities (E. Boserup, 1970, p. 192). Such domestic activities include the lengthy processing of food before cooking, the fetching of water and fuel and the collecting of vegetable food.

Generally, the occupational distribution of a country's labour force reflects the relative importance of different industries as well as the technologies used in these industries. The occupational distribution of the sexes is affected by their relative educational endowments, relative labour costs and customs.

Given the structure of their respective economies, the majority of West African men are farmers, fishermen, hunters, or loggers (Table 2.3). Substantially less than 20 per cent of the men are craftsmen or production process workers and fewer than 10 per cent are craftsmen. As the modern sector is quite small in West Africa, less than 5 per cent of male labour is employed as professional, technical

Table 2.3 Economically Active Female and Male Population by Occupational Group for Four Selected West African Countries, 1960–3 (%)

Occupational Category	Liberia (1962) female	male	Sierra Leone (1963) female	male	Ghana (1960) female	male	Nigeria (1963) female	male
Professional, technical and related workers	1·36	2·12	0·88	1·34	1·12	2·87	1·48	2·70
Administrative, executive and managerial workers	0·13	0·72	0·06	0·35	0·04	0·75	0·06	0·26
Clerical workers	0·39	1·50	0·33	0·96	0·03	2·39	0·49	1·48
Sales workers	2·62	2·72	6·60	4·17	26·73	4·03	38·29	8·02
Farmers, fishermen, hunters, loggers and related workers	93·20	70·57	89·05	66·72	55·08	58·70	22·15	66·41
Miners, quarrymen and related workers	0·14	2·56	0·08	7·05	0·18	1·90	0·00	0·09
Workers in transport and communication occupations	0·08	2·26	0·08	2·16	0·12	3·04	1·13	1·96
Craftsmen, production process workers, labourers not elsewhere classified	0·78	12·51	1·92	10·52	9·74	17·50	11·62	12·07
Service, sport and recreation workers	0·69	2·65	0·27	2·18	1·49	2·32	5·18	4·62
Workers not classified by occupation	0·50	2·33	0·70	4·50	5·21	6·51	20·56	2·34
Total	100·00	100·00	100·00	100·00	100·00	100·00	100·00	100·00

Note: The 1960–3 period was chosen for this and the following tables as comparable statistics were not available from all four countries for a later date.

Sources: International Labour Organisation, *Yearbook of Labour Statistics, 1963*, pp. 64–5; *1973*, p. 151; *1974*, pp. 148–9.

workers or as service workers. Administrative executive and managerial workers constitute an insignificant percentage of the male labour force.

The relative importance of the occupational categories for women workers is quite different from the male pattern. Moreover, the percentage of the women's labour force employed in each category by country shows more variation than is the case with the male labour force (Table 2.3). Again reflecting the economic structure of West African countries, most women are farmers. In contrast to the male pattern, the second most important occupational category is sales workers. The percentage of the female labour force in these two categories varies significantly. Countries tending to have a high percentage of women in the farmer category have a lower percentage as sales workers and vice versa. Craftsmen and production process workers represent generally less than 15 per cent of the female labour force, again with substantial variation by country. Professional and technical workers, clerical workers, administrative and managerial workers are an even smaller proportion of the female labour force than is the case with men.

Within the occupational categories there is not an equal distribution of male and female workers, or rather a distribution which reflects the percentage contribution of each to the labour force. For example, in Liberia in 1962 males represented 64 per cent of the economically active population, while women constituted the remaining 36 per cent. However, men represented 74 per cent of the professional and technical workers, while women workers were only 27 per cent of this category (Table 2.4). Men, therefore, tend to be more highly concentrated in the professions, whereas women tend to be concentrated in the sales workers and farmers/fishermen categories. Modern sector administrative, managerial and professional jobs which require high educational qualifications and which offer substantial social status and good salaries are consistently male domains in the West African countries. In contrast to the experiences of industrial countries, clerical and service workers are also primarily men.

Generally, the occupational status of working women is lower than that of their male counterparts, especially in the urban areas. For example, a recent study of the relative occupational status of husbands and wives in Abidjan found that 74 per cent of the wives had an occupational status inferior to their husbands and 17 per cent had approximately equal status (B. Lewis, 1977, p. 174). Significantly, such disparities in occupational status and income have been noted to have subtle effects on conjugal power and decision-making (Oppong, 1970), an issue which is taken up in Chapter 16 by Wambui Wa Karanja.

With higher investments in female education by West African

Table 2.4 Occupational Employment by Sex for Four Selected West African Countries, 1960–3 (%)

Occupational Category	Liberia (1962)			Sierra Leone (1963)			Ghana (1960)			Nigeria (1963)		
	male	female	total	male	female	total	male	female	total	male	female	total
Professional, technical and related workers	73·4	26·6	100	73·4	26·6	100	80·5	19·5	100	85·1	14·9	100
Administrative, executive and managerial workers	90·8	9·12	100	91·1	8·9	100	96·7	3·3	100	93·2	6·8	100
Clerical workers	87·2	12·8	100	84·0	16·0	100	93·02	6·97	100	90·4	9·6	100
Sales workers	64·8	35·1	100	53·4	46·6	100	19·6	80·4	100	39·7	60·3	100
Farmers, fishermen, hunters, loggers and related workers	57·4	42·6	100	57·6	42·4	100	63·2	36·8	100	90·4	9·6	100
Miners, quarrymen and related workers	96·9	3·1	100	99·3	0·65	100	94·5	5·5	100	98·1	1·9	100
Workers in transport and communication occupations	98·0	2·0	100	98·0	2·01	100	97·7	2·3	100	97·9	2·1	100
Craftsmen, production process workers, labourers not elsewhere classified	96·6	3·4	100	90·8	9·2	100	74·4	25·6	100	76·5	23·5	100
Service, sport and recreation workers	87·2	12·7	100	93·5	6·5	100	71·5	28·5	100	73·7	26·3	100
Workers not classified by occupation	89·2	10·8	100	92·1	7·9	100	66·9	33·1	100	26·5	73·5	100
Percentage of the labour force	64·0	36·0	100	64·0	36·0	100	61·8	38·2	100	75·9	24·1	100

Sources: As for Table 2.3.

governments, the occupational distribution of the sexes may change, more women being employed in modern sector occupations if they are available. A comparison of the Ghanaian occupational distribution by sex for the census years, 1960 and 1970, suggests that such a change has been gradually occurring. For example, in 1970, 23·4 per cent of the professional, technical and related workers were women compared with 19·5 per cent a decade earlier. Moreover, 15·5 per cent were clerical workers compared with 6.97 per cent in 1960 (International Labour Office, *Yearbook of Labour Statistics, 1963*, pp. 64–5, and *1976*, p. 168). However, the redistribution of the sexes by occupational category will probably be constrained by the rate of growth of modern sector employment.

Not only is there a distinctive difference in the occupational distribution of the sexes, but there is also a marked variation in their employment status. The majority of men are employers or workers on their own account, a reflection of the size of the rural and urban informal sectors (Table 2.5). Since the modern sector is small, less than 30 per cent of the men are salaried employees or wage-earners in private or public establishments. A minority of men are employed as family workers. In sharp contrast, a significantly large percentage of women (with the exception of Ghana) are recorded as being family workers and a much smaller group are employers or self-employed (Table 2.5). In Ghana the pattern is reversed, as women control some land and form the majority of the traders. In West Africa less than 5 per cent of the women are salaried employees or wage-earners, reflecting their limited participation in the modern sector.

Table 2.5　*Employment Status of Females and Males in Three Countries* (%)

| | Liberia (1962) | | Sierra Leone (1963) | | Ghana (1960) | |
	female	*male*	*female*	*male*	*female*	*male*
Employers and workers on own account	21·36	53·86	15·05	55·40	72·52	54·67
Salaried employees and wage-earners	3·59	32·81	1·82	15·84	4·17	29·63
Family workers	75·05	13·33	82·42	24·25	18·10	9·18
Others and status unknown	—	—	0·70	4·51	5·21	6·51
Total	100·00	100·00	100·00	100·00	100·00	100·00

Source: International Labour Organisation, *Yearbook of Labour Statistics, 1968*, pp. 46–7, 52–3.

Summary

Traditionally, the West African subsistence economy was based on a division of labour by sex and age within the compound and on the family farm. Generally, the woman could not depend on her spouse for complete support, but had to find independent ways to maintain herself and her children. Some of these ways are depicted in chapters to follow. In different ethnic groups women have had varying rights to land and to control use and disposal of the fruits of their labours. The traditional division of labour has been modified by various changes following colonisation and the subsequent setting-up of independent national governments. These have included expanding opportunities for bureaucratic employment and commerce, limited access to industrial employment, expanding educational systems and urbanisation. Examples of different types of productive work and employment are described in several chapters of this book.

Within West Africa most men are enumerated as being economically active over their lifetimes. In contrast, most women are not recorded as being in the labour force and their pattern of work activities varies among and within West African countries. Generally, in the more southern countries, particularly in the rural areas, women have higher labour force participation rates. These diverse work activity patterns reflect both the differing desires of women to seek employment outside the home and the availability of women's employment opportunities. However, statistics and modes of recording are grossly inadequate and, as Ware has already pointed out, there is a serious lack of detailed observations and time-budget studies. Most men and women are employed in agriculture. With the exception of three countries, a larger proportion of women are employed in agriculture than men. Moreover, the characteristics of male as compared with female agricultural employment are quite different. Men, in many West African countries, are self-employed farmers who raise both cash and subsistence crops, or are wage-earners who work on commercial plantations or as migrant seasonal workers. Women are generally unpaid family workers who grow primarily subsistence crops. Moreover, even in countries such as Ghana where large numbers of women have rights in land and crops farms, the characteristics of these holdings are quite different in terms of crops, acreages and technology from those of their male counterparts.

As modern sector industrial and service employment is quite small in West Africa, relatively few women and men are wage-earners and even fewer are technical, administrative, clerical, or managerial personnel. However, within these occupational categories, there is not a distribution of each sex which reflects the percentage contribution of each to the labour force. Men tend to be more highly concentrated in the modern sector occupations which require higher educational qualifications, offer substantial social status and provide good salaries. With higher investments in female education, the percentage of wage-earners who are women should increase and the occupational distribution of the sexes may change. However, the extent of this change will be determined by the overall growth of modern sector employment which influences the degree of competition between the sexes for these jobs, and by the ease with which women can combine their activities as wives and mothers with work outside the home.

Chapter 3

Patterns of Migration by Sex

ADERANTI ADEPOJU

The countries[1] that constitute the West African sub-region share some economic, social, political and demographic characteristics, relating to the varying degrees of colonial domination (with the exception of Liberia), relative political instability and under-developed economy. Perhaps a more distinctive feature relates to the contemporary demographic pattern, characterised by rapid popula-tion growth and the accompanying population redistribution, through migration, both within and across national frontiers. The rapid rate of population growth has been sustained by high fertility and relatively lower mortality, as described in Chapter 1 by Helen Ware. These features, interacting with a complex of socio-economic and historical factors, largely account for the prevailing pattern of migration.

The pattern of migration in general, and in particular differentials by sex, are closely related to the structures of the economy and the features of urbanisation. Trends in urbanisation in West Africa have been shaped largely by political and socio-economic factors in the pre-colonial, colonial and post-colonial (independence and post-independence) periods. In the process, the rural–urban continuum has become increasingly delineated: the rural agricultural areas lack basic amenities, and incomes have been low, while the urban areas have received a disproportionate share of private and public invest-ment, as a result of which incomes and living conditions have become relatively more attractive. Besides, three distinct types of towns have emerged within the urban network. The first group consists of the pre-colonial, traditional towns that pre-date contact with colonialists, which grew rapidly as a result of their location along major trade routes or as headquarters of chiefdoms: the main occupations there include crafts and trade. The second group of towns, especially those created for administrative purposes, or as transport and commercial centres in response to new economic structures, owe their origin essentially to colonisation. The predominant occupations lie in indus-try and administration. The third group consists of post-colonial cities that have responded to the influence of colonial contact on the economy; such towns have expanded considerably in response to their new functions – in administration, transport, or by new spurts in economic activities such as commerce and industry (Hance, 1970; A. L. Mabogunje, 1975; Gugler and Flanagan, 1978).

The origin and growth of these cities and the economic structure have largely shaped the pattern and process of migration there and, because of the types of occupational structures and skill requirements, their relative attraction for males and females. Besides, the high degree of concentration of industry, services and administration in a few towns, or more usually just the capital city, reinforced by the post-independence development strategies which focus development efforts heavily in capital cities, has inadvertently marked out the migration route, mainly from the poorer rural areas in the hinterland to the rapidly growing cities (Adepoju, 1975).

This chapter is confined to the sex patterns of migration – both internal and international – in West Africa. For lack of adequate data, only eight countries – Gambia, Ghana, Ivory Coast, Liberia, Senegal, Sierra Leone, Togo and Upper Volta – are included in the following tabulations. These countries have recent population censuses with information on migration.[2]

For most countries in West Africa, however, the type of data needed to disaggregate migration patterns by sex into its various forms – rural to rural, rural to urban, urban to urban and urban to rural movements – are not readily available. Few censuses include questions on place of residence at a specified time and place of birth, both of which can provide useful macro data on the volume, pattern and direction of migratory movement in a country. Besides, fewer countries publish the type of data needed for a refined analysis of sexual patterns of migration. Surveys, which have asked detailed migration questions, are usually too severely restricted in scope to give a comprehensive picture of the migration in a country. These limitations are reflected, in varying degrees, in the discussion below. First I shall examine some of the evidence on migration patterns, including sex ratios, and then I shall discuss some of the apparent determinants of sexual differences.

Patterns of Migration

West Africans have always exhibited a high tendency to migrate; the various types of population movements historically serve as a means to restore ecological balance and achieve better conditions of living and are, in most cases, related to the search for more food, better shelter and greater security. Thus, population movement in West Africa is not a new phenomenon; the region had experienced various kinds of population distribution and redistribution centuries before exposure to Western influence (United Nations Economic Commission for Africa, 1971; Addo, 1975b). Movements took the form of group migration; however, as the society became more differentiated and the economy increasingly diversified, the motivations for migration became more complex; subsequently, the direction of migration altered, becoming more voluntary and economically motivated rather than political or forced. This pattern has been paralleled by a shift from group migration, which characterised the era of internecine warfare, to individual movements; consequently, the migrants' characteristics and motivations became differentiated by socio-economic and demographic features, especially age, sex, occupation and education (Adepoju, 1975, 1981).

Early migrations in West Africa took various forms and were associated with specific reasons: internecine warfare, trade, evangelism, colonisation of new lands, slaving, and so on (United Nations Commission on Africa, 1971). The historical discontinuity arising from colonial rule makes it difficult to delineate precisely the frontiers of such movements; besides, colonial rule in West Africa strongly influenced the form and nature, and thereby the volume, motivations and the sexual composition, of migration (Amin, ed., 1974).

In pre-colonial times internal migration occurred largely in response to internal demographic adjustment to the slowly growing population; this was intensified by warfare and the search for new land, safe for settlement and fertile for farming. During the colonial period population movements were mainly from the northern savanna to the coastal regions, as was the case in Ghana, Nigeria and Ivory Coast. The destination regions for migrants were mainly areas of prosperous agricultural activities, especially the coastal forest areas which offered wage opportunities for migrant labourers in the rural areas and to a lesser extent the cities. Movements were on a short-term basis and involved mainly males. The short-term wage jobs in the mines, plantations and cash cropping agriculture provided the means of earning additional money to supplement the poor farm income at the areas of origin and to meet the new financial obligations such as tax (Amin, ed., 1974; Adepoju, 1980a; International Labour Organisation, 1975).

International migration between West African countries has been shaped by economic, political and social as well as religious factors. Of these, economic and political reasons seem to predominate. Intra-West African labour and commercial migration pre-date the colonial era, although the colonial regime altered the motivation and composition of the migration by the introduction of foreign currencies, establishing territorial boundaries and enforcing various blends of political and economic structures. These measures stimulated, and at times altered, population movements across newly created national boundaries. In particular they gave rise to the male-dominated migration which for some countries subsequently became institutionalised.

Movements within West Africa before colonial rule are scarcely documented, available information is scanty and the trends are unsystematised. Besides, the distinction between internal and international migration in West Africa is obscured by several factors. Migration between neighbouring countries with similar cultural, social, climatic and ethnic characteristics takes place on a routine basis; these factors also facilitate the integration of migrants at the destination.[3]

'Commercial' migration, across what migrants regard as artificial boundaries, is a feature of movement in West Africa, which has always been an economic and especially a trading zone within which goods, services and commercial skills have flowed from one country to another. The research by Sudarkasa (1974) among the Yoruba immigrants in Ghana amply documents this very important form of movement. Unlike labour migration, which involves the transfer of sheer physical strength and consists predominantly of single adult males, commercial migrants include males and females. In fact, West African women, especially the Yoruba, dominate the commerical sector, in particular distributive trade, in West Africa.

The major countries of emigration in West Africa include Upper Volta, Mali, Niger and Togo; Ivory Coast, Ghana and Senegal constitute countries of immigration. International migration in Nigeria is negligible, in part due to the large size of the country's population which constitutes about 60 per cent of the population of West African countries. Ivory Coast, Ghana, Liberia, Nigeria and Senegal are coastal countries and are relatively richer, while Niger, Mali (both Sahelian countries) and Upper Volta are land-locked and relatively poorer. In fact, according to the Economic Commission for Africa, some of these countries of emigration are among the least developed African countries. Upper Volta is a major labour-exporting country (Songre, 1973); Ghana and Ivory Coast are traditionally immigrant countries, until recently when Ghana began to experience a turnaround in international migration as a result of its recent economic crisis, which has spurred thousands of Ghanaians to emigrate to Togo, Nigeria and other countries. The underlying causes of the observed pattern of migration are discussed below.

The Sex Ratio of Migrants in Relation to Patterns of Migration

The sex ratio of the immigrant population and the working age-group is used as a rough indicator of the composition of migrants by sex, especially when information is also available on the sex composition of the population of the host country. Such information by age and sex as shown in Table 3.3 is also useful for the analysis of age-sex selectivity of migration.

Table 3.1 shows that lifetime immigrants in Togo and Upper Volta recorded low sex ratios of 93 and 92 respectively around 1975. The relative dominance of females for these countries contrasts sharply with the sex ratio of immigrants in Ivory Coast, Gambia, Sierra Leone and Liberia, which averages over 150 males per 100 females. When the sex ratio of immigrants is compared with the total population in working ages, as in Table 3.2, the male dominance of immigrants in Gambia, Liberia, Sierra Leone, Ivory Coast, Ghana and Senegal persists, indeed is reinforced, in these countries. The sex ratio of the working population in Gambia, Liberia, Togo and Ivory Coast tends towards normal. Senegal provides an exception (Table 3.2).

For the eight West African countries for which pertinent data are available – Gambia, Ghana, Ivory Coast, Liberia, Sierra Leone, Senegal, Togo and Upper Volta – the age-sex distribution of immigrants shows distinct patterns: immigrant males are older than their female counterparts (Table 3.3). The total population contains a high proportion of young persons under age 15 but far fewer persons aged 40 and over, when compared with male immigrants.

On a country level, the relatively younger age structure of female than male immigrants persists for all countries except Togo. In general, female lifetime immigrants are more concentrated in the age-group 15–30 than their male counterparts (Table 3.4). In effect, the proportion of male lifetime immigrants aged 40 and above in the

Table 3.1 *Sex Ratio of Lifetime Immigrants by Age around 1975, West African Countries*

Country	*0–14*	*15–39*	*40–59*	*60+*	*all ages*
Ghana	97	125	263	294	152
Ivory Coast	97	159	310	190	162
Upper Volta	107	71	93	108	92
Senegal	105	98	157	170	116
Sierra Leone	102	166	300	208	156
Togo	99	75	126	141	93
Liberia	103	146	276	272	151
Gambia	91	155	259	235	157

Males per 100 Females / Age Group

Source: Zachariah and Condé, 1980, p. 117.

Table 3.2 *Sex Ratio of Immigrants and Total Population of Working Age around 1975, West African Countries*

| | Males per 100 Females | |
Country	Immigrants	Total Population
Ghana	166	96
Ivory Coast	177	110
Upper Volta	79	94
Senegal	119	84
Sierra Leone	187	97
Togo	88	105
Liberia	164	103
Gambia	181	104

Source: Zachariah and Condé, 1980, p. 128.

countries listed in Table 3.4 is higher than that of their female counterparts; hence the discussion below focuses on the country specific sexual patterns of migration.

The male-dominated immigration to Ivory Coast is evidenced by the high concentration of males in the working age-group 40–59 with 310 males per 100 females (Table 3.1). The migrants in Ivory Coast usually live in urban areas. In Ivory Coast as in Ghana, internal migrants are more selective of females; short-distance migrants within the same department consist mainly of females, while the long-distance movers include more males. Zachariah (1980b, p. 65) suggests that marriage plays an important role in short-distance migration given the age pattern of the observed sex ratios. Interdepartmental migrants had a relatively balanced sex ratio of 112 but the major cities, especially Bouake Ville, attracted more males resulting in a sex ratio of 186.

The differences between male and female migrants in Upper Volta are indicated in the concentration in the young working ages, which is

Table 3.3 *Age Selectivity of Immigrants in West African Countries around 1975*

| | Male | | Female | |
Age Group	immigrant	total population	immigrant	total population
0–14	17·1	46·0	24·4	44·2
15–39	56·6	35·3	58·9	38·4
40–59	20·0	13·3	12·1	12·4
60+	6·3	5·4	4·5	4·9
All ages	100·0	100·0	100·0	100·0

Source: Zachariah and Condé, 1980, p. 120.

Table 3.4 *Age-Sex Distribution of Lifetime Immigrants by Country of Enumeration, West African Countries around 1975*

Country	0–14	15–39	40–59	60+	Number	%
			Age-Group			
			Males			
Ghana	13·0	47·1	28·8	11·1	210,846	100·0
Ivory Coast	10·8	69·5	17·5	4·1	652,388	100·0
Upper Volta	55·6	28·8	10·5	5·6	57,901	100·0
Senegal	18·1	45·8	26·1	10·0	145,997	100·0
Sierra Leone	24·0	54·0	16·4	5·5	48,336	100·0
Togo	49·8	32·3	18·0	4·8	69,293	100·0
Liberia	17·1	60·1	18·6	4·2	35,759	100·0
Gambia	15·5	52·8	21·2	10·5	32,268	100·0
			Females			
Ghana	20·6	57·2	16·5	5·7	139,028	100·0
Ivory Coast	18·2	69·1	9·2	3·5	401,617	100·0
Upper Volta	48·0	36·8	10·3	4·8	62,891	100·0
Senegal	19·9	54·0	19·2	6·8	126,002	100·0
Sierra Leone	36·7	50·6	8·6	4·1	31,078	100·0
Togo	46·7	40·3	9·7	3·3	74,325	100·0
Liberia	25·2	62·3	10·2	2·3	23,699	100·0
Gambia	26·6	53·5	12·9	7·1	20,515	100·0

heavier for females among internal and external migrants. Thus, 53 per cent of females but 45 per cent of male emigrants were in the age-group 15–39 in 1975, as is the case for interdepartmental migrants. The situation is not very different for immigrants, with corresponding figures of 37 per cent and 28 per cent respectively. Condé concludes that 'marriage-related migration could be the main reason behind the high proportion of female migrants in the young adult ages' (Condé, 1980, p. 75).

The 1960 and 1970 census reports of Ghana contain detailed information on internal migration relating to type, duration and distance. Immigrants in Ghana consist predominantly of males; so are inter-regional (internal) migrants.[4]

Regarding internal migration in Ghana, rural to rural migration is female-dominated, with sex ratios of 71 and 73 in 1960 and 1970 respectively. Intra-regional, often short-distance migration is also female-dominated, indicating the tendency for short-distance migration to be selective of females. Zachariah and Nair (1980a, p. 70) suggest that 'most female migration involves marriage, especially in the northern part of the country' (see Oppong, 1967b). This is a phenomenon mentioned subsequently in Chapters 4 and 6 regarding the Limba of Sierra Leone and the Songhai of Niger. In each case virilocal residence after marriage and the necessity for women to move away from their previous home areas is seen as weakening their social and economic positions. Bisilliat even writes of women's essential rootlessness. Other forms of internal migration are dominated by males: in 1960 rural–urban, urban–urban and urban–rural migrants had sex ratios of 129, 134 and 127 respectively. By 1970, however, the sex ratios considerably declined to 107, 113 and 111 respectively and involved more females than was the case in 1960.

In Senegal the sex ratio of immigrants in 1971 was 117 males per 100 females. For all types of internal migration, the sex ratio is consistently low, irrespective of duration of stay. Immigrants to Senegal consist mainly of nationals of Guinea, Gambia, Mauritania, Mali and, in particular, Guinea-Bissau. The latter include refugees dating back to the time of the liberation struggle. Most of the migration is directed to the capital city, Dakar, and as a result the city's population constitutes 48 per cent of the total urban population in the country.[5]

More than 20 per cent of the economically active Togolese live permanently outside their country. It is indicated that the small population size (2·2 million in 1978), low urbanisation, rigid land law, widespread illiteracy and low level of non-agricultural activities in Togo, coupled with historical and political factors, make external migration more important than internal migration.

Very little information is available on migration, both internal and international, on a macro level in Nigeria. For the country as a whole the overall sex ratio was 102 in 1963. The highest ratios occur in the age-group 45–59. Lagos also recorded sex ratios of 119 and 131 in 1950 and 1963 respectively (George and Eigbefor, 1973, p. 406).

The sex ratio among rural migrants in Nigeria indicates that family rather than male-only movements feature prominently: non-migrants have a sex ratio of 102 while migrants recorded a sex ratio of 107–99 for those born in other villages, 103 for those born in small towns and 114 for those born in big towns. Rural migrants attracted to subsistence cropping villages consisted more of males (sex ratio of 112) than those attracted to cash cropping villages (sex ratio of 103) (Adepoju, 1980a). The situation is different for migrants in medium-sized towns, the sex ratio averaging 131 for migrants compared with 106 for non-migrants (Adepoju, 1980b).

Determinants of the Sexual Patterns of Migration

The male-female pattern of migration in West Africa is related to the structure of economic activities, socio-cultural factors defining sex roles and the impact of education on spatial and occupational mobility of females. These factors have reinforced the external factors of colonisation which facilitated population movements in general: cessation of hostilities, diversification of economic activities resulting in rising aspirations and expectations, and improvements in communication and transportation which have fostered greater urban–rural links (Mabogunje, 1975; Adepoju, 1981).

In the colonial period various measures were adopted to attract the right kind and quantity of labour force required for the rapidly expanding administration, commerce and plantation agriculture.[6] The structure of employment required mostly adult men, who tended to migrate alone while leaving their wives behind, permanently or for a short period of time (Addo, 1975a,b).[7]

The observed male dominance in migration, as indicated above, is also related to the direction of the dominant form of migration and, in particular, the economic structure of the destination area.[8] The relative opportunity structures and nature of employment for either sex are determined in part by their relative skills, the prevailing sex segregation and discrimination in the organised labour market, the perceived role of females and the types of occupational structures. These factors have also been shaped, historically, by socio-cultural perceptions of division of labour, which defined the role of women as house-keepers and workers within the household economic system and farm.

Socio-cultural constraints also influence the sexual pattern of migration. To a large extent, West African society is, in general, more permissive of out-migration of boys than girls (Mabogunje, 1975, p. 165). This is paralleled by the cultural bias which favours the education of boys rather than girls, which is discussed in Chapter 15. Since employment in the formal sector is highly correlated with education, few females are able to secure wage jobs in the highly competitive urban employment market. Indeed, the major cities which were integrated into export-oriented market economies offer restricted opportunities for women apart from in trade and commerce (Adepoju, 1981).

In Lagos Ejiogu (1975, p. 319) notes that initially migrants left families at home and visited periodically, but as opportunities expanded they brought their wives to Lagos. Also, as more females migrated to Lagos, the migrant population became more settled and family rather than single migration featured in recent migration streams.[9] At the current level of economic development in Africa most of the male as well as female work lies in the agricultural sector. The cyclical demands for labour in the agricultural sector and the variable timetable of farming – in cash and food production – in various parts of West Africa provide ample opportunity for farmers to migrate to areas of greater labour demand to earn extra money to supplement their poor incomes at home. During their absence, women, who are already actively engaged in farming, bear the extra burden, combining household chores with farmwork. Hitherto immigrants have had lower educational statuses than the nationals of the host countries,[10] but internal migration has been associated with education (e.g. Caldwell, 1969, regarding Ghana). As the level of education in general improves and women attain higher levels of education, and if employment opportunities in urban areas – in both the formal and informal sectors – increase, female internal migration is likely to increase.

Thadani and Todaro (1978) have suggested that female migration should be examined in terms of sex role constraints, thereby de-emphasising the economic motives.

A few studies in West Africa provide empirical evidence to support this approach. Campbell (1978, p. 3) shows, for instance, that in Sierra Leone 85 per cent of female internal migration was sequential to that of males, and while 37 per cent of male migrants went to the city to find work, only 13 per cent of female migrants gave such reasons; 41 per cent migrated for reasons connected with marriage. Sudarkasa (1974, p. 51) found that among Nigerians in Ghana in the 1960s migration of females was closely linked to their marital status. They migrated because of marriage. Among men, however, many migrants have tended to be bachelors. Thus in Ghana in 1970 more than 80 per cent of male immigrants from Togo, Nigeria and Niger were bachelors: for Voltaics and Malians the corresponding figures were 75 per cent and 66 per cent respectively. In 1960 only 9 per cent of Voltaic emigrants were married and among the male emigrants from southern Mossi in 1968, 78 per cent were single. In Upper Volta, over three-quarters of male emigrants aged 20–29 were single, while only 6 per cent of their female counterparts were spinsters, as were 9 per cent for female internal migrants in the same age-group (International Labour Organisation, 1975).

Conclusion

This chapter relates the prevailing sexual pattern of migration in West Africa to socio-economic, political and historico-cultural factors which have shaped the direction of development and types of economic activities; and which have indirectly influenced the role and status of women and their participation in the formal and informal sectors of the economy and, in the process, the sexual composition of migration, both internal and international.

Colonial rule resulted in structural changes in employment, aspirations and needs which in turn led to a reorganisation of the division of labour, and avenues for needs fulfilment. The predominant occupation for both males and females has been, and still is, farming. The imposition of taxation, introduction of foreign currencies and orientation of traditional economies to export production have led to a variety of changes; one outstanding result has been to 'force' the males to migrate to the new centres of wage employment in mining, plantation agriculture and administration, to earn additional money to meet the new demands. The females have remained behind to continue farming, combining this with petty trading, child care and house-keeping. The male migration has been facilitated by the seasonality of agricultural activity and varying demands for farm labour in parts of the sub-region. While a few women participated as 'commercial' migrants, the male-dominated migration, and the implied sex ratio, persisted until the time of independence.

By independence, what initially was forced migration, later coloured with incentives, had already become institutionalised. The gradual spread of education for girls as well as boys and in some cases the increased prospects for employment of women as well as men in urban areas have since increased the tendencies for women as well as men to travel as autonomous migrants.

Again, the recent improvements in urban living conditions for migrant workers have encouraged male married migrants to be accompanied or later joined by their wives and children. This tends to reduce commuting between home and workplace, although there is detailed evidence that in some cases this still continues. Unlike the case of international migration, which still mainly involves males, internal migration, especially over short distances, still includes more females than males, as marriage for the most part still tends to be virilocal.

Notes: Chapter 3

1 These are Cape Verde Islands, Republic of Benin, The Gambia, Ghana, Guinea, Guinea-Bissau, Ivory Coast, Liberia, Mali, Mauritania, Niger, Nigeria, Senegal, Sierra Leone, Togo and Upper Volta.

2 Information derived from sample surveys will be used in the case of Nigeria; the results of the 1973 census which contained information on migration have since been nullified. Most French-speaking West African countries have recently carried out their first census exercise: Ivory Coast (1975), Upper Volta (1975), Togo (1958–60, 1970), Senegal (demographic sample surveys, 1960–1, 1970–1; census, 1976). The English-speaking countries – Gambia, Ghana, Liberia and Sierra Leone – have conducted one or two censuses with useful information on migration: Gambia (1963, 1973), Ghana (1960, 1970), Liberia (1962, 1974) and Sierra Leone (1963, 1974).

3 For instance, Togo and Ghana have close ethnic and linguistic similarities. In fact,

the eastern region of Ghana was formerly part of Togo before it became part of Ghana at the time of independence in 1956. Movements between the two countries, whose borders cut across the Ewe-speaking people, are largely uncontrolled. The same observation is true of the Yoruba-speaking people of south-west Nigeria and the neighbouring country – the Republic of Benin. More important also, for most West African countries, 'the borders are long, recently established and easily crossed and inspections are rare' (International Labour Organisation, 1975, p. 4).

4   The sex ratio remained unchanged for intra-regional (internal) migrants, with a sex ratio of 76 in 1960 and 1970, while inter-regional migrants recorded a slight decline in sex ratio from 129 in 1960 to 120 in 1970 (Zachariah and Nair, 1980c, p. 70). Non-migrants had a relatively stable sex ratio of 101 in 1960 and 100 by 1970. Between 1960 and 1970 the sex ratio of international migrants declined from 175 to 152. The sex ratio of immigrants in Ghana varies considerably by nationality, and over time. In 1960 the sex imbalance was pronounced for immigrants from Niger and Mali, both Sahelian countries, with sex ratios of 802 and 674 respectively. Other nationals had relatively lower sex ratios: Upper Volta 275, Liberia 200, Ivory Coast 154, Nigeria 146. By 1970 both Niger and Mali nationals still have predominantly male immigrants with sex ratios of 677 and 557 respectively. The sex ratios for nationals of Benin and Ivory Coast remained constant for the census years 1960 and 1970, while Nigerians recorded relatively higher sex ratios increasing from 146 to 194. It has been suggested that for some nationals possibly more wives and daughters emigrated from Ghana following the Aliens Compliance Order of 1969 (Zachariah and Nair, 1980, pp. 99–100).

5   Migrants in rural areas recorded the lowest sex ratio of 80, rising to 89 for those in urban areas. The 1970/1 demographic survey shows that Senegal had an excess of females in the total population. The reasons are not clear but it is feasible that the highly selective male out-migration plays a major role in the observed low sex ratio of 91 for the non-migrant population in the country.

6   These include the forced labour recruitment policies vigorously pursued by the French colonialists (Songre, 1973; Conde, 1980); the development of timber and cocoa industry in Ghana (Addo, 1975b); the recruitment of Nigerians to the plantations in Spanish Equatorial Guinea; the recruitment of civil servants from Togo; and the development of groundnut production in Senegambia which attracted 'stranger farmers', to mention a few instances. The forced or induced labour consisted mainly of male, adult workers; for some, such migration later became institutionalised.

7   For example, in Ghana, during the colonial era, the introduction and/or expansion of mining and cocoa farming around the 1870–80 decade and the systematic orientation of the economy towards export production in general created great demands for manual workers which the native population could not adequately satisfy or which they actually scorned. Hence, labourers were attracted or recruited from Ivory Coast, Togo, Upper Volta and Nigeria.

8   In Ghana, for instance, while less than 30 per cent of Ghanaians lived in urban areas, more than 50 per cent of Liberian, Malian and Nigerian immigrants there lived in urban areas in 1970. In contrast, over half of international migrants from Ivory Coast, Togo and Benin lived in rural areas.

9   The point of view, expressed by Little (1970, pp. 18–19), that 'the aim of regulations controlling women's movement was to bind them to the villages as *hostages* for the return of their absent men' grossly distorts the determinants of male/female migration in West Africa.

10 For instance, in Ivory Coast, Ghana, Togo and Gambia nationals are more literate than lifetime immigrants, both males and females. In Ivory Coast, in 1975, of the population aged 6 years and above, only 15 per cent of male immigrants and 9 per cent of females are literate, compared with 38 and 19 per cent respectively of

nationals. In Gambia only 7 per cent and 5 per cent of male and female immigrants aged 5 years and over in 1973 completed primary school, compared with 15 per cent and 7 per cent respectively of nationals (Zachariah and Condé, 1980).

Conclusion to Part One

In this section we have given a comparative statistical framework for the case studies to follow. Certain important themes have been emphasised, such as the high levels of fertility and thus the high burden of child dependency borne by the parental generation, in populations half or more of which may be composed of children, and the associated physical consequences for women in terms of repeated pregnancy and lactation. At the same time women and men are heavily involved in agriculture, in the production and marketing of food. Meanwhile, increasing numbers are migrating townward to seek urban sector employment. Women are noted to be more locally mobile than men, since many leave their natal homes at marriage, but over long distances and across national boundaries men have tended to migrate more. Migration trends are noted to be related to changing access to opportunities for employment and income generation. Thus, for instance, at the present time Ghana, which was formerly a country of heavy in-migration, is now undergoing a period of extensive out-migration.

This overall pattern of variables, including education, has been depicted to form the back-cloth for the series of detailed micro studies to follow. The first set of such cases focuses upon the ways in which the life-spheres of women and men tend to be simultaneously separate and yet interconnected and complementary.

II Case Studies

Part Two

Male and Female Spheres: Separate and Connected

Introduction to Part Two

A notable feature of social and economic life in West Africa is the segregation of the sexes and yet at the same time the sense of connection and complementarity of the roles of women and men is strong and pervasive. In the following series of case studies we shall view this simultaneous ambiguity of separation and connectedness in several spheres of traditional life: in the division of labour; in political and military life; in ritual and ideology; in domestic economies; and in sexuality and procreation. These chapters incorporate studies carried out among the Limba, Akan, Songhay, Hausa and Yoruba.

Themes raised in the earlier comparative chapters which reappear here and are repeated again in subsequent chapters are the effects upon women's position of their frequent lack of a stable residence, because of the dominant pattern of brides joining their husbands at marriage; and the tendency for males to monopolise control of the most important decision-making processes, basic productive resources such as land and crops, and important professional skills. Meanwhile, whatever their activities within or beyond the confines of the home, women maintain a basically domestic or maternal orientation, through the demands of continually repeated pregnancies and periods of lactation, in cultures in which the parental role might be designated the most highly valued and critical of all roles for adult status.

At the same time, however, we are given important insights into female spheres of control and influence and remark female assertiveness in heterosexual encounters; women's alacrity in taking up opportunities for entrepreneurial activities; their maintenance of autonomous female societies and rituals; and their control, management and allocation of critical domestic resources, including food and children's labour.

Ultimately, in spite of emphases upon separation and apparent male domination, the themes of complementation interdependence and mutual need and co-operation are stressed – themes which are continually expressed and reinforced by exchanges of mutually gratifying goods and services between women and men in their capacities as wives and husbands, sisters and brothers, parents and children. In the activities of production and consumption, in the exercise of power and control, in artistic, ritual and symbolic expression, in sexual relations and procreation, female and male roles – their behaviours and expectation – are seen to be intrinsically complementary and interconnected. Neither can exist alone.

Producing and Performing

In communities with simple technologies women and men spend much of their time producing the things that they need every day, including pots and pans, ropes and mats, furniture and houses, cloth and clothing. Such activities are described in Chapter 4 by Simon Ottenberg, writing about the Limba people of northern Sierra Leone. His chapter on the artistic and sex roles of the Bafodea chiefdom provides an example of both the separation and the simultaneous complementarity of male and female spheres of activity and interest. Thus he describes the productive patterns as co-operative and complementary, but males retain the most important social and political control, settling most disputes and making most important decisions, and retaining economic control since they are in possession of the main farm land and the main crop, rice. At the same time they dominate professional and religious fields.

As he describes the society, it is in the sphere of the performing arts that the worlds of the sexes achieve their most perfect communion, in a shared and emotionally laden world of music, dance and dramatic performance. In musical events he perceives achievement of aesthetic solidarity of women and men.

Ruling and Deciding

In Chapter 5 Kwame Arhin describes the Akan traditional political and military systems, noting how a hierarchy of female roles complemented those of males; female rulers sat on councils and were responsible for women's affairs. Such female rulers took part in legal, military and economic decision-making and action and were looked upon as moral guardians of the community and repositories of traditional wisdom, including knowledge of royal genealogies, thus providing critical evidence to support claims to royal succession. On the women depended to a large degree the peace, order and stability of the political community.

Arhin argues that the Akan saw woman as an educator, a moral guardian, and that in the political process male and female roles complemented each other. Meanwhile he introduces a theme taken up again later in Chapter 16, that British colonialism effectively introduced male bias into the political system and shattered the neat balance of male-female power and interdependence.

Ambivalence and Ambiguity

In Chapter 6 on the Songhay, by Jeanne Bisilliat, several fundamental dilemmas involved in sex roles are discussed. The cross-sex sibling bond between brother and sister is one of fundamental solidarity, and yet in a system of virilocal marriage women have to go away to marry. Brothers and sisters have to separate, but forever strong ties bind them and their children, as she illustrates by telling a mythical story. At the same time women who are the bearers of the next generation appear on the surface to be of minor importance in a system, like many others in Africa, in which descent and residence are defined in terms of agnatic ties and male roles. Men control all the main resources and children belong to their fathers not their mothers, who are even prevented by custom from expressing their love for their first-born. However, in myth the closer ties of mothers and maternal kin to children are acknowledged.

Spatial Separation: Inside and Outside

Chapter 7 by Enid Schildkrout is set in Hausa society in northern Nigeria, a cultural area in which the lives of adult men and women are highly segregated. Islam reinforces a separation of the female and male domains by sanctioning the distinction between the private, domestic, domain, controlled mainly by females, and the public domain outside controlled by males. The spatial separation of women and men is meant to protect adults from the potentially chaotic effects of uncontrolled sexuality. Children in this context are the only persons free to move between the female and male domains. Until puberty, by which time sex roles are assumed, children mediate between the public and private sphere. This is evident in their spatial mobility and in their activity patterns which are not restricted by sex. The distinctive roles of children complement the sex-segregated roles of adults and enable this rigid separation of sexual domains to exist.

Women in this context are largely accounted in statistics to be unemployed, as was noted in Chapter 2, and yet observations within the household demonstrate that they are busily occupied in income-generating tasks within the house, processing foodstuffs and other things for sale. Here we are given more insight into reasons for parental reluctance to send girls to school and realisation that schooling will have a revolutionary impact on the domestic economy and sex roles as well as in other spheres.

This phenomenon of spatial separation of adult females from males through their domestic seclusion in purdah in Islamic societies has attracted considerable attention and we are told it is a phenomenon that continues to increase in West Africa. It is seen here to be facilitated by the continued participation of women in the market economy through the assistance of their children. A recurrent theme is the ambivalence of men to the women's income-producing activities and their feigned lack of interest or knowledge regarding the dowries which women are able to obtain. Again, such latent antagonism is revealed in story-telling.

Sex and Birth

The last chapter of Part Two, Chapter 8, is about that sphere of activities which brings men and women into closest proximity – the sexual embrace and the consequent bearing and rearing of infants. Lawrence Adeokun has studied this among two groups of Yoruba. He discusses a critical aspect of the marital relationship – *post partum* abstinence, sexual relations and their curtailment after childbirth. This is a widespread behavioural pattern which has important demographic consequences and individual effects, as Ware noted in Chapter 1, and which may be radically affected by shifts from polygyny to monogamy or by the breakdown of traditional restraints following upon migration and the diminishing restraints of kin. In this particular account, of special interest is the author's observation of small but significant differences in the behaviour and expectations of two neighbouring subgroups of the Yoruba, which have subtle effects on marital relations and fertility outcomes. He indicates how this sexual and procreative behaviour is integrated with patterns of female work outside the home – mainly the production and sale of agricultural goods.

Chapter 4

Artistic and Sex Roles in a Limba Chiefdom

SIMON OTTENBERG

At least three general views can be postulated concerning the relationships of artistic roles and the more general sex roles in a society. One is that the expressive roles and behaviour will be similar to the general sex roles, given the tendency towards consistency in societies and the importance of art and aesthetics in expressing core values and interests. A second is that artistic sex roles will deviate considerably from general sex roles, for here it is possible to give vent to behaviour and attitudes which differ from the norm, for the arts are somewhat eccentric to society. A third possibility is a paradox: that both the first and second views may be true. Artistic matters may reinforce and at the same time deny basic social and sex roles.[1] I shall examine these three views in the context of a specific case.

The Limba of Wara Wara Bafodea chiefdom live in Koinadugu District in northern Sierra Leone (Finnegan, 1965). They are a people of considerable antiquity in their region, transitional between the more thoroughly forest cultures of other Limba, Temne and Mende to the south, and of the savanna Muslim cultures of great tradition, Fula and Mandingo, to the north. In the later part of the nineteenth century a major trade route, the Falaba road, passed through Bafodea, giving it some prominence. This has long since gone and the chiefdom is relatively isolated, without a major trading centre within its borders. The first motor road was built in the south of Bafodea about 1953, and in the north in 1979. This northern part was once a separate chiefdom called Kamuke.

The Bafodeans are rice and groundnut growing peoples, palm wine drinking and palm oil consuming, essentially farmers living in villages ranging in size from several thousand to less than a hundred inhabitants. Smaller farm settlements attached to these villages are endemic. The population density is not high, although accurate figures are not available. The Limba are surrounded by less permanently settled Fula cattle-keepers who fill the interstices of the country. But it is of the Limba that I write.

The major sex roles show features characteristic of other West African societies. Formal political roles in the chiefdom are almost entirely in male hands, be it at the chiefdom level or that of village political structure. The Bafodea paramount chief, section chiefs, speaker and other big politicians are male. At the village level the village head, his speaker and others are also men. There is a traditional head woman for most villages and for the chiefdom, a position in recent years reinforced by government sanction. These women settle some disputes among females, arrange for the feeding of visitors and carry out other duties, but they are not powerful figures. The bulk of decision-making and dispute and settlement remains in male hands – certainly in matters involving disputes over land and other resources, and cases of witchcraft, theft and assault. Women settle quarrels among themselves, but if they remain unresolved men take over the decision-making. Women can make their needs felt as a group to the male heads and their views are taken seriously.

In the histories of the chiefdom and of villages women rarely appear, except as genealogical links, or as a master magician in the days of warfare.

Every adult woman has a male protector. It is said she needs this in the event she dies, in order to have a male to direct her burial, whether this person be a husband, father, other relative, lover, chief, or a big man she has attached herself to as a widow. While men are, of course, very much dependant on woman for food and other needs, an adult male has dependent relationships with a number of women, rather than with one. Marriages are arranged when a girl is young – she may even be yet unborn – and completed when she is around the age of 15, several years after her initiation into the Bondo society. Maybe she marries a young man ten years older than she, a marriage arranged through his father or brother, or perhaps she goes to a male old enough to be her father or grandfather. Because of age differences women often marry two or three times in their lives, thus moving from place to place. They lack the stability of residence of males, a major factor in their subordinate sex role position.

Males enjoy a period of dalliance between adolescence and marriage, although they must perforce largely have relations with married women, but girls have a very much briefer period. Both sexes generally accept arranged marriages, though one of the parties may delay them and if one is very strongly in objection the arrangement may be broken off. Women frequently leave their husbands for periods of time, or permanently, and while parents and other relatives may pressure them to return they are not bound to do so. In marriage matters there is both freedom and constraint.

Land and most property is handed down agnatically, as are surnames. And ruling families can trace their male line of descent through up to ten or more generations. But this is not a heavily patrilineal society. Ancestors on the mother's side, through both the mothers's mother and the mother's father, are reckoned. Most adults trace descent on both father's and mother's side through three or four generations. A male or a female recognises the nearly equal importance of all four grandparents. For both men and women supportive ties exist with the mother's side and various members of her family of birth. Children's relationships with their mother are particularly strong and endure through life. The father, often the head of a good-sized family and preoccupied with various matters, may be a more distant figure. These features, except for the important one of property controls, do not suggest a strongly dominant male bias in the structure of descent. Yet the father or grandfather role is a strong one in the family; he makes the major decisions and settles important intra-family quarrels.

Women do the household tasks – cooking, cleaning, washing, gathering wood for fires and incessantly pounding rice. They are domestically oriented – few have other occupations. They breastfeed a child for two to three years, then quickly produce another infant, whether from husband or lover, for married women may have lovers to complement or supplement their marriages. In these matters females are not shy, but as men, play assertive roles, so that the bonds of an early marriage are not confining. This assertive quality in women is present in other domains, such as in disputes and in demands made to their husbands.

Both men and women farm, often doing complementary work, as in the case of swamp rice growing, and the production of potatoes and some groundnut crops. Other foods are more exclusively female: some groundnuts, beans, cassava and also cotton. Women are not expected to sell crops they grow unless they have a very substantial surplus; these are for household use. Men work upland rice and groundnut farms and they tap palm wine which their wives or other women sell on a share-the-profits basis. The prime rice farming land, the swamp areas, generally belongs to men, although women may be allotted a section to farm by a husband or another male; and the use of this rice is largely controlled by males. The richness of this swampland is such that after the rice harvest a second crops of potatoes, groundnuts, or even cassava, may be grown there through the mutual work of men and women. Upland areas are relatively easy to acquire by either sex for rice, groundnuts, or other crops, for there is little upland shortage in this chiefdom. These features suggest a co-operative and complementary productive pattern, with the crucial controls in male hands, although opportunities exist for female entrepreneurship.

Most professional skills are in the male sphere, including blacksmithing, woodwork, divining, medicine (there are a few female diviners and medical persons), and swear persons who deal with witches and theft. The tools used in the productive life are almost entirely made by men; and the guidance of the religious life, except with regard to secret societies, is largely in male hands, including the carrying-out of many sacrifices and religious rites, though women participate in these.

Both male and female secret societies are found, Gbangbani and Bondo respectively, quite autonomous of one another. These have elaborate initiation rites involving circumcision and clitoridectomy. These rites are secret from the other sex, a privacy well respected at Bafodea. Each society can 'close the town' to the other sex, making them stay behind closed doors. The male society does this with some frequency, the female rarely. Each society has punishments, accepted by the other sex, for abuse of its rules and taboos. Some Bafodea men like to say that the male is more dominant because the Bondo often has a male ritual specialist as a member while the reverse is not true. But the female society is an autonomous and equivalent organisation to the male, making its own rules and controlling its own members and its internal affairs. The female society carries out initiations, burials and certain healing rites; the male society has somewhat broader activities. Neither organization has political power.

In short, Bafodea is a society in which males retain the major social, political and economic controls and dominate professional fields, but where there is a great deal of complementarity of economic and social activities between the sexes, rather than rivalry. Although the north of the chiefdom is Muslim and traditionalist and the south has both these and Christian elements, these general features still obtain. From the point of view of the values of the modern Western world, Bafodea is a place where women's activities are largely limited to the domestic sphere, women do more physical labour on a continual basis than men, control of productive resources is in male hands, and the principle professional occupations are male.

Girls and women are not, in general, in rebellion against the Bafodea organisation of sex roles. Those few who are generally leave the chiefdom. Girls are sometimes a little frightened of the initiation operation but they look upon it as a natural and necessary path to womanhood. Women are more concerned with finding an interesting and supportive husband, in living in peace with a family, in having healthy children, and in fighting off death, disease and troubles stemming from witches, ancestors, or God, than they are with a sense of equality with men. Justice lies in a happy household, with plenty of children, peaceful co-wives, a generous husband and productive farms.

There is no doubt that the society is moving from a more extreme form of patriarchy, which was tied to conditions of warfare in the chiefdom in the nineteenth century and earlier, when husbands played a stronger role with their wives and women did little trading or moving about. Today trading has opened up new possibilities for females, but it is still only on a small scale at Bafodea.

I now turn to those aspects of Bafodea life which customarily are included in the arts by anthropologists without belabouring the question of what is and is not art. Here I will stress the question of choice in design or styling, and the degree of professionalisation, for example, to what extent do persons produce and sell on a regular basis? I begin with material objects.

There are only a few potters now; the plastics and metals of the world have replaced clay containers. The potters, who are female, make small medicine pots, a somewhat larger general purpose container, and a large water storage pot. The scarcity of potters is such that I was fifteen months in the field before I found one actually at work. They have generally learned their trade from their mothers or other older female relatives. None of the present-day Bafodea Limba pottery that I have seen is decorated; it is thick and utilitarian. In the sites of old Limba villages one also finds this pottery, as well as other clay pieces with decorated incisions, some of which are intricate. My information, which is limited, is that the decorated work was of Mandingo or Fula origin, although there may have been Limba women who learned this skill from them. In any case the Limba pottery of today does not manifest much aesthetic expression or choice in design. There is no doubt, however, that the few remaining potters are professionals, in that they produce regularly for sale during the dry season.

Weaving, in narrow bands three to four inches in width, is done entirely by men. Both European and native thread are used. Variation in design lies in the arrangement of the warp or long threads, where European black or white thread is laid alongside native white; occasionally indigo-dyed blue native thread is also used. The sense of style and quality comes in the manner in which men design these warp layouts; the weft thread is invariably white. It also lies in the manner that the weavers, or other men as tailors, arrange the woven cloth bands into garments to create certain design patterns. Again, there is an industry of dying, and then lining and stamping some of the sewn cloths with black designs. This is also done by men.

Native cloths are much used by men as both upper and lower

garments; women often employ them as waist cloths. But females of all ages seem to prefer the brighter, more varied colours of European and Asian printed cloth and wear these most of the time at the waist, upper body, and as headties. Their influence on the production of foreign cloth would be in what they select and reject to buy, but there there is little choice as Bafodea has a small market; what the sellers have the women purchase, unless they go to a city to buy.

Women grow cotton and spin it in their free time, a warp thread and a thicker and looser weft. A woman may give these to her husband to have cloth made for himself or for her, or she may take it to a weaver to make a waist cloth or blanket, or she may even secretly sell the thread to gain some funds independent of her husband. But I know of no professional spinners, in the sense of women who spin fairly regularly to sell thread for a living. Women's contribution to the production of dress at Bafodea is therefore important but utilitarian. Even the crocheted wool caps often worn by men in the chiefdom are made by specialist male workers, using wool from imported second-hand sweaters.

Women have no part in the production of metal jewellery, except as clients of the producers. Jewellery is made from old aluminium pots or sometimes from old coins – ear-rings, bracelets, hair pieces – often with incised or punched designs. They are produced by male Limba blacksmiths. Silver and gold work – not too common at Bafodea – as well as aluminium are also worked by Fula and smiths from other groups. But much of the jewellery worn by women is inexpensive imported ware, some attractive but little that is elegant.

In only one field do women produce attractive dressing objects. This is in the necklaces and waistbands that females of all ages wear and in the headbands that girls in stages of initiation tie around their foreheads. Some necklaces are of native seeds, simply strung on a single thread or cord, but others are of small coloured imported glass beads, as are the forehead bands, strung in more complex ways on some six to twelve or more parallel threads. In the glasswork delightful triangular and diamond-shaped designs occur. Many girls and women occasionally make these; there is no real professionalisation. To produce one done well takes patience, and here there is choice of colour and design arrangement and the skill and sense of style of individual workers comes out clearly.

There is little wood carving at Bafodea. Wood dolls and animals are made by boys and young men at the farm huts, but not for ritual purposes. Simple incised designs, often in the form of rows of Vs, occur on wooden mortars, spoons and combs and on wooden gongs. Crudely carved human heads and figures are associated with the men's society. Sometimes elegantly incised designs are found on the fronts of wooden boxes made by blacksmiths. Women take no part in this woodwork, although they use many of these objects, including the decorated box, often a part of their dowry. As far as I know females have no influence on the production of any of these designs. They accept what is done.

In the world of things made from fibres, especially mats, hammocks and basketry, the work is mainly done by middle-aged and elderly men. The skill in working plant fibres to produce mats, sometimes with simple linear designs, is male, as is hammock production, where more elaborate linear and triangular designs exist. Most storage baskets and a wide range of smaller baskets and bags of various fibres are prepared by males. Many of these objects have V or linear designs on them. There is some professionalisation, especially of hammock-makers and a few basket-producers, and some men who make ceiling mats for sale. However, sleeping mats are widely produced by many persons. Women make only two forms of carrying baskets, using linear designs similar to those of the men, and made by like techniques of workmanship.

From what I have said so far there is little to suggest a heavy concern of women in the arts. There is the production of interesting objects with glass beads, the making of some plain pottery and a little basketry. But in the decoration of the human body the situation is reversed. Men do not have decorative hairstyling as a rule, or body markings.

It is in the styling of female hair that one sees an elegance of taste and choice, as throughout much of West Africa. There are some five or six Limba female hairstyles, one form associated with girls' initiation. It is in the choice of style and the skill of plaiting that real talent lies. Women and older girls do the hair of daughters and other girls, mothers, sisters, friends and the like, although the tool of hairdressing, a decorated aluminium hair piece or a wooden comb, is made by male smiths. To the Limba styles have come others from urban centres to the south, such as Makeni, Freetown and Bo, so that the choice is enlarged, and a selection sometimes of the dresser, at other instances of the dressed, is possible. If women's clothing is, on the whole, not as elegant as Fulani or Mandingo dress, in part due to the poverty of the area, for there is little money about, the hair work is superb, focusing attention on the face and head. Again, female hair-dressing is rarely professionalised; people simply do the plaiting for nothing or for a little gift. Male hairstyles do not involve plaiting and are simple in contrast.

There are also extensive female body and face markings. These are generally done by adolescent girls to themselves and to one another, using glass pieces, knives, the juice of the locust tree bean, or the liquid from an insect found in cow dung. The marks are dots, particularly in older persons, or lines, up to an inch in length. Sometimes the cuts are heavily welted, in other cases they are thin and light, depending on the technique employed and the skill of the operator. V designs sometimes appear but little more elaborate than that – no circles, squares, stars, moons, or the like. The short lines are often arranged in parallel rows. They may appear below and to the outside of the eyes and across the forehead. Boys sometimes make these face markings too but not body cuts. Other favourite areas for females are the stomach, upper chest, shoulder area and upper back. Designs may be elaborate in that many cuts may be made. While these tend to form in parallel rows they are arranged in complex designs, and the parallelism is often imprecise. Extreme accuracy in the work is not part of the aesthetic, as elsewhere in Bafodea. The designs do not normally have names and there is no professionalism of this craft.

In our last concern, the performing arts, there is a rich and versatile aesthetic tradition at Bafodea, and here we find the highest elaboration of Bafodea artistic skills. At first glance male dominance might appear to exist. In the northern part of the chiefdom the women play no musical instrument at all. Even the drums of the Bondo society are played by men. In the southern sections, however, females utilise their own drums and a gourd rattle with glass beads. All of the other forms of instruments – a range of drums, wooden and iron gongs, the flute, the African finger piano – are played by males.

Yet despite this disparity in the sex roles of musicians, also reflected in the number of occasions when women play instruments compared with men, it is in music, song and dance, as well as storytelling, that female aesthetic expression largely centres. That of men is strong here as well, but it is also diffused over other art forms, as we have already indicated.

If you ask a woman which form of musical play she prefers she will probably say 'Bondo'. If you ask her why, she will say it is 'our music'. Men may play the musical instruments of Bondo in the north, males may occasionally come out and dance, or may even sponsor the play, as at a second funeral, but it is an art form dominated and controlled by females in which males are characteristically onlookers at the outer ring of the circle, while women sing and dance.

The Bondo period is at the commencement of the dry season, December to March, when the initiation of adolescent girls occurs and a subsequent (sometimes two or three dry seasons later) final rite takes place, the 'washing hands' of the girls. Usually two or three initiating girls have their own musical group for the first event, with a collection of female followers and helpers of various ages, which mirrors kinship, neighbourhood and friendship ties. There is night after night of practice sessions with mothers, older sisters and other adult females encouraging the initiating girls to dance and sing, but also doing so themselves. The singing is led, at times, by a professional, often a drummer who has organised the musicians, although the initiating girls are expected to lead songs with the female audience as chorus; other women may start songs as well. The songs are varied and rich in text, frequently referring to an initiating girl, to a daughter going to the bush 'tomorrow', to the loss for the mother in housework help; or the song may say: let the girl dance tonight for tomorrow she goes to the bush – almost as if she were not returning. For example:

> My only daughter is going to be circumcised. Lord!

Or another song:

> It is true you own Yebu. It is almost time to go to the bush.

Yebu is a girl's name. 'You' refers to the Bondo women.
Or the songs may mirror personal conditions, as:

> When I die I will not be buried. I will be thrown in the water.

This refers to a woman who has no children. Or in another song:

> If you do a bad thing people will exaggerate it.

Night after night the music plays for hours until on the final occasion, when the initiating girls are specially dressed, there is playing throughout much of the night, the women at an emotional pitch one rarely sees otherwise. The two to five drums are played on the ground, the larger ones with a steady set of beats, the smaller deliberately shifting the beating according to the steps and pacing of whoever is dancing. Skill in playing this smaller drum is what makes for a great Bondo drummer. While many persons can drum and sing, there are some who are professionals – in the north of the chiefdom men and in the south, women. In the case of women, the one who plays the variable drum is also the singer. It is she who is hired, often by the girls themselves, although their parents may pay, and she brings other musicians with her.

Some Bondo music is also played when the girls return from the bush a week or more later; then the gourd rattle may also appear. Bondo music also occurs for the 'washing hands' ceremony. And at the second funeral of a woman, held often from one to five years after her death, the Bondo plays in much the same fashion as at initiations, except that there are no special girl dancers, although girls may join with older women for pleasure or to practise for their own initiation. At these funerals the songs often have texts referring to death or the dead person. Bondo music may also be played in conjunction with a private curing ritual held in a house.

In all of the public Bondo plays there is skilful dancing coordinated with instruments and song. Movements are vigorous and vary according to the tastes of the particular dancer, although dancing is less skilled and varied for girls than for older women. At the height of such activities it is as if the women were inexhaustible as they dance, beat, clap and sing.

There is other music peculiar to women. At the death of a person women relatives and friends gather to wail in the house where the body lies and their wails are interspersed with sad songs, referring to the death. No instruments are played. If the deceased is an uniniti-ated girl they sing Bondo initiation songs, as if she were going to the bush, and not to the grave. If it is an uninitiated boy they sing the equivalent boys' songs (see below). This goes on through the night. There is no professionalism here. Anyone who wishes to sing starts a song or joins in.

At all second funerals, which are only held for adults, there is also a woman's group of five to ten middle-aged or older females who dress up like the dead man or woman, sometimes wearing the deceased's clothes, and who behave as they remember he or she did in life, with peculiarities of speech and movement. They may even sing Fula songs and play crude Fula gourd rattles if the dead person liked this kind of music, but most of the time they sing in Limba. They greet visitors coming for the funeral and do not stop singing until given a 'dash', usually a small sum of money. They interrupt various proceedings of the funeral until so treated, when they melt away for a while, only to reappear later. They act as a constant reminder of the dead person. They are sometimes relatives of the deceased.

Another form of music dominated by females is Gbongbo, the marriage play. While the musicians are usually two male players of wood gongs, the singing and dancing is done by the bride, her girl-friends and by older females, as they move from her home (some-times in another village) to the groom's house as part of the marriage rites. There are special songs and beats, heard only at this time. The singing and dancing is lively.

In some of the southern Bafodea villages there is a secret female society of old ladies, called Kulɔngpan. Unlike Bondo, to which all females eventually belong, not all elderly women of a community are members. Using male drummers and iron and wood gong players, the women sing and dance at the second funeral of a member, these aristocratic-looking ladies carrying swords, cutlasses and knives, and some holding a small iron hand rattle. Their leaders have headpieces of birds' beaks and feathers. The women dance much of the night, mostly moving in a circle, but some coming before the musicians to dance individually, or in twos or threes or fours. What dignity of body and face these old persons possess! It is as if they are saying: 'Yes, even at the end of our lives we can dance and sing and play.'

For children at Bafodea the musical life starts early. Mothers dance when they are pregnant, and at a later time with a young baby on their backs. Children barely able to walk beat metal pieces or dance to their mothers' claps and songs, particularly girls to Bondo, but mothers also encourage boys to do the equivalent Gbondokali steps. Fathers may also do so, but it is particularly the mother–daughter musical tie which is strong and rich and reflects the close ties of both females. And children from the ages of about 5 to 15 play many singing games, especially at night, as well as singing songs from a variety of adult musical plays. In these groups boys and girls sing and dance and play together, as a rule, though one sex may predominate, mirroring later adult behaviour.

There is also boys' initiation music, Gbondokali, heard between February and May, when the boys' initiations occur. In a village practice sessions may be held nightly for a week or more preceding the actual night before going to the bush, when the boys dress in special costume. During and before and after these times younger boys play at these dances without musicians, and also often dance when the musicians are present. The musicians are male, using a drum of some kind, and metal and wooden gongs. The particular dancing that marks Gbondokali involves either twirling or acrobatic cartwheels, back and side flips, and the like. The text of the songs are similar to those for girls – mothers and sisters lamenting the departure of sons to the bush the next morning. But it is not so male-dominated a play as the girls' initiation dance is female-dominated, for women are the major singers at the Gbondokali and they dance along with the boys and men. The event becomes as spirited as the female one as the actual initiation approaches, and it is a play more of an equivalence of sexes than the girls' initiation, even though it is in male hands. It has more of a father and mother aspect than female initiation, where the mother's role appears to predominate.

Again, there are professional musicians for the boys' dances and here the wooden gong players must adjust their beat skilfully to the cues given by the dancing boy's plastic or metal whistle, which he blows at the start of each dance for this purpose. The musicians must also follow the particular manner in which he dances, still as a rule blowing his whistle.

Special dress, brightly coloured and in striking contrast to the usual clothes, is worn at the girl's initiation, at the 'washing hands' rites and by the girl at her marriage ceremony, as well as by the boys at their initiation. In addition some women wear unusual clothes at second funerals. These dressings are put on the person by members of the same sex but costume parts may be made by the other sex, such as the local cloth made by men and the beaded objects produced by females.

Outside its public initiation dances, the men's society, Gbangbani, to which all adult males belong, carries out its activities in total secrecy, giving no public performances. In this it differs from Poro and other men's societies of the Mende and Temne of Sierra Leone, where some public society events occur. In the dry season Gbangbani 'closes' the town perhaps once a week for the night, and its music and song are heard in the streets of the community; this occurs occasionally during the rains as well. It is the most exclusively male musical play of Bafodea. There is some female Bondo music made in secret in the bush, mainly at female initiations, and Bondo occasionally 'closes' the town with accompanying music, but most Bafodea musical activities involve both sexes in public.

There are two music forms, Poro and Kunkuma, related to one another, in which both sexes play major roles. The older is Poro, played usually with a large skin drum, a wood gong, and an iron U-bar hit with an iron rod. Here there is often another musician who is singer, either male or female, although at other times anyone present may lead a song. The dancers are the audience; they also sing as chorus. They are predominantly but not exclusively female, moving around slowly in a circle and one or two coming out to the centre to dance before the musicians. Played at second funerals, on general social occasions, or sometimes just when the musicians feel like it, Poro songs talk of lovers and escapades, and of the jealousy and wickedness of people.

> Your heart will not fight for you. If I have done anything to you tell me, then I will beg you.

The song says that if someone has done something wrong to you, like a lover, it is better not to keep it in your heart but to say it out so that the person can ask forgiveness. Another song goes:

> Sanu sanu, bluff, you will never see a beautiful lady.

This refers to the fact that Sanu will never see a beautiful lady without approaching her. 'Bluff' is a Krio word meaning to put on airs.

Kunkuma is newer in Bafodea, probably coming from the Loko area to the south-west in the past thirty years or so. It uses an instrument called by this name with three metal keys on a wooden box, as well as an iron U-bar gong. Sometimes a wood gong or the African finger piano is also present. The music and songs are similar to Poro, as is the dance. The singer is usually the U-bar or the Kunkuma player, and like the other musicians is male. But females as well as males participate fully in the singing and dancing.

Other musical forms involve both sexes in various ways. In Mayoi, a play found mainly in the north of the chiefdom, there are male wooden and iron gong players and small drum musicians, but there is often a lead female singer as well. The chorus that responds to her is made up of both males and females in the audience. This is perhaps the most male of the public musical plays at Bafodea. While females do come out and dance it is men who dominate the arena, with vigorous, fast-moving steps that sometimes imitate hoeing and other farming behaviour. There is one quite well-known male professional dancer for Mayoi. The play is found at second funerals, and often with a special singer or dancer at work parties.

In the south of the chiefdom Kukangtan is found at some second funerals. Led by a professional female singer and dancer to drum music played by females and wood gongs by males, it has dancing and singing by both sexes. The demands on the female leader, whose musical group it is, are considerable, as the dancing is strong, with much body shaking and very fast footwork, and the singing lies heavily on her with women in the audience as the main chorus. The lead plays most of the night. Several women in the chiefdom are much admired for their skill in this play.

There is also farmwork music, usually led by male players, using the wooden and iron gongs and sometimes one or more varieties of drums. This music is usually played only for organised work-groups. The musicians play and sing during the clearing of land by male workers, perhaps with girl singers. Such musicians also appear at weeding, the work being done by females who sing, at the threshing of rice which is dominated by males, and in some villages also at harvesting.

Ruth Finnegan (1967) had admirably written of Limba stories. In the northern part of the chiefdom there is little story-telling at all, by either adults or children. In the southern areas some old men are very skilled in this art, performing at night in the rainy season in the small dispersed farm villages, to a local crowd of adults and children of both sexes. But middle-aged and young men also tell tales, some very cleverly. The teller is sometimes accompanied by another man playing a wooden gong. Whether so or not, the audience sings and claps to the teller's spoken and sung words, for these stories are interspersed with song which forms an integral part of the tales. Often the male teller stands and acts out aspects of the story, to the delight of the audience. Women and older girls also tell stories, although they generally sit down rather than move about; they sing as well and often tell the same tales as men, and in the presence of males as well as females. There are some magnificent women story-tellers. So story-telling is perhaps only slightly more of a male event than a female one, and like the musical plays discussed above involves active participation by both sexes.

I have described enough of the performing arts to suggest that they are the core of the Bafodea aesthetic. It is through music, song, tales and dance that the major events in the community are expressed for both sexes, especially initiation, marriage and death. Only birth is excluded, probably because of its uncertainties. The texts of the songs are public commentaries on life at Bafodea. For females they are the major form of such public statements, while for men political discussions and case settlement afford other opportunities. So it is not surprising that the song texts often reflect the viewpoint of females.

The other art forms at Bafodea are less well developed than the performing ones, less complex and less emotion-rousing; they are less deeply penetrating to the heart. These other art forms on the whole are male, such as the woodwork, basketry, metalwork and weaving, producing a wide range of objects, leaving only glass beadwork, cicatrisation and hairstyling to females, as well as a little pottery and basketry.

The female material art forms, then, are more restricted, and they are almost entirely directed to the body in terms of appearance and to their roles in the performing arts, while male art forms are broader in range and content. There is also greater professionalisation among males in the art world, although on the whole Bafodea is not a highly professionalised society compared, say, with the Ashanti of Ghana or the Yoruba of Nigeria.

In this sense my first proposition, suggested at the beginning of this chapter, holds true: that the arts, in their sex roles, reflect the general character of the male-female roles in the society at large.

But something else also occurs. In the area of music, song, tales and dance, with the exception of some music played separately by the secret societies of each sex, the world of these particular arts is a joint one, requiring the activity of both sexes to bring it to perfection – or at least the presence of both. The sharing of activities by sex is not unusual at Bafodea, but an emotionally laden world of sharing and joining as equals is; sex status considerations do not seem major here as they do in farming or in the domestic scene. True, there are indications of inequalities here; big men may move the musicians away from one spot to another, and when a man gives the musicians money, usually with a speech in front of the crowd, a few women may kneel down, holding his legs in respect. But the general tone of these performance events is of equality of sex, so that in the very heart of the aesthetic life principles of separatism and sex status tend to disappear, and there is a joining of the sexes, even to the point that performances are times when liaisons are formed or reaffirmed, or secret messages may be sent through song to a lover. It is in the musical events that the aesthetic solidarity of the society is found. In this respect the second proposition, that the aesthetic does not necessarily follow sex role distinctions, is true. The dominant role of the male, its patriarchal quality in life in general, seems absent from performance. And here there is female professionalisation as well.

Thus, in a sense the third proposition is also true, that both the first and the second ones hold. The arts both reflect male-female roles and status considerations in the larger society, and break from them. The paradox is valid. Similar or unrelated paradoxes may occur in other societies.

Notes: Chapter 4

This chapter was written during the seventeenth month (March 1980) of field research at Bafodea, of a two-year stay. I wish to thank the National Endowment of the Humanities, Washington, DC, for a fellowship, and the University of Washington, Seattle, for sabbatical leave, which has allowed this research to be carried out, as well as the Institute of African Studies, Fourah Bay College, University of Sierra Leone, Freetown, for its assistance in this project. I also give thanks to my field assistant Paul Hamidu Mansaray for his comments on this chapter, as well as to Dr Labelle Prussin for many helpful suggestions.

1. A fourth view, beyond the scope of this chapter, is comparative in nature and is that all three of these positions are correct but for societies at different levels of organisation, size and economic development.

Chapter 5

The Political and Military Roles of Akan Women

KWAME ARHIN

The Akan of central and southern Ghana combined political and military roles, the second deriving from the first. The major units of the typical Akan military organisation were the same as those of the political organisation. Consequently, military status was the same as political status. An account of military roles, whether of males or females must, therefore, begin with that of the political organisation. The following account of the Akan political organisation is intended to highlight the actual and potential political and military roles of women. It is based mainly on material on Asante.

The Akan *oman,* the autonomous political community, consisted of a town, *kuro*, and its dependent villages, *nkuraa*, with their satellite settlements, hunting lodges, or cottages, *nnanso*. The town was the earliest settlement and became the seat of the political head of the *oman*. From it families spread out and founded other settlements which in time became the nuclei of groups of villages known as *amansin*, divisions of the *oman*. The *oman*, then, was composed of *amansin*, and the *amansin* were made up of *nkuraa*. The towns and villages were inhabited by members of groups of matrilineages, localised segments of the seven or eight dispersed matriclans which covered the whole of Akanland, in the sense that segments of two or more of them could be found in any of the Akan political communities. In addition to their language, and the dominance of the matrilineal principle among them, membership of the matriclans distinguished the Akan of Ghana from their neighbours, the Guang and Ga-Adanme in the south and south-east, the Ewe in the east, the Gur- and Senufo-speaking peoples of the north-west and the Gbanya- and Gur-speaking peoples of the north.

Of the localised matrilineages in the towns and villages, one was politically dominant. Its members were the owners of the principal stool or political office and the occupant of the stool or the holder of the office was known as the *ohene*. Members of the stool-owning matrilineage were known as the *adehye*, royals or aristocrats of the town or village, and were distinguished from other inhabitants of the town/village by virtue of that title. The former were aristocrats or royals because it was understood by the whole community that their maternal ancestors and ancestresses were the first settlers on the land and that the primacy of occupation made them owners of the land. The *ohene* of a village was known as *odekro*, owner of the land, and he represented the whole of the royal matrilineage. The royal matrilineage was dominant among the other matrilineages in other respects. The members had access to the largest tract of the land belonging to the community, the largest collection of slaves, *nnonko*, which freed their women from most menial services and also the largest hoard of gold-dust. They were, therefore, the wealthiest group, as the Akan conceived of wealth.

Subordinate stools were vested in the other matrilineages which were ranked according to actual or presumed order of the arrival of their earliest ancestors or ancestresses in the community. Ranking carried with it commensurate command of the resources mentioned above. The most important of the stools were known as Konti, Akwamu, Adonten, Nifa, Benkum, Kyidom, Twafo and Gyase. The occupants of these stools, known as *nsafohene,* together with heads of the most important palace associations, the *afekuo,* or functionaries, constituted the council of the unit of the relevant political organisation: the village, the division and the state, or union of states such as the Asante Union which was established in about 1700.

The Akan *oman* or state was first and foremost an organised hierarchy of councils vested with diffuse authority which provided linkages between otherwise disparate kinship groupings in the village, the division and the autonomous political community. The councils passed laws and settled cases arising from breaches of those laws; declared wars and made peace or undertook defensive campaigns; took measures in order to expand the lands of the political community and also allocated land for use, or settled disputes arising from land use; and performed magico-religious rites believed to be necessary for the prosperity of the community. It was the performance of these functions that provided the reasons for the association of the various kin-groups under the headship of the royal lineage.

But it was what Weber called 'custom' that provided the legitimacy for the rule of the aristocratic matrilineage. There were two main elements of custom. First, traditional stories concerning the peopling of the capital town confirmed and validated the primacy of occupation by ancestors of the royal matrilineage. Secondly, Akan religion prescribed that under God and on earth the greatest spiritual guardians and guarantors of communal prosperity were the dead ancestors and ancestresses of the earliest settlers who also founded the town. The major Akan festivals, including the *Adae* and the Odwira, re-enacted and reinforced these two elements of the charter of the rule of the *ohene* and his matrilineage and lengthened their lease of power.

Female Political Roles

Female stools complemented the hierarchy of male stools. In the village the elders, *mpanyinfo,* heads of the matrilineages, who constituted with the *odekro* the village council, had their *aberewa* or *obaapanyin*, who looked after the women's affairs. The *odekro* had an *obaapanyin* who was responsible for the affairs of the women of the village and was a member of the village council; the *ohene*, head of a division, and the *omanhene,* head of the autonomous political community, had their female counterparts known as *ohemma*, female ruler, who sat on their councils. The *ohene* and the *ohemma* were all of the same *mogya*, blood, or clan. The Asantehemma, the occupant of the female stool of the Kumasi state, and therefore of united Asante, since her male counterpart was *ex officio* the Asantehene, king of Asante, was a member of the Kotoko council, the executive committee or cabinet of the Asanteman Nhyiamu, general assembly of Asante rulers.

As members of their respective councils, female stool occupants participated in the legislative and judicial processes, in the making and the unmaking of war, and in the distribution of land, the basic resource of the economy. An *ohemma* of a state also had her own *ntam,* oath, a formula for starting the judicial process, and her own court, as well as her own *okyeame* (spokesman) who in the Akan courts acted as prosecutor and judge.

An *ohemma* was a refuge for a fugitive from the *ohene*'s court who often successfully sought her intervention in cases of the death penalty. Called the 'mother' of the *ohene,* she was the latter's most effective adviser and she had the right to administer to him even a public admonition. The *ohemma* was the *aberewa*, wisdom personified: an Akan court panel preceded their retirement to discuss a case before passing judgement by saying that they were going to consult *aberewa*, the old woman. As the *aberewa* of the town, the *ohemma* was the moral guardian of the females of the political community and a kind of moral censor: she examined adolescent girls before the main puberty rites which ushered them into adulthood and licensed their marriage, and was expected to say whether or not pregnancy had occurred before the rites. A girl who was found to have become pregnant before the rites was known as *kyiribra*, and was punished with ostracism together with her partner. The polity thrived on a sound moral order.

As the *abrewa,* the *ohemma* was also custodian of 'custom'. She was officially the foremost authority on the genealogy of the royal matrilineage, and hence the first and final arbiter on who was quali- fied by blood to be a male ruler; it was said of the *ohemma*'s stool in relation to the male stool that it was the elder stool, *akonnua panyin.* It was the *ohemma* who played the leading role in the selection of a successor to a deceased or destooled (removed from office) *ohene.*

The *ohemma*'s role in the succession to a vacant stool can be understood in terms, first, of the composite nature of most of the Akan matrilineages and, secondly, of the Akan rules of succession. The composite nature of the Akan matrilineage lay not in its segmen- tation over time and space, but in the incorporation into it of 'stranger' segments which in time became concealed; even when it was known it was not permitted for outsiders to point it out. 'Stranger' segments could be descended from slave women or free- born women of another clan who, therefore, were not of pure blood and whose descendants were not eligible for the stool. The *ohemma* was the one who could pronounce on the fitness of potential succes- sors for the stool from the viewpoint of true descent from the found- ing ancestors/ancestresses.

Secondly, while the Akan vested the right of succession in the royal matrilineage, they left open the question of the actual successor among the eligible males, which was resolved by joint consultations between the *ohemma,* as leader of the royal matrilineage, and the members of the village, divisional, or national council. In the process of consultation the *ohemma* and the council were governed by the following rules: brothers should succeed each other before sisters' sons in the order of seniority in age; but age could be discounted in favour of superior wisdom and character in a junior person. Seniority in age could also be discounted in favour of a younger successor, if rotational succession among the segments of the royal lineage had been adopted as a 'convention' by the lineage and the community as a whole. Where rotation had been adopted as a working rule, both the male and female stools rotated among the segments, so that at any moment the occupants belonged to different competing segments.

It was the *ohemma* who operated these rules and ensured orderly succession to the stool. On the decease or de-stoolment of an *ohene,* the members of the council formally asked the *ohemma* to nominate a candidate for their approval, and gave her three succeeding options at the end of which the councillors could in turn present a candidate for her approval. It rarely, if ever, came to this. An *ohemma* consulted members of her matrilineage, her husband, if she had one, and the community at large through discreet inquiries by her *nkotimsefo,* household servants, who, like the palace functionaries, were so selected as to represent the various sections of the community. The candidate she turned up was thus more often than not the result of communal consensus. It was easy to arrive at this kind of consensus in the small-scale, face-to-face communities of the period before colonial rule.

The peace, order and stability of the political community, therefore, depended to a large extent on the *ohemma*. She could give the community a good or bad ruler or defy the customary rules and thus jeopardise the well-being of the community. The part of Yaa Akyiaa, the Asantehemma, in the crisis of succession to the stool of the Asantehene, 1885–8, illustrates the crucial responsibility of an *ohemma* in a keenly contested election. Yaa Akyiaa sponsored her own son, Kwaku Duah III (later Prempeh I), as Asantehene against the claims of Atwereboana, who was both older than Prempeh and belonged to an alternative segment. It was also abnormal for mother and son to occupy both male and female stools at the same time. In the face of objections from the Asante states of Mampon, Nsuta and Kokofu, Yaa Akyiaa organised the Kumasi forces together with those of Bekwai and Ejisu, and thus split Asante into two factions. The result was civil war which, following the turbulent reigns and de-stoolments of Kakari (1567–74) and Mensa-Bonsu (1874–83), weakened Asante and made her an easy target of the British colonial takeover in 1896. Prempeh I and Yaa Akyiaa were both exiled to the Seychelles Islands by the British.

The Akan *ohemma* was not only a maker of the occupants of male stools; she could herself occupy a male stool. The best-known of female occupants of Akan male stools were Dokua of Akyem Abuakwa, who reigned in the nineteenth century, and the Serwahs of Dwaben of the nineteenth and twentieth centuries. Female occupants of male stools performed the duties of their male counterparts, including the rites in the *nkonwafieso*, the room where the blackened stools are kept and which is barred to women in general on account of their ritual impurity incidental to the menses.

Both male and female royal persons were used as linkages in the unification of segments through marriage. An *ohemma* selected a wife for a newly installed *ohene* and the selection was done with an eye on political alliances. It was of great significance that in the course of the consolidation of the Asante Union in the eighteenth century Safo Kantanka, the Mamponghene, head of the non-Oyoko section of Asante, married a succession of Kumasi, Dwaben and other *ahemma* of the Oyoko section of Asante, and thus created filial and affinal ties which supported the formal political and military organisation. Political marriage as a political instrument in Asante and other Akan states is yet to be studied.

Military Roles

It has already been noted that among the Akan the military organisation was given in the political organisation. Political status determined military status. The commanders of the Asante army and its
subdivisions were first elected as heads of territorial divisions or
appointed as heads of palace associations and then assumed corresponding military positions: European visitors to the Akan states in
the nineteenth century referred to the heads of the subdivisions as
'captains'. A female who acceded to a male stool also formally
assumed the corresponding military position and if war occurred she
would be expected to lead her 'men' in war. With the exception of
Yaa Asantewa, however, the Akan know of no parallels to the British
Boadicea; there are only examples of those who urged on their male
counterparts to fight to the death in order to retrieve the national
honour.

Women and adolescent girls were normally camp-followers and
performed commissariat duties. Royal females of Kumasi accompanied the Asantehene, Osei Yaw Akoto (1823–34), at the Battle of
Dodowa in 1826, when the Asante pitched their national shrine, the
Golden (the paramount Asante) Stool, against combined southern
Akan and Ga-Adanme forces led by British officers. It appears from
the events following the war that women were generally desired as
hostages.

The main female military role, albeit played far behind the battle-
lines, was to engage in what was known as *mmomomme twe*, perform pantomime dances and sing dirges in support of the men at war.
It is unclear whether the dances and songs were expected to have
magico-religious effects on the enemy. But they had the practical
effect of shaming potential war-dodgers known as *kǫsaankǫmi* into
joining the war. Women were also authorised to compose songs
which could drive confirmed war-dodgers to suicide.

The situation can be summarised by saying that the essential
female military role was to give encouragement to the men. Giving
encouragement could, however, take a dramatic and more positive
turn, if a woman of high status seized arms, or as the Asante called it
bǫntoa, as an example to the males in order to arouse their sense of
honour and sharpen their martial ardour. This is what the Asante
heroine Yaa Asantewa, *ohemma* of Edweso, did after the governor of
the Gold Coast, Arnold Hodgson, was understood to have demanded
the Golden Stool from the Asante assembly of rulers for him to
occupy in the absence of Prempeh I. Yaa Asantewa then seized a gun
and urged the Asante rulers to fight, and thus precipitated the siege
of Kumasi in 1900. The British exiled Yaa Asantewa to the Seychelle
Islands but she became immortalised in the following Asante-wide

ditty:

> Kookoo hin ko!
> Yaa Asantewaa ee!
> Obaa basia a
> ogyina apremo ano ee!
> Yaa Asantewa!

> *Kookoo hin ko!*
> Yaa Asantewa!
> The mere female who takes a stand
> against the cannon!
> Yaa Asantewa!

Since the Colonial Period

Unlike what happened in the case of the female chiefs of Sierra Leone, the political role of the occupants of Akan female stools became apparently submerged in colonial rule and its supporting institutions, in spite of Rattray's efforts. The military role of indigenous rulers lapsed with the establishment of colonial rule. Women were not recognised on the colonial chief-list, as members of the Native Authority councils and courts. They had no officially recognised shares in the stool treasuries. It is extremely unlikely that the colonial authorities would have recognised a woman as an occupant of a major male stool.

This has been attributed to the British bias towards patriliny and male chauvinism. On the other hand, the tradition of nineteenth-century writing on the Gold Coast as exemplified, for example, in Cruickshank (1853), pointed to the Akan woman as immersed in drudgery while the man loafed about. To British colonial officialdom it was inconceivable that this overburdened creature could have a significant political position or play even an advisory role.

However, behind it all the *ohemma* continued to play her part in the making of traditional rulers, educating them in the lore of the dynasty and of the state, and advising them on regal bearing and courtly etiquette. Today, when education and wealth have nearly become the decisive factors in the selection of traditional rulers, highly educated women and entrepreneurs are increasingly assuming the position of *ohemma* and occupying stools that, in the previous century, would be reserved for males. This is mainly because they can often attract more development projects to their areas, particularly from military rulers, than their male counterparts.

In conclusion, the Akan saw the woman in general as an educator, a moral guardian and a conciliator in the political process. Male and female essentially complemented each other.

For the purpose of this short chapter I have not considered it necessary to provide notes. The reader is referred instead to the following essential works on the Asante and other Akan:

Cruickshank, 1853, 2 vols;
Rattray, 1923, 1927, 1929;
Danquah, 1928a, b;
Fortes, 1950;
Busia, 1951, 1954;
Wilks, 1975;
Arhin, forthcoming, 1982.

Chapter 6

The Feminine Sphere in the Institutions of the Songhay-Zarma

JEANNE BISILLIAT

Among the Songhay people, whose land stretches northward from the bend of the Niger as far as Dendi, descent is reckoned patriline-ally and the Islamic religion is firmly entrenched. These two facts are of considerable significance for the status and roles of women. Physi-cally displaced through the practice of virilocal residence, women are socially displaced as well and this is the structural cause of their basic lack of roots. Indeed, a woman is never fully at home in the place where she lives. Unlike men, her emotional involvement, her sense of past and future, of nostalgia and desire, is permeated by a twofold family space: she is at once a child in her own family and a woman in a family of strangers. This fundamental ambiguity of women, both spacial and social, is taken up and amplified in the cultural elabora-tion of her place in – or rather her absence from – the economic and political spheres. A woman's only source of power lies in swelling the numbers of the male line, in bringing children into the world, in reproducing society. However, this infinite power, her only source of esteem, the role of mother, is at the same time devalued in the male-dominant ideology: she is capable of nothing but motherhood. Thus, what she is granted on one level is immediately taken away on another.

This chapter sets out to clarify the nature of the incongruence of ideology and the recognised fact of the necessary complementarity of the sexes, to elucidate those articulations that give rise to this dual treatment of the female role. To illustrate the workings of a system which simultaneously elevates and oppresses the feminine role, I have chosen to concentrate on the ceremonies of marriage and nam-ing (along with certain related rituals), crucial stages in the process of social reproduction within the family. These stages are acted out within the physical spaces of the compound courtyard and the individual hut on the one hand, and the semantic spaces of men's declarative language and women's symbolic language on the other.

The compound is the space occupied by the family, headed by the senior male of the lineage and his wife or wives, his sons, their wives and their children. Each of the buildings within the compound houses a conjugal family, and each is allotted to a woman, the men having no rights in the huts and, if they are polygynous, moving every three days from the room of one wife to another. Thus the woman has a right to her own room in exchange for her sexual and culinary services. Mobile between her natal and affinal lineages, she becomes unlike the man, immobile within the confines of her spouse's family space. This right to a place of her own is not conferred by marriage alone. It is only after giving birth to a child, in her mother's compound, that her own small house of mud walls and thatched roof is built for her and she is provided with the three hearthstones on which she henceforth has the right to cook. Until that time the young couple sleep in a hut of straw and the young woman only has the right to help her mother-in-law in simple jobs, certain tasks, such as adding salt to the stew, being denied her.

This communal space in which the huts are dispersed thus contains the descendants of one male, 'one seed, one root', all grouped round a number of women. All the man's children are actually divided into matrifocal groups, 'children of one mother', and among themselves the children stand *vis-à-vis* each other in complex relations of inclusion and exclusion, derived from their duties and affections. Thus alongside the juridical unit focusing on the father exists another unit, in a physiological and symbolic sphere consisting of the heart, the stomach or intestines, and milk. These three terms refer to the mother, the mother's family and, in an especially privileged way, to her brother. These bonds are recognised in heredity, since witchcraft is inherited through the 'milk', and in death, since these final groupings are made according to the bonds of heart and stomach. Herein lies a fundamental rift: in this patrilineal system, membership by the heart focuses upon the mother.

Within this general framework I shall explore the different roles that woman plays, on the one hand as a sister and a maternal aunt, and on the other hand as a paternal aunt. If men are aware of the different roles she plays in these different guises, they are mute on the subject. In fact male informants – in my experience – describe the social and family system in the same way as the ceremonies of marriage and naming – solely in terms of what is publicly visible and audible, without reference to the social actors, the women. It is only through working continuously with the women that a hidden, feminine version of life is revealed, an alternative version of which the symbolic function is fundamental, as much for the women themselves as for the equilibrium of the sexes.

At the marriage of their brother, the women as sisters play an economic and symbolic role. They participate in the exchanges of goods between the families. They bring the fee, which entitles the man to enter the girl's compound, to her family, the fee which concludes the engagement and the fee of the hair-dresser who will attend to the bride on the seventh day. They also contribute directly to what is called 'the sisters' money'. Finally, they collect from the maternal and paternal aunt of the bridegroom the money required for the purchase of a black cotton wrapper and a pair of sandals (each set of aunts paying for one sandal). It is worth noting that the sums involved ranged in 1971 from about 15,000 CFA (for the engagement) to 2,000 or 3,000 CFA (for the hair-dresser), and have a value which is not primarily economic. These offerings, which are mainly of symbolic importance and which are the responsibility of the sisters, are basic to the progress of the marriage, which begins from the moment that the man declares his intentions. After spending seven days in a hut in her husband's compound, in silence and almost entirely covered with a white veil, the bride returns home, accompanied by her friends, to have her hair braided. The plaiting of the hair is not only for beauty, for one finds the theme of hair in all the rituals involving separation or integration. The baby's head is shaved on the day of naming, the seventh day after birth. Similarly the bride's hair is dressed seven days after the commencement of the marriage, and the widow's head is shaved seven days after the death of the husband.

In addition to their financial contributions, the bridgegroom's sisters play a more directly symbolic role on the day of the wedding. When the friends of the man pretend to abduct the bride, they carry her across their backs till they reach the man's compound. Shortly after, a procession forms of young men and women, dressed in white cloths to hide their identity, led by the sisters of the bridegroom. Singing and following the newly married couple, they go four times round the straw hut which will be the place where the couple stay until the birth of the first child. Then the married couple enter the hut and the procession disperses. These activities constitute the symbolic acknowledgement of the new bride and her acceptance by the sisters of the bridegroom.

At a naming ceremony the sisters of the young father play a similar role. They collect money from the men and women in the families of the baby's parents, in order to make offerings of millet, rice, enamelled basins and money. In addition they go to ask the cross-cousins of the mother and father for the *giffi kuusu* money. This is for the vessel in which will be prepared all the herbal infusions to enable the baby to achieve the correct physical, mental and social development.

Finally, they share among themselves the cost of the 'umbilical fee', which is distributed to the woman who cuts the cord, the woman who receives the placenta and buries it and the woman who stays in the hut with the young mother on the day of the child's naming. The symbolic value of these offerings is the confirmation by the father's sisters of the child's membership of the patrilineage to which they also belong.

The woman as sister is both an outsider and an inferior: partly included in and partly excluded from her natal lineage, her roles with respect to her kin, and specifically her brother, are split between the passive and the active. The avoidance and 'shame' which characterise the actual and symbolic relationships between brother and sister express perhaps the debt, the claim and the sorrowful distance between them that is imposed by the incest taboo and the necessity of alliance.

But this same woman, in her role as paternal aunt, plays a specific and critical role in the ceremonies of marriage and baptism. On the evening of the wedding it is the men of the two lineages who exchange the words which seal the marriage:

> 'We have come to seek the seed.'
> 'You shall have it.'
> 'Which kind of seed?'
> 'Millet seed.'
> 'You shall have it, the large millet seed,
> you shall have it' . . . etc.

These words are spoken publicly, before a crowd of guests. A little later, in the secluded hut where the bride sits, her classificatory mother pounds incense with perfume and pours it into a calabash. The young girl stands naked and her paternal aunt sprinkles the mixture over her. After that she drags her forcibly to the friends of the bridegroom who are waiting outside. She struggles and cries as they carry her to her husband.

This abduction is not just a pretence. It expresses the semi-real reluctance of the girl to leave her family. This interpretation is reinforced by the fact that the abduction episode is omitted in a marriage of cross-cousins, which is an ideal form because it involves individuals who share 'blood' and 'milk'. The paternal aunt plays a role parallel to that of the men: she establishes the alliance and legitimises it within the secluded sphere of feminine institutions.

Here, as elsewhere, one is confronted with this existential position of the woman: her recognition at the symbolic level is matched by her insignificance at the social level.

At naming, the paternal aunts carry the little tray on which the shaved hair of the infant is placed. They also play an intermediary role between the men outside in the compound, who make the initial choice of names, and the women inside the room, who will make the final selection of the name to be bestowed upon the child. The interplay between brother and sister is thus highly complex, based on the recognition of a fundamental solidarity between those who have consumed the same milk. Oral tradition as well bears witness to the strength of these emotional bonds, as the following story attests.

Woman and Death

A woman raises her child along with one of her brother's children. Death comes to her village. She flees with the children because of the death. She runs to escape to a distant part of the bush where she meets someone. This person asks her: 'Where are you going?'

'I am fleeing.'

'Why do you flee?'

'Because of death I flee with my children, for the death is in my village.'

'I am death who kills all people. But you I will spare on condition that you give me one of your children.'

'I cannot give you any of my children.'

'You must. Give me that one.'

'No. I cannot give you that one.'

'But that is the one I want.'

'No. I cannot give you that one because it is the child of my brother. This is my child. Take it. I give it to you. I can give my child but I have no right to give you the child of my brother to kill.'

'I do not want any child other than that of your brother.'

'In that case you will have to kill all three of us.'

'No. I only want to kill one, the child of your brother.'

'Take my child, but you shall not kill my brother's child.'

They continue thus until the moment of truth when Death grabs the child; the woman screams and Death releases the child.

Death therefore seizes the woman's own child. She tells her brother's child to come away with her. Death calls after her 'Come here', and she does so.

Death says: 'Look, take your child and depart with your brother's child. As for you, I shall not kill you before your children are fully grown.'

Thus there are special bonds between mother's brother's children and father's sister's children. One hears said: 'This one and this one, they are the children of a mother's brother and a father's sister. There is an alliance between them.' There is also a joking relationship between such cousins. The children of the sister enjoy specific rights with respect to their maternal uncle, from whom they can claim many sorts of goods and even steal.

Brother/sister, patrilineal/matrilineal, marriage – one is in the difficult realm of felt emotions and formal sentiments. How should one distinguish which relations belong to which category? It is best to look at oral tradition, which expresses in its compelling way what I have tried to demonstrate. Exogamy is a painful compromise and the incest taboo constitutes for both brother and sister a gap which can never be bridged. The following text, like the one above, has been collected from a female informant. It testifies to the importance of the feminine oral tradition, which has been given such scanty recognition. To ignore it has been to perpetuate the logic on which the inferiority of women is based. One cannot imagine that these women, so silent in public life, are capable of expressing themselves, of having a discourse of their own that goes beyond the monotonous triviality of their daily life.

They speak not of history or the lineages which found cities, but of the intimate and universal story which is the life of each of them, and which clarifies the paradox of the social institution within which they live.

Mother and Child

After the judgement the child goes to hell and the mother follows it, squeezing her breast to kill the fire with her milk. The child is half of the mother's body and the child of the father's money. The father has only married the woman and that is not enough to make him love the child. When the father is angry he says to the child 'I curse you'. The mother, whatever her child may do to her, will not curse it for it is half of her body. For the father the child is not half of his body; it is the child of his money.

When the child dies it is buried in the back of its mother. For when the child dies it is alway in its mother's heart until she goes to join it at her death. Whether it is night or day, it never leaves her heart. The father makes fun of it, the child of his money. If he married another woman he will have another child.

On the day of judgement everyone is assembled. You are called, your father is called. He does not come. He is called and he does not come. The mother's brother is called and he comes.

The father then says: 'This is not my child at all.' The mother's brother says to him: 'It is my child because my sister gave birth to it – so it came out of my intestines.'

On that day the father rejects his child, and it is the mother's brother who comes to act the father. Nobody knows why the father rejects the child. The mother's brother comes because the child is of his 'milk'.

The simultaneous elevation and devaluation of the woman as sister and as paternal aunt is equally apparent when we turn our attention to female productive and reproductive roles.

The Songhay woman participates actively in agricultural tasks, from the sowing to the harvest of the millet, but she has no right of ownership in the harvest. Her right is to be fed, she and her children. She also receives from her husband a small plot of her own on which to raise the crops which constitute the soup ingredients, and she can sell any surplus. She keeps the money from the sale of crops, or of craftwork such as pottery and baskets, or prepared food. Thus she has some financial autonomy, but in reality she has no way to accumulate capital. Only the man has this power. She has no right to the major crops, nor to the large livestock which are the means of production. As a mere tenant, even on her own plot, her economic autonomy is 'conditional' and has been greatly undermined by the effects of monetarisation. Development and developers have systematically excluded women from the economic domain, or included them as an unremunerated labour force, further exposing in a brutal and caricatural fashion the essential fragility of their economic status. Again, the woman's increasingly important role in providing nutritionally balanced food is continually undermined, because the crops which she cultivates fall outside the highly commercialised sector.

In her reproductive role the woman suffers under the incongruous male-dominated ideology. To start with, and this is fundamental, her children do not belong to her. In the case of divorce or repudiation or the death of her husband, the children go either to their father or to his family. Moreover, custom requires her to show a particular style of behaviour towards her first child. She must not, under any circumstances, publicly acknowledge that this is her child, nor should she call it by its name, or pick it up when it cries (unless she does it in secret), or show any concern when it falls sick. She must treat it as a stranger even though she has suckled it at her breast. Thus the woman who achieves the height of feminine status in giving birth to her first child is rigorously denied the joy of identifying with this same child. This is the most glaring example of the phenomenon of nothingness in her own existence, and the deprivation which is the lot of all women.

Conclusion

A brief consideration of aspects of the family system of the Songhay has enabled some light to be thrown upon certain crucial aspects of feminine inferiority, which it has been argued is based on a series of structural ambiguities. The system is patrilineal but the mother–child bond is actually viewed as more genuine, and its strength is vindicated on the day of judgement as the story recounted above shows. In this patrilineal system men play the public and legal roles in institutions, the hidden and symbolic depths of which belong to women. The female roles, although important, are consigned to the imaginary sphere and omitted in masculine discourse. Men remain aware of this feminine side of things, this additional significance of social action. However, in order to maintain a coherent image of themselves and their institutions, they are obliged to dismiss it as meaningless. This refusal to acknowledge the importance of the feminine aspect is so profound that Songhay men even claim not to understand the women's songs, which they hear on numerous occasions and in which are expressed the feminine view of life. Yet, apart from a few archaisms, neither the syntax nor the vocabulary of these songs differs from that which men use in their own traditions. This social deafness furnishes an extreme example of their determination not to hear what the other half of the Songhay world is saying.

The traditional social system was able to maintain a socio-economic equilibrium based upon the complementarity of the sexes. The upheavals which have occurred in this system have up to now, however, been prejudicial to the interests of women. Rejected in the dominant economic mode and in decision-making, neglected in the spheres of education and training, women will lose their own channels of appropriation which, albeit ritual and symbolic and unacknowledged in the male culture, permitted them to carry out their reproductive roles with the dignity required for their roles as socialisers. As complex social systems founded, not upon the values of money, but upon those of exchange, give way, women will increasingly lose those symbolic roles which enable them to act out their conflict-ridden situation. They will retain their status as mothers, but without the symbolic foundations that underlie it.

Chapter 7

Dependence and Autonomy: the Economic Activities of Secluded Hausa Women in Kano

ENID SCHILDKROUT

In the literature on women in West Africa, two factors have been described in some detail: participation of women in the market economy[1] and, in Islamic areas, the institution of purdah, that is, the seclusion of married women.[2] Seclusion is based on the premiss that men provide for the material needs of women and children. Islamic ideology thus gives religious sanction to the dependent status of women and children and enhances the political and social status attached to the economic roles of men. By defining dependency relationships in terms of kinship, this ideology enhances the importance of the family and the institution of marriage. At the same time, religion has thus played a part in curtailing the economic roles of women in many parts of the Islamic world. Since the seclusion of wives is an expression of their husbands' economic success, it has obviously been more prevalent among the middle and upper classes than among peasants and the urban poor. However, in Islamic West Africa there is evidence to suggest that the practice of purdah has been increasing,[3] and in urban areas has become more common, even in families where the economic status of the husband does not ensure the support of women and children. This has been facilitated by the continued participation of secluded women in the market economy.

African women have traditionally played very important economic roles in both rural and urban economies. While purdah restricts these activities ideologically, in practice Muslim women in Africa continue their economic activities – albeit in modified ways. This chapter describes how secluded women in the city of Kano, northern Nigeria, participate in the market, and how this economic activity relates to the formal division of labour by age and sex in Hausa society. It describes how women are able to be economically active through the control they exercise over children. In Hausa society, as in other Muslim societies, the activities of adults are strictly segregated by gender. However, until puberty, children are not restricted by the same religious and cultural injunctions. They are therefore able to act as intermediaries between the male and female domains. Children mediate between the domestic domain of the house and family, which is controlled for the most part by women, and the public domain, which is dominated by men. In the formal division of labour women are defined primarily as consumers, not as producers. However, through their control over the allocation of children's time and labour, Hausa women are able to alter considerably the formal structure of the domestic economy. Children give women access to the market and enable them to subvert some of the implications of purdah. The limited economic leverage which women thereby obtain does not give them status or power in the public arena, but it does give them resources to renegotiate their position in a very restricted domain.

In the first section of this chapter I consider the system of reproduction in Hausa society, focusing on urban Kano specifically. I deal with marriage, the institution of purdah and the expectations of men and women in the domestic domain, exploring the religious ideology on which sex roles and patterns of male–female interaction are based, and the significance of this ideology in segregating male-dominated and female-dominated institutional spheres. The second section of the chapter deals with the economic system, places the domestic economy in a wider context and examines the sexual division of labour in urban Hausa society. The third part of the discussion concerns the roles of children and the division of labour based on age. Children are the crucial links between the domestic domain, which is the arena of reproduction and consumption, and the wider society, including the economic institutions which control production. Here we consider how the economic roles of children vary according to age and sex and also briefly discuss the impact of Western education on the status and roles of women and children. This is a region where Western education has been introduced on a large scale only recently, due to a colonial policy which protected traditional Islamic education by restricting the establishment of Christian mission schools in the colonial period.[4] By removing children from full-time participation in the domestic economy, Western education today is altering the division of labour in the household. More than any other single factor, the enrolment of children in primary school challenges the position of secluded West African Muslim women or perhaps threatens the institution of purdah itself.

Female–Male Relations in Kano

The ideology on which female–male relations in Hausa society are based is similar to that of most Islamic societies in stressing the dominance and superiority of men and the subordination and inferiority of women. While there are undoubtedly male and female versions of this ideology, as have been described for parts of the Middle East and North Africa,[5] the dominant male ideology, sanctioned by religious and political institutions, defines women's status primarily in relation to men. Women are thought to be in need of male care and protection, and there are many passages of the Koran which make this point. Sura IV, for example, states, 'Men have authority over women, because Allah has made the one superior to the other, and because they spend their wealth to maintain them. Good women are obedient. They guard their unseen parts because Allah has guarded them.'[6] Concerning divorce, sura II states that 'women shall with justice have rights similar to those exercised against them, although men have a status above them'.[7]

Sexual activity, except in marriage, is regarded as incompatible with social order.[8] Contact with women, especially those of reproductive age, is always seen as in some sense sexually charged and is antithetical to a state of ritual purity for men. Thus the prohibitions on men touching women after performing ablution, against women entering the main area of the mosque, and against sexual activity during fasting, are examples of many rules meant to protect men and women against sexuality. People can be protected from their own impulses by Allah, by their willingness to follow the teachings of the Prophet Mohammed, and by social institutions which define segregated social spheres for men and women. Hausa folklore[9] and conversation are replete with references to female sexuality and the danger it poses to men and women and to the social order.

The rules of purdah follow from these attitudes and are meant to protect adults from the chaotic effects of uncontrolled sexuality. Neither children nor post-menopausal women are threatened by sexuality and they are therefore able to move much more freely than are men and women of reproductive age, for whom sexuality can be channelled to the legitimate end of procreation only within marriage. As in other Islamic societies, there is a strong fear and disapproval of sexual activity outside marriage, although in Hausa society it is in fact institutionalised in the role of the courtesan, or *karuwa*, as described by Renée Pittin in Chapter 22.[10] However, women who engage in sexual activity outside marriage do lose status and damage the reputation of the men who are related to them as guardians. There is a strong emphasis on virginity before first marriage, but little prejudice against remarriage to either divorced or widowed women. Children born out of wedlock are castigated and courtesans usually marry if they become pregnant. This is a society in which marriage is the most important institution in defining adult status, for both men and women.

The terms used for stages of the life-cycle reflect the importance of marriage and the structural dependence of women on men. All of the terms for stages of the female life-cycle express sexual and/or reproductive status and only approximately indicate age.

Although Western education is beginning to change traditional patterns with regard to the age of marriage, the end of childhood for women still usually coincides with the onset of puberty. Girls are expected to marry as soon as they reach puberty, often as early as age 10. The average age of first marriage for women of all ages in the Kano study was 12 years, and only those girls attending Western schools are marrying later. Young girls move from dependence on their fathers to dependence on their husbands; men have the obligation to support and care for their daughters and wives. Later, when women have passed menopause and are less likely to remarry after divorce or widowhood, they have the right to seek support from their sons and brothers. The minority of Hausa women who spend a good part of their adult lives independently, engaging in those occupations open to women who are not in purdah (as pounders of grain, maidservants, traders, courtesans and, recently, as teachers, nurses, and secretaries) have inevitably been married at some time, even if only in a brief compulsory union arranged by the father. Marriage is an absolute prerequisite for full adult status.

For both boys and girls, first marriage marks the transition from childhood to adulthood, and the ceremony of first marriage differs markedly from that for subsequent marriages. The marriage ceremony involves two very distinct aspects: the union of the spouses and the transition for each spouse to full adult status. The latter obviously occurs only once in a person's lifetime, so that ceremonies for second marriages are usually far less elaborate than ceremonies for first marriages.

For boys, the transition to adulthood depends on economic productivity as well as on reproductive capacity. Even where a boy's economic activity is tied into a family enterprise, as was the case in traditional agriculture,[11] the boy is expected to be economically productive before being eligible for marriage. Young men therefore marry in their twenties or thirties, while the more affluent marry earlier. While women's economic roles also change with marriage, their social status as adults depends more on their relation to men than on their economic activities.

The formal obligations of husbands and wives are clearly set out in both traditional practice and Islamic law. Men are obliged to provide shelter, clothing and food for their wives and children; women are expected to bear and raise children, cook and care for the domestic needs of their children and husbands, and defer to and obey their husbands. Both men and women can obtain divorce, but whereas men need only denounce the marriage, women must take their case to court. Men have custody over all their children after weaning,[12] although they sometimes allow divorced wives to keep one daughter. Wives are expected to heed the restrictions of purdah and thereby protect their husbands' and male relatives' reputations. Women are not expected to question their husbands about their activities outside the house, while men have the duty to control the very limited outside activities of their wives. As we shall see below, they have, however, no control over one crucial area: their wives' incomes – so long as these incomes are generated without violation of the rules of purdah.

When girls are first married their lives change abruptly, for almost all Hausa women are secluded after marriage. As children, girls are free to move in and out of their own and other people's houses. Married women, regardless of how young they may be, are confined to their own houses and are further confined by the prohibition against receiving visitors other than children (who may indeed be older than they are), certain categories of relatives, and other women. Since chronological age is not crucial in defining adulthood for females, married women in purdah are often very young. Most married women are allowed to leave their houses for ceremonial events, for example, to attend naming ceremonies, marriages and funerals. Most are permitted to visit relatives, and to seek medical care. The strictness with which seclusion is enforced depends upon the husband's wishes and the wife's willingness to comply. There are women who do not go out for any social occasion at all, and there are others who simply inform their husbands that they are going out. Most women comply with the restrictions of purdah and go out only at night when in theory they cannot be seen. They take children with them as escorts and cover their faces with shawls. They are not fully veiled, as are women in parts of North Africa or the Middle East, for their shawls often cover only their heads and do not conceal their clothing.

In practice, male control extends primarily over the activities of wives and daughters outside the home, mainly by restricting women's spatial mobility. Purdah also restricts access to secluded women by other males. However, men have little control over the interaction of women and children within the home, for they spend very little time at home. In Kano most men work away from home and are involved with the running of the household only in a perfunctory manner. They provide money and food, but since they are rarely present they delegate major responsibilities for domestic affairs to women. As in many sex-segregated societies, women expect to find most of their companionship from other women and from children. Thus women have considerable power, if not authority, within the domestic domain, while they have very little power and no formal authority outside this context.[13]

Economy

The domestic unit in Kano City is not a significant unit of production. If, in fact, it is more than a unit of consumption, this is only because women have been able to subvert the formal socio-economic structure through their control over domestic labour. In order to fulful their obligation to provide for their families, urban Hausa men must work outside their homes in salaried jobs, or as artisans or traders. A wide range of occupations characterises the indigenous Hausa-Fulani population of Kano.[14] In my own sample of fifty-eight men in two wards of Kano City there were sixteen salaried workers, twenty-six traders, three *malams*, three butchers, two tailors, two washmen, two drivers, two herdsmen, one leatherworker and one baker. Only a few of the male household heads worked at or near their homes – a leatherworker and two kiosk-owners. Most men eat their morning and evening meals at home, although the evening meal is actually consumed outside the house with male neighbours.

The income of Hausa men in Kano varies greatly, and neighbourhoods are not segregated according to income level. Only one of the seventy married women in my sample was not in purdah and the explanation given for her unique position was poverty. In general, the size of households varies with income, more affluent men having more wives, children, dependent relatives and clients. The close correlation between household size and income reflects the obligation of the male household head to provide for dependants.

The salaried jobs of the Hausa men in the sample, reflecting the general pattern, are mainly those which require minimal Western education. Only recently have the Hausa taken advantage of Western education, and the number of men living in the old walled city of Kano (the *birni*) who have completed secondary school is very small. The salaried workers I studied are in the local government administration – formerly many of those of Fulani ancestry were in the emirate administration and in low-level civil service jobs in the state government. Some work for commercial firms controlled by large companies (now Nigerian, but formerly expatriate), and some work for wealthy Hausa merchants. All except the wealthiest men spend most of their salary on domestic needs. In fact, in attempting to obtain data on household budgets, I found that domestic expenses often exceed wages, a situation that can be explained only by the presence of non-wage income (many families have farms outside the city) and by the supplemental – and generally unacknowledged – support provided by wives.

The merchants in Kano also are a very diverse group in terms of income – more diverse than the salaried workers, since their lack of literacy in English is not a barrier in many areas of trade. Those merchants who are literate in English, or who are able to employ people with Western education, are able to operate large firms which play an important part in the national economy. Other traders operate on a smaller, but not necessarily local, scale. My sample includes wealthy merchants who deal in cement, cattle and textiles, and others who operate small stalls selling grain, manufactured goods, kola nuts and other products. The poorest merchants have little capital and work for others. The artisans in the sample are tailors and leatherworkers. Butchers constitute another distinct category (they are usually endogamous) and, like artisans, tend to be in the lower-income group.

The market place in Kano is dominated by men. The well-known West African market woman is virtually absent from view in the oldest large market of Kano City, the Kurmi market.[15] Even the unmarried Hausa women who are not in purdah, rarely set up stalls in the market place. When they do trade outside their homes, they set up stalls in residential neighbourhoods. The virtual absence of Hausa women from the market place in the old walled city is in contrast to the situation in the 'new' market of greater Kano, Sabon Gari market, where Yoruba, Nupe and other Nigerian women from farther south have permanent stalls.

However, despite the absence of Hausa women from the public arena, they are not an insignificant force in commercial life. Virtually all transactions in Kano are on a cash basis, and women participate in the cash economy much more than the formal division of labour within the domestic economy indicates. In a formal sense, the household is only a unit of consumption. Were this the total reality, women would indeed play a very insignificant part in the economy. In reality, women participate in an elaborate network of exchange and generate income for themselves and their children and sometimes for their husbands. Women are able to do this because men in fact exercise very little control over labour within the domestic domain. We must now turn to a more detailed examination of the organisation of the domestic economy to understand how women generate income within the confines of purdah.

The mutual obligations of husbands and wives ensure subsistence for all members of the family, except in the poorest families where the ideal pattern is not realised and where the whole family is in fact dependent on others, or where the wife's income contributes to sub-sistence. In the ideal situation, women and children are consumers, not producers, and women's participation in economic activity con-sists only in preparing food, caring for the house, and bearing and raising children. Hausa men are expected to provide all the ingred-ients their wives need to prepare food for domestic consumption. Women are expected to feed their families three times a day, either by cooking or by purchasing food with the money and provisions given by the husband. Although Hausa women do in fact engage in productive income-generating activity, this is not part of the formal division of labour, for purdah is based on the premiss that a wife need not work – that is, that her labour should contribute only to reproduc-tion, not to production.

The vast majority of Hausa married women do, however, work for an income, albeit from within the confines of purdah. Husbands have no claim to their wives' income and in most cases they do not know what it is; nor do wives know their husband's incomes. Women's actual participation in the cash economy goes far beyond the pur-chase of cooking ingredients, although it is by investing the cash provided by men for domestic consumption that women generate income. In fulfilling their obligation to feed their family, men provide either ingredients or cash for their wives. Most men do both; they purchase staples such as grain and firewood periodically and they give their wives daily allowances to purchase perishable ingredients. All women see that their families eat three meals a day, but virtually no women cook three times a day. In most houses one or two meals are purchased outside the house. Instead of sending children to buy ingredients for cooking, women send their children to purchase cooked food from their neighbours. Alternatively, they buy cooked food from children who come to their house selling food for other women. In my study of sixty-nine women in purdah in two differ-ent wards of Kano, twenty-two women (32 per cent) regularly sold cooked food. Of thirteen women not in purdah (women who were also caretakers of children in the sample), five sold cooked food.

When women cook food for sale rather than for domestic con-sumption, or when they engage in other income-producing activities, all their income is their own. The entire activity is distinct from their obligation to prepare food for their families. The investment a woman makes in her business, even when this business is the prepara-tion of cooked food, is distinct from the household budget. Although a few women do feed their families from the food they cook for sale, the money they invest in their business is conceptually distinct from the money their husbands provide for domestic consumption. Some women, in other words, as wives, buy food from themselves, as food-sellers, to feed their families. Most women, however, purchase two out of three meals a day from other women. The cash that wives receive from husbands for domestic consumption is thus channelled into a female sphere of exchange where women act, not as wives, but as independent producers. In this way men capitalise women's economic enterprises, even though their manifest intention is simply to provide for the subsistence of their own families.

Women raise their initial capital, which is often very small, from a variety of sources: from change in the household budget, from their dowries, from gifts from relatives and female friends, through loans from rotating credit societies, or from spending-money (*kudin batarwa*) given by their husbands. Although Hausa men, unlike the Yoruba,[16] have no obligation to give their wives initial sums of capital, many give their wives regular allowances of spending-money. The amount varies depending upon the husband's income. Although this money is not specifically for trading, many women invest it in business. While a few husbands are strongly opposed to their wives' economic activity, the vast majority simply ignore it. In addition to selling cooked food, women in purdah earn money by trading in small commodities and raw foods, embroidering and sewing, hair-plaiting and running the rotating credit societies.

Since the Hausa husband has no obligation to set his wife up as a trader, he also cannot rely on her as a source of support. Most women do not, in fact, provide subsistence for their families, and those who do are very reluctant to admit it. Non-support is grounds for divorce and women who want to stay married to poor men contribute quietly to their families' maintenance. Most women spend part of their income on clothing for themselves and their children, on gifts for female friends and relatives, and occasionally on luxury items such as cosmetics and jewellery. The greatest part of women's income, however, is spent on the purchase of goods for their daughters' dowries (which consist of household furnishings) and to a lesser extent on contributions to their sons' bridewealth (cash payments, clothing and cosmetics for the bride). The expenses entailed in marriage are said to have risen in recent years with the greater availability of consumer goods. Whether or not this is so, it is clear that the greatest part of women's income is put into the marriage system.

Although males are favoured in the Islamic law of inheritance, sons inheriting twice the share of daughters, the dowry is inherited only by females. From the time they are children, girls work or save from gifts to amass dowries. Throughout their lives, women augment their own and their daughters' dowries. Dowry can be sold; it can be used to generate capital; and it can be used as a source of economic security in case of widowhood, or divorce, or in other times of need. Dowry, in the form of enamel, brass and glass bowls and bedroom furniture, is thus a form of exclusively female property which constitutes capital, savings and insurance for women in a male-dominated society.

The practice whereby women in purdah buy cooked food from other women is significant in several respects. By taking resources which their husbands give them for consumption and diverting them into a remunerated female sphere of production, women are in effect receiving payment for their domestic labour. This is particularly obvious in the case of women who spend their time cooking food for sale rather than for their own consumption. But in any case, by *not* cooking for their families three times a day, all women are thereby freeing their time so that their labour can be used in income-producing activities. Whether or not this diversion of resources from domestic consumption to income-generating activities for women leads to inflation in the cost of subsistence is an intriguing question. Although I am unable to demonstrate this with quantitative data, it is logical to suggest that by adding the cost of female labour to the resources men provide for subsistence, women may inflate the price of subsistence. The cost of prepared food does include the cost of women's labour, which instead of being unpaid domestic labour is now remunerated. In a sense, then, men subsidise women's economic activities by paying a price for food which includes this labour cost. In Hausa society, where secluded women continue to work, this is one price of purdah. Hausa women, although in seclusion and precluded from working outside the home, are able to turn their domestic labour into a productive resource.

Independent incomes allow women to build and maintain emotionally supportive extra-domestic relationships with other women through the exchange of gifts.[17] Most important, women are able to use their income to control the system of reproduction to their advantage. By diverting resources from a male-dominated productive economy into a female sphere of exchange, women obtain limited social mobility. They are able to withstand the loss of male support after widowhood or divorce and in some cases their incomes enable them to instigate divorce and manage independently outside marriage. They are sometimes able to use their independence to negotiate more advantageous marriages for themselves and their daughters. Thus through their control over the daily operation of the domestic economy, women gain a measure of control over their own lives which is denied to them in the formal definition of sex roles in Hausa society.

Since most of women's assets are spent on marriage expenses for themselves and their daughters, the question arises as to what effect this has on Hausa economy and social structure. Men still participate more significantly in production and generate most of the income in the community. However, women gain greater control over their own lives and, in a more abstract sense, over the system of reproduction. Their formal dependence on men for status and support is somewhat reduced and they are able to manage independently and renegotiate their marriages. The ability of Hausa women to transform the domestic domain from being solely an arena of unpaid domestic labour to being an arena of production and exchange seems to represent the persistence of a particularly West African female behaviour pattern within a family structure defined by Islamic values regarding the sexual division of labour.

Children

In attempting to analyse the nature of this economic system, a factor which has to be considered in some detail is the role of children. It is the labour of children that enables secluded women to carry on their economic activities, and it is women's ability to control this source of labour which is the key to their limited success.

Women in purdah are extremely dependent on children for performing their obligatory activities as wives. Although women are expected to be able to carry on all their domestic chores at home, in fact many of their tasks require communication with the world outside their own homes. Children are secluded women's primary and often only means of communicating with the outside world. They do almost all the shopping for cooking ingredients. Most husbands supply their households with staples such as grain and firewood, but children are sent daily to buy meat, vegetables and other perishables. They take grain and soup ingredients – peppers and tomatoes – for grinding and purchase sundries such as kerosene, mosquito coils, matches, medicines and thread. They take refuse out of the house and sweep the external gutters. They take clothes to the washman, the tailor and the seamstress. Many women send cooked food to their husbands' relatives in neighbouring houses and children carry the empty dishes and steaming bowls of food from house to house. Children are crucial in carrying messages, news and gossip from house to house. They also accompany women when they attend ceremonies, visit relatives or go out to seek medical care.

While all women rely on children (or paid servants, in the wealthier households) for domestic help, there is considerable variation in the extent to which secluded women rely on children in their income-earning activities. Some occupations require more help from children than others: embroidery, machine sewing, and hair-plaiting require minimal help. These occupations are usually pursued by women who have no children over age 5 or 6 to help them, or by women whose children are all enrolled in school. Even these occupations, however, require some assistance: someone must collect raw materials and deliver the finished products. Women change their occupations frequently during the course of their lifetimes, and changes in occupation are almost always related to the availability of children under a woman's care. Women's incomes likewise vary in relation to the availability of child labour. In my study, women whose children were engaged in full-time street trading were earning an average of two to three times more money than women whose children were not trading.[18]

The predicament of women without children is recognised in the willingness of men to allow their divorced wives to keep one child, usually a daughter, after divorce. Women without children often foster co-wives' or relatives' children, and older women frequently foster grandchildren. The term in Hausa for fostering is *riko*, derived from *rik'e*, to hold or to keep. This term is used in reference to children whose parents are still alive (as distinct from orphans, who are not foster children), but whose parents have delegated parental responsibility to others. Foster parents are known as *mariki* (male) or *marikiya* (female). The dictionary definition of *riko* is interesting in that it refers specifically to marriage and focuses on females: *riko* is defined as 'keeping a child with a view to marrying her when she is old enough' or 'keeping a child for a particular suitor until she is old enough for marriage'.[19] Fostering can, in fact, occur with children of either sex, but the emphasis on females and on marriage highlights an important aspect of the relationship. The foster parent has the responsibility of arranging, and paying most of the expenses of, the child's marriage. Since boys are usually economically independent and considerably older before they marry, the link between fostering and preparing for the child's marriage is not as evident. For boys, fostering is often associated with apprenticeship: the foster parent is more frequently a non-relative and is responsible for teaching the boy a skill or trade. In the case of children of both sexes the foster parent has the right to the child's services.[20]

Until the recent increase in primary school attendance, subsequent to the implementation of Universal Primary Education (UPE) in northern Nigeria in 1976,[21] children were available to help their mothers or female caretakers most of the day. Formal education is not new in northern Nigeria, for children in the past attended Koranic schools from an early age. However, since the government began a campaign to increase primary school enrolment in the north, the number of children in Western schools has increased substantially, from 160, 340 in 1975/6 to 341,800 in 1976/7.[22] For many children this means that up to six hours a day are now spent in formal education, since in addition to four hours in primary school (and more after Class 3) many children spend several hours a day in Koranic school.

There are a number of reasons for traditionally low enrolments in primary school in northern Nigeria, including the close association in many people's thinking between Western education and Christianity. However, of equal or greater importance are the need for children to perform domestic tasks and the nature of the marriage system with its emphasis on early marriage for girls and large initial expenditures for both brides and grooms. The need for domestic help is clearly linked to purdah, as we have seen, for without children or servants purdah becomes virtually impossible, given the division of labour between adult men and women in Hausa society. Wealthier families can sometimes afford household help in the form of housemaids (usually poor widowed or divorced women from rural areas), Koranic students (often children), or clients of the household head. Among these wealthier families the enrolment of children in school does not cause as much disruption as it does for poorer families. Since purdah has become almost ubiquitous, in families where children are the only domestic help the children are burdened with household tasks, particularly errands, after school.[23]

Opposition to Western education is greater for girls than boys for many reasons, not least of which is the early age of marriage and the perceived need for girls' assistance in raising their own dowries. In 1975/6 out of 160,340 children enrolled in primary school in Kano State, 24 per cent were female. This was, in fact, a decrease of 3 per cent from 1968 when 27 per cent of the 49,580 primary school children were female.[24] Among the reasons cited for this situation by the Kano State Education Review Committee in 1976 were the traditional antagonism towards Western education, based on its association with Christianity, the very early age of marriage of girls, the perceived moral laxity in the schools, the lack of strong leadership by educators, the lack of encouragement given to working women in the society and the negligible adult education facilities for women. In addition, this influential government report noted the association between children's economic activity, particularly hawking, and school attendance.

It is customary in Hausa society for a bridegroom to expect his bride to bring to his house, as her bridal gifts, an assortment of cooking utensils, plates, dishes for decorative purposes and loads of clothes. The family of any bride who fails to respect this custom is often jeered at. It is for this reason that mothers, who are locked in their houses, use their daughters as their main contact with the outside world. A girl's hawking career therefore prevents her from going to school and unless a father is rich enough to provide for his daughter all her bridal requirements the mother will always have her way in controlling her daughter [sic].[25]

There is clearly an inverse relationship between children's participation in economic activity and primary school attendance, and this affects girls even more than boys. While boys and girls are important in assisting their mothers with household tasks, girls play a greater role in income-earning activities than do boys. They also assume greater household responsibility, but not until about age 10.

Gender is not very relevant in defining children's roles before puberty. In fact it is precisely the asexual way in which childhood is defined that allows children the spatial and social mobility to assist women in purdah. There are no restrictions on the movement of children inside and outside their own and other people's houses. Before puberty, boys and girls can interact with secluded women freely. Both boys and girls assist women in minding younger children, in doing errands and carrying messages, and in shopping. Girls play a slightly greater role than boys in helping their mothers cook, but if girls are not available, boys will help with sifting flour and cutting ingredients. It is in income-earning activity that the greatest differences emerge between boys and girls. Most of children's income-earning activity is in the form of street trading, and girls are more active than boys in this regard. In a sample of 109 school-age children, 57 per cent of the girls and 14 per cent of the boys did not attend school and engaged in street trading most of the time (see Table 7.1). Daily diaries obtained from these children over a ten-day period showed that children who engaged in full-time street trading spent approximately six or seven hours a day in this activity. They would leave in the morning to sell one item, return with the money and be given another tray of items to sell. This would continue throughtout the day with breaks for meals, prayers and domestic chores including errands. Most children traded for their own mothers or caretakers but some traded for more distant relatives or non-relatives on a commission basis (usually 10 per cent of the value of

Table 7.1 *Primary School Attendance and Street Trading among Kano Children in Two Wards by Sex*

	Attend school/ do not trade		Attend school/ trade		Do not attend school/ trade		Do not attend school/ do not trade		Total	
	No.	*%*	*No.*	*%*	*No.*	*%*	*No.*	*%*	*No.*	*%*
Boys	38	60	8	13	9	14	8	13	63	100
Girls	12	26	4	9	26	57	4	9	46	101
Total	50	47	12	11	35	32	12	11	109	101

the goods sold). The overwhelming reason why girls are more active than boys in income-producing activities is the perceived need to raise dowry and the responsibility of the mother or female caretaker for raising a good part of this dowry. Girls must have this money by puberty but boys have a longer period in which to earn the money they need for marriage.

There are two categories of children whose labour is used to contribute to subsistence before it is used to raise dowry or bridewealth. These are children who are not living with secluded women, and who therefore are unable to rely on a father's support. The *almajirai*, or Koranic students, are boys who have come to the city to study the Koran with a particular *mallam*. These children are expected to support themselves, and sometimes reward their teachers by contributing labour or income to the teacher's household. These boys beg, do odd jobs, such as cleaning gutters or portering at railway and truck stations, or do hawking (*talla*) for traders for a fixed commission.[26] Of nine boys in the Kano study who traded and did not attend primary school, three were *almajirai*. These children are available to work for people who have an insufficient number of children in their households. Although they do attend Koranic school – often for longer hours than other children – none of them is in primary school. The other category of children who work for subsistence and do not attend primary school are those girls who live in female-headed households, usually with divorced or widowed mothers. In the Kano sample these girls, like their mothers, all contributed to their own subsistence.

Among the children in male-headed households there is still an inverse relationship between certain forms of economic activity and school attendance. While all children engage in some form of economic activity, some activities are more compatible with school attendance than others. Domestic tasks and errands, child care, and escorting women when they go out, are chores done by all children. In the sample of 109 school-age children, some children attended school and sporadically did *talla*. A child whose mother's primary occupation was embroidering or hair-plaiting might do *talla* when the mother cooked food for sale on the weekend. Street trading, however, can only be done as a full-time occupation by children who are not in school. As we have seen, the incomes of the mothers and caretakers of these children are considerably higher than the incomes of women whose children's main economic activity is unpaid domestic work and errands.

When children are engaged in income-producing activities, this is usually described as a means of earning money for marriage, except in the case of the poorest children and the *almajirai*. When children earn money they generally give it to their mothers or caretakers to keep for their dowry or bridewealth. Children also occasionally engage in independent economic enterprises, for example, cooking small pancakes for sale to other children, or renting their toys or bicycles to other children, or doing errands for strangers for money. They usually spend this money on snacks; older children sometimes also save it for marriage expenses. Since children, like women, have considerable control over their income, they generally feel that they are working for themselves, not for their parents. Therefore, from the age of 5 or 6, girls spend most of their time and energy on accumulating dowry. Those girls who attend primary school increasingly rely on gifts from suitors to buy their *kayan daki*.

There is a clear division of responsibility between husbands and wives in meeting the expenses of dowry. Fathers, or male caretakers, are supposed to provide furniture, including a bed, mattress, pillows, linens and a cupboard. Mothers, or female caretakers, are expected to provide *kayan daki*, literally 'things for the room', in unlimited quantities. In addition to the traditional enamel and brass bowls, glassware and modern appliances are increasingly becoming part of *kayan daki*. It is difficult to overemphasise the importance of this form of dowry as a status symbol and as a form of stored female wealth. However, it is interesting to note that men, even prospective husbands, are only marginally concerned with their bride's *kayan daki*. Because of the rules of purdah which strongly limit adult male access to female living space, a groom's friends and male relatives, with few exceptions, never see the bride's *kayan daki*, and many profess to know little about it. The women who attend a marriage ceremony, however, are extremely interested in evaluating the quantity and quality of the brides's *kayan daki*.[27] The wealth stored in *kayan daki* reflects on the status of the bride's family generally, but particularly on her mother or *marikiya*. Since most women build this dowry through their independent economic activities, this aspect of female status does not necessarily reflect the status of the men on whom women are otherwise dependent. The limited interest which men express in *kayan daki* may be a reflection of their ambivalent attitude towards women's income-producing activities.

An interesting Hausa folktale[28] reveals, however, latent antagonism between men and women over women's independent economic activities. In the story *kayan daki* actually reverses the status of the favoured versus the despised wife, but the husband eventually retaliates against the economically active wife. In this tale a man has two wives, each with a daughter. He favours one wife and supports her more generously than the other. A friend of the poor wife notices her plight and loans her money to trade. The poor wife and her daughter eventually build this into a large sum. The father then finds husbands for his daughters: a rich merchant for the daughter of the favoured wife and a poor man for the other. After the marriages, the husband of the favoured daughter discovers that the wife of the poor man has brought many fine things to the marriage: metal basins, fine calabashes and imported carpets. After seeing this, the wealthy husband beats his wife until she runs home to her father. He smashes her calabashes and pots and says: 'Good-for-nothing slut – you and your mother too, your father's favourites and you haven't even any decent utensils. While the daughter he doesn't like – and her mother too – why, she's got a hut full of things!' Then the father beats the despised wife, accusing her of being the cause of his favoured daughter's getting a beating.

Among that segment of the population that has accepted Western education for women, it is expected that the bride will contribute to her dowry from the courting gifts of cash that she receives from men. Although courting gifts are traditional, their amount has increased and the use to which these gifts are put has also changed. Whereas formerly much of this money may have been spent before marriage by the bride or her family, it is now used for the purchase of *kayan daki*. Formerly these gifts were not returned if the marriage did not take place. They consisted of small amounts of money given when the suitor went to visit the bride. Nowadays the amount of money given is often larger and if the suitor is unsuccessful the money is often returned. In some cases, a successful suitor will reimburse an unsuccessful one. There are two interesting implications of the new pattern. The first is that the economic burden on men is increasing before marriage. This is a matter of frequent complaint by some university students and other men who want to marry Western-educated women. Secondly, it suggests that an area of activity – the accumulation of the part of the dowry – that formerly represented female autonomy is increasingly provided by the husband. Housewares may then become part of a conjugal fund, rather than representing an exclusively female store of wealth.

Conclusion

Despite the fact that seclusion is an ideal form of Muslim marriage, the practicality of purdah obviously varies with economic circumstances. The difficulty of keeping women in purdah among rural peasants and among the urban poor is obvious. In an economically stratified society women's contribution to production is essential, at least among the lower classes where men simply cannot produce enough to support numerous dependants. In comparing female–male relationships in Kano with those in other parts of the Islamic world, one is struck by the strength and the particular form of the institution of purdah in northern Nigeria. In Kano City, which by any account is economically stratified, few married women are not in seclusion. Even when husbands cannot fulfil all their wives' and children's material needs, as they are enjoined to do by Islamic law, women are secluded. Out of sixty-nine households of all income groups in this study, in only one case was a wife not in seclusion, due to poverty. Purdah is seen as a sign of high status, and despite its restrictive character it reflects positively on the social status of both men and women, given the adherence to Islamic values in the population.

In some ways the strictness with which seclusion is enforced in Kano (and probably elsewhere in northern Nigeria) appears to be greater than in other parts of the Islamic world. In North Africa, in Morocco for example, women use the veil to segregate themselves from men and from public male space;[29] women in Kano, however, rarely go out at all during the day, not even to go to market. Their spatial seclusion is even greater than in places where the veil enables women to move through, if not in, male space. The ubiquitous adoption of purdah in Kano is possible precisely because secluded women do continue to play economic roles and generate income, at the same time as they participate in the myth of being totally dependent on men. In fact, behind the walls of individual houses, the degree of dependence varies considerably. Women in Kano seem to be continuing the long West African tradition of female involvement in economic life. They are able to do this because of the control they exercise over the activities of children. The availability of children and the way in which children's roles are defined enable women to carry on economic activities, both domestic and extra-domestic, in the manner of market women elsewhere in West Africa.

Because of purdah, northern Nigerian Muslim women are not economically active in ways that are revealed in labour force statistics, as Eleanor Fapohunda noted in Chapter 2. They do not participate in the formal economy, but rather in what Polly Hill has described as the 'hidden trade'.[30] While this activity gives them some mobility within the domestic domain, and enables them to improve their living conditions as wives, it does not lead to further participation in the male-dominated areas of economic and political life. Women are able to move resources around within a very limited sector of the economy, that sector which is basically involved in consumption. They are unable to gain control over significant areas of production and they remain dependent on manipulating the limited resources that men give them for subsistence. Moreover, the limited profit that individual women amass is reinvested almost immediately in the very marriage system which defines their position in the first place. By spending most of their profit on dowry for themselves and their daughters, women and young girls are, in a sense, working very hard to move in a circle. The pattern of female dependence repeats itself generation after generation, as it should, given the Islamic value-system. Despite their prodigious economic activity, Hausa women do little more than protect their autonomy in a sexually segregated society.

Today, however, the division of labour by sex and age in Hausa society is being severely disturbed by the introduction of universal primary education. Even in the short run, the enrolment of all children in primary school threatens the institution of purdah and the sexual division of labour. Without children available to participate in domestic work, the West African version of purdah is impossible, except in the upper classes where adults can be employed to replace the labour of children. In the long run, Western education is likely to create new expectations about marriage and about work on the part of young women and perhaps on the part of young men. Whether these expectations will be met with new employment opportunities for secluded and non-secluded women is a question I cannot answer. Whatever the ultimate result may be, Western education inevitably challenges the structure of all but the wealthiest families in Islamic West Africa. The positive benefits that many people – Muslim and non-Muslim alike – acknowledge from Western education can be attained only with the alteration of the traditional division of labour by sex and age and the transformation of the family structure that is based on this division of labour.

Notes: Chapter 7

The research on which this paper is based was conducted in Nigeria between 1976 and 1978 with support from the American Museum of Natural History, the National Science Foundation (grant no. BNS76–11174), the Social Science Research Council and the Wenner-Gren Foundation for Anthropological Research. I am extremely grateful to Carol Gelber for assistance in analysing the data and to Jan Brukman for commenting on an early version of this chapter and making many helpful suggestions. The Ford Foundation generously supported the analysis of the data.

1 For example: Bashir, 1972; E. Boserup, 1970; Brooks, 1976; Hill, 1969, 1971; Hodder and Ukwu, 1969; Lawson, 1972; B. Lewis, 1976, 1977; McCall, 1961; Mullings, 1976; Peil, 1975; Robertson, 1974, 1976; Sanjek and Sanjek, 1976; Schildkrout, 1973; Sudarkasa, 1973.
2 Barkow, 1972; Hill, 1969, 1971, 1972; Ogunbiyi, 1969; Schildkrout, 1978, 1979; M. F. Smith, 1954; M. G. Smith, 1952, 1954, 1955.
3 Barkow, 1972; Hill, 1972; M. G. Smith, 1954.
4 Fafunwa, 1974; Hiskett, 1975; Hubbard, 1975; Ogunsola, 1974.

5   Dwyer, 1978; Rosen, 1978. Mernissi (1975) argues that Islamic attitudes towards sexuality affirm the power of the female. She therefore maintains that inequality is not a characteristic of the Islamic attitude to women.
6   Dawood, 1959, p. 358.
7   ibid., p. 345.
8   Mernissi, 1975.
9   Rattray, 1913, pp. 200ff.; Skinner, 1969, *passim*.
10 As Renée Pittin (1979b, p. 3) points out, there has been a fallacious emphasis on the literature on the Hausa on the institution of *karuwanci,* as exemplified by M. G. Smith (1959, p. 244) and A. Cohen (1969, *passim*). As Pittin stresses, the status of 'non-marriage' *(jawarci)* is also an option for divorced or widowed women. In Kano the term *bazawara* is more commonly used to refer to divorced women. *Jawara* is used in Katsina where Pittin worked.
11 See Hill, 1972, 1977; M. G. Smith, 1955; and Wallace, 1978, for varied descriptions of the way in which the traditional *gandu* system worked.
12 In this respect the Hausa practice varies from that of other communities which follow *sharia* law. The Koran stipulates that boys should remain with their mothers until puberty, after which they are given an option of which parent to live with; girls should remain with their mothers until they go to their husbands' houses (Anderson, J. N. D., 1970, p. 214). There is one provision in the Koran, however, which exempts Hausa practice from this rule: that mothers retain custody 'unless they marry outside the immediate family', which indeed is the general practice in Hausa communities.
13 Although the public/domestic distinction seems pertinent to a sexually segregated society such as the Hausa, the criticism of this dichotomy as a theoretical construct by Schlegel (1977, pp. 17ff.) is valid.
14 Paden, 1973; M. G. Smith, 1959.
15 M. G. Smith, 1962.
16 Sudarkasa, 1973.
17 See Raynaut (1968), whose account, which the present author discovered after writing this chapter, describes a similar situation in rural Hausaland.
18 Schildkrout, 1981.
19 Bargery, 1934, p. 856.
20 This is common in West Africa, where fostering is often regarded as an obligation between kin. See E. N. Goody, 1969, 1971, 1978; Oppong, 1973; Schildkrout, 1973. The use of children as pawns for debt does not seem to have been common among the Hausa.
21 Bray, 1977, 1978; *West Africa,* 1979a, 1979b, 1979c.
22 *Educational Statistics for Kano State 1975—76*, p. 7
23 In a study of Yoruba schoolchildren in Lagos, Oloko has found that there is a strong negative correlation between school achievement and trading, whereas domestic work does not seem to affect school achievement adversely (Oloko, 1979).
24 *Educational Statistics for Kano State, 1975–76*, p. 7. See also Trevor, 1975a.
25 *Kano State Educational Review Committee, 1976*, p. 35.
26 In a study of beggars in Zaria city, Mensah (1977) noted that the majority (59 per cent) of beggars were male children, many of whom were Koranic students.
27 Bashir (1972) reports that women will borrow *kayan daki* for these occasions if they feel inadequate about their holdings.
28 See N. Skinner, 1969, pp. 357ff.
29 Mernissi, 1975.
30 Hill, 1969.

Chapter 8

Marital Sexuality and Birth-Spacing among the Yoruba

LAWRENCE A. ADEOKUN

This chapter is about marital relationships and child-bearing among two ethnic subgroups of the Yoruba – the Ekiti and the Ikale. The different sexual practices of the two groups following childbirth allow an investigation of attitudes to child growth and of the relative role of the lactation sexual prohibition and of *post partum* amenorrhoea with regard to childbirth spacing and fertility, in an area in which little has been documented about child development and little is known about birth control. Both the Ekiti and the Ikale are Yoruba, mainly farmers and Christians, with high levels of illiteracy especially among females. And yet there are subtle differences contrasting the two groups, which are located in Ondo State in the south-west of Nigeria.

In 1963 the Ekiti numbered more than a million and this number has probably doubled since then due to improvements in general living standards. They have a reputation for being strongly united and are noted agriculturalists, who have maximised the advantages of their hilly and rain forest environment for the growing of their favourite tuber – yam. For reasons of their location in the interior, away from the modernising influences from overseas, they are regarded as latecomers to the economic mobility game. However, their dedication to education as a means of escape from the drudgery of agriculture has produced high secondary and university registration rates and a correspondingly high mobility in the public services (Imoagene, 1976). Until recently, education and out-migration were closely linked in the area because of the scarcity of schools, the outcome of the relative neglect of the 'interior' by both the colonial and indigenous administrations.

Although the Ekiti benefited from the introduction of cocoa, the loyalty to 'real' farming – that is, the growing of yams – still remains. The certainty of subsistence from yam crops contrasts with the uncertainty of reward from cocoa, due to the instability of the external market and the huge profits made at the expense of the farmers by the local middlemen and the marketing boards. The respectability of a farmer is still linked with the size of his yam crop. In pursuit of this respectability, every member of his household constitutes his primary labour pool.

Socially, the Ekiti are considered as pleasant rustics, lacking in the finer graces of speech and manners of *ara isale,* or those of the lowland and coastal areas who had earlier European contact. Partly on account of this late contact, the Ekiti are considered conservative in matters of sexuality as well as in morals. The girls from the area are sought after as making reliable wives and good mothers. It is conceivable that the submissiveness of the lowly educated Ekiti wife to her husband is an important part of her attractiveness.

The industry of the wife in support of the family is also a feature of the life and image of the Ekiti woman. Partly because of the limited but growing market for local and imported goods, the activities of Ekiti women focus on the sale of farm surpluses, crude manufacture of farm produce and the sale of the same. In the conduct of these activities, the women are locked into a circuit involving the family compound, the farm and the local periodic and day-markets (see Sudarkasa, 1973). The need to combine these itinerant activities with child-rearing places some strains on the mother, who has to carry an infant over considerable distances and promotes willingness to leave the children at home with others as soon as it is practicable to do so. But the financial returns from these activities also encourage an early training of the growing child, and especially the females, into the work routines of the mother, as soon as the conditions are right for the child to be so integrated.

Participation in outdoor marketing has given women an opportunity to socialise outside the home, which has been facilitated by the advent of an easier road network and the expansion of trading activity to include some urban contact for the purchase of manufactured goods.

Partly because of the conservatism in sexuality and fertility behaviour, the main customary features of Yoruba child-rearing practice, such as the extended breastfeeding on demand, the taboo on sexual intercourse during lactation and the devotion to child welfare and family-building persist in Ekiti. Although subject to change and modification with the socio-economic transformation of the society, the combination of these practices and the high infant mortality, resulting from limited access to modern health care and the lack of basic amenities, assure that children are born at substantial ages apart

(Orubuloye and Caldwell, 1975). Consequently, there are marked distances between age-group associations.

The stature of an Ekiti mother increases with the amount of sacrifice she makes for her children, and at times, the struggles of a sterile or sub-fertile woman in her search for children add to her stature. To transfer the sacrifice into sexual restraint is not so very difficult, when there are the supportive taboos and quasi-religious association of sexual laxity and ill-health in children. There is nothing that a Yoruba woman would not do for her children. Sexual abstinence is one such sacrifice.

Given the puritanical image of the Ekiti, it is consistent that they should be considered as demanding in the upbringing of their children. The main features and virtues expected in children are strength, which is taken as an indication of good health; honesty, which is reinforced by a number of food taboos and corporal punishment; and intelligence, often conceived in terms of adaptability to the Western education system.

Although the Ikale and the Ijale, another Yoruba group, occupy a territory about two-thirds the size of that of the Ekiti, the population size and density are much lower, due to the difficulties of the riverine and coastal environment in which they live. The population of Okitipupa division in 1963 was just over a quarter of a million. As in Ekiti, recent improvements in general standards of living and a high population growth rate may have resulted in the doubling of the population by now.

The coastal location gave the Ikale and the Ijale an early contact with external trade and encouraged the exploitation of their natural resources, mostly palm produce in the rain forest and fishing along the creeks. But their role in external trade declined, when the trade routes to the interior switched to the easier land routes from Lagos through Ibadan and western Yorubaland at the end of hostilities between the various Yoruba sub-kingdoms at the middle of the nineteenth century (Akintoye, 1971). With the reduction in transit trade through the area the poverty of the environment in terms of subsistence agriculture, and the neglect of the area because of its peripheral location to the new route and the seat of colonial administration, resulted in the relative underdevelopment of the area.

The main food crop in the area is cassava, grown for the tuber, and the semi-processed food, *gari,* which is popular and in demand in other parts of Yorubaland. In common with other subsistence groups, the cultivation of the crop is primarily for the use of the family, with the sale of surplus conditioned by market prices. Recent increases in food prices and access to the Lagos metropolitan market via the creeks have encouraged an upsurge of fishing and agricultural activities. As in Ekiti, the processing of food and fish for the market and actual marketing is the preserve of females and provides an opportunity for socialisation of female children into adult activities. The development of oil palm plantations in the area has created a local capacity for paid agricultural labour. Although the Ikale had depended on the immigrant Urhobo community to exploit the wild palm trees (Otite, 1979), they have been prepared to seize the opportunity of paid labour in the plantations themselves.

The main elements of the social structure are the same here as in Ekiti. The conjugal family based on a network of kinship obligations is important. The residence group is increasingly the nuclear family, mostly owing to the change in house construction methods – from the communal sprawling compounds, built with cheap materials and little skill, to the more expensive and individual smaller houses, built of cement and corrugated iron sheets.

One indicator of sexuality of a group, often employed by the Yoruba in the assessment of their own and other ethnic groups, is the frequency of confinements and/or the urban female behaviour. It is generally held that the coastal people are more fecund than the upland tribes and that this is the result of greater sexuality. It is also believed that Ikale marriage customs are more flexible than those of the more conventional Yoruba. The extent to which marital sexuality and family formation among the Ikale differ from those of the Ekiti was, however, not apparent until the collection of my data was well under way.

Briefly, the rule concerning sexual abstinence during lactation does not apply to the Ikale. Not only is there no such taboo, but the duration of a *post partum* sexual avoidance is considerably shorter than, and independent of, those associated with the taboo. Besides, the abstinence is practised for reasons of uncleanliness in the woman, rather than for the health of the infant as is the case in Ekiti.

What, then, is the Ikale attitude to children and what is the position of the child in the general scheme? The theme of a mother's trials and concern over her children is prevalent here too. The entry of the child into the work pattern of the family as an individual is reported to start with the child running errands around the household. The reported traits of a good child repeatedly included the physical strength, ability to communicate and the ability to 'look after itself', a phrase covering the avoidance of simple domestic and environmental nuisances, such as the open fire, and recognition of some harmful weeds and insects. The fulfilment of these traits and conditions creates a long gap between the time when the Ikale woman is open to the risk of pregnancy, because of the early resumption of *post partum* sexual activity, and the time when the decision on another pregnancy and the next child may reasonably be made.

Differences in Fertility and Family Formation

Contrary to the suggestion of a higher frequency of births among the Ikale, the survey revealed that the crude birth rates for the two groups were virtually identical at 54·4 and 54·7 per 1,000 for Ikale and Ekiti respectively. Similarly there was only a negligible difference in the crude general fertility rates at 236·4 and 240·6 per 1,000 women of reproductive ages in Ikale and Ekiti respectively. But with reference to total fertility rate, the Ikale do have a slightly higher rate, with 7·07 live births at the end of the reproductive span compared with 6·85 for Ekiti women.

It is, however, with reference to the age-specific fertility that some life-cycle differences emerge between the two groups, revealing some contrasting attitude to the issue of 'grandmother pregnancy' or the idea of a mother and her daughter becoming pregnant at the same time. For most Yoruba women, the inconvenience that might arise from such a situation leads to early onset of terminal abstinence (Adepoju 1977, p. 137; Caldwell and Caldwell, 1977). The mean birth rates per woman in the several age-groups reveal contributions at all reproductive ages to the general fertility rate in Ikale. In contrast there is no recorded birth in the last age-group (45–49) in Ekiti.

Post Partum Sexual Attitudes

The trauma of parturition and the centre stage occupied by the newborn impose some period of sexual restraint on the male in most species. This instinctive avoidance period has been extended for varying lengths of time through the use of several social and cultural devices in different societies. Such extension has direct implications for the timing of the subsequent resumption of sexual activity and, in a non-contracepting population, for the occurrence of the next birth.

There is general agreement among Ekiti and Ikale women and men that the recovery period for the mother after the delivery of a baby is typically three months and, for some, less. Fewer than 10 per cent of any group or sex would consider that more than six months was needed. In effect, the three-month recovery period sets a lower limit to the resumption of sexual activity. The question asked was, how does this perception affect the recorded shortest period of *post partum* sexual avoidance? It is here that striking differences between the two groups emerged, for while 59 per cent of the Ikale women and 76 per cent of the males reported the shortest *post partum* abstinence of six or fewer months, the corresponding proportions of Ekiti were less than 1 per cent and 4 per cent of the females and males respectively. And while 85 per cent of the Ekiti sample would wait for a year or more before resuming sexual activity, only 15 per cent of the Ikale sample were so prepared and less than 5 per cent waited beyond the twenty-fourth month.

When the existence of traditional prohibitions concerning *post partum* sexuality was investigated, the following similarities and differences between the two groups emerged. Both groups are agreed that sexual intercourse leading to a pregnancy during breastfeeding was not good for the surviving child. And both groups would stop breastfeeding on account of an early pregnancy because the quality of the breastmilk was assumed to deteriorate. But only in Ekiti is the mere fact of coitus during breastfeeding considered as having an adverse effect on the baby. From the responses obtained in Ekiti, it was clear that the prohibition on sexual activity during breastfeeding no longer carried the life-and-death consequences associated with the breach of the taboo. However, while Ekiti women report a *post partum* avoidance period which is consistently longer than the breastfeeding duration by a mean of seven months, Ikale women were, by implication of early resumption of sexuality, prepared to run the risk of an early pregnancy, stop breastfeeding if they became pregnant and, according to one woman, 'make it up to the surviving child by taking extra care of it'.

The Ikale believe that the survival of a child aged 1 year or less could be threatened by the magical power of an early pregnancy. It is stated that the foetus will attempt to kill the surviving child by making it suffer from a condition called *apa*, the symptom of which is the tiny size of the surviving child and incessant illness. But the term *apa* is applied to the foetus rather than the condition of the surviving child. Some native medicine can be given to the child to save it and these medicines are relatively difficult to obtain. Consequently, most couples would rather take the trouble of avoiding becoming pregnant than attempt a cure.

In Ekiti, on the other hand, the link between sexuality and the health of the child was established through the often-cited effect of sexual activity on the deterioration of the breastmilk and the malnutrition of the surviving child. The condition of the child is described in terms very similar to those employed for *apa* in Ikale. Apparently the different attitudes to *post partum* sexuality between the two groups coexist with a similar concern for the welfare of the surviving child. In effect, the relevance of child welfare and development to the postponement of the next pregnancy appears of paramount importance. Thus attention is now turned to the issue of child development and its link to the duration of breastfeeding, the reason for terminating it and the circumstances that encourage a decision affecting timing of a subsequent pregnancy.

Breastfeeding Duration

Breastmilk assumes greater significance in developing countries because it provides the most reliable source of a baby's needs in the first six months of life and because of the inadequacy of weaning foods, which are little more than watered or mashed forms of adult food. Consequently, the termination of breastfeeding is an important indicator of the mother's assessment of the adequate development of the child at that point in time. In this context, it is easy to understand why the differences in attitude to *post partum* sexuality between the Ikale and the Ekiti has not produced any significant difference in breastfeeding pattern.

In both groups, only negligible proportions of women would breastfeed for less than six months. At the other extreme, while 7 per cent of Ikale women would breastfeed beyond two years, 13 per cent of Ekiti women were breastfeeding that long. In effect, both groups clustered around the mean of seventeen months for Ikale and twenty months for Ekiti. The three-month difference between the groups can be explained by the higher incidence of termination of breastfeeding in Ikale resulting from pregnancy.

In Ikale there is apparently a higher awareness of the association between extended breastfeeding and the delay of the onset of menstruation. This is because the very short period of *post partum* avoidance there places a higher probability on the occurrence of pregnancy soon after the onset of menstruation. Available evidence on the association of breastfeeding and amenorrhoea (Van Ginneken, 1977) would suggest that the slightly shorter breastfeeding duration in Ikale by itself is not enough to produce significant differences in the onset of menstruation. The extent to which onset of menstruation and early pregnancy influence the decision on the termination of breastfeeding is investigated next.

Given the importance attached to breastfeeding and the added fact that, in Ekiti, its termination is a necessary prelude to the resumption of sexual activity, I asked who decides that breastfeeding should be terminated.

In Ikale 89 per cent of the females and 74 per cent of the males hold the view that when breastfeeding should be terminated is the decision of the wife. Less than 10 per cent of either sex consider the decision to lie with the husband alone. This pattern of response is consistent with the observation that the resumption of sexual activity in Ikale is disengaged from breastfeeding. In effect the mother's assessment of the needs of the child takes precedence in the termination of breastfeeding.

In Ekiti, however, there is a contradiction between the sexes. While 63 per cent of women claim that they are responsible for the decision to terminate breastfeeding, the proportion of Ekiti males who would agree is only 19·0 per cent. In contrast, while 32 per cent of the females claim that it is the husband's decision, nearly three-quarters of the males believe that they are responsible for the decision. This pattern of response would appear to be related to the existence of the taboo on sexual activity during lactation and therefore an indication of male anxiety that breastfeeding be terminated for reasons of resuming sexual activity. Inquiries regarding the reasons for terminating breastfeeding and the possible existence of husband–wife conflict did not support this hypothesis with respect to anxiety about sexual activity.

Significantly it is in Ikale, where there is the real probability of a pregnancy occurring before the termination of breastfeeding, that a small proportion of both sexes, less than 5 per cent of females and 2 per cent of males, give the reason that a mother's pregnancy is the reason for terminating breastfeeding. However, in both areas the dominant factor in the termination of breastfeeding is the development of the child, which is variously conceived in terms of physical development or in terms of chronological age. For example, while half of Ikale males and females give the ability of the child to walk as the trigger for weaning, the proportion of Ekiti respondents who give walking as a reason is much smaller. More than half of Ekiti females and males give an age specification of between 2 and 3 years old as reasons for weaning the child, the corresponding proportion for Ikale being 18 per cent of the females and 29 per cent of the males. In general, though, the ability to walk is typical of Ikale responses, while the age specification is typical of Ekiti.

The importance attached to the physical growth of a child and to the role of breastfeeding in that development is also illustrated by the responses given to the inquiry as to why there might be conflict between a husband and wife regarding the termination of breastfeeding. There is hardly any difference between the two groups. About a third of women claim that there could be no such conflict. The rest who could see why a conflict might arise cite poor health, that the child is not old enough, or that the child cries a lot, as reasons for possible conflict. The corresponding proportions of the total female sample citing these three reasons are 34 per cent poor health, 23 per cent inadequate child's age and 4 per cent the child crying a lot.

When note is taken of different implications of weaning for the resumption of sexual activity in the two groups, then the convergence of opinion about the importance of the physical growth of a child is more striking. The irrelevance of weaning for sexual activity in Ikale rightly shifts the emphasis to the age and health of the child. And in Ekiti, where the motivation for weaning is supposed to be linked with sexual activity, the concern is also for the attainment of the right age and good health by the child.

In Ikale, discussions with couples reveal a strong awareness of the inevitability of another pregnancy at the end of the amenorrhic period. And some couples accept the inevitability, since it accords with their own view of adequate birth-spacing: 'I do not worry my mind about pregnancy, we keep on having sex and as long as she keeps on breastfeeding nothing can happen. Once she has stopped and her period has returned than we know it is time for her to become pregnant again.' This husband had reasons for complacency. His wife breastfeeds a child for an uncharacteristic twenty-five to thirty months for each of her children and has a range of child-specific amenorrhic period of between fourteen and nineteen months.

In the absence of modern contraception and in view of the early onset of *post partum* sexual activity, another Ikale couple were asked how they achieved observed birth intervals which did not accord with the very short breastfeeding or amenorrhic periods reported. The use of *coitus interruptus* and some traditional herbs was mentioned. The couple conceded, and the same sentiment was echoed by others, that because they both enjoy sexual intercourse and both have the welfare of their surviving child in mind, the extra trouble of assuring safe sex was well worth it. (The survey did not yield any evidence of higher incidence of abortion or pregnancy wastage in Ikale. The overall pregnancy wastage for the two groups stands at the same level of 84 per 1,000 pregnancies.)

When Ikale couples were asked directly what they looked for in a child before they thought it was time to have the next child, the ability to walk dominated the responses. But to this ability were added the carrying of small loads over given distances, the wisdom to cope with the environment and the ability to respond intelligently to directives from elders.

It is in the discussions carried out in Ekiti that the physical attributes are highlighted and used to explain the circumstances that produce a substantial post-weaning abstinence of about seven months mentioned earlier (see Adeokun, 1979). According to one parent: 'Part of the joy of having children is to be able to send them on errands. What I look for in my own children is that they should be able to work. When a child can carry things like a gourd of palm wine with appropriate care, bring a day's supply of yams for the family or a day's supply of firewood from the farm, then the child is old enough.'

Further discussion of the health and care of individual children helped to confirm that variations in physical development are noted in terms of simple landmarks in physical growth and that allowances are made for this in the postponement of the next birth. As one parent remarked of one of his children, 'he walked very early but he was so sickly, always complaining of headache, and that is why we have not decided to have another child after him'. The best assurance of good health in children is seen to be adequate spacing. According to an Ekiti mother: 'There are some women who have children at the same time with me and later have another before me. But when you see our children, you see that my own look better. That shows that I have the patience in nursing my children.' When the woman was asked what she saw as signs of good health, she continued: 'His behaviour will be good, he will be strong and able to go to the farm. There is no point in carrying him on the back when I am pregnant again.'

The openness of the Yoruba conjugal families means that kin and in-laws take part in the decision-making about child-rearing and the timing of a next pregnancy. They are also participants in the actual socialisation of the child into the life of work and service to elders.

About half of the women, especially the Ikale, had been involved in conversations with friends and relatives about sexual behaviour of husbands – whether they were early or late in making sexual advances to wives at the end of the customary abstinence period. Fewer had exchanged comments about actual pregnancies. Only 8 per cent of Ikale women and 20 per cent of their Ekiti counterpart reported such exchanges: understandable, because of the reluctance of Yoruba people to comment about a current pregnancy, except with very close relatives or friends, since any untoward outcome of the pregnancy commented upon could lead to accusations of 'evil eye' (Ebrahim, 1978, p. 17). Even fewer were involved in comments about the timing of additional children. This decreasing pattern of interactions illustrates a willingness of outsiders to the conjugal family to be involved at the pre-decision stages, but to withdraw once the response of the parents to the prompting to have another child is favourable.

Some Conclusions

This chapter calls in to question the emphasis given to lactation abstinence as the main determinant of birth-spacing. Such emphasis is based on the assumption that extended breastfeeding and the associated amenorrhea and abstinence constitute the only choice for parents in non-contracepting societies to achieve desired pregnancy intervals. Clearly, the Ikale case shows that such an assumption is not valid and that alternative family-building patterns are possible. In Ikale communities where lactation abstinence is not practised extended breastfeeding still constitutes the main source of nurture and basis of child growth and development. In such societies, as in those which practise lactation abstinence, it is the monitoring of the physical development of the surviving child that forms the basis of the next child decision. The shift of emphasis in the next-child decision-making from *post partum* sexuality to child development points to an important element for consideration in the formulation of family advisory and planning programmes. As marital sexuality becomes disengaged from the timing of additional children or from lactation, as is the case in Ikale, the means of combining sexual activity with desirable birth-spacing may be increasingly sought after. At that point, the replacement of folk methods of contraception with compatible modern contraception will become important to the determination of fertility levels.

This chapter has shown the significance of variations in traditional marital sexual practices which might affect the ways in which decisions are made about the timing of additional children. It has also shown for the Yoruba the important position occupied by the physical growth of the surviving child in the next-child decision. The study of such growth and development within the context of birth-spacing and family formation is an area of further investigation and analysis. Such studies will require the collaboration of demographers, nutritionists and sociologists.

The data reported here are taken from the author's 'Next Child' Project funded by a Ford Rockefeller Population Research Award. The study was designed to investigate the relationships between biological, social and cultural variables involved in the sequence of events within a single birth interval. The quantitative data consist of two schedules administered to 995 mothers and their 778 husbands. Discussions with a panel of families were also recorded. In Ekiti the villages of Eporo and Emure were selected. In Ikale the villages were Ikoya and Iltirun. The data were collected in 1977.

Conclusion to Part Two

Certain constant patterns in West African societies have now been sketched both in outline and using specific case studies as illustration. These have included what we might term the tremendous continuing 'familism' – the persistent strength and salience of ties of kinship and marriage, in contexts where high fertility remains a valued norm and in which virtually all are married for the greater part of their adult lives, at least once if not more frequently; and in which ties of kinship continue to constitute the important social roots for individuals, their sources of material and emotional security and sustenance and their guide to community relations. The two sexes are seen to depend upon each other, especially as man and wife, and brother and sister, or in other kin roles. Sexuality is observed as a pervasive force which must be contained and controlled through secret societies, through seclusion of one sex, or other methods. Even sexual relations within the privacy of the conjugal bed are noted to be carefully controlled by social pressures of kin and neighbours.

We have seen examples of ways in which diverse ethnic groups from different countries organise their artistic, political, ritual, economic and parental roles in terms of gender. Separation and interdependence have been themes. Hints of latent tension have emerged, often surfacing in story, myth and ritual.

In Part Three we turn to a more exchange-centred approach and a focus on individual expectations and bargaining behaviour. Given the foregoing constants and pervasive patterns, we now ask how women and men organise their daily lives in marketing, fishing and farming and domestic consumption in one broad cultural area: that of southern Ghana.

Rights, Exchanges and Bargains: Co-operation and Conflict

Introduction to Part Three

In West African societies domestic groups of co-residing kin and affines and kin groups, based on ties of common descent including lineages (or unilineal descent groups), continue to be important units for economic cooperation, for co-ownership and production of goods and services and means of generating an income for consumption. The forms which these groups and sets of individual men and women take, however, are highly varied and flexible, splitting up, reassembling and taking new forms over time, as male and female relationships and resources alter. Such changes are often preceded by tension and conflict, as we shall see documented in some detail in the various chapters of Part Three, in which the theme is the reciprocal rights and duties in terms of goods and services; the exchanges and the bargains between women and men in domestic contexts in their roles as wives and husbands, sisters and brothers, kinswomen and kinsmen. These relationships are explored here in legal contexts, among traders, cash croppers, food growers and fishermen and fishmongers.

Food production, processing and distribution, agriculture, fishing and trade remain the chief sources of livelihood and forms of subsistence activities for both women and men in West Africa. Husbands and wives characteristically co-operate in various ways in these activities to maintain themselves and their dependent young and old; and yet, as previous commentators have clearly demonstrated, conjugal units are not discrete property-owning units. Joint conjugal property in a polygynous or potentially polygynous context is a virtual impossibility. Moreover, in most contexts kin, not spouses, are legally recognised co-owners and heirs. Marriage itself is more of a complex process of events, which may in many cases be speedily reversed, including return of marriage gifts and presents. Given the complexity and diversity of conjugal ties and forms of domestic organisation, and the ever-present daily need to co-operate in providing food and sustenance for selves and dependants, what are the characteristic patterns of conjugal co-operation and management of time and resources? What are spouses' respective rights and duties and how do they assume them?

The next five chapters consider such issues in terms of reciprocal expectations, exchanges and bargains between spouses and kin. Significantly, conflict, latent and manifest, and tension are features of each of them. All are set in southern Ghanaian contexts and in recent contemporary time. The first chapter sets the complex legal context for changing marriage norms and practices and claims of kin.

Legal Battles

Chapter 9 by Dorothy Vellenga focuses on the confusion surrounding the social and legal implications of a variety of heterosexual relationships in Ghana. First the historical origins of this confusion are traced; secondly, different types of marriage are examined; and thirdly, the post-independence legal reform movements are outlined to demonstrate the differing interests of various groups within the society.

Three interrelated and still unresolved questions are seen to be of critical importance: the extent to which the interests of spouses should be or are in fact joint and unique and differentiated from all others, especially in terms of ownership and inheritance; the capacity of men to marry more than one wife and the consequent rights of such multiple spouses and their offspring; and the rights and duties of kin with respect to property and maintenance in contrast with those of spouses. Vellenga's presentation and discussion of evidence shows that these remain matters of concern and debate and that as a consequence the rights and duties inherent in the conjugal bond are more varied, fluid and fragile than they are in some other cultural areas of the world.

Vellenga's discussion provides the background of changing and conflicting legal and customary norms necessary for the subsequent chapters.

Hers and His

In Chapter 10 Katharine Abu describes conjugal relationships in an Ashanti town. Her emphases are upon the separate nature of spouses' resources and activities and the extent to which wives and husbands overtly make bargains in their exchanges of goods and services with each other. She illustrates how the expectations and activities of matrikin and fear of potential sexual rivals contribute to the lack of security, trust and solidarity in the conjugal relationship. Husbands and wives are noted to maintain separate, individual economic interests, and provision for the domestic needs of themselves and their children is a matter for negotiation. Frequently the conjugal family, husband and wife, parents and children, do not co-reside. The flexibility and variation in relationship and economic arrangements are associated with observable tensions and conflicts.

Siblings and Spouses

In Chapter 11 Christine Okali discusses in detail aspects of the roles
and relationships existing between women and men, kin and spouses,
as they co-operate in producing food and the cash crop cocoa in
Ghana's rain forest. Her discussion underlines the significance of
customary property relations and patterns of exchange of goods and
services for explaining male female relationships as well as the micro
organisation of cocoa production. Her chapter emphasises clearly that
conjugal and sibling ties between women and men need to be considered within the context of customary expectations attached to these
roles, concerning maintenance, long-term economic security, inheritance, and so on, and in terms of availability of required resources,
whether land, labour, crops, or other finite goods.

Her detailed presentation of data from individual cases and
arrangements demonstrates the complexity of domestic economic
arrangements and the diversity, in situations in which multiple marriages for men are common; in which women frequently bear several
sets of offspring with different spouses; in which matrilineal norms
and practices still prevail concerning descent and inheritance; and in
which sibling solidarity has more traditional support than conjugal
solidarity. Arrangements for co-operating in production and relationships of dependence and support are flexible, varied and often *ad hoc*
with individuals, men and women continually assessing and reassess-
ing their current often ambiguous situations and adapting their
activities and expectations accordingly, subject to constant pressures
to change.

Fish Catching and Selling

Chapter 13 is about fishing and fish-processing and marketing on the
coast of Ghana using traditional canoes. The canoe fishing industry is
noted to have employed 5 per cent or more of the Ghanaian labour
force, and almost half of the workers are women who process and sell
the fish. Emile Vercruijsse depicts in considerable detail the exchange
relationships over the short and long term which exist between the
fishermen and the women, noting their close interdependence and
the frequency with which these relationships are simultaneously
bonds of marriage and kinship. Mechanisms for obtaining necessary
credit are described, and the ways in which income and the harvest of
the peak season is managed and preserved so as to last the fisherfolk
and their dependent kin and children through the lean months of the
year.

In passing, Vercruijsse notes how this interdependence and autonomy of males and females is mirrored in the Akan lineage norm, which stress the continuing close bonds of matriliny, thus inhibiting the formation of functionally and financially individuated domestic conjugal units.

In Chapter 14 George Hagan describes a fascinating pattern of family life among the Effutu, in which boys live with their fathers and male agnates and girls live with their mothers and female matrikin, and in which women only join their husbands at nightfall after cooking and sending supper to them in the evening. Meanwhile in the daytime husband and wife co-operate to catch, smoke, dry and sell fish. The men fish and the women process and market the catch. Many also buy and sell food. The women are recognised as the economically dominant force in the society. At the end of the fishing season they pay their husbands for the fish harvest and keep control of their own profits. What is particularly interesting and striking about the chapter is the way in which marriage and divorce and family relationships are shown to be intricately interwoven with the annual economic cycle of fishing and travelling, so that there are demonstrated to be peak times for divorce. And the incidence of polygyny and family welfare are shown to be intimately bound up with the fate of fishing harvests and the careers of fishing crews and boats. Meanwhile the complex and changing system of residential arrangements is also intimately tied up with control of catches and participation in fishing crews and marriage timing.

Chapter 9

Who is a Wife? Legal Expressions of Heterosexual Conflicts in Ghana

DOROTHY DEE VELLENGA

Ghana is an interesting society in which to observe some of the processes and effects of a plural legal system regarding heterosexual
relations. It has had several centuries of contact with Europeans
leading to the development of a coastal, Afro-European culture
(Priestly, 1969). The indigenous culture in the south has been dominated by one group, the Akan, who form less than 50 per cent of the
whole population. Although marital and family practices differ
somewhat from one ethnic group to another in Ghana, many of the
underlying principles of systems with corporate descent groups are
similar. In the first part of this chapter I shall outline some of the
major sources of conflict between European and Akan conceptions
of marriage and the family and then turn to some of the sources of
conflict within the Akan tradition itself. I shall then illustrate some of
these conflicts as they have been manifested in two arenas: the more
personal arena, in which specific situations are made public and
brought before some established authority for resolution, and, secondly, the political arena in which public debates and social movements attempt to resolve some of these questions (Wright Mills,
1959). For the first analysis, I shall draw upon data from cases
brought before traditional authorities.[1] For the second, I shall draw
mainly on public debates in the press and parliament.

Conflict between European and Akan Conceptions of Marriage

In the conflict between European and Akan conceptions of marriage
two broad areas were particularly problematic. One was the form of

marriage and the second was the consequences that arose from such forms, particularly in the area of property and financial arrangements. The Akan were more sophisticated and subtle than the Europeans in their explicit recognition of the variety of forms that heterosexual relations could take. One source lists names for as many as twenty-four different forms of heterosexual relationships (see Vellenga, 1974, pp. 52–83). These varied according to the amount of kin involvement in and knowledge of the relationship, the number of material exchanges that had taken place between families and the class relationship between the partners. Relationships also differed in terms of the exchange and rituals performed between partners and their kin. A relationship could go through concubinage, betrothal and marriage with the steps marked by the types of gifts given and the recipients of those gifts. Finally, there were marriages in which both partners were domestic dependants or in which one partner was a commoner or royal and the other a domestic servant, dependant, or 'pawn'.[2] The higher-status person could be either a male or a female. In the matrilineal society of the Akan, the marriage of queen mothers were not always to other royals, but sometimes even to servants, craftsmen and traders of different ethnic origins.[3]

Some of these forms were considered more permanent than others, but generally it could be said that marriage was considered more of a *process* than a state of being. One hears Ghanaians say 'I am marrying so-and-so'. The somewhat tenuous and fluid nature of the marital bond among the Akan is in contrast with the ties binding matrikin, and with the indissolubility and ritual significance of the clan or lineage bond.

To Europeans, both missionaries and colonial officials, this appeared to be the opposite of what they considered 'normal' and much of colonial legislation on the family was aimed at clearly defining and strengthening the marital bond in opposition to the lineage bond.[4] They were continually perplexed by the consequences resulting from Akan marital forms, particularly polygyny, the lack of a common budget between husband and wife, and inheritance of property by matrikin rather than the widowed spouse.

In summary, the major sources of conflict between Europeans and Africans in the area of heterosexual relationships arose from the attempts by European administrators and missionaries to define marriage and its consequences strictly. In a culture in which there were many definitions of marriage and heterosexual relationships and in which the most binding family ties were with kin rather than spouses, this created not only confusion, but the opportunity for manipulation of various authorities: the British, the churches and the traditional rulers.

Conflict within the Akan System

The Akan society also had within it sources of heterosexual conflict. One of these is built into the matrilineal situation in which ties to the lineage are in competition with ties to the spouse. Some forms of marriage, such as cross-cousin marriage in which a man's daughter or son might marry his nephew or niece by his sister, were ways of alleviating the strain. The pattern remained, however, in which a man's ties to his wife or child were largely determined by affection and were not supported by the institutional power of the lineage. A further problem was the competition between older and younger men for the available women. Since so many marriages were arranged when the woman was very young and elders had the means to contract more marriages, many young men had to wait years to marry. The elaborate system of adultery fees in Akan society is testimony to the fact that many of the older men had trouble controlling their wives (see Vellenga, 1974, pp. 101–6; 1977, pp. 132–4). This has created a preoccupation with the adultery of women which has continued to the present. Such adultery might not even be restricted to sexual intercourse, but could include gifts of money given by a man to a woman or even the touching of the woman by a man other than the husband. In a culture in which polygyny was the norm, these very different definitions of adultery for men and women created another major source of conflict.

Cases Illustrating Heterosexual Conflict at the Personal Level

The debate surrounding the Marriage Ordinance of 1884 reflects the conflict between British and African concepts of marriage. In its original form it stipulated that marriage under the Ordinance was to be monogamous and upon the death of the husband intestate, his self-acquired property was to go solely to the wife and children of the Ordinance marriage.This would be a consolidation of property in the nuclear family. There was such an outcry against this that the Ordinance was modified in 1909 to provide that one-third of the man's estate would go to his lineage and two-thirds would go to the widow and children. Although a very small proportion of the population marry under the Ordinance now, a larger proportion were married under the Ordinance in the earlier part of this century largely due to pressure from the churches.[5] Consequently there were many legal battles between a widow and children of an Ordinance marriage and the lineage of the deceased, not to mention any other wives and children he might have had.

The arena in which such confrontations between widow and lineage came about was the High Court, which had sole jurisdiction over Ordinance marriages. One such case which illustrates the confusion caused by different forms of marriage is that of Yaotey V. Quaye in the High Court, Accra, 16 October 1961.[6]

In that case as in others the determination of whether a woman was a wife or a concubine revolved around the nature of the relationship between the families of the two parties. If there is some indication of family recognition and approval of the relationship, then it is considered a valid marriage. Such recognition could come through gifts and drinks given to the woman's kin by the man's kin, or the performance of funeral customs for the kin of the spouse. In some of these cases, Christians would argue that a valid marriage had not taken place unless the gifts had also gone through the church elders in addition to the relatives. Here, again, this is the recognition of the importance of the two kin-groups and community over and above the agreement between the man and the woman. This distinction between giving money and gifts to a woman directly as opposed to giving money through a network of relatives, church elders, and so on, again reflects the more basic conflict between the consolidation of property and wealth in the lineage as opposed to the conjugal family.

This conflict is heightened by the practice in the rural areas of women serving as agricultural labourers for their husbands. The terms of this arrangement are often ambiguous and after the husband dies or divorces the woman all her labour may have been for nothing when the man's kin take over the farm (as Okali describes below in Chapter 11). Some husbands resolve this dilemma by helping their wives to establish farms on the woman's family land, but many situations are unresolved. Such cases do not often find their way into the conventional courts.

One of the arguments for women against investing both wealth and emotion in the marital bond is the continued presence of polygyny. In a culture where men are allowed, and even expected, to be involved with more than one woman, and where adultery for women includes a wide range of activities, there is the built-in potential for conflict. Men can only be accused of adultery if they are involved with a married woman, whereas for a married woman all men are taboo. In the lower courts, all adultery cases are directed against wives and their suspected lovers. In the High Court, however, the situation is reversed. Since Ordinance marriages supposedly support monogamy for the woman as well as the man, most of these cases are against husbands and their suspected lovers. Even the minority of educated women, however, seem cynical about the potential for genuine monogamy in Ghana (as Dinan illustrates in Chapter 25), and much of this is reflected in the public debates over the impossibility of a 'common budget' between husband and wife. Women seem determined to keep a separate budget for themselves and both the demands of kin and other women would argue against the practicality of husbands and wives pooling their income (as Katharine Church describes in Chapter 10). Yet such pooling does sometimes take place and several cases in the courts are testimony to the conflict this produces when the relationship breaks down. Furthermore, women are increasingly suing their husbands for maintenance.

Heterosexual conflicts in Ghana, then, reflect more than just the battle between the sexes. They are embedded in the basic conflict between corporate kin-group systems based on sibling solidarity, descent and filiation, and conjugal family systems based on the conjugal bond.

Expressions of Conflict at the Political Level

When heterosexual conflicts emerge at a political and societal level, they usually take the form of social movements and factions pressing for and against various policy changes. Ghana is no exception to this. Early in the 1950s Ghanaian women began organising to pursue issues particularly relevant to women, although they were also concerned with the larger political questions of independence for Ghana (or the Gold Coast, as it was then called). One of their first concerns was the confusion over various forms of marriage and the difficulties this created particularly for wives married under customary law. They wanted a more secure position for wives married according to custom, especially when it came to matters of inheritance and property settlements. This movement, called the Federation of Ghana Women, eventually brought about the appointment of an Inheritance Commission in 1959 to revise the inheritance laws. However, the question of defining a legal wife caused insuperable problems and the commission's report was never published.

Over the next twenty years, through civilian and military governments, various groups sought to change the marriage and divorce and inheritance laws. In 1961 a Marriage, Divorce and Inheritance Bill was introduced, went through several revisions and was eventually not passed. In 1963 a Maintenance of Children Bill was introduced and eventually passed in 1965 in a much modified form. In 1969 an amendment encouraging the protection of women and children was introduced in the Constituent Assembly and eventually passed. In 1971 a new divorce law was passed.

All these exercises are interesting for what they reveal of the attitudes of various factions in the population as reflected in commission reports, parliamentary debates, newspaper letters and articles, position papers published by different organisations, and reports of discussion groups. These factions include the politicians, the legal profession, the churches, the traditional chiefs and, finally, the different women's groups. The main questions raised by all these legislative moves were 'who is a wife?', 'what are a legal wife's rights?' and 'what are the rights of the children?'.

Different groups appeared to want different cut-off points between a wife and a non-wife. The politicians, above all, were in a dilemma. While outwardly reflecting views that were progressive on the equality of men and women, many were polygynously married or had concubines. This dilemma is reflected in the provisions of the Marriage, Divorce and Inheritance Bill, which provided that one wife was to be the 'registered wife' and would be considered the legal wife. Other wives would not be registered, but all children, whether by registered or unregistered wives, would be legitimate children and heirs. This dilemma faced by the politicians is reflected in conflicting statements from party leaders. Eventually the party made a clear statement supporting monogamy, but from the parliamentary debates that followed it is difficult to believe that such a position was actually supported by the majority of politicians.

The Marriage, Divorce and Inheritance Bill was finally defeated, but this conflict continued into the next debate on the Maintenance of Children Bill, which stipulated that women could collect money for maintenance from the fathers of their children. This brought a great outcry from the male politicians, many of whom expressed the fear that women would 'trade in children'.[7]

By this time, however, female politicians were coming into their own. President Nkrumah had appointed ten women to Parliament. Furthermore, the Minister of Social Welfare was a woman, Miss Susanna Al Hassan. There were obvious differences between men and women Members of Parliament in their perceptions of the causes of the neglect of children, the men being more likely to consider the prostitution and promiscuity of women as important factors.[8] Eventually the Maintenance of Children Bill was passed, thanks in large part to the efforts of the Minister of Social Welfare, and the support of President Nkrumah and the work of the women MPs. However, the Bill emerged in a much-diluted form. Meanwhile, study of applications for maintenance in the Accra area showed that the vast majority of women seeking maintenance for their children were women who had been in a recognised relationship, in many cases a customary marriage, before the break-up and neglect. These were definitely not prostitutes 'dealing in children'.

The legal establishment in some cases overlapped with the politicians. Many lawyers were also MPs. The legal establishment as a whole, however, was often at odds with the political parties. The lawyers and judges were concerned about the contradictions existing in marriage law, but were even more disturbed by the confusion in the reform efforts.

Some lawyers and judges felt that case law was handling many of the discrepancies in the conflicts between customary and Western law regarding marriage. It was an elite legal society, the Mensah Sarbah Society, that eventually got the Marriage, Divorce and Inheritance Bill withdrawn, but it was also the lawyers who got a revised Divorce Bill finally passed during the Busia regime.[9]

The mainline churches – the Presbyterians, Methodists and Anglicans – had already built up considerable experience in a kind of case law of their own. Church elders often settled marriage, divorce, seduction and inheritance disputes. In the early part of the century they even had their own hierarchy of adultery fees. Church members who were traditionally married could have their marriage blessed in the church. This blessing meant that they were to remain monogamous and, at least in the Presbyterian Church, at the death of the husband intestate, one-third of his estate would go to his wife, one-third to his children and one-third to his lineage. Many church leaders felt that the various legal reform movements would only make the situation more ambiguous especially regarding the case of unregistered wives.[10]

The traditional rulers – chiefs and court officials – also had considerable experience with case law in the traditional courts. By the time these Bills were being debated, the chiefs had formally lost their courts to local magistrates. Chiefs might still hear cases informally but much of their power was eroded. Previously chiefs were concerned with the validity of a marriage to know whether to assess adultery fees against a wife's lover or seduction fees against a man who had seduced an unmarried woman. One of their concerns in the pre-independence days was the number of women who were not properly married (i.e. with parental consent and exchange of some gifts and money). Some even went to the extreme measure of locking up such women until their lovers would pay a fee to release them, thus legitimising the relationship.[11] The chiefs' concern with some of the post-independence Bills was similar. They were convinced that even more women would be running around 'loose'. Two reactions to the proposed Marriage, Divorce and Inheritance Bill are the following.

The houses of chiefs in the Volta, central and northern regions were concerned about what the registration of only one wife would do to polygynous unions, and the Volta chiefs, in an *Evening News* article headlined 'Volta chiefs pray for Osagyefo and say they prefer polygamy', said they objected to the registration of only one woman because they saw polygamy as the safest and surest way of checking prostitution by letting young girls marry as soon as possible.[12]

As we can see, women who wanted a comprehensive law protecting wives married under customary law faced some formidable obstacles. It is clear from the above analysis that there was a strong tendency to 'blame the victim'. Women who were forced to be independent because the fathers of their children would not support them were then seen as scheming to take advantage of the men. Evidence from court cases and welfare agency records would go against this accusation, but rational arguments would not convince most men, except those such as ministers and welfare officers who had had direct experience with hardship cases.[13] Also, several factions within the debate saw case law in the local courts, church courts and welfare and labour agencies as taking care of the situation. Against this argument, women could counter with the opinion that many of them were embarrassed to take such cases to any court, even an informal one. Also there seems to be a preference among many Ghanaian men for making a lump sum or property settlement rather than paying a woman on a regular basis.[14] Such lump settlements might satisfy a woman for a time and discourage her from taking a case to court, but it would not give her any long-term security or provision for her children unless the settlement was enough to give her some investment capital.

The strategy of different women's groups varied. The early organisation, the Federation of Ghana Women, threatened to stage protest marches.[15] This strategy created a counter-attack in the male-dominated legislature and the Inheritance Commission which resulted came to nothing.

As more women were appointed to parliament and given access to cabinet posts, they were more successful in their efforts and finally got a Maintenance of Children Bill passed. One of their strategies in this regard was to pack the galleries with the wives and concubines of the male MPs, apparently an effective ploy.

When the limitations of this Maintenance of Children Act became evident (among them problems of enforcement and collection of money and severe restrictions on the amount of money that could be paid by the father), an amendment for the protection of women and children was introduced into the Constituent Assembly which was writing the Constitution for the Second Republic.[16] This assembly had eleven women representatives.

There was some opposition from the men on this clause, but a number supported it and it was eventually passed. It had little impact on policy formation, but as Dr de Graft Johnson suggested, it may have had the following functions.

(1) It will provide a standard against which the legality of legislation and governmental action, as also the activities of private individuals, may be judged.
(2) It will establish a norm to be followed.
(3) It will contribute to the moulding of public opinion.

Conclusion

Behind all these expressions of conflict lies the basic contradiction between systems based on corporate kin-groups and the functionally individuated conjugal family. With the breakdown of the security of a lineage system, many women want a stronger emphasis on the conjugal bond. Although the lineage may not provide much security any more, however, many of its forms linger on. Polygyny, in one form or another, is still widespread, but again without the security of former times. Many men will claim that a woman who would be considered a wife under traditional law is only a concubine and thus not deserving of support once she no longer 'serves' the man. The distribution of property within the lineage rather than between marital partners is still strong.

How have we seen these conflicts expressed in the law? The confusion over various forms of marriage has been expressed both in case law at the personal level and in policy debates at the political level. Such confusion in the pre-independence period could work to the disadvantage of the husband, who could obtain adultery fees only if he were properly married to the woman. On the contemporary scene such confusion works to the detriment of women, who can lose out both at inheriting property on the death of the spouse and over obtaining maintenance money from the living father of their children.

There is also evidence of the strong feelings that men have against giving money directly to women. Such direct transactions imply that a woman is a concubine and entitled to keep whatever gifts she receives. As a concubine, however, she is not entitled to regular maintenance payments. If the money is given through a third party, this legitimises the relationship again, giving some men second thoughts about this type of remittance. This puts pressure on the women to obtain as much money as possible as long as a relationship is viable, thus giving the impression that such women are 'gold-diggers'. The amazing thing is that more women do not act in this way.

For many men, then, the status quo is fairly satisfactory. The widespread practice of multiple sexual relationships occasionally leads to conflict, but it is possible for many men to evade the issues. For most women, the status quo is not satisfactory. Some, a minority, would like the enforcement of genuine monogamy. Most women, pragmatically, want stronger supports for traditional marriage, even though such marriages may include polygyny. While some men who work directly with hardship cases are sympathetic, such sympathy is not enough to support nationwide changes in the laws. Such changes are only likely to come about when women gain more political power, as we saw in the debates over the Maintenance of Children Act and the

Constitutional Amendment. This means power in the inner circles of government and not only as a lobbying force.

Notes: Chapter 9

The fieldwork on which much of this chapter is based was sponsored by a variety of grants for which I am most grateful. These include the American Association of University Women, the African Women's Programme of the United Methodist Church, the Mack Foundation and the Social Research Council.

1   The 280 cases analysed as a basis for this discussion all dealt with conflicts in heterosexual relations that erupted on the personal level and were then brought before some kind of court for resolution. The 1930 cases were taken mainly from the records of a chief's tribunal in a largely Akan area, Akuapim near Accra – these dealt mainly with claims for adultery fees, or damages for seduction of a wife (thirty-five cases). The rest were from the records of the High Court in Accra. These were five divorce cases. The four 1940 cases were taken from church records in Akuapim. The 1950 and 1960 cases were taken partly from records of the local magistrates' court, which had replaced the chief's tribunal in Akuapim. These forty-eight cases included several concerned with seduction, maintenance during pregnancy of unmarried girls and wives' maintenance claims for themselves and children. From this period there were thirty-eight cases from the Accra High Court – mainly divorce cases. The third source for this decade was the Labour Department archives in Sunyani, Brong Ahafo, which were mainly claims for property from an ex-spouse by either a divorced husband or wife. A report of the Social Welfare Office in Accra, 'Services offered under the Maintenance of Children Act, 1965, in the Greater Accra Region', dated 1967, provided evidence of 136 cases of claims for maintenance for self and children by neglected wives.

2   A pawn was someone who was given over to another person or family as security for a loan. When the loan was repaid, the person could return to his or her own family.

3   For an interesting description of the marriages of queen mothers of the Akan state of Bono see Antubam, 1947.

4   J. Goody (1971, 1973) sees the Eurasian and African conceptions of marriage as representing two ideal types which in turn reflect very different types of society. The former, with its emphasis on the conjugal bond, monogamy and a dowry presented to the couple on marriage, is related to a social system that emphasises the concentration of property in nuclear families and class endogamy. The African form of marriage, with its emphasis on the involvement of the two lineages, polygyny and a bridewealth presented to the woman's family by the man's family, is related to a social system that stresses the circulation of wealth through kin ties and class exogamy.

5   The Blue Book of 1909 lists 237 marriages under the Ordinance for that year, a rather substantial number considering the small size of the colony (CO, 100/59, *Gold Coast Colony Blue Book, 1909*, Accra: Government Printing Office, 1910). According to another source, the Registrar General of Ghana, in 1935 there were 399 Ordinance marriages out of a population of around 3,160,000. In 1967 there were 494 Ordinance marriages out of a population that had almost doubled, to 6,727,000.

6   Yaotey V. Quaye in the High Court, Accra, 16 October 1961, mimeographed for Family Law Course, Faculty of Law, University of Ghana, Legon, 2 February 1967. In this case the deceased who died intestate had married under the Ordinance and had three children by this wife. He then divorced her and married

another woman by customary law and had a child by her. He also had a concubine and had a child by her. The children of the Ordinance marriage claimed that they had sole right to the two-thirds of the estate set aside for the widow and children of an Ordinance marriage; the customary wife claimed that she was the legal widow and should get the one-third of the two-thirds that would go to the widow; the concubine claimed that her child, but not she, was entitled to a share in the portion that would be allotted to the children of the deceased. Although the children by the Ordinance marriage claimed that the customary law marriage was not a valid one, the court ruled that it was since the deceased had lived openly with the woman as his wife. Also she had performed funeral customs for him, and upon retirement he had given her some money as gratitude for her services to him and this money was delivered through her relatives. The judge made the point that if the woman were a concubine, the gift would have been given directly to her. He also determined that the child of the concubine should share in the portion of the estate allotted to the children. Thus the widow, a wife by customary law, received $\frac{2}{9}$ of the estate, the children by the Ordinance marriage, the customary marriage, and the concubine – five in all – received $\frac{4}{9}$ of the estate, and the man's lineage received one-third of the estate. Such a decision seems to emphasise the continued importance of blood ties rather than marital ties, since the widow received less than one-third of the estate and the concubine was left out altogether. Nevertheless the customary marriage was held to be valid and all children participated in the estate distribution.

7   See Republic of Ghana, *Parliamentary Debates*, first series, vol. XXXI, 1963, col. 651.

8   The reasons given for child neglect by Members of Parliament are analysed in *Parliamentary Debates*, vol. XXXI, 1963.

9   Given that this was largely a technical exercise, and the Bill had the professional backing of the lawyers, they still had to reply to such observations as the following:

Clause 28 (1) concerns something which always brings about controversy – 'financial provision to cease on remarriage or death'. In the case of death, it is well understood. But what about that of remarriage? Many a woman does not remarry, but she goes about more than one who has a husband. Should such a person still be supported by the respondent? Should not there be any clause restraining the woman from openly indulging in such acts resembling marriage while she is still being financially provided for by the unfortunate man? (Republic of Ghana, *Parliamentary Debates*, vol. VII, no. 10, June 1971, cols 347–8)

This MP expressed the prevailing opinion among many of the men that unattached women were little more than 'gold-diggers' (see Chapter 25).

10   'Comments on the White Paper on marriage, divorce and inheritance submitted on behalf of the Presbyterian Church of Ghana', Accra, 9 June 1961, typescript.

11   See the discussion in file no. 1383/3, sub-file no. 3: 'Forced marriage of African girls, prevention of', 12 June 1939, in the Ghanaian archives; and 'Letters to the editor', *Gold Coast Independent*, 25 January 1930.

12   'Central region chiefs say marry one woman', *Ghanaian Times*, 14 June 1961, and 'Volta chiefs pray for Osagyefo and say they prefer polygamy', *Evening News*, 15 June 1961.

13   Republic of Ghana, *Parliamentary Debates*, first series, vol. XXXI, 1963, cols 664–5.

14   Debate sponsored by the Women's Society for Public Affairs on the proposed Constitutional Amendment, 3 April 1969. The cedi was then worth around $1·40.

15 J. O. Kuevi, 'Ghanaian wives may stage protest march', *Daily Graphic,* 9 April 1959.
16 Republic of Ghana, *Proceedings of the Constituent Assembly* (Accra: Government Printing Office, April 1959).

Chapter 10

The Separateness of Spouses: Conjugal Resources in an Ashanti Town

KATHARINE ABU

The most striking feature of the marriage relationship in Ashanti is the separateness of spouses' resources and activities and the overtness of the bargaining element in the relationship. This chapter describes expectations and activities concerning house space, food, sex and money and the dynamics of the conjugal relationship, how it derives from the wider family structure, and the motives of the individual women and men in struggling to get what they want from spouses and lovers.

This discussion is based on research carried out in an Ashanti town of about 10,000 inhabitants. The subjects of the research were natives of the place in the sense that it was their home town whence they traced their forbears and in which they had many kin.[1] The town is a district headquarters for government offices and is relatively well endowed with schools and medical services. There were considerable numbers of 'strangers' living there, and 'locals' themselves were frequently well travelled, having at various stages, in connection with jobs, trade, or marriage, lived in other towns and cities including Accra.

The town is of a size for it to be considered an urban area, yet both its economy and its inhabitants are intimately connected with the rural area in which it is located. Many of the women trade in locally produced foodstuffs. Some of the urban dwellers combine trading with farming, walking or taking buses to reach their farms. Thus while urban facilities are present, the tie with the rural area is strong.

Ashanti is considered to exhibit markedly the imprint of its descent structure upon its social organisation. For the purposes of this chapter it will be sufficient to draw attention to those aspects of matriliny which actually affect conjugal resources.[2] The conjugal family is weak in residential, economic and emotional terms compared with the matrilineage, and spouses frequently live apart, the children residing with either or neither parent. The continuity of matrilineal norms regarding descent and paternity means that the paternal role may be relatively unimportant, particularly if the father is inclined to pay little attention to his offspring, and women may be left comparatively free from the conjugal authority of husbands, though still inclined to benefit from their economic potential wherever possible.

These points are an essential background to the understanding of marriage relationships in Ashanti, yet it would be a great mistake to push them to extreme conclusions, and to imagine, for instance, that paternity was quite irrelevant or that men had no control over their wives.

Ashanti marriage involves only a limited reordering of social relationships, and customary rites are simple, inexpensive and private. There are no public celebrations to which guests are invited. The parents and elders of the couple partake of token quantities of kola nut and alcohol to signify their consent to the marriage. The atmosphere is more that of a contract being concluded than an important stage in the life-cycle being celebrated. There may be lively argument about the sums to be paid in respect of different parts of the marriage fees, the woman's family being anxious to show that they value their daughter highly and are not going to give her away easily, even though the fees are in fact low enough to be considered symbolic.

As well as full customary marriage there is *mpena awaree* (lover marriage) which describes marriage by mutual consent or a fairly long-term lover relationship. It is not uncommon for a woman after one or two divorces to reject customary marriage. She may enter into a longstanding relationship with one man or have a series of shorter-lived relationships. All of these liaisons can be described as *mpena* relationships. When a young woman who has never been married takes an *mpena* she usually tries to hide it from her parents and elders since such a relationship is illicit. In practice most marriages are preceded by this sort of relationship. Bleek (1976) reports an increase in what he describes as 'free marriage' and attributes it to women's dissatisfaction with the protection and support supposedly guaranteed to them under full customary marriage. In so far as there are any rules and conventions attached to *mpena awaree,* they are that the woman should have no other man friend, that customary marriage take place if a pregnancy occurs (which is not always done), and that the man give the woman some money or presents regularly, however small.

Although the form of customary marriage is the same for remarriages as for the first marriage, parental influence is likely to be much less upon somebody who has been divorced or widowed once. People do talk, however, of matrikin, especially mothers, encouraging sons to take on additional wives and introducing them to favoured girls in the hope of diverting their affections from the first wife, when they feel that his attachment to her is at their expense. Some mothers also encourage daughters to divorce men whom they feel are not sufficiently well-off, if they have a better prospect in mind for them.

There is strong evidence to suggest that freedom of choice for the individual in marriage has increased during the twentieth century, as has the spatial and ethnic distance across which people are prepared to marry. More important than freedom of choice and marriage partner, however, would appear to be mobility and distance from relatives. Bleek's (1975) findings indicate greater stability among migrant than home town dwelling couples.

The traditional practice of going to the parents to ask for a girl before courting her seems to be very rare these days. Of the younger women in the Ashanti study, only two had been involved in such a marriage process and they had both been somewhat reluctant brides. They had been married as third and fourth wives respectively to well-to-do local businessmen. In both cases the men had wooed the parents with expensive presents and the girls had been persuaded to drop their less affluent boyfriends and marry the 'big man' suitors.

> One young man described the process of marriage as follows. You take a girlfriend and get her pregnant – then she will be asked by the parents who is responsible – then you have to answer and perform the customary rites – but if you do not want to marry the girl, you don't send any booze to the parents, but the child is still yours. Alternatively, rather than taking her as a girlfriend first, you can go straight to the parents and ask for her. Not many people do this these days. There are plenty of girls so there is no need to bother yourself with formalities.

Increased mobility has facilitated ignoring of parental responsibilities by young men. Use of courts to get money out of them is still not very popular, both because of the inconvenience and publicity involved, and because up till very recently the courts have not been in a position to award substantial payments. A study of paternity cases in Koforiduana shows the most frequent category of men involved to be the most mobile workers, such as policemen and agricultural officers who are subject to regular transfers (Lowy, 1977).

Residence Arrangements

An important aspect of married life in Ashanti is the fact that spouses frequently do not live together.[3] This is particularly common in the home town where both husband and wife have their own matrilineal homes to live in.

In my Ashanti study 45 per cent of married women lived with their husbands, most of these being in the middle age-range (25–40 years). The youngest married women tended to stay in the matrilineal home in order to have help in looking after their infants, and also because their husbands, being fairly young as well, were unlikely to be able to provide accommodation for joint residence. Matrikin do not like the idea of a young girl leaving home to face the problems of domestic management. Particularly in the field of baby care, young mothers are not considered competent to manage alone. Among the older women, the child-rearing period of their lives being almost over marriage has become less important, and once again they orientate themselves more towards the matrilineage and their roles as grandmothers and maternal aunts. Thus fewer of the married women in the older age-group lived with their husbands, and moreover the currently married accounted for a little less than half of the older women.

Migrant situations, where the couple either move to a satellite village to farm or to another town to work, are associated with conjugal co-residence. Although the ideal is for a married man to build a house and have his wife living with him, in practice very few can afford to set up house independently from the matrikin. Since both women and men find the idea of living with in-laws highly undesirable, duo-local residence remains a common arrangement in the home town.

More people of both sexes expressed a preference for joint conjugal residence than actually practised it. The main reasons given by women for preferring to live with a husband concerned financial management and discipline of children. They emphasised that if a man is living with his wife and children all incidental household expenses will perforce be brought to his notice, and that a wife can expect to receive more financial support if the husband is living with her. The practice of sending food to the husband's house in the evening is less economical than having him eat in the place where the wife lives. One woman suggested that the ideal arrangement would be to have the husband eat in the house but sleep in his matrilineal home. That way the food money would go further and the wife would be sure of seeing him every day to discuss the children's behaviour with him. At the same time she would not feel disgruntled if he habitually left the house after dinner because she could assume that he was going straight home. The sound upbringing of children is also a motive for spouses to live together.

However, a substantial minority of women and men consider the difficulties involved in conjugal co-residence to be insurmountable. Men and women both fear the quarrelling that can arise when the couple live together. Men do not wish to have their movements closely observed by their wives. Some women feel that to live with a husband would be to submit themselves to agonies of jealousy every time he left the house, especially if he spent nights away from home. This would provoke them to quarrel with their husbands and might lead to a divorce.

> If I lived with him, then every time he came home I should be convinced that he was coming from another woman's place and every time he went out I would think that he was going to another woman and I should speak harshly to him.

Others opposed the idea of living with the husband on the grounds that it would give them no privacy.

> If my sister came to stay where would she sleep? If my husband was entertaining guests in the room, where would I go?

This kind of comment reflects a life-style so geared to duo-local residence that the domestic arrangements of conjugal co-residence appear problematic. Another very serious disincentive to living with the husband is the fear of what will happen in the event of the husband's death. The man's relatives would be likely to invade the house as soon as he died and turn out the widow and her children, sometimes preventing her from taking her own clothes with her, on the grounds that the husband might have paid for them and that therefore they were part of his estate.

Many women consider ideal the arrangement whereby a man rents and furnishes a room for them but lives elsewhere so that at least the household property remains theirs in the event of his death. However, very few men could afford to provide for their wives in that way.

People stressed that spouses living together was only feasible in a monogamous marriage. The polygynously married man usually lives with none of his wives. The type of polygynous culture such as Dagomba or Ewe, in which women grow up learning how to interact peacefully and accept the authority of the senior wife, is absent in Ashanti. Except at royal palaces, polygyny has been associated with separate residence for spouses.

The Substantive and Symbolic Roles of Food in Marriage

The transfer of food or money from man to woman occupies a central place in marriage and lover relationships in Ashanti. 'Chop money', the Ghanaian-English phrase for 'money for food', is the subject of much marital strife. The Akan verb stem *di* (to consume, enjoy) refers both to eating and to sexual relations. Moreover, the Ghanaian-English verb 'to chop' refers to both food and sex.

The symbolic relationship between food and sex is quite highly formalised in Ashanti. In a polygynous marriage the cooking and sleeping arrangements rotate together; that is, the wife whose turn it is to sleep with the man also cooks for him. The post-parturient woman ceases to send food to the husband for as long as she is not sleeping with him. A man can initially show his sexual interest in a woman by giving her money to cook for him.

A wife becomes extremely suspicious of a husband who eats with poor appetite or who refuses to eat at all, and concludes that he has been giving another woman money to cook for him. A man who is annoyed with his wife can deliberately offend her by refusing to eat her food. The norms of conjugal interaction are such that it is difficult for a woman to tell her husband to his face that the 'chop money' is insufficient. As one man explained:

> Some women will just prepare food for one-fifty [cedis] which is very small, and refuse to add to it, but most women will add to the 'chop money' without telling their husband that his contribution is not enough. We don't discuss these things; you can't ask your wife how much she is adding to the 'chop money'.

If the wife is not satisfied with the amount of money the man is giving her, he can only know it by the contents of the soup or stew. If the man lives with his matrikin, thin soup sent by the wife could be a source of embarrassment to him. One of the advantages of conjugal co-residence is a measure of privacy for the couple regarding the contents of the soups or stew. Sisters living together and in a position to observe the contents of each other's cooking pots are easily aware of how well each is supported by her husband or lover. This can lead to jealousy. Some women are said to boast or lie about the amount of 'chop money' they receive. Comparing the 'chop money' is considered to be a prevalent feminine vice. Thus a bride may be cautioned against comparing the amount of 'chop money' she receives with what her friends get.

'Chop money' is both a practical economic arrangement and a symbol of love. A man's interest in a woman is indicated by how much effort he makes to supply her with her needs. It is perhaps because of the relatively loose structure of Ashanti marriage (duo-local residence, easy divorce, limited control of woman by man and vice versa) that the provision of 'chop money' occupies such a central and visible role in the marriage. The social forces constraining a man to look after his wife and children are relatively weak and there is a considerable voluntary element in the arrangement. As a result, except amongst the very wealthy, 'chop money' provision is seen as an indicator of the quality of the marriage.

Allocation of Financial Responsibilities within Marriage

The separation of spouses' financial responsibilities is closely connected with their retention of their separate individual economic interests at marriage. This concept of separate interests in marriage was stressed by the early exponents of Akan customary law, John Mensah Sarbah and J. B. Danquah, who were anxious to draw attention to differences between British and Akan concepts of marriage.[4]

In Ashanti marriages both the orientation of the spouse towards the matrilineage and the presence or potential presence of additional wives or girlfriends, as well as the potential fragility of the union, work against the pooling of conjugal resources. When husbands and wives co-operate closely, as some forms of production require, the separate financial interest of each may be recognised and arrangements made so that each gets separate returns from the venture.[5]

In more recent times it has been observed, as Christine Okali describes in Chapter 11, that a wife who, with her children, assists the cocoa farmer during the early, non-profitable years of establishing the farm frequently receives a small farm for herself as a reward for her services. The gift has to be made in time for the wife to work on her own farm and profit from it. Wives who feel that they have been kept waiting too long are apt to cut their losses and divorce.

I attempted to assess people's attitudes towards the dual obligation of men to matrikin and wives. Men and women stated that a man should provide his wives and children with basic necessities such as 'chop money' and school fees, but that in capital investment, such as houses and cocoa farms, the matrilineage should have priority.

> The family [i.e. matrilineage] are to have the house built for them first, but if he doesn't have much money he must feed the wife and children first. (Woman)

> One has to help one's wife and one's family [matrilineage]. If one builds a house for the wife first, the family will never allow it. People these days have to give their wives more financial help in the sense of giving them money to trade. Men cannot provide for their wives completely as they used to but they must do their best. (Man)

> You have to help your wife first. After all, your sister also has a

husband but if relatives get into trouble, for example with court cases, then you have to help. (Man)

The question of how a man should allocate his income, then, does not produce any theoretical conflict in the sense that there is widespread consensus that he should look to both his conjugal and his matrilineal family. However, assuming a scarcity of resources, these norms are likely to produce tension in the form of competition between conjugal and matrilineal units for individual men's resources.

In times of unprecedented rates of economic change, tensions resulting from norm conflicts will inevitably be exacerbated. These tensions are further compounded by the fact that a man can have more than one wife. People say that men should only have as many wives as they can afford, but that in practice they often marry more than they can afford, frequently as a result of girlfriends becoming pregnant. Moreover, to state that men may marry 'as many wives as they can afford' begs the question of how much economic support wives and children are entitled to. There is wide scope for disagreement between interested parties as to how men should dispose of their income. Ashanti women have always contributed significantly to the maintenance of their conjugal families through their farming efforts. Under urban conditions their activities are directed towards earning cash.

The question of wives' allocation of their incomes provoked more controversial reaction than that of husbands' allocation of income. Those who asserted that women were not traditionally supposed to make any cash contribution to the maintenance of the conjugal family and that the practice should be upheld were in a minority. In fact the majority of men and women stated that it was necessary for wives to contribute financially to the maintenance of their children. Several of the men's comments contained a kind of collective apology for the male sex in its inability to fulfil the traditional obligations towards wives, and for the compromise to which changed economic conditions had brought them.

> Formerly it was the man's duty to look after the children but these days the wife has to help too. I believe in working everything out together. Since it is not compulsory for the wife to bear some of the household costs you have to be very sure before you marry that you understand the girl well and that she will agree to it. Otherwise you marry and then find the girl unhelpful and you cannot force her to help. (Man)

The idea that contribution to financial maintenance of conjugal family is not really a duty but an act of voluntary goodwill is endorsed by responses from women in the group.

Household finances are a matter for negotiation between husband and wife – whether he is to provide entirely or she is to help out. It is not compulsory for her to help. (Woman)

I would not like to see my husband suffer by paying for everything if he were poor. I would rather get some useful work and help him. (Woman)

If they have no means of getting a salaried job, women living in urban areas usually take up some form of trade. The capital for trading is supposed to come from husbands. A young man with a job is advised to save so that he can provide a wife with the necessary capital for her to earn a living. However, many husbands do not have the means to give their wives trading capital and the latter have to beg or borrow a small sum from a relative or friend in order to begin to trade on a very small scale. A number of women interviewed traded in tomatoes, palm wine, or akpeteshie and said that they had chosen these particular lines of trade because the capital required to start was small. Women starting with larger amounts of capital supplied by husbands traded in things such as tinned and packaged foods, head-ties and sandals. To provide a wife with capital for trade does not exempt a husband from the responsibility of providing 'chop money' and school fees. It does mean, though, that in some future time of financial difficulty she is more likely to be supportive and less likely to divorce him. In that sense, a gift of money at the beginning of the marriage is an investment in the security of the marriage and an insurance against the wife and children's destitution.

Many women seemed to accept that a wife's financial contribution to the running of the household was a necessary fact of life. For them it was less a question of how their income ought to be disposed of than of how they were able to dispose of it. Many had no choice but to spend their earnings on basic necessities, and made assertions to the effect that if the husband did not have much money the wife would be forced to add to the chop money and contribute to the school fees. At the same time, they felt that the husband should pay for expenses as far as he possibly could, and they were prepared to use whatever means they could to force him to do so.

If the husband was rich I would expect him to pay for everything. Later on if I see that he cannot manage I will help him to recuperate. (Woman)

Very few husbands are good and pay all the household expenses. As soon as they find out that the wife has money they will force her to contribute, because if he fails to contribute, there is nothing that the wife can do about it. (Woman)

Women express willingness to help husbands who are doing their best to provide for the conjugal family, but some of the older ones in particular state with bitterness that a wife may help her husband and see him through a difficult period by her own diligence, but that he is quite likely when financially better off to neglect and even abuse his old wife and marry a young girl. When discussing the topic of conjugal finances there was much talk by men and women of the need for trust between spouses, alongside evidence of a pervasive atmosphere of mistrust. The following statements from respondents illustrate areas of mistrust:

So long as a man has another wife I will force him to pay for everything. I will only help if I know that he is really trying and cannot manage. (Woman)

If a woman is working she should not ask for much help from a man. Even a Fante woman has to be reasonable about that kind of thing these days. The amount of chop money she should contribute depends on what kind of work she has. If you marry an ordinary girl who cannot help herself she will be a burden and you will be treating her as a maidservant. Most women want to become rich on their own account. You can't trust them. They want you to pay for everything. You won't know the truth about their income. If your mother or sister needs help you have to give it but it's better not to let your wife know or she will criticise you for being too sentimental with your sister's problems. If you tell her that you are helping your family she may resent it or want to do the same one day. (Man)

The latter discourse by a man on the subject of marriage shows reluctance to contribute much at all to the support of the wife and children and anticipation of total mistrust. He wants the wife to be self-sufficient yet is critical of women's desire to become rich. It was rare, among the people interviewed, to find husband and wife both reasonably satisfied with their conjugal financial arrangements. Where this exists there is a discernible contribution pattern, which is the nearest thing one could describe as an ideal norm for present-day economic conditions.

Under this pattern, the husband pays for most things and the woman contributes a little of her income. For example, the man might pay school fees and 'chop money', and the woman would buy her own clothes, the children's clothes and, if any of them are at boarding school, their provisions and pocket money.

Collaboration over domestic budgeting is clearly considered to be innovative and to be dependent on the understanding nature of the wife. One young construction worker described how fortunate he was that his primary school teacher wife was helpful.

> While she was having the baby I sent her to stay with her mother for a while. I had to give my mother-in-law money for this time, and as I only had ₵30 my wife added ₵30 of her own money, making it ₵60, and she let me give the whole sum to her mother as if it had all come from my pocket. Because my wife is co-operative my mother-in-law thinks well of me. She thinks I provide everything. I was friends with my wife for eight years before we married so we know each other well.

Women showed markedly less propensity to think of conjugal resource allocation as a matter for discussion and planning between spouses than did men. This is probably because men are more in control of their incomes than women are, in that they can choose to be irresponsible fathers without dire consequences. They can be sure that however little they contribute the mother will do her best to maintain the children. On the other hand, a man who wishes to see his children well cared for stands to gain by having a wife who trusts him, understands his problems with regard to the matrilineal family and willingly contributes a share of her income to maintaining the children. In other words, he has nothing to lose by a system of planned co-operative budgeting.

A wife, on the other hand, may fear that if she voluntarily contributes to household expenses the husband will take his responsibilities lightly. At the same time, a young wife's attitude to helping the husband in the early years of the marriage is likely to be coloured by awareness of the possibility of his neglecting her in favour of a younger woman when she gets older. With this in mind, she may take the attitude that it is best to get as much as possible out of him while she can and save her own money. Several younger women respondents explained that it could be difficult for a woman, if she wanted to co-operate with her husband in domestic budgeting, because if her mother found out about it she would discourage her.

Although men say that they cannot force their wives to contribute to household expenses (though they clearly can by neglect), they generally have much more to say on the 'oughts' of conjugal resource allocation than do women, whose attitude is rather to deal with each situation as it comes; they do not appear to feel that they have much control over events. To them there is not much point in asserting that 'fathers are supposed to provide for their children'. They tend to talk more in terms of facts, for example, 'Some men are good, some are not', or 'Everyone has to do what she can for her children'. Thus if a husband and wife plan their budgets together this is likely to be the result of the husband's initiative. This is because the man effectively has the more choice as to how he will dispose of his income and because joint budgeting is in his interest, so long as he puts a high priority on his children's welfare.

Since so many Ghanaians, whether otherwise employed or not, operate some kind of trade, it might be thought that husband–wife enterprises would be quite common. This is not the case. Respondents were asked whether they thought it a good idea for a husband and wife to join together in business. Men and women were unanimous in rejecting the idea. They pointed out that divorce could happen at any time and that one partner might not get his or her money back. Women feared that men would spend the profits on other women.

To do business with a husband is not a good idea because he is likely to cheat you. It's better for each to do his or her own work so that neither knows how much the other is making. If he knows that you have money he will ask you to pay for things that he should pay for, so you have to hide your profits. (Woman)

A wife should have her own trade. You should not join hands in business because at any time there could be a divorce. She will accuse you of using your money on other women. She will keep a very strict eye on your expenses. The man will end up the loser. (Man)

If your husband is out of a job, you have to keep your trade going to support him, but it is not good to join hands in business with him. It may be that you the wife are doing better at business than he, but if you join him he may take full control and all your money will be wasted. (Woman)

There are cautionary tales of women who were so rash as to join their husbands in some business venture or in the purchase of some large item. Women cite these cases as warnings of the dangers of too much financial co-operation with the husband.

Since allocation of financial responsibilities is not the subject of an explicit and widely held set of consensual norms, and yet is of great material interest to the parties concerned, the scope for conflict is great. The traditional Ashanti pattern of resource allocation paralleled the division of labour for a largely subsistence agriculture. The encroachment of the exchange economy into the sphere of the domestic economy, and with it the greater potential for resources needed in the home to be spent elsewhere, have upset the old order of economic relations between wife and husband.

Throughout this discussion emphasis has been placed on the separateness of spouses within marriage. The reordering of social relationships which marriage entails is limited. This is reflected in the informal nature of the marriage ceremonies, and the prevalence of consensual unions.

Similarly, residence arrangements for married people are highly flexible, and are determined by individual convenience, factors such as availability of living space. It is in moving away from the home town and their respective relatives that spouses are often forced to share cramped quarters and to operate an apparently more joint mode of conjugal living.

The tension and stress in relationships between women and their husbands is most prevalent in the area of the allocation of financial responsibilities. Separate identities, allegiances and interests can lead to strife. The very flexibility and variation in arrangements for provision of domestic needs gives scope for conflict. Moreover, great variations and fluctuations in the respective income-earning capacities of husbands and wives militates against the evolution of the kind of norms which would establish a standard pattern for the allocation of financial responsibilities.

Notes: Chapter 10

1   For a full account of the findings of the fieldwork, see my thesis 'Women and family life in an Ashanti town' (Church, 1978).
2   For earlier studies of the effects of matriliny on conjugal relations including resources and residence, see Bartle, 1978; Bleek, 1975, 1976; Fortes, 1949b, 1950, 1969; Okali, 1976; Oppong, 1972, 1974.
3   The 1960 population census of Ghana, Vol. 3, shows only 51 per cent of married Ashanti women living in the same house as their husbands.
4   It has been dealt with at length recently in Oppong, 1982.

Chapter 11

Kinship and Cocoa Farming in Ghana

CHRISTINE OKALI

The transformation from subsistence to cash crop production without doubt creates dramatic changes in the economic relationships of farmers. In many situations contractual exchanges with unrelated persons supersede those based on kinship and marriage. Furthermore agricultural changes reflect ongoing changes in other sectors of the economy, all of which are directed towards a reallocation of productive resources from the traditional channels to the open market. Consequently numerous commentators on contemporary farming systems have predicted and even demonstrated the breakdown of customary units of economic co-operation. This subject is explored here with reference to the matrilineal Akan of Ghana and cases of investment in cocoa farms are used to demonstrate the extent to which patterns of male–female interactions are still determined by a matrilineal kinship ideology and practices.

Multiple Interest in Farms

The Ghanaian migrant cocoa farmer working in a frontier area has frequently been cited as an independent operator, free from the need to rely on customary kinship relationships for his production. However, on the basis of reports of citizen (local) and stranger (immigrant) farmers, regarding their pattern of cocoa farm investment and details of actual labour used on farms over twelve months, it has been demonstrated that these relationships are still important, and indeed in a number of cases made the migration and farm development possible (Okali, 1976).

A significant feature of the details of the resources of farms from two contrasting communities, one an old settled village, Akokoaso, and the other a newly established migrant village, Dominase, was the value of assistance from matrikin, fathers and even in some situations affines. Indeed, wives and offspring were contributing substantially to their husbands' and fathers' cocoa farm development at Dominase by providing labour. That this was the pattern earlier on for farmers at Akokoaso has been suggested briefly by the work of Beckett (1947). Labour for which immediate cash payment does not have to be made, principally that of wives and offspring, was noted to be particularly valuable to farmers just starting their cocoa holdings.

Wives working on new and young farms were always aware that they were not working on joint economic enterprises. They expected eventually to establish their own separate economic concerns, as indeed those did who were in a position to do so. Female citizens were in an advantageous position in this respect, since they had separate resources such as land; while women who had co-wives appeared to have more freedom of movement to work on their own than their counterparts with no co-wives. At Dominase women were responsible for much of the food production on the young farms, as had been the case earlier at Akokoaso.[1] As strangers, however, their cultivation rights were restricted, so they were unable to establish themselves on their own, since they were unable to pay for the land. They therefore continued to work in the only way possible, on their husbands' farms. How the various investors view their contributions, the security of their claims in view of potentially conflicting rights in farms, and how these claims are satisfied, are the theme of this chapter.

Returns to Investment

People who assist in farm development are likely to consider that they have rights in the farm. Whether these assumed rights are considered binding or mere expectations is significant not only for interpreting farm investment patterns, but also for looking at the way in which returns are distributed. Detailed documentation of the dynamics of cocoa farm management has demonstrated that although male farmers rely on their wives, offspring and matrikin, the roles which each perform and the associated expectations vary (Okali, 1976).

Returns may be visible in the form of cash, food crops from young cocoa farms, land, or other assistance for the establishment of separate properties, and may include ultimately the transfer of ownership of the farm itself following the death of the owner. Returns may not reflect inputs in farms, but may be related to other services rendered or to other obligations of the farmers involved. The question of returns is further complicated by the fact that reciprocation for assistance may not be immediate, especially where cash and farms are involved, since cocoa farms may take up to ten years to mature, depending on the type of seedlings planted and the number of labourers. Cocoa farming is a long-term investment programme and this fact is even more significant for stranger farmers, who pay for cultivation rights, and who are subject to various cash constraints.

Cocoa farming needs to be placed within the context of the total rights and obligations of the individuals involved. This aspect of production is discussed by examining the expectations and rewards of those who have invested in farms at Dominase and the ways in which farm owners attempted to meet these. Not unnaturally, unfulfilled expectations led to strain and conflict.

Returns to Wives

In Ghana hired labour is used widely in cocoa production but relatives still contribute substantially to work on farms, especially wives on their husbands' farms. At Dominase farmers with new and young cocoa farms received little assistance from relatives other than wives. These farms were the principle source of food crops, and as the women concentrated their labour on them they were recognised at least in part as owning the food crops. The amount of control which each wife exercised over these varied, however.

Food crops are the only source of income from young cocoa farms and estimates of returns indicate that it can be considerable, especially that deriving from the plantain and cocoyam (Rourke, 1974; Okali, 1975). The amount of food crops planted, however, seemed to be correlated with the distance of the farm from the market and also the size of the farm. The farther away from the main road or village or the smaller the size of the farm, the less food crops planted.

Payment for hired labour in young non-bearing cocoa farms is made annually, usually from sales of food crops. Where the production unit consumed all or much of the food produced – which was the case with most of the farmers with younger groups of farms which were also small – there was no question about the sharing of food crops among assistants. Where possible sales were involved, the rights of wives were clearly defined. At one extreme were the wives who had comparatively free access to the food crops they had planted on young farms. In cases involving more than one wife the young farms were divided between them. At the other extreme were the wives among whom, because there was more than one wife, the new farms were again divided for the purpose of planting and harvesting certain food crops. But their husbands received the money from any sales of corn, cocoyam and plantain, even though each was already a comparatively successful cocoa farmer within the community.

The growing of food crops is an essential part of the farming programme and once such crops from the new cocoa farms are no longer sufficient for consumption needs alternative arrangements are made. Food crops are not usually mentioned as being part of the returns to women, but land or farms are. Indeed, it is the incidence of men giving land or parts of farms to wives and offspring which has led observers to comment on changes in relationships between spouses and offspring arising from cocoa farming. In many cases these gifts are being made for assistance received in the past in the development of cocoa lands. Although the continued involvement of women in food production at Dominase has been emphasised, labour data also indicated that they did other jobs. Even if this work could be viewed as pertaining to the food crops, the wives were both directly and indirectly assisting with the cocoa. Nevertheless, the participation of the women including wives decreased, as the farm aged, while that of their husbands and male matrikin increased. The women still harvested the food crops and apart from weeding and assisting with cocoa harvesting by collecting the pods into heaps, they did other work, such as carrying water to mix with insecticide for spraying. Generally, however, in spite of the women's continued participation, the mature farms were considered to belong to the men.

Wives did not assume that they had established a joint concern with their husbands (with equal rights), although they did expect some compensation other than the food crops, possibly even a fraction of the established farm. Several of the farmers who were just beginning to establish themselves independently did not mention having made any arrangement for establishing farms on behalf of their wives or their children, although in addition to providing labour their wives were also contributing financially to domestic needs, either by trading or by other means. Those farmers would have been hard pressed to have established any additional farms at that time without such financial assistance and depended heavily on income from other sources to make their work at Dominase possible. In addition wives, by completing the work on the new farms, were saving half of the labour costs. One or two wives who obtained loans from their husbands to trade with were expected to repay them. Such financial arrangements were regarded in a totally different way from the gift of farms or land to farm, where no question was raised about returning the initial investment which the husband himself might have made.

In contrast to the group of farmers with younger holdings among the others almost all had at least stated their intention of making some separate provision for their wives and offspring, by providing land, farms, or labour. Nevertheless, this was many years after the husbands established their own first farms. For the most part they were not considering any entirely separate property for their wives or children and arrangements were, to say the least, often vague.

Five of the sixteen wives observed at length had already started working on separate farms, including one who spent all of her farming time on them. Only one man was reported to be working on his wife's farm. Another provided money for labour to be hired. It was not, however, only the men who were investing in these separate properties of wives. One wife said that she used part of her share of the proceeds of a bearing farm for hiring labour to clear her land, even though her husband was assisting with labour.

Other women had been promised parts of established farms, but these were not being operated as distinct units; one husband claimed that he made a larger farm the year he arrived in Dominase, which was to be shared between his two wives, but the senior wife, dissatisfied with her position, left before any transfer was finalised. Another farmer also claimed that he has made provision for his wife but no specific area was indicated.

These provisions were being made for wives when the farmers were themselves well established. Thus, for example, a wife who was starting her farm eleven years after first coming to Dominase had been married almost sixteen years. She said that she had always worked for her husband till she started this farm. Most of the women had been married a number of years, even if this was not their first marriage. Some farmers obviously made promises late, as was demonstrated by one man who was in the process of purchasing a separate plot for his junior wife just before he died. Fortunately for her, the heir finalised this arrangement.

The size of farms involved was comparatively small, although the women did not voice dissatisfaction and there was in any case no agreement about how much land or farm a woman might expect to have. It was not possible in all cases to measure the size, partly because the farmers were themselves sometimes vague, but the young farm for one farmer's three wives was only 2·2 acres and even if they took over the whole of the young bearing farm, which was unlikely (since the farmer did not even wish to discuss the matter), only an area of 4 acres was involved. Another man had given to each of his two wives 2 acres from his 37 bearing acres. One woman probably had a comparatively large acreage with three young farms covering 4 acres. Assuming a production of ten loads to an acre, which was high in view of the then average production in Ghana as a whole, and the practice of giving a third of the proceeds to caretakers, it was still possible at the time for her to build a dwelling place, for instance, with these returns, assuming she had other sources of income for maintenance.

Finally, and probably the most important point about all the reported provisions, was that none of the women had finalised any of the customary transfer arrangements for either the land or parts of the farms indicated. This included a woman who had been operating independently for three years and the three co-wives, the senior of whom said she was ready to take over the bearing section within a year of the farm being surveyed for transfer. She planned to give her part to a caretaker and her husband said that she could use the proceeds for building a house in her home town for her children. This delay in farm transfers was related partly to the fact that husbands were bearing part of the establishment costs, which they would probably no longer be prepared to do once the transfer was complete. On the other hand, if the transfer was not effected in time a woman might terminate the relationship by divorce.

It has been suggested that wives are given land or farms on behalf of their children. A number of the women had grown-up children who had been educated by their fathers, and this could be regarded as an alternative to providing them with a trade or business which would benefit the mothers. Even in such cases some separate arrangements for their mothers were made, suggesting that wives could receive returns in their own right. Some women received farms when they had not themselves invested in those of their husbands, as in the case of young wives with small children married to elderly and well-established husbands.

Returns to Offspring

Adult offspring who have assisted their fathers on farms are also likely to expect some return. Their contribution to farm development at Dominase, like that of their mothers, was in the form of labour and again was restricted mainly to the younger farms. At Akokoaso the analysis of production units indicated that few adult offspring were assisting their parents and at Dominase, among the fifteen cases investigated, they were exceeded in number by matrikin. Nevertheless, where offspring did assist on a permanent basis their contribution was relatively substantial. Thus one farmer's two elder sons were entirely responsible for the development of his property and one of them had worked for six years at the site. Another farmer's sons were the only ones among the adult offspring who actually received a separate piece of land to farm on from their father, who had already established three farms before migrating to Dominase. The children were in a fortunate position.

In another case a farmer relied on his married son at Dominase, although he himself was present at the site most of the time and his daughter was working in the bearing farms at home. He claimed that he had offered part of a 27-acre young farm to all his twenty-one children to share, but he admitted that no single one of them was prepared to care for the farm and then share the proceeds with everyone else. Thus he was looking after the farm himself. His son assisting at Dominase was certainly not satisfied, one of his complaints being that his father had refused to pay for his secondary education, and he was preparing to return to his home town to plant cocoa on land provided by his mother's brother. Being a comparatively wealthy man, he had provided separate plots of land for his sister's daughter's son, and five sisters and their sons. Two other relatives had been given part of the land he was developing at Dominase. Only one of his children was being catered for by the provision of a separate plot and both he and his junior wife, the mother of this child, travelled to a nearby site to do the work. The position of caretaker is considered to be the best among the possible contractual arrangements for labourers, and by reserving this work for a senior daughter and spouse he could be seen to be caring for her needs separately. It would hardly have been possible for this exchange to have been anything other than direct, since it involved both the daughter and her husband who had no binding rights on him as did lineage members. Thus his married son, although younger, was preparing to leave. Once his father had failed to provide for his future and an alternative was offered, there was no question of his staying at Dominase.

The duty of a father with respect to his offspring has been clearly stated by Fortes (1950), who observes that it was to feed, clothe, educate and later set them up in life. Bearing this in mind, offspring would seem to be in a more secure position than their mothers with respect to claims since, as Fortes points out, there can be no question of offspring being obliged to assist their fathers. Once they receive sufficient land and have the resources to develop it, which at Dominase appeared to include a wife, male offspring will work on their own. Nevertheless, offspring, like their mothers, may be involved in a long-term investment programme and may be disappointed. A 35-year-old married son had always worked with his father till his death. He not only worked at Dominase but also travelled to their home town to harvest his father's self-acquired bearing farm. The main development of his father's holding was a 14-acre new section, which was to have at least partly provided for his wives and children. The development of this farm was curtailed by his sudden death. The disappointment of his eldest son, who was given a 4-acre portion of the new farm, is reflected in his own comment on the situation: 'If you follow your father you are a fool for nothing.' Not only was the farm still young, but it was neglected for some time following his father's death and its division into various parts. He was still therefore in a very dependent economic position, but was retained by his father's heir as caretaker of the two bearing farms at Dominase, for which he would receive a fixed share of the crop. Thus the heir was fulfilling his duties of caring for the economically dependent offspring of the deceased by entering into an exchange which was direct, immediate and fixed.

Most of the farmers with adult sons had in fact educated them and they were not working as farmers. However, as illustrated, the fact that fathers may be working closely with sons on farms hardly seems to present a serious threat to the corporate rights of descent groups.

Returns to Matrikin

Two categories of matrikin who have invested in farms must be clearly distinguished: those who from the information might expect a return and those who do not. In addition, when considering rights and obligations of matrikin, we are looking both at individuals and at the matrilineage as a whole. Among the individuals are nephews working for their mothers' brothers while having no independent income of their own. Of the Dominase farmers, several were working with their sisters' sons on a permanent basis. Matrikin were also supervising work on bearing farms elsewhere, but these were more senior kinsmen who themselves had farms, and for them there was no question of expecting a direct return for assistance given. Among this second group of matrikin are mother's brothers and a large number of temporary assistants, who included mothers, sisters, a brother and sisters' sons. Most of the twelve male owners studied at Dominase had received assistance from this category, who were in a position to give rather than to receive. In a number of instances this was in the form of contacts, money, or land to make the venture possible in the first place. In some cases part of their financial backing came from the proceeds of farms which they had inherited and which were therefore lineage property. The position of this group can only be understood if account is taken of the corporate nature of descent groups and the sense of obligation existing between members, doing things for one another because they must, particularly men for their sisters' sons. A good mother's brother is expected to help his sisters' sons, thereby obliging the latter to reciprocate in the next generation either through their own sisters' sons or through other matrilineal dependants (Fortes, 1950). Returns are not always therefore related directly to inputs on farms. Three farmers had each made gifts of farms or land to matrikin which could not be related directly to inputs. One had purchased four pieces of land for the children of four sisters, and one for his oldest sister which was to have been for his own mother, who died before he was able to complete the project. A second had offered land to the adult offspring of his mother's sister. In the first case the only assistance he claimed to have received from matrikin was labour from a grand-nephew when he first arrived at Dominase; whereas the second man did rely financially on matrikin and used the proceeds of a family farm which he had inherited, although he had until then received little help from his grand-nephews. The third farmer said that he had purchased land for a brother who had not worked for him.

Among the most unsatisfactory relationships at Dominase were those between a man and his sister's son. This can be partly ascribed to the uncertainty of the latter's appointment as heir, since although sisters' sons inherit in accordance with seniority by age of their mothers, character is also considered and the heir must be approved by the lineage head and his elders. Thus one sister's son who was working on his uncle's farms did not inherit the property. If it is accepted that there are two types of transactions between matrikin, direct and indirect, it is also possible to see insecurity increased by assistance being regarded as part of the whole series of exchanges. Thus the claims of sisters' sons may be merged with the rights of the corporate concern. It is possible, therefore, that sisters' sons feel even less economically secure than offspring. The position of sisters' sons as recipients of assistance may also not be enviable, since it incurs the obligation to reciprocate.

The rights of the descent group as a corporate unit are ultimately established through inheritance. There was only one farm at Dominase which was divided in this way during the fieldwork period. In this case that part of the holding which was already established and yielding cocoa all went to the heir and included two inherited farms and two which the deceased had acquired himself during his lifetime. The younger farms of 15 acres, where the oldest trees were two years old at the time of his death and which still required considerable investment, were divided among his two wives, his own and his sister's son who had worked for him during his lifetime. The heir had never worked on any of the farms himself and had earlier even been in a position to offer assistance.

Although farmers at Dominase had already gifted or arranged to give parts of farms to wives and offspring, overall the remaining acreage was still the larger proportion. Certainly earlier investigations at Akokoaso, using the same sample of farmers as Beckett (1947), demonstrated that the larger part of the acreage of the ten holdings was inherited by matrikin (Okali and Kotey, 1971), even though wives and children were reported by Beckett to have contributed substantially to the workload. But, as with Dominase farmers, this occurred mostly when the farms were still very young and when they were still therefore the main source of food for consumption, and still required substantial labour inputs.

Clearly Busia's contention, based on research completed in the 1940s, that the cocoa industry had grown as a result of individual toil and enterprise or that all the work had been done by the farmer assisted by his wives and children or by hired labour paid for by himself, was only partially correct. At the same time, however, our conclusions correspond with those of Fortes (1950), Oppong (1972, 1982) and Van der Geest (1974), all of whom have demonstrated the continued importance, with respect to the management, allocation and transmission of resources, of the customary rights and duties based upon matrilineal descent and inheritance even in urban areas and among the educated in Ghana. They also support the findings from elsewhere in West Africa that organised kin-groups play an important role in the promotion of business activities. Here we have been particularly interested to see their effects upon the interactions of men and women, principally in their roles as husbands and wives in cocoa farming in Ghana.

Note: Chapter 11

The inquiries on which this work is based were carried out during 1971–3. In 1971 a farm management survey covering the families referred to here was started and completed twelve months later. Subsequent interviews with individual women and family members provided other details of their expectations. The final work, which included survey data and supporting material from court records, was presented to the University of Ghana, Legon, as a PhD thesis in 1976.

1   The food consists of plantain and cocoyam, the foliage of which provides shade for the young cocoa seedlings.

Chapter 12

Fishmongers, Big Dealers and Fishermen: Co-operation and Conflict between the Sexes in Ghanaian Canoe Fishing

EMILE VERCRUIJSSE

Canoe fishing by means of dug-out canoes is still practised in Ghana. The canoes are launched from beaches and mainly still propelled by human labour-power. It has thus been commonly characterised as 'primitive' and 'traditional' and therefore as being 'inflexible' (e.g. see Lawson and Kwei, 1974). However, in the past decade fishing by dug-out canoes still accounted for half of Ghana's marine fish landings, and production is known to have been raised by some 300–400 per cent.[1] This feat has been accomplished with a labour force which has remained about the same size. The considerable increase in the productivity of labour was achieved by the replacement of a large fleet of medium-sized canoes with a smaller fleet of larger canoes, multi-purpose (*ahwea*) nets and outboard motors. Two basic forms of production are distinguished: one in which the fishermen work as crew members for a boat- and net-owner and are paid for their labour contribution with a share of the catch (*ahwea* fishing), and another in which as net-owners together with the boat-owner, they join his boat for fishing with their individual (*tenga*) nets.[2] Under the first, halfway capitalist form, *ahwea* fishing, they are in some respects like wage-labourers and when at sea have to obey the boat-owner or his representative, who acts as the organiser of production; under the second form, since they also own a net, they are on a similar footing to the boat-owner and may deliberate with him on the time and target of the fishing trip as equals, as they do on how and where they will cast their nets. The boat-owner's only prerogative is to receive a part of everyone's catch as payment for a share of the boat.[3]

The Preservation and Marketing of Fish

The fishermen keep some of their catch for household consumption. Small pails of fish are carried to crew members who have stayed behind because of illness and a few fish are doled out to the *apaafo,* that is, to those on the beach who helped the fishermen to land and unload. The biggest part of the catch is sold. With most of the labour force in Ghanaian fishing communities mainly engaged either in fish production or in preservation and marketing, fish is produced as a market commodity.[4]

A *tenga* fisherman usually passes his catch and an *ahwea* crew member his share on to the woman who cooks for him, that is, to his wife or, if he is not married, to his mother or his sister. She may in some cases resell to fish-smokers or to bigger dealers, especially if the supply is so plentiful during bumper catches that her limited smoking facilities cannot cope with the quantities landed, or if the fishermen are in immediate need of cash. I shall here focus on the more common case, where both the preservation and the selling remain in the hands of the fisherman's 'fishwife'.

The main technique for preserving fish, smoking, is carried out in cylindrical ovens made out of mud and covered with corrugated iron sheets. It involves the collection and carrying of firewood; the scaling of fishes; the packing of the oven; the firing and unpacking of the oven; and lastly the packing of the smoked fish into baskets for transport. In small-scale *tenga* fishing most of the labour is provided by the fishwife, who will at times be helped by younger female relatives. Once the fish has been smoked it can be stored in the same ovens, which for that purpose are packed much more compactly, and kept for as long as eight months, provided the ovens are heated at intervals of four days to a week. Normally fish is not stored much longer than a few weeks, until a sufficient quantity is collected to make its transport to one of the main regional markets such as Kumasi or Tekyiman worthwhile.

Very small fishes are also dried on flat sun-baked surfaces and some species of large fish are preserved through salting and drying. Preserved fish is sometimes sold to bigger wholesale dealers either from the same village or travelling through the village, but mostly the fishwife will market the fish herself. If ready cash is needed, she will retail it in nearby markets. When fish is plentiful four or five women may team together to hire a lorry to transport fish inland where prices are higher. Or she may sell in faraway markets through an agent, to whom she sends her baskets of fish by regular lorry.

In whatever way she disposes of the product she is in the main selling as well as processing on behalf of her husband (brother, son). She does not pay a price for the fish that she collects from him at the beach, but rather after selling, she makes a complete account to him. This includes expenses incurred for transport, board and lodging and marketing, as well as for small personal purchases. The husband is likely to keep a close eye on the quantities of fish that he has given 'on commission' to his wife. He is generally well informed regarding the prices that can be obtained in different markets and the accounts are a potentially controversial issue between spouses. Husbands who feel that they have been cheated too badly or find their own wives not sufficiently competent as a trader may, consequently, decide to give their catch to a more professional trader, leaving their wives only a token amount to sell.

Of every ₵2 for which she has properly accounted the wife will be given 30 pesewas (formerly referred to as three shillings in the pound). The sum remaining will be divided equally, one part for the immediate expenses of the man and the other part to be kept by the wife until further notice. The items for which the fisherman is most likely to be in need of ready cash are the repair and maintenance of his nets, the education of his children and his obligations towards his relatives. Occasionally he will also have to spend money on food for his household, that is, at those times when there are reasons to assume that his wife cannot afford to contribute the 'chop money' from her own purse. With her half of the earnings the wife will be expected to trade, so as to feed the household with the profit she makes, after most of her commission has been spent for this purpose. The trading capital built up in this way during the main season is bit by bit claimed back by the husband during the lean season to be spent on repairs and maintenance as well as on food.

The exchange relationship of supplier and agent between the fisherman and his wife is sometimes interrupted and replaced by a purely commercial relationship. This generally occurs during the main season, especially when catches are plentiful. At such times the husband is not able to keep an overview of the quantities of fish which he is supplying, so that proper accounting is out of the question. For the time being he will therefore accept to be paid in cash by his own wife against the prices for fresh fish that prevail on the beach.

It is said in Ampenyi about such times that 'no man will be so stupid as to give his wife any "chop money" '.

The Articulation of Production with Distribution and Exchange

Let us now see what an analysis of the relationships described above reveals about the articulation between production on the one hand and distribution on the other.

First there is the clear-cut sexual division of labour which leaves the processing and selling entirely to the women. The question is whether there is anything in the structure of marine fishing as a form of production that more or less directly determines the prevailing sexual division of labour or whether it is a question of what Marx called 'an extension of the natural division of labour imposed by the family'.[5] The meaning of the word 'natural' (*naturwüchsig*) in this context could refer to the heavy and hazardous character of fishing, which may keep the fisherman away from home for days on end, while the wife has to stay behind to look after the children. I would, however, see no contradiction with the alternative of locating the determination of the division of labour in the structure of production, more specifically in the process of material appropriation. This in itself would exclude the women from going to sea, but would not at the same time exclude the fishermen from taking part in processing and selling. That they are, in fact, excluded from these activities is also determined, I suggest, by the characteristics of the labour process in fishing. The time taken up by travelling to the fishing grounds, with setting the nets and with returning there regularly for inspection of the catch, and in addition the long hours spent in mending nets, leaves the fisherman – at least during the main season – with little occasion for anything else but sleeping. Consequently, the small subsistence income he earns this way does not exactly present him with an opening for subsidiary economic activities.

Quite another matter is that the mode of women's participation in production and exchange assures them a money income of their own. Significantly, the man and his wife as members of different *ebusua* or localised matrilineages have separate kinship obligations which they can never transfer to their common household.[6] Adult, married persons are full members of their matrilineages and, as such, are expected to attend whenever the family holds counsel. They are also obliged to make a financial contribution whenever this is required, especially at festivals and funerals. A woman may be expected to contribute to the needs of her sister's daughters and, if she can afford it, she should in later life make an effort to build her own house and offer house room to her female kin. It is only during a particular stage of her married life that the wife is expected to live under her husband's roof. Both Fortes for the Asante (Ashanti) and the present author for the Mfantse (Fanti) found less than 40 per cent of married women residing with their husbands.[7]

The relative independence of a woman's economic activities is characteristic of the Akan kinship system. In the subsistence activities of the traditional lineage mode of production, Akan women have had an economic role of their own, while their rights and obligations are defined within the legal structure of the lineage. With the continued existence of the Akan kinship system in present-day Ghana, the pre-scribed norms continue to stress the relative independence of a woman's economic activities in terms of their importance for her own lineage (to which her children belong) instead of defining her earn-ings unrestrictedly as income of a common conjugal household.

The exchange relationship between husband and wife works to maximise the earnings from fishing for them individually. Meanwhile both spouses have an obligation to feed their children. Moreover, the 'banking' function which the wife performs, and which acts as a buffer between the fisherman and indebtedness, is very much tied up with her trading role. Any other exchange relationship would have dis-tributive properties that might less effectively reproduce *tenga*-fishing as simple commodity production.

I have no information on the extent to which *tenga* fishermen get into debt during the lean season for purchasing repair materials and food. But I do have data to show that the indebtedness for the financ-ing of their nets is not of great consequence.[8] Accordingly I conclude that no heavy indebtedness arises from *tenga*-fishing and that it does not draw *tenga*-fishermen into new exchange relationships which are beyond their control.

There may be an element of commercial dependence in the few loans (five out of the sixteen) on which more than straight repayment is required. In these cases the creditors are fishmongers, who assure themselves of a supply of fish by demanding reimbursement of the principal in the form of a share in the catch. They hold regular weekly or bi-weekly 'accounts' when the fish is valued at the price which was set on the beach when a particular share was received, and they agree on the moment at which the last penny has been repaid. The profits gained (or the losses incurred) on the sales of the shares do not enter into the accounts. The profits accrue to the lender by way of interest.

As fishmongers are looking for ways and means to assure their supply of merchandise, there is a tendency for these credit relation-ships to continue after loans have been repaid and to become perma-nent. In the present study all creditors noted are close kin, if they were not already selling the fisherman's catch and cooking his food. Indebtedness of this kind does not endanger the structure; on the contrary, it contributes to its continuity. It is not difficult to surmise, however, that with non-relatives as creditors and with larger sums of money involved, indebtedness could operate to dissolve the current structure of relationships.

'Middlemen' and Wholesale Traders

In terms of employment the canoe fishing industry is of some signifi-cance. According to the 1960 Ghana census of population it engaged more than 100,000 workers or about 5 per cent of the labour force. By comparison, the employment effect of the capital-intensive modern sector is negligible.[9] Nearly half of the canoe fishing labour force, or 47,000 workers, are women who carry out the processing and selling of fish. This amounts to a ratio of eighty-five women traders to every hundred male fishermen. If Lawson and Kwei (1974, p. 23) are correct in their assertion that the census underestimated the number of fishmongers, the ratio is about 100:100 or even higher. In the two fishing communities studied I found that the ratios were 85:100 for Ampenyi and as much as 110:100 for Kromantse. Thus for every productive worker there is about one circulation worker.

Fishmongers, as sellers of the one *birefi* (share) which their husband (or their son or brother) earns as a crew member, are commonly known as 'middlemen'. This is to say that they deal in limited quantities of fish, which they retail after processing at nearby village markets or sell to wholesale dealers.These may be from the same locality or visitors passing through the village. It is for this last reason, selling to bigger traders, that the average 'fishwife' refers to herself and is referred to by others as a 'middleman'.

The distinction between the subsistence trading of the 'middlemen' and the specialised commercial trading of these wholesale dealers is mainly a matter of scale, in the first place defined in terms of processing capacity. Wholesale fish traders, operating either as individuals or as co-operative groups, stand apart from the ordinary 'middlemen' by owning a score of ovens instead of a single one, so that they can take on the smoking of a multiple number of shares. And smoking – and more generally processing – is an indispensable element in the production of fish as a saleable commodity.

Fish traders who own ten or more ovens, medium-sized or large, are quite common in Kromantse where the wholesale trading sector is far more developed than in Ampenyi and matched by the much larger processing capacity. In Ampenyi not more than twenty bigger dealers are operating and they have only a limited number of smaller ovens at their disposal.

In Ampenyi nearly all the twenty-three ovens were built by fishmongers themselves, and at 1977 prices they represent a capital investment of between ₡320 and ₡380. Construction prices reported for Kromantse are much higher, and at 1977 prices the 1,453 Kromantse ovens taken together represent an investment of between ₡22,000 and ₡30,000.

The 'big dealers' are able to make themselves useful in the main season when the normal processing capacity of the fishwives is insufficient for coping with the temporary increase of fish landings. They are also able to use their ovens for storing smaller quantities of smoked fish and for accumulating these until they have collected

enough to be profitably marketed. For the same reason the big dealers are attractive trade partners for the *ahwea* fishermen with large
boats and nets who need bigger outlets.

The 'size of operation' as a characteristic distinguishing the
wholesale fish traders from the 'middlemen' is closely related to the
different marketing function which they fulfil, by regularly transport-
ing and selling in bulk at regional market centres such as Kumasi,
Obuasi and Tekyiman, where they enjoy better prices for the fish.

Labour Requirements in Wholesale Trading

Dealing in big quantities requires the employment of a considerable
amount of labour, since the preparation of the fish, as well as the
packing of the ovens for smoking and of the baskets for transportation, is rather labour-intensive. In addition, a regular supply of wood
to fire the ovens has to be ensured. In view of the prices charged for a
bundle of firewood, many fish traders arrange to have the wood
collected themselves.

For the trader the problem of having sufficient labour at her disposal when required might start at the moment when the fresh fish
has to be carried from the beach to her house. This will only become a
problem, however, when she buys from irregular sources, such as
from a boat not belonging to her home town but landing its catch
there. For if she buys from 'middlemen' they will themselves deliver
the fish to her door; and if she has a regular commercial relationship
with certain net-owners, they will pay some men in kind to do the
carrying. Only when she buys fish *ad hoc* does she have to engage
carriers herself; the women who undertake this work as casual labour
receive 40–50 pesawas (₡·40–₡·50) for carrying a full pail (1975
prices).

In view of the fact that the labour requirements for scaling and
packing are very seasonal and, apart from that, affected by all the
vicissitudes of fishing and therefore highly irregular, wholesale traders frequently engage piece-workers at peak periods, to whom they
pay 40 pesawas per hundred fishes (*kokore*, shad) or 20p for the
scaling and 20p for the packing of the oven per hundred. The packing
of the smoked fish into baskets which contain 600–800 *kokore* is
remunerated at ₡1 per basket (1975 rates). The workers employed
are without exception females, most of them being either young and
unmarried, or old and widowed or divorced.

The wholesale, regional trade in fish is based on credit. At every
transaction on the beach, where dealers buy a number of shares, they
accept the obligation to pay the greater part of the sum agreed upon
after the fish has been marketed. Thus the regular solution to the

labour problem has to be one whereby the trader does not have to pay wages. She either solicits help from relatives – mainly sisters, daughters, or grand-daughters – or co-operates with some of her colleagues (who might be relatives but often are not), because they can be paid with a share in the proceeds after a sale has been made. In those cases where labour is provided by female relatives who are mostly too young or too old to be in business themselves, they share the profit at such rates as 3:2 or 7:5. At times they take equal shares, although this is more often the practice of traders who, as non-relatives, have formed co-operative groups. In such trading co-operatives all members are fish-dealers in their own right and each of them brings in a number of *birefis* to the sale of which she can lay claim. Thus whenever catches are small and irregular, at least one out of a group of traders is likely to be supplied with fresh fish by some net-owner, so that as a group they stay in business much more regularly. At the same time they divide the work of scaling, smoking and packing among themselves. Although exceptions occur, most co-operatives pursue strict equality of their members. Labour of all types is equitably apportioned among them, while profits and losses are equally shared. This will be the case even though one among them acts as a leader and though the site for processing is located at her house. Such a co-operative trading group can afford to build a larger number of ovens and will also be able to negotiate transportation at lower prices, as it will more regularly be engaged in sending large quantities of fish to the regional markets. And while one co-operative might not have sufficient capacity, two co-operatives if they team up might be able to hire an entire lorry. Another advantage is that they can afford to have a representative continuously stationed at one of the regional market centres, to whom they send the processed fish by regular lorry and who does the selling for them. Sometimes individual traders, who engage the help of female relatives, may do the same by stationing a daughter or a grand-daughter as their sales representative at the market centre.

The Actual Marketing of the Fish

Fishmongers who travel to the inland markets in groups of four or five need at least a couple of days to complete their sales. Although they do not retail the fish but sell 'in hundreds' to both wholesalers and retailers, it usually takes them four days to a week before they have disposed of their entire load. This problem of accommodation is easily solved by the existence in Kumasi and some of the other centres of special 'pensions' run by former colleagues, who have themselves come from one of the fishing villages. It is thus common for a fishmonger to stay with a landlady from her own home town who caters for the particular needs of the fishmongers. In these boarding houses the fishmongers generally pay nothing or very little for their board and lodging. They are rather charged by number and size of their baskets for the special services which are rendered to them by the landlady, such as the safekeeping of their baskets of fish, the security of their person and their property – after having disposed of their goods they are likely to carry considerable sums of money on them, and the transport of the heavy baskets to and from the market by the landlady's servants. Alternatively they may leave the fish in the market stall where they then need a reliable watchman to keep it safe.

At the market place they are involved in further costs, including a market toll levied per load and the rent of a stall or shed. Some have a standing relation with colleagues who reside at the market centre, and who sublet a part of the market stall which they have on long lease. In this way marketing costs can be considerably reduced.

The Secret of Market Control

The role of the big dealers in the exchange system is specifically dependent upon their control over a processing capacity much larger than the simple fishwives have at their disposal and on their consequent ability to sell at a profit in the more distant regional markets. Thus big dealers are able to capture a part of the market, especially when the processing and selling of larger quantities of fish are involved. For in the peak season the 'middlemen' cannot cope with the amounts which their husbands (or brothers or sons) supply to them. The same problem of oversupply occurs because the owners of large boats and nets (as in Kromantse) have not one or a few but a sizeable number of shares to sell, so that some times even outside the peak season they have to dispose of quantities of fish which exceed the fishwives' capacity. There is still, however, in canoe fishing about one circulation worker to every production worker and circulation workers are 'fishwives', who can lay claim to selling at least some share of the catch. The question which arises is how the 'big dealers' are able to ensure themselves of a supply of fish all through the year which will allow them to continue the trade at their own level.

The answer to this question lies in the limitations on the way in which the product is distributed. We have seen that a fishwife, as the seller of a fisherman's shares, keeps half of the proceeds to trade with. The underlying idea is that in this way the profits she earns will help to buy food whenever catches are insufficient to feed the household. Meanwhile, in the off-season, when the husband's earning capacity is reduced to nil, her small trading capital may be used for that same purpose. There is no doubt, however, that this 'buffer'-mechanism does not always suffice to keep hunger at arm's length. It is at such moments that additional sources of income are relied upon. Thus many fishwives engage in shallot and vegetable farming during the off-season. Should the availability of credit become of vital importance, however, the big dealers enter the scene in a role that not many others in the fishing community can fulfil, that is, as sources of credit.

The average fisherman is constantly confronted with the dilemma that it takes at least a number of days, if not weeks, before his fishwife can supply him with some money income from the sales of his share in a particular catch. If the fisherman is the owner of a boat or net he may in the meantime have to meet the costs of repairs which he is not able to pay. This is one of the reasons he may have to turn to the bigger dealers for credit. Indeed, the need for ready cash increases with the scale at which fish is produced. The need has considerably increased with the introduction of outboard motors, as well as with the scale of the operation in *ahwea* fishing, thus giving the big dealers a hold on the supply of fresh fish which the fishwives cannot take away from them so long as they are regular and reliable in providing the boat-owners with ready cash.

There is, however, another, far more substantive need for credit; namely, the financing of fishing equipment – boats, nets and motors. To the extent that the big fishmongers are able to advance sums of money to the fishermen, enabling them to become the owners of the means of production, or, being owners, to renew, improve, or increase the capacity of their equipment, they may attempt to negotiate terms which guarantee a continuing supply of fish. And because sources of long-term, large-scale credit are scare, the wholesale dealers have been able to dictate terms which oblige the fishermen to supply them regularly all through the season with a certain number of shares of the catch; in fact, to continue the supply of fish at an agreed level as long as the loan has not been repaid.[10]

The threat of the fishwives as competitors for the shares of the fishermen to whom they are in one way or another related is, however, constantly there. And the big dealers are aware of it. They know that with diminishing catches and, therefore, with shrinking supplies of fresh fish (as at Ampenyi), they will gradually be locked out as precedence will (and must) be given to the fishwives' claims. The result is that while business will increasingly depend on credit to keep it going, the sources of credit are actually drying up.

The Producer–Trader Terms of Trade

For a fisherman there could be no greater difference than between having his catch sold by a fishwife with a view to turning it into a money-income, and having it sold by a fish-dealer with a view to repaying a loan. In the first instance accounts are made in terms of sales prices for processed fish, as well as in terms of processing, transportation and marketing costs, so that he does not have to relinquish control over the results. He can, moreover, claim as much as 85 per cent of the revenue accounted for, while he will also indirectly benefit from the portion given to his fishwife. In the second instance costs and profits are none of his business. In view of the fact that accounts are made in this case solely in terms of cost prices for fresh fish, we can only conclude that he has lost control over the outcome. All he can demand is that the worth of the fresh fish which he has supplied, valued at current cost prices, is booked off from his loan. The consequence of this credit relationship therefore is to give the traders a hold on the supply of fresh fish as well as turning the terms of trade against the fishermen.

Conclusions

In conclusion we may say that in the sexual division of labour the tasks of preservation (an integral part of fish production) and selling (the necessary realisation of the exchange value of the fish) fall to the fishwives. This puts them in a position from which the entire process of fish production might be controlled, a position which they are not likely to relinquish easily. Even if a system of wage payments could be introduced that would be satisfactory to the crew members themselves, it would most certainly meet with resistance from their fishwives. Put differently, both fishermen and the fishwives have a part in the control over fish production, in consequence of which they find themselves in opposition to each other. I suggest that it is this structural opposition, arising from the established systems of distribution and exchange, which together with the newly arisen capitalist relations of production in *ahwea* fishing is a determining factor in the shaping of the sharing system.

To see this in its proper light we have to realise that the boat- and net-owners would only be able to do away with sharing in favour of wage payments if they could either gain control over smoking and selling or avail themselves of much larger amounts of credit. In the first case they would immediately find the fishwives as well as the bigger dealers pitted against them, apart from having to oppose the full weight of their own kinship traditions. In the second case they would in all likelihood have to depend heavily on the bigger dealers – who have developed into quite a powerful class in Kromantse – to whom they are in a real danger of losing their part of the control over fish production. It is for this reason, with their need for credit constantly on the increase, that the boat- and net-owners will be likely to look for sources of credit other than the big fish traders.

My conclusion is that as long as the commercial role of the women continues as at present, the process through which *ahwea* fishing as a form of production has materialised will not develop much further and cannot reach the point where labour becomes a commodity freely exchangeable for money.

Notes: Chapter 12

1 According to Lawson (1968, p. 93) the average canoe catch before the introduction of mechanised craft in the early 1950s was between 20,000 and 30,000 tons of fish annually. Average fish landings in the early 1970s amounted to more than 100,000 tons per annum.

2 *Tenga* fishing as a form of production does not exist in a pure state. Owners of *tenga* nets find that they can only at times get the opportunity to join a boat for *tenga* fishing if at other times they agree to take part in fishing with the boat-owner's larger *cedi* net as a crew member. This is to say that the owners of the (smaller) *tenga* nets will only be able to avail themselves of their nets in the off-season if during the main season they work as crew members in *cedi* fishing with the larger net of the boat-owner.

3 The main data on canoe fishing, relating to fishing equipment and techniques as well as to the organisation of production and distribution and to the role of exchange, were collected in Ampenyi and Kromantse, two fishing communities in the Central Region.

4 *Tenga* fishermen are simple (or petty) commodity producers in the sense that, as direct producers, they own the means of production with which they produce on a small scale for exchange in the market. In view of the fact that the exchange of their output is *systematic* and not spasmodic, *competitive* and not monopolistic, and moreover not of a marginal nature, they do really exchange according to the law of value. Most small producers in pre-capitalist formations do not engage in exchange which is both specialised and generalised. For them use value is predominant. In this sense, *tenga* fishing as a form of production may well be called an 'odd case'. See Amin, 1977, p. 34.

5 See Marx, 1965, p. 122.

6 On how the composition of Akan households relates to the lineage structure, see Vercruijsse, 1974, pp. 50–5.

7 See Vercruijsse, 1972, p. 8.

8 On seventy-five *tenga* nets of all types, twenty-eight Ampenyi fishermen spent ₵8,250 or about ₵110 per net and about ₵310 per owner. On no more than sixteen of these nets, i.e. slightly over 20 per cent, loans were taken at an amount of ₵61·50 per net or ₵110 per owner. All the others were financed from 'own savings', earned either in fishing or in craft activities. Most of the loans (fourteen out of sixteen) were taken from relatives (notably mothers, brothers, sisters, some in-laws), with the consequence in ten out of the sixteen cases that on the principal no interest has to be paid and that periods of repayment are not very strictly enforced.

9 For 1974 I estimate total employment in the modern sector at about 6,000.
10 Indebtedness of *ahwea* fishermen at Kromantse is, consequently, much heavier than of the *tenga* fishermen at Ampenyi. While the average loan for the latter amounted to ₵178, the former had borrowed as much as ₵1,660 on average. This is directly related to the level of investment, which at Ampenyi was not more than ₵410 on average for *tenga* fishing and ₵765 for *cedi* fishing compared with as much as ₵4,900 for the *ahwea* fishermen at Kromantse.

Chapter 13

Marriage, Divorce and Polygyny in Winneba

GEORGE PANYIN HAGAN

In the traditional family system of the Effutu of Winneba, a coastal fishing community of Ghana, husband and wife have distinct but complementary responsibilities for providing for their own needs and the needs of the children. This system, as it operates among fisher-folk in particular, tends to create functional crises for the hus-band–wife relationship with consequent possibilities of divorce or co-location of two or more women in the role of wife in relation to one man. The discussion here is intended to throw light on two facts about conjugal crises in Winneba. First, that there is an annual cycle of divorces which coincides with the seasonal fluctuations in fishing activity among the fisher-folk and, secondly, that there is a gradual increase in divorce rates as one moves from the lower age-groups to the higher age-groups of both men and women.

With reference to the family as an operating social unit, these observations suggested that divorce might relate to two domestic cycles: first, the annual seasonal cycle in the domestic economy and, secondly, the developmental cycle of the domestic group and the conjugal family. Both of these cycles exhibit interesting alterations in the conjugal relationship, which are directly related to the system of providing for the needs of the conjugal family. Polygyny plays an important part in these cycles in relation to men's idea of their own welfare. Several people noted that while acting as a salve to some of the domestic crises, polygyny also tends to lead to the dissolution of marriages.

Situated some forty miles west of Accra, Winneba with a popula-tion of 30,000 holds the southmost tip of a long line of Guan-speaking communities which occupy the great divide between the matrilineal-dominant Akan spread and the congeries of other ethnic units which practise patrilineal descent. In spite of their long contacts with the Fanti on the one hand and the Ga on the other, they have maintained a distinctive cultural identity and institutions which one does not find among either the Ga or the Fanti. The traditional economy of Winneba has been based almost exclusively on fishing, in spite of the fact that they have large tracts of arable land.

Among the Effutu marriage is duolocal. A married man normally stays in his father's house with his brothers or a group of people who trace their descent through a common progenitor. (The agnatic household is called *prama*.) A man's wife does not move in to stay with him. She rather stays with her mother and sisters in her mother's house (called *igyiase*) and visits her husband in the evening to sleep with him. While a married woman might perform all her chores in the *igyiase*, she rarely sleeps there.

Like the *prama*, the occupants of typical *igyiase* trace common descent from a known progenitrix and thus consider themselves to constitute one lineage or a segment of a lineage. The segregation of women in women's households and of men in their households constitutes a critical breach in Effutu social organisation which is articulated in almost all aspects of the individual's social life.

The polarisation in Effutu society seen in the household composition is a reflection of the practice of dual descent, by which a person traces descent through, and inherits from, both father and mother. The *igyiase* constitutes a lineage segment – a matrilineage in this case – the male members of which are scattered over several *prama* according to their fathers' derivation from different agnatic households. A *prama* is, on the other hand, composed of a core of male agnates, whose female lineage members live in several *igyiase*, according to their mothers' derivation from different *igyiase*. It is on the basis of the *igyiase* and the *prama* that domestic life is organised.

From birth, and till they marry and become mothers and die, daughters stay permanently in the *igyiase* with their mother. It is they who enlarge and perpetuate the corporate maternal group. Boys stay with their mothers in the *igyiase* till they are just old enough to go without their mother's care. At 8, 9, 10, or earlier, according to their physical constitutions, boys move to stay with their fathers in the father's *prama*. It is the sons and not the daughters through whom the agnatic household is perpetuated. In this phase of family development, then, a sibling group is sexually divided, the mother keeping the girls and the father receiving the boys as they grow up.

For boys, as they move from the mother's house and sphere of women to the father's house and his authority and care, there seems to occur a traumatic umbilical separation, which makes them independent and forces them to begin to live by their own devices. Before moving from the *igyiase* a boy depends almost entirely on his mother for food, clothing and shelter. With the move he comes to depend on his father for shelter, but food and clothing continue to be provided directly by the mother. Life, however, loses its assured regularity. In the father's house he is assured of the regularity of one meal only – the evening meal. When a father goes to sea and comes home late, it could quite well mean a boy goes without breakfast, unless he runs to the mother's house. Here too the chances are that the mother may be away on the beach or off to sell fish or about some errand. In her absence a mother's sister or a mother might take care of the child and feed it. Boys adjust in different ways to this change. Most boys keep hovering between the father's house and the mother's house, often escaping from the spartan life of the former to seek relief in the latter.

In Winneba a woman cooks just one meal a day for her husband. In some female households, one large pot of food is prepared from which the sisters and the married women in the house dish out portions to be carried in different directions to their husbands. What remains after the portions of the husbands have been served is for the women and their children. Some women sit together with their children and eat from a common pan, while others serve their portions and eat from individual plates. In other houses individuals cook their individual pots of food and eat them at the same time as their husbands and children. The husband, of course, does not stay in the house, and his portion is carried to him at his *prama* by the wife or one of the children in the house. The Effutu recognize the all-around beneficial effects of the first kind of group cooking: if a woman has travelled, or is indisposed, or just not free to cook, her children and husband are still fed.

When the food reaches the *prama* the husband does not set up a lone table to eat his meal by himself. He puts his food aside, and as the meals of other married men in the *prama* arrive from their wives' *igyiase* each man sets his aside. At meal-time all the different dishes are brought together and the men sit around to eat them together. A portion of the food is then left over for the children and young boys in the house to eat. After this the young boys carry the vessels back to the wives or mothers in their *igyiase*. Eating together is a daily expression and reaffirmation of the solidarity of the *prama*. Besides this practice serving to keep the men together, it also provides each man with a wide selection (not very wide in this case) of different dishes – different both in kind and in quality of preparation. Because of this collective eating a man feels ashamed if his wife brings too little food or badly cooked meals. This is considered grounds for divorce. The question naturally arises, where does the money come from for the provision of food, clothing and the several needs of the married couple themselves and their children? How is the economy of the conjugal family organised?

The Domestic Economy

Among the fishing community, the family economy rests on a system of division of labour based on sex and on conjugal co-operation. Only men go to sea; and only women handle, smoke, dry and sell fish. Fishing is a group activity. Men in a single *prama* tend to fish together. They may organise expeditions in a single boat or join men in other *prama* to go to sea. When they make a catch, one portion goes to the boat, another to the net, and the third portion is shared equally by the members of the crew. Right there on the beach the wives of the crew members come and collect their husbands' shares for the market. If a woman smokes her fish she may get help from her mother or sister. This of course depends on whether they themselves have obtained fish to smoke or sell. The sale of fish makes the female population of Winneba the most mobile sector in the society. The women carry their fish to the market centres of Swedru, Ayim and several others up to Kumasi. The marketing activities of the women make them not only those who control the husband's purse strings, but also the one sector of the society which controls and moves money around.

Fishing is not the only economic activity in which women are involved. A large number of women engage in selling agricultural produce which they bring in from outside. The leading women in this group are surprisingly wealthy and the ordinary food-seller would appear to be wealthier than the ordinary fishmonger. Unlike the fishmongers who are buffeted from season to season by market forces, the sellers of yam, plantain, and so on, have evolved a system for controlling these forces. They have organised themselves into a union which settles conflicts which tend to erupt in the market place. The union members also have a monopoly over the sale of the kinds of foodstuff they sell. While keeping out any new members, particularly women from outside who would like to bring in large quantities of plantain, cassava and yam and sell in the Winneba market, they also ensure a safer market for each member by operating a system which I have called 'the system of circulating monopoly'. The women have shared the market days, so that each day belongs to one person or one group of persons who have the market exclusive to themselves. This way they keep competition from their ranks and ensure that each person's foodstuff is bought and does not rot in her hands. The big members arrange the supply of food to prisons and educational institutions. They circulate the contract to the prisons. The highest prestige (though not necessarily wealth) attaches to the women who have stalls at which they sell cloth and things such as household eathenware and silver. The interesting point about this sector is that the better the fishing season, the better their sales. But whatever the kind of economic activity, it is recognised that it is the women who control the commanding heights of the town's economy. In the traditional system, which is now mainly prevalent among the fishing sector of the community, the domestic economy reflects this dominant if not domineering female role in the maintenance of the split conjugal family.

The economic fortunes of the conjugal family depend on the fishing activities of the husband, and between fishing seasons on the business acumen of wives. The major fishing season in Winneba begins in the second half of July and ends in September. The end of the year is marked with the celebration of Akomase, a harvest and thanksgiving festival. During the whole season the catch which a man makes is given over to the wife to sell at a fixed price – what they call the beach price – which changes from day to day and indeed from morning to evening. At the end of the season the wife makes accounts to the husband. The husband is entitled to claim from his wife the price of the fish he gave to the wife during the whole season. If the woman has made losses the man does not seek to know. So the wife has to make up for any losses. When the woman is not able to do this the husband feels cheated. Under normal circumstances a man must make as much as any person in his crew. 'Other crew members who had the same amount got ₵60 out of their catch, why should I get half as much?' This, according to the fishermen, often leads to divorce when it persists over a number of seasons. As one fisherman put it: 'We do not have any bank: we do not have any source of income. Our wives are our banks and our sources of income.' It is mainly from the peak season's activity that a man gets money to look after his wife and children. So if a woman does not carefully look after the financial affairs of the family, it becomes difficult to maintain herself and the children.

When a woman makes her account to her husband he gives to the wife *atondze* (literally the thing for selling or the sales commission). On every ₵1 the wife makes, she get 10p. So if she has made ₵100 on the fish according to the beach price she is entitled to ₵10 or 10 per cent commission. The husband deducts this and gives it to the wife. Of the remainder the man must give to the wife all the money she may have borrowed for the upkeep of the family. This is in respect of hospital fees, school fees and books, clothing for the children, indeed, all expenses the woman may have incurred in looking after her husband, herself and her children for the whole year from the previous fishing season.

This is where the men, according to the women, are often unreasonable, and the women, according to the men, break faith. Often some men, realising how high their debt to the wife is, pay only a small amount or even refuse to pay any of the debt, even though the woman may have incurred the debt in genuine expenses on the family. On the side of the women, it is said some women actually cheat their husbands by so engulfing the man with debt that he is left with nothing. After the debts have been settled, the man then takes out of the remaining money a good amount – according to the man's own financial standing – and gives it to the woman. The highest amount I heard mentioned was ₵30–40. This figure was from the men. The women put it round ₵16. It is this that is called the year's 'chop money'. When a man gives this money to the woman, he expects her to feed the family with this for the whole of the ensuing year. Hospital fees will be paid out of this, and all the needs of the children. If the husband does not travel in the off-season – and the older ones appear not to – he expects one solid meal every day out of this money. The wife meets this staggering obligation by trading with the money. And this demands great business acumen and immeasurable energy and dedication on her part.

With the closing of the fishing season towards the end of September the pattern of family life changes, and the man's breadwinning role comes to an end. Several men, particularly the older fishermen, remain absolutely idle. Several assist their wives by bringing in some money from the out-of-season catches they make. Some of the men migrate westward to Apam, Sekondi and other places to fish. Most of those who do this are young men with growing children, and they leave their wives behind. This separation of husband and wife has its attendant risks. Wherever the men go to fish they take on women who cook for them, see to their welfare and sell their fish for them. The pattern of life they live with these women is not like that they practise in Winneba with their own wives. The relationship is on purely business lines. Yet the privations of months of separation from wife and children lead the men to enlarge the scope of their relations with the women. Many liaisons and several marriages result from these connections.

During this seasonal separation a man leaves all the children to the care of the wife. With communication between husband and wife cut, the woman has to bear the care of the children on her own shoulders. If business turns out to be bad she may rely entirely on her mother and sisters. She may borrow or even commit adultery to make ends meet. Knowing full well how strong this latter temptation is, some men set spies to watch the movements of their wives. In casual conversations the men point to the profligacy of their wives when they are away as the cause of divorce, and the women attribute polygyny and the occasional lapses in marital fidelity to these travels.

Many of those who travel return home for Christmas. Upon their return their wives expect them to pay any of the standard debts which they may have incurred from September to December. But this is not mandatory. A considerate husband will give the woman something before going back to continue his fishing activities, if he intends to return. By April all the men are coming back home to prepare for the annual festival of 'The Deer Hunt'. April to June is the period for mending old boats and nets, buying new nets and boats and getting ready for the major fishing season in Winneba. Apparently when the men come back in April many come either quite wealthy, or very poor, depending on the fortunes of the seas. This is the time when the women expect some relief; and I myself have seen a woman bring her husband before the Tufuhen to find out from the husband why he had not bothered about the costs of maintaining the family in his absence. The marriage was dissolved after the case had been heard. It turned out the man had actually got a second wife where he went to fish. Thus April, the month of family reunion, tends to be the month of divorces.

A Survey of Marriage

From the data collected in a household survey in Winneba from July to August 1972 it emerged that 73 per cent of all married men interviewed were monogamous and only 27 per cent were polygynous (N = 328). Of the polygynous husbands, 47 per cent were fishermen. This included a third of all married fishermen. Meanwhile 27 per cent of all men interviewed had been divorced, and the figure for fishermen was as high as 41 per cent. Men gave misunderstanding and the infidelities and bad character of their wives as the main causes of divorce. Women mentioned misunderstanding and irresponsibility as their main reasons for leaving their husbands. Misunderstanding in both cases was dominantly economic and not sexual or religious. Co-wife conflict and problems with childbirth ranked among the next most frequent problems, indicating that polygyny is itself a precipitant of divorce, one critical reason being that henceforward the woman begins to get half the husband's fish catch to sell, instead of all as formerly. Children are considered especially important to a marriage as they are the only guarantee of a couple's welfare in old age, and old age in the fishing community is known to be nasty, brutish and often long. Divorces seem to occur with a definite periodicity apparently related to the cycle of fishing activity. Analysis of the registration of divorces for three years 1969–71 indicated two peaks: one in April and one in September, with the first slightly higher (see Figure 13.1).

April is the month when all men come home to prepare their nets. I have already explained why their return may coincide with heavy divorces. First, the high incidence may be on account of the men's

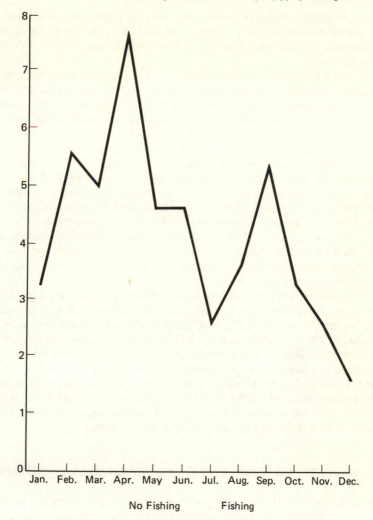

No Fishing   Fishing

Figure 13.1   Registration of divorces, 1969–71.

unwillingness to give the wife some further financial assistance or on account of adultery or polygyny. But it could also be on account of the general increase in the population at this time – for the festival. Often couples who have travelled together return because of the Deer Hunt festival to settle their marital misunderstandings. Complaints against husbands and wives are brought forward and often the couples divorce before the husband or wife goes back to work.

September is another peak. Here divorces are accounted for by two main reasons – polygyny and the woman's failure to look after the financial well-being of husband and children. Polygyny, as I have indicated, is often seen as a marriage-saving device – or as a divorce precipitant.

When a fisherman discovers his wife is dissipating his money and is not able to trade or make enough money out of the fish he gives her, he seeks to divert some of his catch to a woman on the side. Rather than keep secret this affair, a man may inform his wife and take the woman as a second wife. To take a new wife, the man gives the first wife what is called *abiendze,* a fee for pacifying the woman and securing the wife's formal approval for 'splitting her basket into two'. The diversion of part of the catch means a diversion of part of the wife's capital for trade and a reduction of the woman's capacity to meet the obligations of looking after her children. The women, therefore, do not take this lightly and may seek divorce on this account. As far as the wives are concerned they may never meet; each woman stays with her mother in her *igyiase* and they definitely take turns to visit the husband. So except for the chance encounter on the beach the two wives may never cross paths.

The second main cause to which people attribute polygyny is the seasonal separation between husbands and wives. It is said that often the women with whom the men treat when they travel become their wives. But more often when the first wife grows old or acquires many children and is less able to trade and look after the man he may feel inclined to marry a younger woman who will be able to look after him and travel with him. In many cases in such conditions the first wives tend to be more ready to give their personal approval to such marriages. All these facts acquire added significance when we relate divorce and polygyny to the different age-groups.

Developmental Cycle and Domestic Groups and Divorce

In a breakdown of both polygyny and divorce according to age there seems to be a gradual rise among both older men and women (see Figure 13.2). Polygyny reaches a peak in the 60–69 age-group and starts diminishing from that point. Divorces for both men and women reach a peak in the 50–59 and 70–79 phase, and appear to fall in the 60–69 phase. For men aged 70–79 there is a sharp rise in divorce; while for women there is only a slight upward kink in a steady downward drift in divorce.

To explain family life in relation to welfare, we have so far referred to two points in the developmental cycle of the split conjugal family: first, the marital union and the birth of children; secondly, the sexual separation of the sibling group as the boys reach 7 or 8. The third

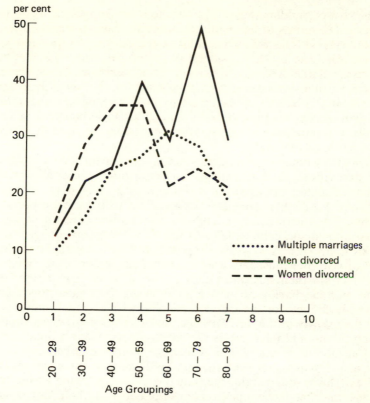

Figure 13.2 Divorces by age group in Winneba.

point in the cycle occurs when the children begin to marry. This point is closely linked with the developmental cycle of the mother's domestic group, the *igyiase,* and the developmental cycle of the father's household group.

Interviews with people divorced and non-divorced suggested clearly that significant changes occur in the pattern of family life which tend to affect its stability. The first is that about the age of 50 for the husband the conjugal family begins to go through a phase of growth in generational terms. First the children marry and begin to have their own children. This affects the domestic lives of both their father and their mother. For when a man's son comes of age and marries, according to Effutu practice, his father must leave his room and give it to his son to stay in. If the first son to marry has other brothers behind him, as each takes a wife the older brother occupying the father's room vacates for the newly wed to stay in. In earlier days the father teamed up with his sons to put up a new men's house. Due to the cost of building these days, this does not happen now and the father often retires to his maternal home to stay with his sisters or goes to stay with his wife when there is accommodation in the wife's *igyiase*. The wife is often reluctant to permit this when the man has not assisted the woman to expand living accommodation in the *igyiase*. Even in cases where a man has done this, it is most likely that the rooms will be directly taken up by his grown-up daughters. For the men, except for the very rich, accommodation becomes quite a problem, and their wives may not feel very happy going to sleep with them as they used to do.

From the woman's point of view, when the daughters have children and start visiting their husbands at night the good mother feels reluctant to abandon the daughters' children to go and sleep with her husband. While her daughters go to sleep with their husbands a woman is left with her grandchildren to tend and care for at night. She cannot abandon this role to go and fulfil her marital obligation to her own husband. Also women report that they feel it slightly indelicate to visit their husbands and meet their daughters at the gate all coming from their husbands: they knowing what their mother has done and she having no doubt about what they have done. This makes it difficult for the married couple to have sexual intercourse and they slowly drift apart. Divorce, however, may not occur on this ground alone. The financial change which occurs in the economic cycle is by far the most crucial issue which the women emphasise.

When a man's sons start fishing, his fishing career stops and he retires. This is round about the time the sons start taking wives. This means that the economic relationship between their father and mother changes: it tends to break down. For when the father stops going to sea he does not get fish to give to his wife. This means that he becomes a liability to his wife. She has to look after him in addition to any of the children who have not married and formed their own economic units independent of their parents.

Usually at this stage of the developmental cycle a father comes to depend upon his sons for food, while a woman depends on her daughters and sons. At this stage the children may be using their father's boats and nets, if he has acquired any before retirement. In this case the portions for the boat and net may go to their father, who then has a basis for giving fish to his wife. But of course it is not every man who invests in boats and nets. Indeed, whether the father does this or not depends on how hard perhaps their mother has worked for their father and how prudently he has saved. So it would appear that the extension of marriage beyond this phase of change depends upon the women as much as the men. The portions which a net- or boat-owner receives are large, and the man can afford to split one between two women and satisfy both. Often in view of the age of the wife a man might take a young woman who would have the capacity to maximise his wealth. This might account for the high incidence of polygyny in this age-group and phase of change, coming to a peak in the 60–69 age-span. At this peak of polygyny, divorces fall: women most likely show less desire to divorce on account of polygyny.

In the 70–79 age-range women are not of much help to men in the preparation and marketing of fish. And the women, if the men are indolent, would have no wish to look after them. This would seem a reason for the high divorce rate at this stage. Another aspect of this high rate of divorce in the 70–79 age-range is that the obligation to look after the children which would be one of the strongest ties holding husband and wife together would by then have passed.

In this chapter I have related divorce and polygyny to some important features of family life, demonstrating that they appear to be influenced by seasonal changes in the fishing activities of men and women. But more important, they relate to changes in the roles of husbands and wives as the conjugal family develops.

This chapter, of which a slightly different version was first published in the *Ghana Journal of Sociology*, vol. 10, no. 1, 1976, originally formed part of a thesis for D.Phil at the University of Oxford: 'Aspects of social change among the Effutu of Winneba', 1974. The material was collected during fieldwork from 1970 to 1973.

Conclusion to Part Three

In Part Three the focus of concern has been the relationships between men and women in the domestic economies of several southern Ghanaian communities. Two of the studies are set in provincial inland communities and two in coastal fishing villages. Discussion has centred on the transactions in money and domestic resources between wives, husbands and kin. Several themes common in studies of West African domestic life recur here: the complexity and diversity of domestic organisation – including patterns of co-residence and the types of transactions between marriage partners, parents and children, and kin; the considerable economic individualism of women and men and yet at the same time the financial interdependence and co-operation between wives and husbands, who carry out separate but complementary income-generating tasks and whose meetings in the conjugal relationship appear circumscribed and defined by multiple ties and constraints; and a continuing bargaining element in conjugal exchanges, which is more or less latent but sometimes becomes manifest and may erupt in observable crises leading to separation and divorce, resulting from the unmanageable tensions and conflicts inherent in a relationship, in which continually fluctuating domestic resources have to be managed to provide for the continuing maintenance and welfare of dependent offspring and kin.

It is not surprising that a common theme of discussion is food and the wherewithal to purchase it, in communities which have moved out of the simpler subsistence mode of production into production of commodities for sale and depend upon goods which money can buy to survive, including daily food. And these are people for whom expenditure on food requires daily transactions and decisions. Food is a perishable commodity which must be bought in the market daily and it is a basic norm in each of the communities described that husbands should be ultimately responsible for its provision. But as we see, they are often unable or unwilling to fulfil this obligation in the desired manner, and wives play varying parts.

A notable feature of the studies is the energetic and dedicated work roles of both women and men. The market women of West Africa have been rightly famous for their industry, power, flamboyance and marketing abilities. Indeed their control of retail trade has led them in some countries and time-periods to be the national scapegoats in periods of scarcity of desired commodities, both local foods and imported manufactured goods.

In Part Two the women traders described in detail were the unseen traders who buy and sell from the privacy of their own homes and who can only continue to ply their trade through employing the services of their own and fostered children as go-betweens. In Part Three we have been given insights into the lives and strategies of women fishmongers in particular, seeing how they control the trade in fish from coastal villages to inland towns in Ghana and how they are linked by ties of marriage, kinship and credit to the men who catch the fish, who are their husbands, brothers, sons and lovers. A significant fact emphasised in these accounts is that women have no right, and do not expect, to be totally maintained by their husbands. They have to work to support themselves and their children.

The other important category of workers are the food growers and cash croppers and the case described here has been that of Ashanti cocoa farmers and growers of plantain and cocoa yam, staple foods in the tropical rain forest. In this account we were given an important indication of the potential effects of shifts to a cash economy on the relative resource balance of the sexes, a theme taken up again in subsequent chapters.

Female–Male Power

A recurrent theme in all the case studies so far has been the relative control over critical resources and power over others exercised by men and women, through their roles in political affairs, ritual activities, ownership and allocation of productive resources and channels of communication, or circulation of goods or control of labour. Within the West African region we assume that the power relationships between men and women are variable from one culture to another and that the relative power and resources of each will be subject to alteration over time, consequent upon their changing access to scarce resources and opportunities. Another factor to bear in mind is one which several observers have stressed: that a male monopoly of prestigious public roles and resources may only give an appearance of male dominance. The reality of female power may be pervasive.

Again it is frequently reiterated that the processes of modernisation, Westernisation and development in countries currently attempting to industrialise are detrimental to women and that relatively egalitarian situations have changed into contexts of male dominance and female dependence. It has, moreover, been contended that women's status in sub-Saharan Africa has been seriously undermined by colonial policies in the past (Etienne and Leacock, 1980, p. 7). In Parts Four and Five some of these themes will be taken up. First we shall look at some of the changes occurring in availability of scarce resources and see whether there can be said to be a male bias.

Part Four

Resources and Opportunities: Male Bias?

Introduction to Part Four

In this series of case studies the focus is upon critical resources and opportunities in the modern world, including political power and office; domestic authority and ability to make household decisions; and access to training and desirable employment and to income and social support.

Political Roles

In Chapter 14 Kamene Okonjo considers the traditional political systems of three large ethnic groups in Nigeria, the Hausa, Igbo and Yoruba, and describes how women as well as men had official roles of power and prestige, in contrast to the present-day situation in which women are largely marginal to national politics. The process of marginalisation is seen to have begun during the colonial era, when the female political roles were ignored and even systematically destroyed, a process which was not unique to Nigeria and which has been perpetuated in the present day.

Education, Training and Employment

In Chapter 15 Carol Martin looks at how young women aged 18–24 who have been to primary school obtain employment in the private sector and what training and other factors appear to influence this process. The views of government planners and employers are also considered and their perceptions contrasted with those of the potential employees.

Domestic Authority and Ideology

It is Wambui Karanja's contention in Chapter 16 that men in Lagos play a dominant role in the domestic domain as well as outside the home, which is supported by customary norms regarding authority. Her evidence of reports of decision-making tend to support her. There are, however, differences according to the relative resources in terms of education and levels of employment of the spouses which remain to be further explored.

In Chapter 17 Nimrod Asante-Darko and Sjaak van der Geest have examined the portrayal of women and men in Ghanaian highlife songs. They argue that the views on love and marital problems expressed in them often serve as ideological charters, expressing the male point of view and supporting an ideology of male supremacy. They conclude, however, that this male dominance is only a facade which enables women to retain power and independence in more hidden domains.

Factory Workers

In Chapters 18 and 19 we shift to wage employment in urban factories described by Eugenia Date-Bah for Accra and Catherine di Domenico for Ibadan. In the process of technological change many of the things formerly being made at home as well as new products are now starting to be made in urban factories. In the cases described it is mainly clothes and processed foods and cigarettes and matches. As in most newly industrialising countries around the world, women form a minority of this new workforce and they work with certain drawbacks less apparent among their male colleagues. They are shouldering larger burdens of domestic and parental responsibilities, for they are mainly mothers as well as workers. Thus it is not surprising to see that in one case they are being discriminated against in employment opportunities and being phased out of the workforce because of their too frequent maternity leaves.

E. Boserup (1970, pp. 112–13) asked the question over a decade ago: 'Why is it that we find so few women among the industrial workers when there are so many among the independent producers and home industries?' She went on to explain that for one reason or another most employers tend to prefer male labour, and di Domenico describes how this process is taking place in Ibadan. Even factories which formerly employed many women are gradually phasing them out.

Eugenia Date-Bah examines some aspects of relationships and differences between men and women workers in a garment factory in Accra. The major difference in their lives is the expected one. The women have to cope with heavy burdens of housework and child care in addition to their factory work, with the result that they are more often late or absent from work than their male counterparts. Furthermore the close ties obtaining between female supervisors and staff inhibits the former from playing the appropriate disciplinary role in the workplace.

Social Contacts

In the concluding chapter of Part Four Margaret Peil examines survey data from several urban contexts in Nigeria and The Gambia. According to the quantified data items assembled and analysed, women appear to be more prone to relative social isolation and dependence upon males, especially husbands, than is the case for men.

Chapter 14

Sex Roles in Nigerian Politics

KAMENE OKONJO

The role of women in community and state governments has been variously interpreted by students of African societies in the past. On the one hand it has been minimised,[1] and on the other African women have been portrayed as traditionally holding high positions and having high statuses within their communities.[2] Using historical and contemporary Nigerian data this chapter illustrates how women held very high political posts in the traditional community organisations of three large ethnic groups, the Hausa, Yoruba and Igbo, among whom there are seen to have been specific political roles to be played by both women and men.

The colonial era disturbed the functioning of these traditional institutions by suppressing them and imposing alien systems.[3] Women are seen to have suffered more from these changes than men, for having enjoyed their political roles in earlier traditional forms of organisation, they discovered themselves under colonialism systematically excluded from any participation in the new systems which the intruding colonial powers had hastily formulated and which ignored their customary roles.[4] We shall see how this occurred first among the Hausa, then among the Yoruba and finally among the Igbo. Subsequently, the present diminished political role of women, and their increasing political marginalisation in Nigeria today is perceived as largely due to the introduction into the country of a type of political system following British colonial rule which has effectively displaced the traditional ones with their roles for both sexes. In this regard the effects of the anti-feminist bias of alien religions, Christianity and Islam, is also mentioned.

The Case of the Hausa

There is evidence that at least until almost the end of the fifteenth century the status of women in Hausa society was very high, one factor being that the culturally dominant people belonged to a civilisation characterised by matrilineal succession in the ruling class, and women held high political office. For example, in the fifteenth century Queen Amina of Zaria, after succeeding to her father's throne on his death, conquered all the towns around Zaria as far as Kwarafa and Nupe, and dominated these regions for thirty-four years. In fact the introduction of fortifications into Hausaland is attributed to her (Palmer, 1928, p. 109).

Although Islam had reached the Hausa states by the fourteenth century, it made slow progress and was usually practised only by foreign communities settled in the towns and a few of the Hausa rulers. Islam therefore functioning as a class religion in the Hausa city states did not gain a hold upon the Hausa cultivators, the Hausa being mainly cultivators, skilful artisans in leather and matting work and enterprising traders, until after the Fulbe conquest of the Hausa over the period 1802–17.[5] By 1900, when the British took control of northern Nigeria, some 50 per cent of the Hausa were animists, although by 1959 Islam had spread so rapidly that some 75–80 per cent of the Hausa had become Muslim. Large blocks of animists collectively known as Azna or Maquzawa still survive, but they are coming more and more under Islamic pressure (Trimingham, 1959, p. 16).

Thus although as early as 1485 the ruling monarch in Kano, Muhamad Rimfa (1463–99) had established the custom of *kulle* – wife seclusion (Palmer, 1928, p. 112) – both Muslim and pagan women in the Hausa city states enjoyed considerable freedom and high social status. This was especially true in the case of the Muslim women because all Hausa women were economically independent of their husbands. Being responsible for the maintenance of their children, they engaged in commercial activities in order to enable them to do this. With the progressive Islamisation of Hausa society following the Fulbe conquest of 1802–17, the unstable nature of the period, the increasing sexual laxity and the greater use of concubines by men which accompanied it, respectable citizens felt forced to adopt strict seclusion and segregation of the sexes in order to protect women from unwelcome male attentions. Islam now invested the husband with absolute authority to decide where the conjugal home could be, which often led to conflict where matrilocal customs existed, and with the progressive seclusion of women and the loss of their freedom to engage in economic activities they became more and more dependent on the men, with their obligations being confined exclusively to domestic work (Trimingham, 1959, pp. 117, 176, 189). And without an economic base women could hardly influence politics. Moreover, I would argue that the influence of Islam on the participation of women in traditional Hausa politics has been one of depoliticisation.

The transitional colonial period for the Hausa started with the Fulbe conquest. Subsequently, far from liberating Hausa society from Fulani religious, economic and political domination, British colonialism, which followed in 1900, through its policy of indirect rule confirmed this domination and permitted the expansion of Islam. This had deleterious effects on the participation of women in political and economic life; for the habits of the nobles and wealthy in the towns, in adopting the institution of purdah, spread to the poorer peasants in the rural areas, with the progressive Islamisation of Hausa society. In these circumstances the participation of women in Hausa politics was minimal. Only a very few cases of women participating in politics in northern Nigeria are recorded during the colonial period. One such case was the nomination of two members, the Sagi and the Niniwaye, to the Bida Town Council in 1937 (Hogben and Kirke Green, 1966, p. 279).

The position of the Hausa prostitute, (*karuwai*), especially in the Hausa diaspora in southern Nigeria, is in marked contrast to the seclusion of the majority of Hausa women from current politics: prostitutes being, it must be noted, 'the freest, most versatile and often the best educated women in Islamic West Africa (Trimingham, 1959, p. 178). Since the institution of prostitution freed many women from their natal settlements in the north and rendered them mobile within the Hausa diaspora, they thus became a fundamental source of Hausa housewives for the pioneering men (A. Cohen, 1971, pp. 266–81).

In some of these settlements like the Sabo settlement at Ibadan there is an officially installed 'chieftainess' who attends to the welfare of these women. With the introduction of party politics to the settlements in 1950, the prostitutes organised themselves in separate branches of the two major southern Nigeria parties – the NCNC and the Action Group – and in contrast to the housewives 'barred' from public life, they have been very active politically, registering their names on voters' lists and casting their votes in federal, regional and municipal elections (A. Cohen, 1963, p. 63).

On the other hand, the influence of Western education so far has been to encourage educated Hausa women to challenge the present socio-political status of women in northern Nigeria, and a few Hausa women hold important positions in their states and hold them creditably. However, as I have argued, the two colonial dominations and the introduction of Islam and wife seclusion have led to a restricted and segregated role for women, very different from that portrayed in early myth and legend. At the present time the women apparently most free to assume chiefly office and to play a part in national politics are those unfettered by conjugal obligations.

Women's Participation in Politics among the Yoruba and the Edo

The Yoruba and the Edo are taken together, since they are geo-graphically neighbours and were from 1954 to 1963 both grouped in what was then the Western Region. Before the advent of British rule in the later part of the nineteenth and earlier part of the twentieth centuries both the Yoruba and the Edo had established empires – the Yoruba under the powerful hegemony of Oyo, an empire which can be traced back to the sixteenth century, while the Edo empire, with its capital at Benin City, has a history that pre-dates the tenth century. Politics in these empires was centred essentially on the king in his capital and his palace.

The Oyo political organisation was built on a system of checks and balances centring on the *alafin* (the king), with his administration, comprising a complex hierarchy of priests, lineage chiefs, military leaders, lieutenants and judges. Watching over all the administration were the *alafin's* many wives, who acted as his eyes and ears and as his secret service in the course of their trading activities throughout the empire.

Among these 'Ladies of the Palace', as they were called, who contributed to the smooth functioning of the political machinery, there were eight titled ladies and eight priestesses. Of the eight titled ladies of very high rank four deserve special mention. First, there was the Iya Oba, who was the king's 'official' mother – the king's biological mother, if she was still alive, being quietly 'put to sleep' on her son's accession to the throne; secondly, the Iya Kere wielded the greatest power and authority in the palace, being the custodian of the palace treasures including the royal insignia and the king's para-phernalia of office, as well as being responsible for crowning the king in the coronation ceremony. Her position was one of great political significance, because as custodian of the royal regalia she could sabotage any of the king's public appearances by refusing to allow him the use of his garments of office, especially if there was dissatisfaction with him and his leadership. A third very powerful political figure was the Iyalagbon – the mother of the crown prince – who, like the king, wielded great authority and ruled over a part of the capital city. The fourth of these important ladies of the palace was the Iyamode, who was responsible for the king's spiritual well-being. Her function was to guard the graves of departed kings and to act as an intercessionary and intermediary between the living king and the spirits of his dead predecessors. The king's unprecedented respect for her exalted position was evident in the manner in which he addressed her, calling her 'baba' (father), since she was the official representative of the departed kings, and saluting her on his knees. No other human being enjoyed that honour (Johnson, 1966, pp. 63–7).

This group of women formed an effective group of spokeswomen for political stability and humane rule, as well as for the interest of women at the highest political level in the kingdom, bound up as their lives were with that of the ruling monarch, with whom they were expected to depart to the land of the spirits in the event of his death.

The generality of Yoruba women are also known to have established in the pre-colonial period very effective political pressure-groups, through which the political authorities were persuaded to attend to issues which were of immediate concern to women or deal with broader political issues. There is evidence that this practice continued in the Yoruba kingdoms until shortly after 1914, when with the amalgamation of the northern and southern Nigeria protectorates into the Colony and Protectorate of Nigeria, Nigeria passed formally under British colonial rule (Fadipe, 1970, p. 253). It should therefore be evident that traditional Yoruba society accorded women high political status and permitted the participation of women in politics at all levels. Moreover it is erroneous to believe that the socio-political status of women was depressed in traditional Yoruba society. In fact it is my thesis that the depressed status of women in politics developed after the imposition of British colonial rule.

The high socio-political status of women in traditional Yoruba society can also be observed in Edo society. There, for example, the queen-mother always received the title Iyoba from her son, the king, three years after his ascension to the throne and was thereafter sent to Uselu (a part of the kingdom) where she reigned as the Iyoba of Uselu and sat in the king's executive council as one of his four most senior and important chiefs. This practice of installing a queen-mother, who then participated in the running of the affairs of the Benin kingdom, was begun by Oba (King) Esigie. In 1506 Esigie installed his mother, Queen-Mother Idia, who was reputed to be politically shrewd, warlike and to have helped her son win a war against the Idah kingdom, as the first Iyoba of Uselu. This custom continued until 1889 when the British, as one of their first steps on conquering the kingdom of Benin, abolished the post of Iyoba and refused the installation of the new Iyoba (Egharevba, 1968, pp. 75–6). But tradition has, since the end of colonial rule, partially reasserted itself; and the political eminence of Queen-Mother Idia has lately been recognised by the government of Bendel State, Nigeria, which has named the first girls' secondary school in Benin City, established and owned by the government of the state, after her.

The transitional phase in Yoruba and Edo political evolution, ushered in by the imposition of the 'Pax Britannica' and British colonial rule at one fell stroke, eliminated women from their exalted institutional positions in traditional politics, replacing the traditional political system by a Western-oriented system in which women had no place. A new female political elite perforce emerged, establishing themselves through their success in colonial commerce by acting mostly as factors to the foreign commercial companies. One such Yoruba woman was Madam Tinubu, a truly outstanding woman by any standards, who won herself wealth, position and power through trade in slaves and tobacco with Brazil. Because of her position she fought, with success, for the return and reinstatement of Oba Akitoye, the exiled Oba of Lagos, following the British seizure of Lagos in 1861, and thereafter she became the power behind the throne of Lagos, a role which she continued to play until Akitoye died and his son, Dosunmu, became king. Her political power was so great that she was seen as a threat by some prominent chiefs in Lagos, who appealed to the British colonial administration in Lagos to remove her. The British complied, and she was banished from Lagos to Abeokuta, the capital of the then independent kingdom of the Egba to the north of the colony of Lagos. She quickly established herself as the political and military power behind the throne of Egba-land and, through successful trading in guns and gunpowder, played a key role in organising the successful defence of Egbaland against the kingdom of Dahomey in the 1860s. Understandably, the Egba rewarded her for her activities in the war with the title of Iyalode (First Lady) of Egbaland (Biobaku, 1960).

The colonial era proper also threw up its own female political activists in Yorubaland. A good example was Mrs Funmilayo Ransome-Kuti, who died recently. She made an impact on the political life of Egbaland, and with independence continued her political activities. As head of the Nigerian Women's Union, she led the women of Egbaland in the 1940s in revolt against the taxation of women by the Abeokuta local authority and forced the then Alake of Abeokuta, the king of Egbaland, into temporary self-exile (Sklar, 1963, p. 251).

With the introduction of party politics in 1950, Yoruba women became active politically, organising women's wings of political parties. With the end of colonial rule and the achievement of independence in 1960, it would be expected that their political potentialities would acquire new dimensions since they had obtained the right to vote and to be voted for.

Yet they have not benefited as women in the exercise of this their right, for not one female was voted in as an elected representative of the people in the Nigerian national legislature during the decade 1950–60. The record of the political parties in this respect was dismal, despite the undoubted activity of women in forming women's wings of political parties and on election day helping to mobilise both men and women to vote. Of the two major southern political parties operating in Yorubaland then, which admitted that women had a right to participate in politics (the Northern People's Congress did not), only the Action Group was prepared to nominate women candidates in the pre-independence federal election of 1959. Its candidate, Mrs Wuraola Esan, lost her fight. In the case of the NCNC the party refused to nominate Mrs Ransome Kuti of Egba fame, who had been an NCNC women's wing organiser and leader, and instead gave the nomination to a man who had once been a clerk in the school where Mrs Kuti's husband had been headmaster. She contested as an independent and lost (Post, 1963, pp. 264–5).

We turn now to the third major Nigerian ethnic group: the Igbo.

Women and Politics in Eastern and Mid-Western Nigeria – the Case of the Igbo

The Igbo live mainly in Anambra and Imo States. With this ethnic group we encounter perhaps the most illustrative example of women's traditional participation in the political lives of their communities. Frequently characterised as aggressive, frank and ambitious, the Igbo (especially those on the eastern side of the Niger) have a political system which can be said to belong to the segmentary category (Fortes and Evans-Pritchard, eds, 1940). It does, however, have some centralised administrative and judicial institutions and cleavages of wealth and status corresponding to the distribution of power and authority (Jones, 1963, p. 4).[6] Leadership was achieved, not ascribed, and authority was dispersed widely within each autonomous unit, so that it is not easy to single out any particular individual (male or female) who played an outstanding role as is the case among the Hausa, Yoruba and Edo. Afigbo (1972, pp. 13–26) points out that these segmentary political systems also depend, for the regulation of political affairs between territorial segments, on non-kinship associations such as title and secret societies, with each equivalent segment within the federation of equivalent segments that constitute the central goverment within each autonomous unit retaining a large measure of power and authority and regarding as binding only those decisions to which it has given its assent. Afigbo further distinguishes two types of these political systems: the 'constitutional village monarchy' type, to be found among the riverine and western Igbo, and the 'democratic village republic' type to be found among the rest of the Igbo – both systems characterised by the small size of the political units, the wide dispersal of political authority among the sexes, lineages and kinship institutions, age-grades, secret and title societies, oracles and diviners and other professional groups, the lack of clear separation between judicial, executive and legislative functions, and lastly the lack of distinction between the political and the religious in the governmental process.

In both types of political system each sex generally managed its own affairs and had its own kinship institutions, age-grades, secret and title societies. Independent evidence exists of this right of women to manage their affairs in traditional Igbo society. Sylvia Leith-Ross, the British government anthropologist, writing in 1939, observed that Igbo women were politically and economically the equal of Igbo men and that such industrious, ambitious and independent women were bound to play a leading role in the development of their country. She had been astounded at the way Igbo women had organised and accomplished 'a movement as original, and formidable as the Aba Riots, known to them as the Women's War, which necessitated the calling in of military forces before order could be restored and the subsequent appointment of a Commission of Enquiry' (Leith-Ross, 1965, pp. 19–20). Her impressions were that, more than the men, the women seemed to be able to co-operate and to stand by each other even in difficulties and to follow a common aim.

Although the Women's War took place during the colonial era and was a protest against the rumoured taxation of women and the excesses of the indirect rule system in Igboland, the socio-political factors which made an organised protest embracing an area of about 520 sq. km possible are to be sought for in a traditional structure, which recognized the rights of Igbo women, to manage their own affairs.[7] Although in Igbo political history, as is the case in the political history of most of Africa, it is not easy to ascertain the exact dimensions of women's political powers, yet it is obvious from their elevated socio-political status at the turn of the century, when Nigeria came under British rule, that Igbo women enjoyed a great deal of political independence and that they had their own women's councils which enacted laws.

Prominent among the institutions evolved by women in both types of political system for the running of their affairs were the *ikporo-ani*, the *umu-ada* and the *inyemedi*. The *inyemedi* (wives of a lineage), comprised of all women married to men of one lineage, was responsible for settling all disputes between the wives of that lineage. In meetings of the *inyemedi*, the *anasi* – the most senior wife in terms of length of marriage to a man of the lineage – presides. Disputes of a more serious nature, or infractions by women of sexual morality as in cases of adultery, or disputes between lineages, villages, or village groups, were dealt with by the *umu-ada* comprising the widowed, married and unmarried daughters of a lineage, village, or village group. Because of the lineage exogamy practised in Igboland, the married daughters acted as arbiters between their natal lineage, villages, or village groups, and the lineages, villages and village groups into which they were married, and were thus able to prevent wars. They also took a keen interest in the local politics of their natal lineage and village and, when necessary, took a common stand on an issue, forcing the political authorities of their villages to implement their wishes or demands. The *ikporo-ani*, on the other hand, was made up of all the adult women in a village or village group and consulted and took decisions on all matters which affected the generality of women.

Peculiar to the 'constitutional village monarchy' type of political system to be found among the riverine and western Igbo is the female institution of *O*mu. The *O*mu has been styled 'queen' of the village or village group, since her role in society closely parallels that of the king, but the *O*mu is neither the king's wife nor his relative. She is simply the 'female counterpart of the king' in his role as father of the community, or the traditional 'mother' of the village or village group.

As the official mother of her society, the *O*mu, usually a woman distinguished by her wealth, intellect and character, has responsibility for the affairs of the women of the community and presides at meetings of the *ikporo-ani*. She selects her own counsellors just as the king (Obi) does and with identical titles, and reigns from a throne just as he does. She also had the right to don the colonial-type white helmet, felt hat, or red cap (in *O*nitsha) to signify her political equality with her male peers. Since her major political function centred on women's affairs, and since trading was a major social and economic function of women in traditional Igbo society, she and her counsellors reigned supreme in the markets – fixing prices of goods, settling quarrels arising in the market and imposing fines if and where necessary. To her also fell the duty of acting as a court of law for all cases involving women, encouraging traditional title-taking among women and cleansing and releasing widows from protracted mourning. She and her counsellors acted as custodians of the welfare of the village or village group, performing propitiatory rites and sacrifices, when necessary, in order to ensure the welfare of the village or village group and its markets as well as to prevent the occurrence of epidemics and wars.

It is not surprising in the light of its action in abolishing the post and title of Iyoba of Uselu after conquering Benin in 1889, that the British colonial administration either failed to see or, having seen, refused to recognise, the political institutions evolved by Igbo women for their governance. Conditioned by their experience to seek in their newly acquired territories for a social organism which would evolve into the Western European type of nation-state, and regarding the Igbo with their segmentary political system as acephalous, primitive and stateless, the British sought to create an administration modelled after the emirates of northern Nigeria which had formed the basis of the famous system of indirect rule. However, they did not find in the democratic political system of the Igbo political figures equivalent to the emir, district and village heads in northern Nigeria. So the colonial government proceeded to create and appoint warrant chiefs without consulting the Igbo, and to introduce a native administration system in which the warrant chiefs played a primary role. It is not surprising to find that the warrant chief and native administration system as proposed by the British proved unacceptable to the Igbo. The failure of indirect rule in eastern Nigeria, the collapse of the warrant chief system and the success of the revolt of the women in 1929 known as the 'Women's War' all point to the unsatisfactory nature of the colonial solution.

Not integrated into the new male-dominated colonial framework of politics, Igbo women suffered a dimunition in their collective participation in politics during the transitional colonial period. Yet, as in the case of the Yoruba, new leaders emerged through achieving outstanding success in colonial commerce. These new leaders attempted to unite in their persons traditional political power and colonial political influence. A case in point is the famed Madam Okwei of Onitsha and Ossomari, otherwise known as Omu Okwei (1872–1943). Using her wealth acquired in her trading with foreign merchant companies to acquire political power, she engineered the appointment of her husband as a member of the Onitsha native court – a position of considerable political importance in the colonial administration of the period. She finally became the Omu of Ossomari, functioning in her role of Omu as 'foreign minister' or 'ambassador-at-large' between her people, the foreign commercial firms and the British colonial administration. She held her post of Omu so creditably that she is still regarded by many as the greatest Omu in Ossomari political history.

In the period of the transfer of power from the British colonial administration to the hands of local politicians in the decade 1950–60 women participated in party politics in eastern Nigeria, mobilising the women and organising women's wings of political parties. Again as in western Nigeria, despite their acknowledged activities, which benefited their parties immensely, they were not accorded the recognition which they deserved.[8] Thus in the seven years of post-independence civilian politics not one woman was elected into any of the national or regional legislatures, although the southern parties attempted to correct this situation by appointing their party faithfuls to various legislatures.[9]

Conclusion

In this brief review of politico-religious roles in the three largest ethnic groups of the most populous nation in West Africa, I have shown how in each case in these societies there have traditionally been certain specific roles reserved for women and for men. Both sexes have had their own recognised spheres of power and influence. But I have pointed out that with the imposition of colonial rule women's active participation in the political life of their communities diminished, a situation reinforced by the generally anti-feminine prejudices of many followers of Christianity and Islam.

It has been indicated that the current male-dominated nature of national politics, itself only a slight modification of the imported prototype of a Western representative governmental model, continues to stifle women's participation in politics in the Nigerian setting; while national leaders, unconsciously seeking for solutions to a felt but unrecognised problem, appoint women to posts at the highest political level, by-passing the established political machinery. I have further shown the strong nature of the indigenous political systems, incorporating female and male roles, which have continued to flourish at the local and sub-national levels, despite the non-integration of women in politics at the national level in their own right.

Notes: Chapter 14

1 For example, the Ottenbergs (eds, 1969, pp. 48–9) minimised the role of women in their popular overview.
2 See Bohannan and Curtin (1971, pp. 107–8): 'African women by and large have a high social position, legal rights, religious and political responsibility, economic independence. Women in Africa are not, in short, a deprived group as they were in the nineteenth-century Western world.' See also Afigbo, 1974, pp. 2–4.
3 cf. Lebeuf, 1963, p. 94, and Van Allen, 1972.
4 As Lebeuf wrote: 'Completely swept aside by this new development, they found that both the material and the psychological basis upon which their authority had rested had crumbled, and that gradually their privileges were disappearing.'
5 So Barth, writing in 1857, was able to observe: 'It is evident that the larger portion of the population all over Hausa, especially that of the country town and villages, remained addicted to paganism till the fanatic zeal of their conquerors the Fulbe forced them to profess Islam, at least publicly' (p. 118).
6 Meek (1937, p. 3) describes the characteristic feature of Igbo society as the 'almost complete absence of any higher political or social unit than the commune or small group of contiguous villages whose customs and cults are identical and whose sense of solidarity is so strong that they regard themselves as descendants of a common ancestor.' See also Green, 1964, pp. 3–5.
7 For a fuller discussion of the causes of the Women's War (Ogu Umunwanyi), otherwise known in Nigeria colonial literature as the Aba Riots, see Afigbo, 1972, pp. 207–48.
8 Mrs Margaret Ekpo, the dynamic leader of the women's wing of the NCNC in eastern Nigeria, sought but failed to obtain her party's nomination in order to stand as its candidate in the Aba urban constituency. Mrs R. T. Brown who was nominated by the Action Group to contest in Port Harcourt lost the election, while Mrs M. R. Nwogu, who stood as an independent in the Orlu South Eastern constituency, also lost.

9 In this way Mrs Margaret Ekpo (NCNC, eastern Nigeria), Mrs Kerri (NCNC, mid-west), Mrs Janet Mokelu (NCNC, eastern Nigeria) and Mrs Elizabeth Adekogbe (Action Group, western Nigeria) were all appointed to the Senate, the upper house in Lagos. This trend was continued in the East Central State by the appointment of Mrs Flora Nwakuch as Commissioner in the military government of that state. This was followed by the appointment of a woman lawyer as the Attorney-General of Anambra State when the East Central State was divided into the two states of Anambra and Imo following the political reorganisation of 1976. She however resigned this august appointment soon afterwards, 'for personal reasons'.

Chapter 15

Skill-Building or Unskilled Labour for Female Youth: a Bauchi Case

CAROL MARTIN

In West African societies, as well as globally, women have long lagged behind men in educational attainment and skill training as the statistics in Chapter 1 demonstrated. This lag has been somewhat offset by the entry of young women into the private informal labour sector, where they have sought their livelihood as well as acquired work skills as was shown in Chapter 2. Meanwhile, influenced by the expansion in basic education, the private labour sector is increasingly requiring that workers have certain intermediate skills, such as literacy and some technical or managerial knowledge. Yet for most females primary education is terminal, and it is producing thousands of young women searching interminably for jobs as an alternative to further education. To compound the situation further, as the private sector expands, training schemes and the allocation of jobs have tended to favour males, equally desperate in their search for a livelihood.

Social constraints as well as limited access to education advancement have essentially entrenched women in the marginal confines of the labour market. For social restrictions defining women's roles in society not only pervade planners' perceptions, but may also lend some bias to private sector employers, faced with choosing helpful employees among the hordes of female and male job-seekers.

The example of Nigeria can be taken to demonstrate the characteristics surrounding women's vocational training and employment. Nigeria's universal primary education scheme (UPE), launched in 1976 to give children equal access to basic literacy, will have enrolled an estimated 14·1 million youth by 1982, of which 2·1 million will graduate in that year ('Blueprint. . . ' 1979, p. 2127).[1] For those who do not go to post-primary institutions, the national Third Develop-

ment Plan 1975–80 projects that only a third of primary school leavers will actually join both wage and non-wage employment sectors
(Anaza, 1975). The remaining 66 per cent will be cast into unemployment.[2] Mindful of the fact that only 15–20 per cent of the female
primary school graduates are given the opportunity to acquire further
education in Nigeria, the projected unemployment rate will mostly
affect the young women, some of whom eventually migrate into marginal areas of self-employment and wage labour. For instance,
according to the 1963 national census, Nigeria had a total labour
force of 18·3 million of which 13·9 million were males and 4·4 million
were females (United Nations Economic Commission for Africa,
1973, p. 2). Lending further evidence to this limited opportunity
structure, Unesco has projected that the discrepancies between male
and female enrolments in primary and secondary level education in
West Africa will increase by 1985, in spite of the relative increases in
female primary school enrolments (Unesco, *Statistical Yearbook 1977*,
p. 37). Women's education in Nigeria appears to be no exception.

The current educational expansion and subsequent implications for
women's further training and entry into employment can be exemplified in the case of Bauchi State in northern Nigeria. A new state,[3]
carved in 1976 from the formerly large Northeastern State, Bauchi
State between 1972 and 1979 increased its enrolment of females in
the primary school system by over 900 per cent, thanks to the UPE
scheme, but female enrolments still only increased from 30 per cent
to 38 per cent of the total. However impressive these increases may
be, access to post-primary education institutions is still only available
to 15 per cent of the female UPE graduates, a quota set in 1974.
Also, having tried a coeducational system at first, the state has now
adopted sex-segregated education at the post-primary levels. Given
financial as well as these policy constraints, the extent to which
women's general education and vocational training can be developed
poses a real question. In the meantime, the 85 per cent of young
literate women not placed in schools find their way into the labour
market, sometimes in search of opportunities missed or denied elsewhere.

This chapter focuses on how young women acquire employment
and the factors, including training, influencing their success or failure.
It also discusses perceptions of government planners and private
employers towards women's access to training and employment.

First, the private sector is examined as it relates to Nigerian
women's economic activities. The discussion does not include the
public sector, which usually requires higher school qualifications that
eliminate most primary school leavers. Secondly, the educational and
training opportunities open to women in northern Nigeria are briefly
indicated. Thirdly, a case study of selected working and non-working

women in Bauchi State is discussed, in particular their patterns of job acquisition. The perceptions of planners from ministries in that state and from ten private sector employers are discussed and, where possible, related to the women's experience.

The Private Labour Market

Participation in the informal private labour sector has been one redeeming alternative in the otherwise limited structure of educational opportunity that exists for women in Nigeria.

It offers extensive possibilities for casual self-employment. Analysts have positively characterised this labour sector for its ease of entry, low capital outlay, ability to generate reasonable levels of earnings, and its capacity to teach skills through structured, informal apprenticeships (King, 1977; Sethuraman, 1977; Steel, 1977). It displays a shock-absorbing effect by allowing the school leaver – the 'sub-proletariat' of youth – to enter this non-wage sector for temporary relief. Females tend to predominate in the lower-income groups, according to several studies conducted by the International Labour Organisation (ILO).

While the private sector does offer women opportunities for real income-producing activities, it also has limitations affecting women. According to Standing (1976), the private sector has created a 'sexual dualism' brought about by industrialisation and urbanisation in the market place. This dualism has relegated the less-educated women to peripheral, intermittent secondary jobs. For instance, 'traditional' crafts mostly involve women in the low-technology areas of pottery-making, spinning and petty trading, whereas the technical trades and administrative jobs have been assumed by men since colonial times. Since women's crafts are less mechanised than men's crafts, they earn the label of being less 'modern' (Koll, 1969). In the northern Nigerian context, such a dual job pattern has been characteristic. Remy's study (1975, pp. 359–62) revealed that women's home industries in Zaria are undermined by competition from manufactured products. Men able to accumulate capital from wage employment could invest it in more technical trade and craft production. Access to economic opportunity was further constrained by the prevailing belief that a woman's economic activities should be confined to the domestic sphere. One noted example of domestic productivity which is exclusively female-dominated and comprises much of women's income-generating activities is food-processing (e.g. Simmons, 1975).

While Muslim women are largely excluded from field agriculture, women's general participation in industry continues to lag (Steel, 1977). Women's low-income status is further perpetuated by beliefs that child-care responsibilities prevent them from maintaining the regular, full-time working hours required in modern industry. Also, the presumption that men should be the primary income-earners favours the development of training programmes for them (Steel, 1977, pp. 10–11). The structural inequalities in women's employment become a vicious circle, in turn regulating the opportunity levels open to young women. Better training programmes lead to more modernised ways of producing goods and services, and more modernisation tends to loosen cultural constraints. Yet women have usually been excluded from participating in those sectors which undergo more progressive change. Instead, their sectors are deprived of any modernising interventions. An examination of training opportunities for women reveals the familiar dearth of preparation for such modernisation and, hence, the predominance of women in private 'marginal' sectors of development.

Training Opportunities

Training worldwide for the basically literate woman has traditionally focused on her social (as opposed to economic) role as a reproducer and on family management, home economics and rural life skills. This trend has tended to produce social elites rather than producers of goods and services hardened by gut experiences of modern labour markets, realities.

One explanation for this pattern and for parents' basic reluctance to send girls to school is that they prefer that their daughters learn crafts at home in preparation for early marriage. Also, education takes valuable labour away from mothers in seclusion, who use their daughters to dispatch goods made in the home for sale to the public as Enid Schildkrout has described in Chapter 7.

Apart from traditional literacy classes, the Women's Programme Unit of UNECA (United Nations Economic Commission for Africa, 1973, p. 45) has cited a paucity of women's programmes in the north-eastern part of Nigeria. Vocational training centres predominately emphasise male trades. Craft centres and only one secondary level polytechnical school admit girls, who specialise mostly in commercial and secretarial subjects, needlecraft and home economics.

These training programmes prepare women principally for government public sector employment, but we have already noted that the majority of Nigerian women are actually self-employed in the private sector. In 1965 only 7·2 per cent of the total wage employment population of the public sector were women. In contrast, a 1966/7 sample survey of industrial distribution showed 62 per cent of economically active women in agriculture (mainly in the south) 14 per cent in manufacturing and 22 per cent in commerce (ibid., p. 46). Significantly, these are occupations for which women were *not* trained but which offer a ready opportunity for them to make economic gain. This is due largely to the alacrity with which Nigeria's unrestricted private sector responds to entrepreneurial activity.

If these employment areas offer labour options to women, why is vocational training generally unavailable to answer such market demands? Are planners and policy-makers aware of the implications of a training policy which draws women into the competitive, dualistic, wage-regulated, formal public sector, yet leaves out those who are actively acquiring skills through experience, as well as an understanding of and value for work itself, within the busy confines of the private sector? Are they also aware of the theme of sex-specificity, which both the labour market and present vocational training schemes associate with women, thereby narrowing women's chances to participate in the wider development processes of the society? Answers quite clearly lie in the women's own experiences of acquiring jobs and training, as well as in the examination of planners' perceptions and training policy. All are inseparably bound to concepts and practices concerning women in the development of their societies.

Women and Work: the Bauchi Case Study

In early 1980, 121 women between the ages of 16 and 24 who had received primary education were asked how they had found income-generating activities and what had appeared to influence this process.[4] Their experiences in obtaining post-primary schooling or training were investigated to see what obstacles were faced in getting further training and how the training they chose to pursue related to work preferences. Working women were selected from both urban and district level settings in Bauchi State according to the work they were doing within eight categories of the private sector known to involve women. Women without significant income-generating activities were also interviewed to provide comparative material. Work activities included agriculture, trade, services, sales, crafts, clerical, small-scale manufacturing and transport and communications.

After leaving primary school, a series of events determines the direction the young woman takes concerning employment acquisition and the establishment of a family. First, an important determinant is whether she passes or fails the Common Entrance Examination, her passport to further education for post-primary placement in a secondary school or teacher training college. Most women indicated a preference to continue their schooling. However, for Muslim girls the preference was considerably subdued since their families generally prepare them for marriage.

Secondly, girls usually remain with their parents on finishing school and engage in household errands and gardening. Half of those interviewed did some form of farming while at home, work in which they still retained a positive interest.

Their reasons given for working were many, though primarily to provide financial contributions for family needs. The women in the urban setting had migrated to the capital either because their husbands' work located them there or because the women, if single, were in search of employment and training. Many took on jobs requiring few skills. For instance, a quarter of the urban-based women interviewed had held two or more jobs since leaving school, three to four years ago. In contrast, the district women conducted income-generating activities sustained by craft skills already learned from either their mothers or the schools. These included mainly sewn products and processed food items.

If further schooling did not appear to be a likely alternative, many of the school leavers looked for work both within and outside of their districts. For the urban women, a mixture of reasons for working emerged ranging from the need for financial independence and financial aid for family and relatives to financing further training. Similarly, the district-based women worked largely for financial reasons and for parental support. Encouragement to work or not to work largely appeared to be a function of parental or conjugal need for financial aid or family preference that daughters establish families. For those who were neither working nor seeking work, the prevalence of family restrictions was the main reason rather than actual labour market constraints. Many of the urban non-working women expressed either a dislike for work, the husband's refusal to allow them to work, or the desire to continue schooling. The second two reasons also may explain why women develop negative attitudes towards work.

Finding work seemed to present more acute difficulties for the urban-based women than for the district-based. People assisting the women to find work were relatives, principally male, parents and friends. Husbands were the main assistants for the married women. While parents offered much encouragement, they were not significant information sources in finding work, or assistants in the application process.

Non-working women gave a variety of reasons for why they were not involved in any income-generating activities. While three-quarters of the urban non-working women (twenty-six in all) said their family situation was not a deterrent to their working, over half were not doing anything to find work. For the ten district women who were not engaged in any income-producing activity, their reasons pertained more to their perceived inabilities, including restrictive husbands and lack of qualifications and job opportunities.

Studies of individual women indicated a strong desire on the part of many to change their vocations. Two significant conclusions arise from these data. One is that work preferences are directed towards the traditionally 'female' occupations, such as teaching, nursing, midwifery and clerical work within the *public* sector. The second point is that training is preferred in an occupation which is not related to the women's present line of work, but which would lead to competence in the familiar trades mentioned above or to the public wage sector. Thus twenty-six of the thirty-seven urban working women wanting to change their work aspired to prestigious public sector jobs. In contrast, the district women preferred more diversified types of work found in both the private and public sectors. In terms of training preferences thirteen of the twenty-two urban working women who had had some training or education beyond primary level wanted to switch to jobs for which they were not trained. Two home-economists-in-training, for instance, expressed preference for nursing and typing; all four drivers-in-training expressed preferences for other work. One teacher did a typing apprenticeship for six months, even worked as a typist, but preferred to continue teaching.

These switches in vocation give evidence that young women may view work which requires no training as a stepping stone to larger opportunities in the public sector. Nevertheless, 70 per cent of the total sample indicated that they hoped to be working in five years' time and 17 per cent hoped to be in school. This tends to refute traditionalists' beliefs that young women merely want to establish families rather than pursue their education and participate in the labour market.

Twenty-six of the thirty women who had further education had started training programmes after considerable investigation, between one and four years after leaving primary school. Most also entered training after they had worked for a while. The completers were those who had undertaken shorter-term, job-specific training of six to twelve months' duration, such as in clerical institutes or as apprentices. Women appear to have divided opinions about the type of training they would prefer to do if given the chance: 42 per cent of the total sample held rather high aspirations to continue with longer-term training taking over three years.

Other factors were found to influence work acquisition among young women, such as employer attitudes, women's organisations, child-rearing responsibilities and their self-image and work performance. Seven urban women interviewed expressed a conscious distrust of employers' attitudes to hiring young women with such remarks as:

It is sometimes hard to find a job if not married.

They really don't want women because they are lazy and always getting pregnant.

Some will like to befriend you sexually before giving you work.

Some officers will want an affair with a working woman.

However, the majority of women thought positively that employers were generally willing to hire, while a third had no opinion.

Ten private sector employers in the urban centre were asked to rank women's work performance.[5] They employed 19 women out of a total of 220 employees. A discrepancy was seen to exist between women's highly positive self-image about their working abilities and employers' relatively negative perceptions of women's working abilities. In contrast, the ten male employers thought women weak in about all of the abilities, the widest discrepancy existing for manual work capacity. One implication of these different perceptions is that working experience seems to reinforce a positive self-image in women, but a clash of interests and aspirations appears to operate between a young woman's perceived chances of meeting employer expectations and the employer's own views about a woman's chance of success.

With regard to the effects of child-raising on work performance, the fifty women with children in the sample confirmed that child-raising responsibilities may frustrate, but not entirely impede, both the continuation of work and the acquisition of training. Urban and district women differed mostly in that the district women felt it less necessary to change to a higher paying job in order to raise additional children, indicating that the level of self-sufficiency gained from self-employment in the rural areas is felt to be adequate for starting a family. Fewer rural women perceived constraints from child-rearing, a factor that could also reflect the need for child labour to help in the mother's catering and trade activities.

Planners' Perceptions and Recommendations

Fifteen planners, three of them women, in six ministries of Bauchi State, discussed how they viewed the private sector's response to the job demands of the female school leaver.[6] The planners differed widely in their views, suggesting that a philosophy or direction of development for this problem had still to be carefully delineated.

Small-scale industry/manufacturing and transport/communications were considered to offer the least opportunities for employing young women, who were thought to be often excluded from small-scale industrial participation because they lack capital and are not ready to take risks.[7]

Some planners thought that clerical work offered few job opportunities since such work required training before employment and only certain minority ethnic groups tend to take up clerical work. Opportunities in other fields, such as trade, services and crafts, were thought by some to be closed to many, due to the system of close family working ties among richer family members successful in these fields. They were of the opinion that most attention was being given to encouraging employment for women in the clerical and service categories.

While agriculture was thought to rank third highest in receiving attention from planners, there are in fact no organised activities for women in agriculture apart from the small percentage of women enrolled in the state's School of Agriculture and Animal Husbandry which takes candidates at the post-secondary school level.[8] Planners emphasised that attention should be given to encouraging women's entry into the labour force in agriculture and small-scale industry. These occupations were supported because they could be considered with domestic work. Likewise, industry was favoured because women were thought to need a work opportunity that does not require a lot of training. Crafts were considered suitable for housewives in purdah. Significantly, themes of isolating women into home-based and female-specific activities appeared to be quite dominant.

With regard to training, the clerical, services and sales categories were viewed as offering the most opportunities and were thought to be areas where women could be easily trained because there were existing facilities.

The availability of schools, programmes and places in specialist schools is actually quite limited in the state, so that the planners' comments were perhaps rather optimistic. For example, the number of female trainees admitted to the state Post and Telegraph Training School is very small. Also, there is no agricultural training or extension for women other than occasional primary school gardening schemes. Those areas believed to offer least opportunities for training young women were agriculture, transport/communications and industry, categories also thought to provide the fewest job opportunities.

A consistent recommendation of the planners was that attention should be given to areas hitherto ignored, including trade/commerce and crafts. Although some planners did not think that child care responsibilities posed a serious obstacle to women's employment, most favoured government establishment of child care facilities over those provided by employers.

Teaching rural life skills through government extension was also strongly recommended, thereby placing more women in extension activities which focused on self-employment. Short courses in specific skills were also highly favoured, because married women with families would be more encouraged to attend, thus making such training more socially acceptable than longer training. Government backing was thought to guarantee the success of the course. Employer involvement could help diminish the usual high rates of employee and trainee drop-outs.

Most planners felt that a deliberate vocational training design for women was needed, segregated from that for men, particularly to promote women's reorientation to the world of work. Only a few planners reiterated that vocational training should not be limited to female jobs only. When asked, those planners were unable to give specific examples of other types of jobs. Many suggested that women's vocational training should teach tailoring and local weaving, home management and poultry-raising, using more modern machinery and techniques. Three to four weeks were considered to be the most suitable duration for courses. Sex-segregated vocational training was thought to be appropriate since coeducation had been ended throughout the state. Planners expressed neutrality in advocating training in the traditional female crafts. These occupations were thought to be neither prestigious nor financially attractive to young women. Nor does such training offer skill diversification for other jobs or a modernised opportunity to compete with non-locally manufactured products.

Employers and Hiring Women Employees

Exploratory discussions were held with ten private sector male employers in Bauchi town. The purpose of the discussions was to solicit their views about hiring young women who have only a basic primary education. As noted earlier, employers tend to rank working women's work performance more negatively than do the women themselves. Employers considered trustworthiness and the ability to take instructions as the most necessary capabilities young women should possess for employment. Employers also demanded the following abilities of a prospective woman employee: write and speak English clearly, salesmanship, politeness, simple accounting skills, some previous work experience and some experience in public relations. They thought the following were barriers to female school leavers' getting employment: lack of skills, inability to speak, read and write English well, lack of seriousness, parental restrictions, immaturity and lack of work experience, and the lack of enough employing establishments to employ the women. Single women were preferred over married women since the latter tended to 'lack concentration due to their matrimonial duties and family problems' and pregnancy. Single women, on the other hand, could 'put in more time to work, overtime', but were less mature than married ones.

Concerning training a novice employee, seven of the ten employers said they could train through an on-the-job apprenticeship or by sponsoring the training if it is short-term. However, most preferred that the woman have had training before taking up employment. Employers suggested that a government-sponsored basic skill training in the various trades should precede any expectation that the private sector absorb the amorphous talents of the unskilled.

As a result, employers' attitudes towards hiring women with a basic education were ambivalent. In this respect, planners had assessed employers' reluctance realistically, though perhaps for different reasons. Employers' views tended to embrace the common stereotype of women as docile workers. While they favourably considered adolescent women as relatively innocent, honest and able to 'take orders', any weakness in women's task performance was viewed as a problem that could be overcome through training.

Planners' expectations also seemed to match employers' dispositions towards collaborating with the public sector for training purposes. Planners felt that as long as the government led the way in financing and planning programmes, some reasonable co-operation would result. However, such co-operation should be short-term and immediately beneficial to the employer.

Perceptual Differences

Interviews and discussions with the three different groups of young women workers and non-workers, government planners and private sector employers brought out the fact that three distinct levels of perceptions about women's employment and training opportunities exist. The women school leavers have perceptions of themselves eventually entering the female-specific trades and professions, taking training for granted. They are also consciously obedient to what their societies expect from them as productive citizens. Women hold perceptions of job market realities marked by success and failure rates usually well known from peer experiences.

For their part, the employers hold perceptions with realistic rigidity. They are not development-oriented but profit-seekers and material exploiters of local resources. The planners act as technical advisers who must respond to information in making their proposals. Yet their perceptions of women's work issues lack contact with realities which the other two groups constantly experience.

One obvious remedy to help planning for women's employment options is training. However, training alone cannot be expected to overcome all the constraints experienced by young women entering the labour market. Social and economic alterations will need to be made, which structurally affect labour market practices, as well as public attitudes and social beliefs about women's skill roles in the labour force.

Conclusion

In spite of the vertical growth of Nigeria's primary education system attributed to the Universal Primary Education scheme (UPE) which began in 1976, a large majority of female primary school graduates in northern Nigeria do not continue their education due to the lack of opportunities available for them. Cultural, social and economic factors tend to deter educational progress as well. Alternatively, a sizeable percentage of young literate women enter the informal labour sector, where they earn a subsistence income for their livelihood as well as informally acquiring some job-related skills and attitudes. However, opportunities to develop their job-related skills are minimal.

If UPE and subsequent educational expansion is to have impact, educational planners and policy-makers will need to be aware of the present realities: the perhaps unintended yet real exclusion of most females from formal training on the one hand, and the reluctance of the private sector employers to absorb the unskilled school leavers on the other.

This chapter has explored several issues related to the development of opportunities for young women in employment and training in Bauchi State. These include perceptions of government planners about factors influencing young women's access to private sector employment and training; employers' perceptions and attitudes towards hiring young literate women; and the process of acquiring jobs and further training by a sample of young women. The implications of the findings for female education and training, both formal and non-formal, are numerous. Of particular interest are the contrasts illustrated between the perceptions of the predominantly male planners and employers and the realities experienced by the women themselves in employment and in the acquisition of skills.

Notes: Chapter 15

1 Females now represent an average of 40–45 per cent of the total primary school enrolment in Nigeria compared to 37 per cent in 1970, a decade ago (see United Nations Economic Commission for Africa, 1973, p. 45).
2 Anaza (1975) has discussed this issue of narrowing the gap between the supply of school leavers and available job opportunities by suggesting that policy-makers have three alternatives:

   (1) slow down the output of school leavers so as to allow available job opportunities to catch up;
   (2) continue the pace of educational development but at the same time greatly expand employment opportunities for school leavers;
   (3) leave supply and demand alone but manipulate the wage rate to clear the market. (p. 34)

3 The estimated population of Bauchi State is 3·57 million according to projections from the Bauchi State Ministry of Information and Communications in 1979.
4 The women chosen for study are meant as an exploratory base from which major issues emerge, not as a statistical representation of the characteristics of women in similar age-groups. Any inferences drawn, therefore, pertain to the group under study only.
5 The abilities ranked included manual work, ability to take instructions, capacity to supervise others, ability to write reports, mathematical and accounting skills, ability to work with others. These abilities were ranked on a four-point scale from very weak to very strong.
6 The eight private sector categories mentioned earlier were used during interviews with the planners as reference points. Six questions concerning the employment and training capacity of the private sector were presented to planners who were asked to rank their answers.
7 Significant changes are occurring in Bauchi State. One is that there is a concerted effort now to extend loans to entrepreneurs of small cottage industries and offer training for loanees in building a business. While there have been applications from women, such applications have failed to be considered, due, as one planner put it, to the fact that 'women who are married cannot chase up their application with the men at the headquarters'. Loans are available for such industries as blacksmithing, tin-cutting, leatherwork, polythene bag-making and furniture-making, vocations which traditionally have not included women.
8 The 1979/80 female enrolment figures at the Bauchi School of Agriculture and Animal Husbandry indicated that only thirteen women or 6 per cent were enrolled out of a total of 210 students (researcher's/author's personal visit).

Chapter 16

Conjugal Decision-Making: Some Data from Lagos

WAMBUI WA KARANJA

Two antithetical observations have been made regarding the relative equality of African sex roles. On the one hand women of Africa are said to be dominated by their menfolk in practically all spheres of life. Their inferior status has even been likened to that of 'beasts of burden'.[1] On the other hand, it has been argued that women's position is neither superior nor inferior to that of men but simply different and complementary.[2] As Paulme (ed., 1963, p. 6) put it: 'The influence exerted by women is due to their liveliness, their independent spirit, and their inexhaustible energy, rather than to rights recognized by custom.'

There is a widely accepted argument that the development of market economies superimposed on predominantly agricultural systems has eroded the status of many African women. Factors such as increased rural–urban migration which favour the young and male, unequal opportunities for educational advancement, the stratification of distributive functions, the undermining of the traditionally complementary sex-division of labour, and so on, have all been seen as contributing to exacerbate further the decline in the status of African women (Karanja-Diejomaoh and Scott, 1976). Indeed the form of economic dependence for some women reported, for example, by Oppong (1982, pp. 139–42), and the case reported by Aronson (1978) and which we know to exist in some African cities, is a recent phenomenon which is quite alien to most traditional African social structures. Be that as it may, the specific question that immediately concerns us here is the extent to which African women were dominated by men in more traditional structures and the extent to which such dominance may survive in a modern urban context.

When we turn to ethnographic evidence it appears that a significant proportion of women, especially in West Africa, have always enjoyed economic independence and relative freedom of movement and association.[3] This has been particularly true of Yoruba market women in Nigeria. However, despite the unprecedented growth of Nigerian cities, the position of Nigerian non-market women remains to a large extent undocumented. Using evidence from a survey of reports of prescribed norms for conjugal decision-making (who should decide a number of defined issues in domestic and social life) the present analysis is an attempt to provide some relevant evidence by (1) documenting people's responses regarding norms for differential distribution of conjugal power (Sweeney and Clignet, 1978, p. 565), (2) discerning the extent to which women's reported norms are different from those of men, and (3) contributing another piece of evidence to the existing polemical debate as to whether African women are dominated by men or not.[4]

In the survey, of which the results are summarised here, twenty-two 'key' questions, designed to elicit data on conjugal decision-making, were posed. The sample included equal numbers of men and women from high, intermediate and low socio-economic levels, all employed by the University of Lagos and the federal civil service. One of the considerations in undertaking the inquiry was to ascertain the degree to which conjugal decision-making was *husband-dominated, autonomous*, or *syncratic*. Thus responses were broadly categorised as 'husband alone', 'wife alone' and 'both husband and wife together'. The questions included an array of issues such as child-bearing and rearing, the use of leisure-time, work outside the home and the co-residence of kin and in-laws.[5]

Majority support was voiced for husbands making decisions alone in such areas as housing and the husband's work, leisure and training and who should co-reside.[6] Substantial support was reported for the husband deciding alone such issues as those pertaining to children (family size, birth control use, education, discipline), the wife's use of time for work and leisure, and domestic expenditure and time-use. There was only one issue for which there was majority support for the wife making decisions alone and that was the domestic food menu. Substantial support for the wife's autonomous decision-making was reported in such areas as the wife's work outside the home and domestic help and her use of free time and contraception. The majority of those surveyed thought that husband and wife should both decide on issues concerning family size, wife's work, contraception, children's discipline and domestic expenditure. Significantly there were more females than males who reported thinking that these decisions should be joint. The more highly educated women were especially more in favour of joint decision-making in such areas as family size, contraception and household expenditure. Among issues on which there was substantial support for joint decision-making were co-residence of relatives, family leisure, household help and wife's employment. Again differences were observable between the several socio-economic and educational categories. In summary, it was found that a much greater proportion of total respondents thought that husbands should make decisions on their own rather than wives.

Our Lagos survey data thus indicate that people from different socio-economic categories of employees, both men and women, admit an unequal distribution of domestic power which favours husbands. Moreover, I would argue that our data reflect to varying degrees what obtained in 'traditional' societies,[7] even though it is from a 'modern' urban situation.[8]

A closer look at the responses of males in the lower and intermediate socio-economic categories, compared with those of males in the highest socio-economic category, shows that the former support greater levels of husband dominance. Furthermore, the senior male employees approve to a greater extent joint or syncratic conjugal decision-making. Explanations could be offered in terms of 'Westernisation' or 'modernisation'; the adoption of assumed European cultural norms for conjugal relations by those with higher levels of education and more extensive exposure to foreign models. Or it might be argued that the higher socio-economic category are more likely to have higher-educated and higher-status wives, whose resources in the modern urban setting may encourage a more equal division of domestic power (cf. Oppong, 1970). Certainly the most highly educated professional and administrative category of women in the survey differed in their responses from the other women and were less likely to state that husbands should make decisions alone.

Our stance here, then, is as follows: that the status of African women is likely to lie somewhere between two extreme positions, on the one hand the view of earlier scholars who took women's position to be abject[9] and on the other that of advocates of the neither superior nor inferior position, but simply different and complementary. Certainly it would seem imperative to undertake the sort of classification provided for us earlier by Gluckman (1950) in which the ordering of rights and obligations in different societies are spelled out. This seems preferable to generalised statements about the position of African women which holds variations of different orders constant. For example, researches reported in *African Systems of Kinship and Marriage* (Radcliffe-Brown and Forde, eds, 1950) showed that the ordering of male–female relationships differs from one society to another depending on the particular form of descent structure. Fortes (1950) has attributed the relative equality between husbands and wives among the Ashanti to their matrilineal descent structure. In some cases spouses may acquire reciprocal rights at marriage, but it is also true that in many African societies the husband frequently acquires additional rights (rights *in rem*) over his wife which enable him to claim damages if his wife commits adultery (Radcliffe-Brown, 1950, p. 50).

To return to the particular data I have examined, both men and women in the Lagos sample feel that when it comes to decision-making the husband should dominate the wife. But men in lower-level employment seem to adhere to this prescribed norm more than either senior male or female workers, particularly the latter. The data reported here are mostly from Yoruba or Lagos. The women in this part of Nigeria have long been famous for their 'economic independence'. But it is also a fact that Yoruba society is highly stratified. Husbands and wives here, as in much of Africa, carry on most of their activities independently of each other.

However, at the juncture where they meet, and this is crucially important, the wife is expected to show deference to her husband. This is also the case among the Baganda of East Africa and a host of other people in West Africa, where a wife acknowledges the husband's *authority* over her by kneeling down for him as the occasion demands. Is this not entirely consistent with relations of domination? That is, does the act of kneeling not tell us something about the husband's locational position in the power structure?

My other researches among market women in Lagos, to be reported elsewhere, clearly demonstrate that these women are more sensitive to power (*agbara*) relations (albeit not 'analytically') than investigators are. When asked to rank men and women in Nigerian society, they invariably ranked men above women. When asked to elaborate on *agbara*, they cited the various cognates of power, such as prestige, influence, authority, and so on, but invariably added physical power. A rhetorical question frequently uttered was: 'If you had a quarrel or disagreement with your husband, could you beat him up?' This must be what Gough (1975, pp. 70–1) means when she says: 'Although men seldom use weapons against women, they possess them (or possess superior weapons) in addition to their physical strength. This does give men an ultimate control of force.'

In ending this discussion I acknowledge once again the significance of the recent research findings indicating that at an empirical level African women are relatively freer, like the working-class women in Western societies, than their Western middle-class counterparts. This is a valuable contribution to knowledge. However, I seriously question the grounds on which some researchers assert that African women are *not* dominated by men. The spheres of action and association are not so *totally* segregated that men and women *never* meet. What happens at the point where they meet cannot be taken as a given or held constant. That is, in associational situations questions of authority cannot be wished away. These vary with space and time, requiring constant re-examination. As Dahrendorf (1957, p. 173) has forcefully argued:

> If either nobody or everybody had authority, the concept would lose its meaning. Authority implies both domination and subjection and it therefore implies the existence of two distinct sets of positions or persons. This is not to say, of course, that there is no difference between those who have a great deal and those who have merely a little. Among the positions of domination there may be, and often is, considerable differentiation.

Our research findings show that the 'position' of women with regard to prescribed norms for decision-making is relatively inferior to that of men in the context of our study. They are expected to defer to men in practically all areas of domestic decision-making chosen for our research. Most important of all is the fact that men can intrude on women's activities if and when they so desire. In the scheme of subordination-superordination this state of affairs by definition *cannot* be said to amount to a *neutral position*, or *different* but *complementary* thesis, *nor* is it reducible to a 'beast of burden' thesis.

Notes: Chapter 16

The data reported here are part of a research project which was financed by the University of Lagos, the Ford Foundation and the Wenner-Gren Foundation for Anthropological Research, to whom I am very grateful. The opinions expressed, however, are my own and in no way the responsibility of these organisations.

1 As Leith-Ross, 1965, p. 19, notes, the image portrayed was one of a 'downtrodden slave or unregarded beast of burden'. Another observer relates that they seemed to be valued only to the extent that they attended to the whims and caprices of their menfolk (Clarke, 1843).
2 Little, 1973, pp. 6–7, asserts:

> it is tempting and fairly accurate to describe the role of women as *complementary* rather than *subordinate* to that of men, even though women are as a rule *under* the *control* of males. This is generally so, both before and after marriage, and is usually the case in *matrilineal* as well as in *patrilineal* systems because in matriliny a woman comes under the *authority* of her mother's brother or her own brother (emphasis mine)

Another contributor (Kaberry, 1952, p. 152) writes:

> It is believed in Nsaw that women are more sensitive, quick tempered and capricious than men, and hence less capable of adopting the dispassionate attitude necessary for the judgment of cases. Women change their minds. . . Women are like children. . . Women are not sure what they want. . . 'If you give the country to women, some will spoil the country. They have no intelligence like men. Anger burns women greatly and they have grieving hearts indeed. If you

say something a man hears it with indifference. If you say it to a woman, then she is deeply pained.'

I was told that 'Women can't rule because they can't control themselves. They vex easily, they lose their heads. . . Yes, a woman is like God, and like God she cannot speak. She must sit silently. It is good that she should only accept.'

3   Evans-Pritchard, 1940, 1965; Fortes, 1950; E. N. Goody, 1962; J. Goody, ed., 1975; Harrell-Bond, 1975; Hodder and Ukwu, 1969; Sudarkasa (1973), Marris, 1961; Oppong 1982.

4   The data to be analysed here are based on a disproportionate stratified sample of 300 male and female respondents randomly selected from a list of Nigerian federal civil service workers in Lagos, which also included the University of Lagos. Stratification is by broad income groups which, until recently, broadly divided workers in Nigeria into senior, intermediate and junior categories, which also corresponds roughly to educational attainment. The research was carried out during 1978 and 1979: most of the questionnaires being administered during the months of June to August 1979.

Through a simple random sample, I selected 150 males: 50 senior, 50 intermediate and 50 junior staff; as well as 150 females, also distributed equally in the above three categories.

5   (a)   Similar questions have been raised by earlier analysts, for example, Blood and Wolfe, 1960.

6   Anyone wishing to see the questionnaire or detailed tabulation on answers should contact the author, c/o Sociology Department, University of Lagos.

7   My other intensive investigations among market women in Lagos (to be reported elsewhere) demonstrate forcefully that the women themselves perceive male–female relationships in terms of dominant male models (E. Ardener, 1975a,b,; S. Ardener, ed., 1975).

8   A question which arises, however, is whether rural and urban are such discrete entities (Banton, 1957, pp. 218–19) to be analysed in simple dichotomous terms; or whether the two should not be viewed in terms of a continuum, in which change, institutional or structural, is seen in terms of degrees rather than in kind.

9   Such as Malinowski, 1913, p. 287, who argues that 'the relation of a husband to a wife in its economic aspects is that of a master to a slave', and Ashley-Montagu, 1937, p. 23, who compares women's position with that of a domesticated cow.

Chapter 17

Male Chauvinism: Men and Women in Ghanaian Highlife Songs

NIMROD ASANTE-DARKO AND SJAAK VAN DER GEEST

Literary sources enjoy increasing attention from social scientists, who scrutinise them as valuable sources of information. Feminist authors and other students of women's roles have been particularly active in this field.[1] In this chapter we investigate how husbands, wives and lovers are depicted in popular Ghanaian songs called 'highlife'. Throughout we confine ourselves to Akan highlife songs and to Akan society as such. First we shall discuss some methodological problems of this exercise. Next we give a brief description of the general role of highlife music and we continue with some remarks about Akan marriage and male–female relationships based upon anthropological evidence. Finally we analyse a number of highlife texts, relating them continuously to anthropological evidence. Our view is that highlife songs on the subject of marital problems often function as ideological charters expressing the male point of view.

Our data derive from two different types of research: participant observation[2] and collection, transcription and translation of highlife songs.[3] Although these two research approaches vary considerably, they are in this case closely connected. The importance of highlife songs in Ghanaian daily life dawned upon Van der Geest only through his fieldwork. People's love for both music and texts of highlife became clear to him on many occasions. During funerals the young people neglected the traditional drumming and danced to the tunes of highlife (cf. Bleek, 1975, pp. 68–9). Every evening young people grouped together near a canteen to listen to highlife. In the compound where Van der Geest lived children and grown-ups eagerly played the few highlife songs which he happened to have on cassette.

Participant observation also provided a framework for the interpretation and analysis of the songs. Van der Geest carried out investigations into some of the very problems which are dealt with in highlife songs: marriage and divorce, love affairs, inheritance, witchcraft and death. The anthropologist, therefore, can provide background information to clarify the meaning of highlife songs. But can the songs help the anthropologist understand life in this society? In other words, can the songs be used as ethnographic material? There is no simple answer to this question. The ethnographic use of songs and other forms of popular art is beset with methodological problems. Fabian (1978, p. 321) lists a number of questions which need to be answered before an anthropologist can treat any form of popular art as ethnographic information. These questions refer, among others, to the identity of performers and public, and social setting of the performance, its purpose and the use of poetic figures.

Some authors suggest that novels, songs and other forms of literature should be treated simply as information given by an informant. There remain, however, some thorny problems with such an approach. In the first place, there is a vast difference between information collected during face-to-face interviews and information which is transmitted through, for example, a song on a record. The anthropologist in an interview situation is, to a large extent, able to judge the reliability, the validity and the meaning of the communication. He knows the setting in which the information is transmitted, he knows the informant and he himself is the listener. Further, he himself has determined the purpose of the conversation, and when the informant's purpose deviates from his he will probably notice it.

An anthropologist using art material as data lacks this privileged insight and it is uncertain whether he will find answers to all the questions formulated by Fabian. There is a great danger that he will fall into *Hineininterpretierung*, which may lead to false conclusions about the meaning of the content.

A second problem is that the purpose of an interview usually differs greatly from the purpose of a popular song. A song usually wants to entertain, an interview to collect accurate information about certain topics. It is possible that the artist has to discard reality in order to entertain his audience. Science fiction, fairytales and fantasy literature, such as Tolkien's writings, seem to confirm this. The point is, however, that an author who tries to escape his social or political reality in his writings reveals another – ideological – reality (see Blécourt, 1979). To take the two extremes: an artist may try to entertain his audience by portraying their life situations as closely as possible, or by allowing them to fly far away from their actual life. In both cases, however, the artist holds a mirror in front of the public. In the former instance the mirror reflects their lives, in the latter their wishes and fears. Art which does not reflect anything of the public is unlikely to entertain or move them. The spectators will feel unconcerned. The degree of popularity of a particular song or story may well be an indicator of how successful the artist has been in depicting a particular feature of the people's life, but it remains a difficult task for the anthropologist to find the exact point of reflection: whether he has to do with actual behaviour, repressed behaviour, or wishful thinking.

The same difficulty arises when we attempt to analyse highlife songs. But our knowledge of marriage problems in Ghana, based on everyday experience and fieldwork, gives us important clues as to how each song should be interpreted. Some are based on true events, others may be rationalisations and others again idealisations. Looking very critically at this chapter we must admit that the texts have augmented our understanding of Akan marriage only a little, but rather our acquaintance with this topic has helped us to understand the songs.[4] Our insights into Akan husband–wife relationships have prompted us to regard highlife songs not as simple accounts of the problems which occur in married life. Although many songs probably describe true events, they do more. They give an interpretation, a biased view, of the events which are related. In this interpretation the male point of view is instilled into the listener's mind. Highlife songs on marriage, therefore, assume an ideological character. They form part of a cultural complex which – at various levels of consciousness – is to uphold the ideology of male supremacy. In this respect these highlife songs are similar to other songs which have a clearly political or social function. One may think of military songs and protest songs which aim at rallying support for a political case (see Zimmerman, 1966, cited by Doornbos and Cook, n.d.) or bring about feelings of solidarity in suppressed groups (see Hannerz, 1969).

Highlife in Ghana

Highlife is a blend of traditional Akan rhythms and melodies with European musical elements. It encompasses a variety of artistic expressions: music, dancing, singing, story-telling and theatre. It originates from the end of the nineteenth century, but its exact source is not known. From the 1920s onwards, however, its history is well documented (see Bame, 1969, 1975; Darkwa, 1974, pp. 138–48; Collins, 1976a 1976b). It started on the coast but has now spread over the whole of southern Ghana and other West African countries. It seems that at first urban life and social mobility were predominant themes in highlife songs. The term 'highlife' suggests that too; it reflected the life of the 'high (Ghanaian) society' in towns. Collins estimates that at present there are about fifty highlife bands in Ghana, but there are probably more than a hundred. Some are famous and have lasted a long time; many, however, disappear after a short time and sink into oblivion or start again in another composition and under a new name.

Highlife is in the first place music. People enjoy its rhythm and if they do not like the music the song will never become popular. But the text is important as well. Highlife is played in homes and in drinking bars, at parties and at funerals. At market places and lorry parks people gather near radio boxes to listen to highlife during 'listeners' choice'. There are national competitions for highlife bands which attract a lot of people. Highlife is played during intervals of football matches, at trade fairs and other public occasions.

Highlife is so popular and its texts are so well known that it lends itself as a medium of communication. It is sometimes used to send a political message, more or less in disguise. During Nkrumah's regime E. K. Nyame composed a highlife song saying:

> Before it is going to rain
> the wind will blow.
> I warned you
> but you did not listen.

Nkrumah's opponents interpreted the song as a critique of his government and Nkrumah banned the song. Similar incidents took place under Acheampong and during other regimes.[5]

Popular highlife texts can also be borrowed for phatic communion among friends and acquaintances. One song, for example, entitled '*Okwaduo*' (a type of wild ox), tells a story about how the ox managed to set itself free from a hunter. It then became a fashion among friends to refer to each other as *okwaduo* if someone was considered to have been lucky. At the same time this song assumed a political meaning as well (see Bame, 1969, pp. 68–9).

The popularity of highlife shows itself also in the fact that titles of successful songs are given to particular cloth designs. It is not clear whether this happens spontaneously (Boelman and Van Holthoorn, 1973, p. 239) or whether it is a marketing strategy.[6]

Male and Female in Akan Marriage

There is something ambivalent in marriage among the Akan. On the one hand people do not seem to consider it very important. Young people try to avoid it as long as they can (Bleek, 1975, 1976; Dinan, 1977, ch. 25). Married people easily separate, divorced people are not always willing to start a new marriage, and relatives look askance at a marriage in which husband and wife develop a close relationship (Bleek, 1975).[7] On the other hand, people cannot do without marriage. It still marks the transition to adulthood, young people have romantic expectations of marriage and there even seems to be a growing sense of 'illegitimacy' when children are born outside marriage.

A similar ambiguity is to be found in the husband–wife relationship. On the one hand women are, to a large degree, independent of their husbands. Economic assets and incomes remain strictly separated, almost half of the women in rural places live apart from their husbands, the matrilineal principle marks the husband as a kind of outsider *vis-à-vis* his wife and children, and women as often as men initiate divorce, as has been described in several earlier chapters. On the other hand, a – perhaps slightly superficial – observer notices considerable subservience and respect on the part of the wife towards the husband.

Female subservience, however, should not be taken literally. An increasing number of authors, who have observed women's subordination to men in various societies over the whole world, take the view that so-called female subordination is often a facade hiding a large degree of equality between the sexes. They view it as a power game, in which women buy off a large quantity of practical power in exchange for allowing men public respect and status (see Rogers, 1975).

This model seems to fit the Akan marital situation reasonably well (see Bartle, 1978), but there remains one enigma which resists the glib application of the equality model. This is the inequality in opportunities for husbands and wives to contact additional sexual partners, either within or outside marriage. Only men can afford to take a second partner in marriage; only men can afford to commence extra-marital liaisons more or less openly. This inequality has found its way into highlife songs. This inequality itself is, however, not criticised in the songs; on the contrary its roots are confirmed. The songs function as an ideological instrument proclaiming the superiority of men.

Husbands, Wives and Lovers in Highlife

Singing, playing and composing highlife is mainly a male affair. Female performers are rare and the few who do exist[8] are probably male oriented as well. As a rule male singers play the roles of both men and women. It is likely, therefore, that highlife songs confirm the ideology of male supremacy. The female partners in a polygynous marriage are presented as competing for the husband's favour. Significantly, the Twi term for co-wife is *kora* (rival).

In a song entitled *Asiko Darling* the singer, Eddie Donkor, describes the co-wife relationship as follows:

> Uncle Kwasi, I shall tell you a story.
> There were two co-wives.
> The youngest of them was the senior wife.
> A quarrel broke out between them.
> The younger one said to the older one:
> 'I win the husband through the
> delicious soup I make.' (twice)
> You know, when women quarrel they
> want to insult each other.
> So the younger wife said that she pleased
> the husband most because of her soup.
> The older wife replied: 'Eei, you win
> him with soup? Then I shall win
> him with love-making, haha.'[9]
> Good soup or love-making . . . over to you.

Nana Ampadu, who at present is probably the most popular high-life singer, uses the co-wife relationship as a setting for a symbolic story about alertness in a hostile environment. The song is entitled *M'ada me ho so* ('I am watchful'):

> 'If my words are bad,
> summon me before the elders in the chief's palace
> and I will open my defence.'
> There lived co-wives,
> it seemed they liked each other,
> it seemed they did not like each other.
> One day the younger one decided to travel.
> When she said farewell
> the older one gave her money
> to buy something for her on her return.
> The younger wife took the money and asked
> what she should buy for her.
> The older one said she should buy something
> called 'If I get the opportunity, I will harm you',
> she should try and buy this article.
>
> When the younger wife returned
> she told the other that she could not get
> what she had asked her to buy.
> Instead she had bought something called
> 'I-am-watchful'.
> The elder became annoyed and took offence.

The younger replied that she had not done
anything wrong.
'If my words are bad,
summon me before the elders in the chief's palace
and I will open my defence.'

The same singer, Ampadu, in another song uses the polygynous marriage as a proverbial example of rivalry and jealousy, whereas the husband appears as the only sensible – but troubled – person. The song is entitled *Somu gye w'akrantee* ('Take your grasscutter'). In the song the husband is a civil servant. One day, when he returns from work, he buys a grasscutter and an antelope. He takes the grasscutter, which is considered as one of the greatest delicacies, to his elder wife, and the antelope, which is less appreciated, to the younger one. The younger wife becomes annoyed and refuses the antelope. She starts a bitter quarrel with the husband and the other wife. The older wife is also not satisfied with the grasscutter and so she also gets annoyed and starts quarrelling with the husband. The next day the man must take an examination. He is so confused because of the incident that he only writes his wives' abuses on the paper. He fails the examination and is dismissed from his work. The man then divorces both women. Jealousy as the basic pattern of co-wife relationships is also mentioned in another song by Ampadu: *Aku Sika* ('Golden Aku').

These songs show the effects of polygyny from an extremely male point of view. Reasons why polygynous unions are decreasing in number are more complex than is suggested by these songs. It is not so much jealousy between the wives of one man which creates problems for the polygynous household, but rather the entire socio-economic position of men and women. An analysis of this complex of factors – in the form of a story – would not result in emphasising male supremacy. It would rather show the absence of male dominance and the existence of equality and independence on the part of wives. For a song with this content it is still too early.

Songs which disturb the ideological facade of male superiority endanger the power relationship between wives and husbands. Even women, therefore, prefer to keep the facade intact in order to safeguard their interests. The following incident, reported by Kleinkowski (1976, p. 63), is typical. For the annual meeting of a Ghanaian women's organisation a (Twi) song was composed which said: 'The belief of the past that men are superior to women gives way to a new era: men and women are equal.' The women liked the song but did not want to sing it because, as they said, their husbands would stop giving them 'chop money' if they heard the song.

Another song to illustrate our point also describes rivalry between two women. One woman is superseded by the other as a man's marriage partner. Although the title of the song *Okunu pa ho ye na* ('Good husbands are rare') suggests criticism of men, the song really describes the foolishness and wickedness of women. The singer is again Ampadu.

> If you find one get hold of him well, sister,
> A good husband is rare. (refrain)
>
> Before Nana Yaa left the house to stay with her
> husband, her grandmother called her and gave
> her advice. Nana Yaa took a chair and sat down.
> The grandmother started:
>
> 'Be careful with the venture you are going to take.
> Marriage is a very long thing, that is why it is called
> *awaree* [a very long thing].[10] You are a child going
> to taste marriage life for the first time. But don't
> go and think childishly. Don't reject the advice
> of an elderly person. Don't go and make many
> friends, don't listen to gossip – because gossip
> leads to the downfall of a town. Don't go and
> make many friends because it is due to making
> many friends that the crab lost its head.
> Nana Yaa, obey your husband in all respects. If
> he offends you, report the matter to your landlord
> so that he will settle the dispute. A house
> affair is not a rag which can be washed and
> dried in the open. It is not something which
> should be known by everyone. Since you will be a
> stranger in that new place people will be
> interested in what you buy at the market every day.
> The glory of a home lies in the woman, and the
> glory of a woman lies in the husband.
> I hope that the little I have said will sink into
> your ears. A wise child is talked to
> in proverbs and not in ordinary speech.'
>
> When Nana Yaa left to stay with the
> husband, the husband used to give her
> four shillings daily as chop money.
> Nana Yaa never complained and spent the
> four shillings accordingly.
> After about six months, she got a certain
> friend called Awura Afua – who was single.
> When the two of them met at the market, Awura
> Afua asked Nana Yaa:
> 'Nana Yaa, how much money does your husband
> give you every day as chop money?'
> Nana Yaa answered: 'Four shillings'.

'Nana Yaa, what can you buy with four
shillings at Obuase – here?
Even I who am a spinster sometimes go
to the market with six shillings – sometimes
I spend even ten shillings a day.
How many cloths has your husband bought for
you since you became his wife?'
Nana Yaa (exclaiming) – 'Since I came to
live with him, he has not bought any cloth
for me. Not even a headkerchief.'
'Nana Yaa, you are too submissive.
If I were you, I would divorce the man.
I once had a husband who treated me in the
same way. Since I divorced him, I am
living peacefully and feel very free.
Nobody is my master.'

When the following day Nana Yaa's husband gave
her four shillings, she refused to take it.
She told her husband Kwaku Yeboah that four
shillings was too little for a day's meal
because Obuase was a town where prices are
high. She asked the husband to add more.
The husband replied: 'Since you came here,
is it not four shillings that I have been
giving you every day? What has prompted you to
ask for more?'
Nana Yaa became annoyed and insulted the husband.
The husband also became angry and slapped her.
'Agyaee' (screamed Nana Yaa). 'He has killed me,
this marriage is finished. My mother did not
bear me for you. How could you slap me like this?
I am going to my town.'

When she reached home, she told her story that
the chop money given her by Kwaku Yeboah was
not enough and that when she complained, Kwaku
Yeboah had slapped her. She had therefore decided
to put an end to her marriage with Kwaku Yeboah.
From then, Nana Yaa went to live in Kumasi
where she tried all sorts of things without
success. So she returned home and asked
her grandmother to go and plead to the
husband to enable her to go back to stay
with him.
'Had I known is always too late.'
Nana Yaa and her grandmother went to Obuase.
When they reached home, Kwaku Yeboah had not
returned home from work. A woman in the

compound told them that Kwaku Yeboah's
wife was in the room (climax).
Nana Yaa was startled and asked
who the new wife was who had taken her place.
When Nana Yaa entered the room, she realised
that the new wife was nobody but her own
friend, Awura Afua.
'Eei, Awura Afua, that's how you are.
You advised me to divorce my husband so that
you could take my place.
You said four shillings was not sufficient
and now you are living on that.'
The other replied: 'Nana Yaa, I want you to
understand that you have not bought Kwaku Yeboah.
In this world, some people even like the intestines
of a civet cat (everyone has his own taste).
You did not like Kwaku Yeboah and I have replaced
you. If it pains you, go and die.' (4 times)
'I will never leave Kwaku Yeboah until I die. If
it pains you, go and die.' (2 times)
Nana Yaa began weeping. She wept and continued
weeping.

When Kwaku Yeboah came home he refused to accept
Nana Yaa back as his wife. He told Nana Yaa
that it was too late for her to return to him
because her place had been taken by somebody else.
So if you get a good husband hold fast to him
because good husbands are rare. (refrain)

The copious use of proverbs in this song is striking. Proverbs are frequently quoted in highlife songs. They too present the male view of life and help to keep up the facade of male dominance.

The theme of the above song appears also in a song by Konadu. Here too another woman has pushed the lawful wife aside. She assumes a very superior attitude and abuses the former wife. The most superior person in this triangle is, however, the husband, because it is for his love that both women are competing. We only cite a few lines. The song is called *Wobewu a kowu* ('You can go and die'). The intruder is speaking:

Yes, you can go and die.
It was your property
but you joked with it
and somebody has taken it now.
Yes, you can go and die.
You had every opportunity to drink it,
but you joked with it
and now somebody has drunk it.

The male point of view is also present in songs which describe extra-marital love affairs. It is nearly always married *men* who have such affairs and although there is a tone of criticism in the songs, they express at the same time secret admiration of this male prowess. Songs showing secret admiration for extra-marital affairs of *women* are unthinkable.

In a song called *Sensam* ('Weeds') Ampadu relates a quarrel between a married woman and another woman who is suspected of being her husband's girlfriend. The married woman challenges the other as follows:

> Useless weeds, useless weeds,
> you are just growing under the palm tree.
> Come and live in the house
> as a recognised wife.

She continues to say:

> My husband takes you as a wooden bed
> but me as an iron bed.

In a song by the City Boys Band a man speaks to women about love in a very viricentric way. The title of the song is *Ankwanoma Dede* ('Lonely Bird').

> Our sisters, the women
> don't understand what love is.
> Some women, when they are asked
> to talk about love,
> behave very strange.
> When a young man calls a woman
> to talk to her about love,
> the response is: 'As for me, as for me. . .'
> *Agyei* [expression of pain],
> Women, sisters, love is expensive.
> Love is like a necklace,
> Someone wears it, another one wants it.
> Therefore, women, sisters,
> if a young man calls you
> to talk about love,
> you should be patient and listen to him,
> because love is expensive.

In a number of songs a deserted girlfriend complains that people laugh at her because she has been 'sacked' by the man. An example is *Odo san bra* ('Darling come back') sung by Pat Thomas:

> Darling we have stayed together for a long time
> I don't know what I have done against you,

but you have sent me away.
My enemies are laughing at me.

The theme of shame is a powerful instrument to instil ideas of male superiority. Another way is to describe the intentions and behaviour of women in a denigrating manner, as happens in the song below. The song is entitled *Mmesiafo yi* ('These girls') and is sung by Pat Thomas:

These girls, if you have money,
they go with you.
The day you don't have money,
they will broadcast your poverty,
to give your enemies the chance
to laugh at you.

The same denigrating tone is found in a folk-song which is sung by young (male) children to make fun of girls:

Kooko aben, nkanfoo aben
Nea mmaa pe ne apotonsu

The meaning of this song is that women like to eat food which is ready. They will come as soon as it is ready and when it is finished they leave unceremoniously. It is striking that such children's songs expressing sexual antagonism can exist, whereas there is no doubt that in actual life eating and cooking behaviour by men and women tends to be the opposite of what is suggested by the song. It shows that the possibilities of ideological inversion of reality are almost unlimited.

The supposed superiority of the male lover over the female one is, finally, well expressed in a song with the telling title *Si Ejisu* ('Get down at Ejisu'). The song is sung by Konadu:

I was travelling with my lover to Accra.
Ampofowa, your character
prevented you from seeing the sea
Darling, get down at Ejisu. . .

The journey had hardly started
when you started misbehaving.
So, get down at Ejisu.
If you marry an educated woman,
you become her interpreter.
Ampofowa your character prevented
you from seeing the sea.
Get down at Ejisu. . .

> I won't stay with you any more.
> Go away with your mortar,
> I take my pestle. . .

The song confirms in a very authoritarian way that women should be obedient to men and that inequality between the two sexes is necessary.

Conclusion

The aim of this exercise has been to show the ideological character of a number of popular songs which are usually considered as pure amusement. Highlife songs in Ghana which deal with marital problems, particularly problems connected with the polygynous and 'polycoitous' nature of marriage, often present a highly biased account and interpretation of these problems. This bias consists of a systematic emphasis on male superiority. Highlife songs, therefore, form part of a general cultural complex which upholds male superiority over women.

The fact that songs about polygyny and polycoity express male dominance most vividly is not surprising. Legal polygyny and extramarital love affairs are still largely reserved to men and pose an enigmatic phenomenon in a situation where a high degree of equality exists between men and women. This phenomenon, therefore, lends itself pre-eminently to exalting the male ideology.

The result of this ideological function of highlife music is not, however, true dominance by men. On the contrary, there are indications that the cultural complex of male dominance is tolerated and even desired by women. A facade of male dominance enables them to retain power and independence in more hidden domains.

It should be taken into account, however, that musical entertainment such as highlife does not necessarily reinforce existing ideologies. Songs may as well assume a revolutionary and educative function by propagating new ideas and pleading for suppressed groups. It is not unlikely that this will happen to highlife when more female musicians enter the stage.

Notes: Chapter 17

Nimrod Asante-Darko and Sjaak Van der Geest conducted fieldwork together in 1971. Apart from the two authors, many more people have been involved in the collection, transcription and translation of highlife songs. We are especially indebted to Samuel Asamoah, Kwasi Anim, Boakye Danquah, Margaret Hall-Badoo, Veronica Ampofo, Kofi Asiedu and Gifty Anin. We are also grateful to Kwame Arhin and

Christine Oppong who commented on an earlier version of this chapter. Funds for the research came from the Institute of African Studies, University of Ghana, from the Netherlands Foundation for the Advancement of Tropical Research (WOTRO) and from the University of Amsterdam.

1 A few examples from Africa are Case, 1977; Essomba, 1974; Hammond, 1976; Kilson, 1977; Lee, 1974; Lippert, 1972; Mutiso, 1971; and Zerbe, 1974.
2 Participant observation was carried out mainly in two six-month periods of field-work in a rural town in southern Ghana. A part of the first period of fieldwork was carried out by both authors together, the remaining fieldwork by Van der Geest alone. It should, however, be noted that Asante-Darko, as a native of the Asante in southern Ghana, brings into this chapter the most intensive 'participant observation' possible. A substantial part is based on his personal experiences and observations within his own community, with regard both to husband–wife relationships and to highlife music in general. This chapter is the result of close co-operation and long discussions between an insider (Asante-Darko) and an outsider (Van der Geest) to Ghanaian society. The latter, as an anthropologist, asked most of the questions; the former attempted to answer them or reformulate them.
3 Collecting texts of highlife songs is an entirely different research activity. All songs collected by us exist on records manufactured by Ghanaian companies. Recording, transcribing and translating them was chiefly office work. Most of this work was done by Asante-Darko but various other people were involved as well (see above). Until now, 107 songs – not a representative sample – have been transcribed and translated, many of which touch upon problems in the marital relationship. In this chapter we discuss one theme which appears particularly frequently in highlife songs: rivalry and feelings of jealousy which occur in marriage. Although the two research approaches mentioned above vary considerably, they are in this case closely connected.
4 The ethnographic use of highlife songs was more directly profitable in a study of the image of death as depicted in the songs (Van der Geest, 1980).
5 The political meaning of highlife songs is dealt with more extensively in Asante-Darko and Van der Geest, n.d.
6 There are more similarities between cloth designs and highlife. Boelman and Van Holthoorn (1973, p. 243) point out that clothes can have communicative functions. Certain occasions prompt people to wear certain designs, e.g. a design called 'handcuffs' was worn to protest against arrests under the Nkrumah regime.
7 Someone who loves his wife too much is disparagingly called *mmaafodie*, i.e. someone who hangs around women.
8 Three quite famous female highlife singers are Vida Rose, Janet Osei Donkor and Rose Awura Amma Badu.
9 The joke, according to a translator, is that it is older wives who are famous for cooking and young wives who are better at love-making.
10 *Awaree* means both 'marriage' and 'it is long'.

Chapter 18

Male and Female Factory Workers in Ibadan

CATHERINE M. DI DOMENICO

Nigeria has been the scene of rapid economic change, particularly during the 1970s after the civil war drew to an end and money from oil wealth began to flow. This contributed to rapid inflation through-out the country, causing much hardship for the poor, but also pro-vided more employment opportunities for migrants coming into the urban centres. Both men and women proved eager to work in the new factories in order to make a living for themselves and their children, and even to save capital for their own businesses. However, it appears that some of the new employers of factory labour are less interested in employing women than men. It is therefore interesting to consider how men and women in factories – managers and operatives – per-ceive their relative positions, and to compare their attitudes and aspi-rations for the future.

It is frequently assumed that both women and men prefer wage-employment and only work in the informal sector of the economy if they are excluded from jobs in the formal sector; and that women especially opt for self-employed status when they perceive rejection and discrimination against themselves as wage-earners. It appears, however, that these assumptions are misplaced with regard to many workers in Nigeria, both female and male. Research undertaken in Ibadan, a traditional Yoruba city growing rapidly as a commercial, administrative and educational centre, suggests a rather different perspective. The present analysis is based on insights originally developed in the late 1960s and early 1970s in a study of the Nigerian Tobacco Company in Ibadan (Di Domenico, 1973). This multina-tional company (a branch of British American Tobacco and the big-gest single employer of industrial labour in Ibadan) was at that time apparently commencing a policy of running down the employment of women and increasing the proportion of male workers. From inter-views with both men and women in the factory it was evident that in terms of commitment to income generation and attitudes to work and family, and a number of other indices, women and men resembled each other closely. Work was seen in very instrumental terms by both men and women, as a means to the end of improving their life positions, especially their family welfare and economic security. This instrumental orientation reflects prevailing social conditions and societal expectations. Women in polygynous societies such as those in Nigeria are often obliged to support themselves and their children either partially or completely. Like men, they have basic economic family responsibilities to fulfil. In the NTC study it was found also that they as much as the men were ambitious to leave formal work and set up their own businesses in the informal sector. The opportunity to establish a business suits the trading orientation of the Yoruba and affords individuals the chance to achieve their personal ambitions as well as allowing greater flexibility and the more successful merging of home and work life for both men and women.

The research undertaken began with the collection of basic data on male and female factory workers in both the public and private sectors. Secondly, it involved an analysis of the structure and conditions which men and women face when looking for factory employment. These include the attitudes of managers and policies of government officials towards the employment of male and female factory workers. Thirdly, the attitudes of factory workers of both sexes were examined towards factory employment and one another, especially in terms of their perceptions of equality of treatment. To these ends, workers and managers were interviewed in various factory locations in Ibadan. This chapter presents a brief résumé of some of the observations.[1]

The Setting and Location

Ibadan is a vast, densely populated and fairly homogeneous Yoruba city in the west of Nigeria dating back to the early nineteenth century. Although modern governmental institutions and industries are now common features, the city dwellers continue to follow traditional ways of life and surrounding land is still used for subsistence farming as well as commercial production by townsfolk. The main occupations within the town itself are trading and craftwork. The transition of labour to industry is often from trading or crafts, and does not generally imply long-distance migration. The industrial labour force remains small in comparison with government, commercial and craft employment in the city, and comprises an insignificant proportion of the total population. In 1973 an estimate put the industrial population of Ibadan at between 7,000 and 8,000 workers (Di Domenico,

1973) and Koll (1969) estimated that there were perhaps six times as many persons involved in the craft sector as there were employed in registered firms with more than twenty-five employees.

Manufacturing and processing industries of the factory type have only recently arrived on the scene. Nevertheless, the rate of growth of industrial enterprises has been extremely rapid, principally since independence, in Ibadan as elsewhere in Nigeria. While some of this growth involves large-scale multinational concerns, such as NTC and the more recently established (1979) Leyland Nigeria Ltd, which each employ well over a thousand workers in Ibadan, most workers in the industrial labour force are employed in smaller-scale Nigerian- and Lebanese-run establishments. Official statistics indicate that over 80 per cent of the approximately sixty Ibadan firms with a workforce of over twenty-five persons employ less than 100 workers. Only a few concerns employ more than 200 people (*Nigerian Industrial Directory*, 1970). Although some factories and most of the printing presses are publicly owned, the majority of industrial enterprises are privately owned.

An Overview of Male and Female Participation in Industrial Establishments

The present discussion begins with an overview of male and female participation in those industrial establishments in Ibadan which dominated the industrial scene in the city during the period 1976–80. A total of sixteen enterprises were surveyed. Two were government-owned factories; ten were factories under predominantly private ownership; the remainder were printing and publishing establishments, all but one of which were government-owned. Relatively small-scale establishments with fewer than 100 employees were excluded from the survey, on the grounds that they not only had too few workers but were also basically traditional in nature (operating with apprenticeship systems) rather than modern organisations.

The majority of the industrial labour force working in the survey firms are men. Women comprised only 12·6 per cent of this group in 1980. The ratio of male:female employees is higher in the private sector than the public, being approximately 13:1 and 3:1 respectively in 1980. Almost all the employees in the two government-owned factories in the survey (both food-processing industries) are women, although senior and supervisory positions within these establishments are held almost exclusively by men. Females comprise only a small part of the labour force in the predominantly privately owned factories. Relatively few women are employed in the printing and publishing concerns surveyed.

Not only is women's participation in the industrial labour force much less than men's but it also appears to be decreasing. In 1976, 15·5 per cent of the labour force in the selected factories was female, but this proportion has fallen to 12·6 per cent four years later. The number of female employees in these establishments increased by only 4·4 per cent while that of male employees rose by 33·3 per cent. The change appears to be largely due to a decrease in the employment of women in private factories. Although the number of men employed in private factories increased by 37·5 per cent over this period, the number of women actually decreased by 9·3 per cent.[2] Thus, while the proportion of women remained fairly constant (1976–80) in the government-owned factories and in the presses and publishing houses, it dropped from 11·4 to 7·8 per cent in the private factory group.

A profile of the type of factory where men are likely to secure jobs compared with women is summarised in Table 18.1.

Women are more likely to secure employment in the public rather than in the private factory sector. Their chances also seem to be higher in establishments involved in the processing of foodstuffs which are

Table 18.1   *Factory Profiles*

I Factories more likely to employ women	*II* Factories more likely to employ men
Public ownership*	Private ownership
Food processing: dealing with food-stuffs traditionally associated with women (e.g. fruits, nuts)	Manufacturing/processing of non-foodstuffs and modern food and drinks production (e.g. Coca-Cola, Pepsi)
Light work: requiring nimbleness/dexterity (e.g. match manufacture)	Heavy work (e.g. log-processing)
Temporary/part-time work: seasonal employment corresponding with crop harvests (e.g. fruits, nuts)	Permanent employment
Small-scale concerns	Large-scale concerns
Lower wages (paid less than men)	Higher wages (paid more than women)

*In so far as such establishments are under public ownership, the employment which they offer is akin to other government employment (posts may to some extent be likened to sinecures). They are not basically profit-oriented in the manner of factories in the private sector.

subject to seasonal fluctuations in the employment of labour. Thus, both the Cashew Nut and the Lafia Canning factories employ predominantly female labour forces. By way of contrast, very few women are employed in the two factories concerned with the production of soft drinks. They are recruited only for secretarial and clerical posts and regarded as unsuitable for the operation of 'technical and sophisticated' machines. As we have noted, increasingly few women are employed in other areas of modern manufacture, namely, in tobacco-processing at the NTC factory and at the new Leyland (Nigeria) vehicle assembly plant, where again they are confined to clerical and secretarial jobs. Employers in Ibadan factories appear to make the distinction between 'light' or simple work for women and 'heavy' or technical work for men. Thus, significant numbers of women are employed for the manufacture of matches by Niger Match, while the sister factory, Safa Splint, employs women only in a secretarial or clerical capacity. Niger Match was originally established on a Swedish model, in which female labour comprised the majority, although the company does not employ as high a proportion of women as was initially expected. Safa Splint is involved in wood-processing and in the production of chipboard from logs (its 'waste' products being sent to Niger Match), and only men are employed for this heavy work. Even within one factory this distinction between light women's work and heavy men's work in the production process may be observed. For example, at the NTC factory men are involved in the primary processing and women in packing. It seems that men are also more likely than women to secure permanent employment, for the latter's job opportunities are located in food-processing establishments, in which employment is both temporary and part-time due to seasonal fluctuations in the raw materials concerned. Finally, it appears that women are likely to be employed in smaller-scale concerns than men and are also likely to be paid markedly less than male employees.

The foregoing profiles highlight the different situations of men and women in the industrial labour force, even though both sexes appear to share the same attitudes, values and responsibilities. Women are apparently more willing than men to take up seasonal employment and to work for lower rates of pay. In addition, they appear less likely to articulate grievances or to strike, although there is no evidence to suggest they are any less bored or alienated by working on tedious and repetitive tasks. What seems to be important is the range of available alternatives. For women, being less mobile than men, there are fewer choices (Di Domenico, 1973).

Convention within the industrial world has it that women are better suited to boring jobs and those requiring a degree of manual agility and dexterity. By the same token, women are regarded as unsuited to heavy work, or tasks requiring some strength and stamina or unpleasant working conditions. However, traditionally women were and continue to be engaged in heavy manual labour. Thus women at the Cashew Nut factory were employed in the store to lift bags of produce weighing about 100 kilos. Subsequently, with a change of management, this task was reallocated to male employees. Women are now principally employed to peel, grade and pack the nuts.

Comparable notions and biases have, until recently, characterised sociological contributions in this field of study. Industrial sociology has tended to be male-oriented, and when the position of women in industry is analysed they have often been dismissed (on little or no evidence) on the grounds that they are satisfied with monotonous work and low-status positions, in so far as their commitment is to their families rather than to their jobs (see Blauner, 1964, p. 81). The research carried out in Ibadan does not lend support to this traditional stereotype of the female worker.

Unfortunately, some of the new large industries being established in Nigeria, such as the Leyland Nigeria truck assembly plant in Ibadan and the Peugeot and Volkswagen plants elsewhere in the country, fit the second profile, as industries most likely to employ men. Furthermore, those large-scale concerns which before had a reasonable proportion of women are now running down their female labour force. This appears to be due to a number of factors. First, government regulations, drawn up to protect women also serve to discourage employers from employing them. Of chief consideration (from the employer's viewpoint) are time lost (through three-month maternity leaves, for example) and the difficulties of organising shiftwork schedules. (With the exception of a limited number of categories such as nurses, women are not allowed by law to work on the night shift. Secondly, employers' choices are influenced also by the availability of male alternatives. Female labour generally belongs to the unskilled and semi-skilled categories, but these are also the categories for which there is a large potential male workforce. Few women belong to the highly skilled (or managerial) category, where workers are often in short supply. Neither is it the prerogative of women to work in factory catering or clerical jobs. Men are frequently employed as clerks, typists and office messengers, and in the company canteen. Thus the labour market which is developing inhibits the employment of women in factories.

Attitudes of Male and Female Factory Workers

Both sexes share to a considerable extent the same norms, values and perceptions regarding work and income generation. Both men and women are family-oriented in terms of sharing multiple financial obligations to dependent children and kin and both share an instrumental attitude to factory employment. Neither sex favours long-term industrial employment, however, preferring temporary attachment to a firm rather than permanent involvement in the industrial way of life. Indeed, factory workers are often already involved in part-time business activities outside the factory. In the early NTC study, for example, half the women workers were engaged in such activities as sewing and trading which often impinged upon the factory itself. Women sold clothing, cloth and other items in their cloakroom during break-times, even in contravention of management rules. Similarly, it was found that female workers in the Lafia Canning factory also engaged in trading activities and many hoped to leave the factory when they had acquired enough capital to expand their trading ventures. This was especially so among casual workers whose remuneration from factory work was very low (Fagbemi, 1978).

Although all workers, regardless of sex, tend to see the future in terms of independence and business entrepreneurship, commitments to kin combined with very high rates of inflation are making it difficult to save capital. Hence, workers, whatever their sex, grade, or skill, tend to be employed and perceive their immediate employment on a semi-long-term basis. In the public sector employees may work until voluntary retirement at age 45, and a majority wish to do so. In this way, a period of full-time wage-employment may enable a worker to achieve the hope and dream of a self-owned business, in a world of commerce which has traditionally been a woman's as well as a man's world. Yet, given the opportunity structure within the industrial sector, men are in a better position to accumulate capital and are thus better able to buy in greater bulk and sell at lower prices and thereby lower the rate of profit of less advantaged female traders. Nevertheless, both a lack of formal employment and a reduction of opportunities means that the realisation of the Nigerian worker's dream, male or female, is becoming more and more unrealistic and unattainable. For example, in the early 1970s during the oil boom period employees left the NTC factory regularly to take up trading, contracting and other business activities. The opportunities to do so are now considerably reduced and workers are more reluctant to gamble with their hard-won jobs.

Although both men and women regard wage-employment in the industrial sector as an important avenue to acquiring sufficient capital for establishing a business, women workers find their opportunities more limited than those of their male counterparts. There is competition for wage-employment in the urban areas, but women's opportunities are restricted to a narrower range of jobs.

Employers tend to be perceived by workers as exhibiting preference for men, due to the extent to which women's family commitments are seen as impinging upon their role as workers. This perception is a realistic one. In Ibadan the majority of workers take up
employment in factories in their twenties and thirties. Retirement is
possible as early as at 45 years in the public sector and it is also
generally earlier in the private sector than in industrialised countries.
Factory work is, therefore, concentrated in the period during which
women are most likely to be child-bearing and child-rearing. It coincides with that part of their life-cycle when they are expected to be
primarily responsible for taking their children to schools, doctors, and
so forth. For example, few female factory workers' husbands were
responsible for taking children to school, and two-fifths of such husbands did not participate at all in domestic chores. Studies of women
workers at the Cashew Nut factory and at the Lafia Canning factory
confirm this finding (Arinola, 1978; Fagbemi, 1978). Owing to the
nature of the contemporary urban environment, in particular the time
involved in travelling about the city, such tasks may take several
hours a day. This may be why women come to be regarded as less
satisfactory workers than men. The time taken off work may be considerable. Maternity leave is obligatory for six weeks before and after
child-bearing, and women tend to bear on average five to eight children, generally having a child every two years. Protective legislation
designed to promote maternal and child health allows lactating
women to finish work one and a half hours earlier than usual in order
to breastfeed.

Conclusion

The unpopularity of women workers is thus due mainly to the fact
that child-bearing and child care are largely female tasks. This
accounts for the decrease in female labour participation through
replacement of female employees by males. This policy on the part of
employers is apparent in a number of firms, especially in the profit-
oriented private sector. The situation is somewhat different in the
public sector, as the country's constitution supports women's claims.
The attitudes of male managers towards female labour tend to be
very negative, combining traditional and modern prejudices. Thus although women are expected to work outside the home and to contribute to family maintenance, they are regarded as inferior employees to men. Some of the managers interviewed at the NTC factory
accused women of being less committed to their jobs than men,
although this is not supported by records on absenteeism and lateness
on duty (see Laws, 1976).

Both men and women share basically similar needs, attitudes and values regarding employment, but the way they are perceived by potential employers and able to work as employees differs considerably. Apparently as a consequence, income-generation opportunities for women in factory employment are currently decreasing and the percentage of women employed in the modern economic sector is likely to remain small, compared with their high level of participation in other spheres; even though there is nothing intrinsically different in the occupational attitudes and aspirations for playing an effective role in factory production and economic development in Nigeria, there will have to be a reallocation of child care tasks and responsibilities to facilitate a more equal participation of both sexes in the labour force. Otherwise women in Nigeria will be forced into a position of increasing structural ambivalence, trying to resolve conflicts associated with the performance of domestic roles combined with modern work roles. As it is now, women are increasingly relegated to a narrow restricted area in the modern factory sector and their lot is likely to be one of part-time, low-paid seasonal employment in light industries such as state-owned food-processing enterprises. This sex-typing and restriction of employment opportunities for women, and the consequent unequal and imbalanced occupational distribution of employed women in the modern labour market will play a potentially critical part in the perpetuation of the unequal status of women and men.

Notes: Chapter 18

The author would like to acknowledge Dr. J. Leishman and Mr O. O. Taiwo, both former postgraduate students of the Department of Sociology of the University of Ibadan, for their invaluable help. The former assisted with the analysis and helped to edit this chapter. The latter helped at the data collection stage. The author would also like to acknowledge the help of the sociology students who assisted at various stages of the project.

1   The study was first developed as part of a larger project on working women in Ibadan and Abeokuta undertaken in 1976. The data on factories and their employment of men and women were collected as part of a general survey of male and female employment in various locations in the two cities. It was decided to conduct follow-up studies in Ibadan and to undertake more in-depth analyses. In order to do so, managers in each of the industries were interviewed at length by the researcher or student assistants. Approximately thirty managers were interviewed over the period 1976–80, representing not only the broad spectrum of both public and private organisations but also departments within organisations such as personnel and production. Six managers who represented the various industrial and departmental sectors and who were exceptionally co-operative were interviewed in greater depth over the whole period.
    A random sample of 52 men and 55 women were interviewed in 1976 by two research assistants at the NTC factory, four other privately owned factories in a few

of which there is some state government participation although control is in private hands (e.g. the Nigerian Bottling Company factory), and a private and publicly owned press; 150 interviews (75 men and 75 women) were conducted at the same company in 1980 by O. O. Taiwo and others, and between the two sets of interviews various groups of undergraduate students conducted projects in the factories and reached conclusions which give support to the findings presented here.

2   A chi-square test of significance showed that these changes in male and female private factory labour are statistically significant at the 0·001 level.

Chapter 19

Female and Male Factory Workers in Accra

EUGENIA DATE-BAH

One situation which provides the observer with a good opportunity to view relationships between women and men in the African urban setting is the workplace. The workplace is one of the 'key environments', the others being the neighbourhood and the church, where contacts with ethnically diverse people or strangers are fostered in the African urban context (Gugler and Flanagan, 1978, p. 75). The workplace, however, differs very much from the other two contexts because the worker has no choice regarding who become workmates. This chapter sets out to examine, among other things, the kinds of relationships which emerge between women and men when they are brought together to work in a factory in an African city.

To talk about the relationships between females and males in factory employment in Ghana is to describe something not very typical, because very few Ghanaian men and even far fewer women are found in factory employment. Women form only 3 per cent of the total labour force in industrial wage-employment in Ghana. Indeed, the small number of females in factory employment seems to be a common feature of African countries. According to E. Boserup (1970, p. 109), 'in all developing countries women in industrial occupations account for less than one fifth of the employees' and 'even in West Africa with high female literacy, by African standards, very few women are employed in the modern sector'. In Ghana the women are more frequently self-employed (as traders, bakers, seamstresses), and for a number of reasons appear to prefer it to industrial employment because with the former they can have more flexible working hours. This constitutes a great advantage for married women with small children, especially in the urban areas where they less frequently have kinswomen to give a helping hand in caring for the children (Oppong *et al.*, 1975). Self-employment, however, has a disadvantage, namely, the irregularity of the income derived from it. Many of the Ghanaian women in the study to be discussed below disclosed this to be their main reason for choosing regular wage-employment.

Very few studies are reported in the literature which try to compare female and male workers in factory employment in the African urban context. One is Elkan's study of the employees of a tobacco factory at Jinja in Uganda (Elkan, 1955). Another is a study of a small cosmetics factory in Accra, where sex appeared to be a very important factor in the formation of friendship groups or clusters found among the factory workers. Most of the workers with friends in the factory mentioned only friends of the same sex (Date-Bah, 1972, p. 95).

The present chapter reports on a study carried out in another factory in Accra. It tries to spell out not only the differences in social characteristics between the females and males there, but also differences in absenteeism and lateness, supervision and informal relationships. Sex is seen to be an important variable, which accounts for many differences among Ghanaian industrial workers in the urban work situation with respect to their behaviour and relationships.

The data to be discussed were collected through interviews and observations in 1972–3 in a study of a Ghanaian garment factory in Accra. At the time of the study the factory had been in operation for ten years and the average length of service of the employees was 8·6 years. These facts stress the point that the employees had been working together for a long enough period for relationships which had emerged between the sexes to have become stabilised.

A garment factory was chosen as the subject of the study for a number of reasons. The first is that it is in the garment industry that we find a substantial number of the few Ghanaian women who are in industrial wage-employment. Secondly it is here that we see many of the women engaged in actual industrial work rather than the secretarial and clerical duties which are their common lot. This is because sewing, the main work done in this factory, has been found, in addition to trading and baking, to be among the occupations which seem to attract Ghanaian women (Peil, 1966, p. 36). Women thus formed 48 per cent of the factory's 283 employees. We first discuss the similarities and contrasts between these Ghanaian women and men in their life and social characteristics and working behaviour. We then move on to analyse the various types of informal relationships which have emerged among the employees at the workplace, in order to ascertain whether sex is an important factor accounting for these relationships.

Among the similarities between the male and female workers is the fact that they were almost all first-generation entrants into industrial wage-employment since their parents were mostly farmers and/or traders. Although there were Ga (people from Accra) among them, most of them were migrants to Accra, coming mainly from the Eastern, Central and Volta regions and very few from Ashanti and Brong Ahafo. Almost all were educated, mainly up to elementary school level. This high proportion of educated people in the factory, in a country where 56 per cent of the population have had no education, is explicable in terms of the factory's deliberate recruitment policy, to employ people with some education, since the tailors and seamstresses have to be able to measure and to read the instruction cards on the garments to be sewn. Again, there was no difference between the sexes with respect to the skill they had, namely, sewing, which they had all learned before their recruitment into the factory. Both sexes appeared also to be mostly parents and married under the customary law. Both groups appeared again to bear obligations to kin in the form of monthly monetary and other remittances to parents and others. Apart from these few similarities between men and women workers, there were also some differences with respect to other aspects of their social characteristics. The women were slightly younger than the men. The average age of the females was 33 years while that of their male counterparts was 36 and this was related to the stage reached in their working career. Those who were in their first full-time job tended to be mainly women, while quite a few of the men were in their third, fourth, or fifth jobs.

Although most of the employees (86 per cent) were married, there were differences between the sexes with respect to the extent of monogamy and polygamy. A higher percentage of the women tended to be in polygynous marriages (23 per cent) while only 10 per cent of the men were. Again, a higher percentage of the women than the men were divorced or separated: almost a fifth of the women (19 per cent) compared with only 3 per cent of the men.

Some differences between the sexes were also noted with respect to who cared for the employees' children while they were at work. Here more than two-thirds of the male workers (68 per cent) relied on their wives while only 2 per cent of the women mentioned their husbands. Most of the factory women tended to rely on parents/grandparents, maidservants and relatives (65 per cent). Again, twice as many women (17 per cent) as men (8 per cent) had children who were old enough to look after themselves while their parents were at work.

Other differences found were with respect to household obligations and activities engaged in after work. While the average time for getting up each morning for the women was 5 a.m., that for the men was around 6 a.m. This difference in the hour of waking up is related to the difference between the sexes with respect to the household chores performed before leaving the house for work each morning. While the men generally did nothing except get themselves ready for work, the women swept the house and fetched water from a nearby pipe, because most of them were living in working-class or poor residential areas where dwelling units did not possess their own water supplies. They also lit the coalpot or fire and boiled water to bathe their children and themselves. This was followed by the preparation of breakfast and also washing of children's clothes. Those with helpers in the form of maids or other relatives got assistance, but those without assistance performed all these chores single-handed before leaving the house for work.

The off-the-job activities engaged in by the employees after work and at the weekends also showed a marked sex difference. The women spent a lot of their time in household chores, such as cooking, washing and cleaning the house, while the men had a lot of free time to devote to recreational activities and resting. Generally, however, both these men and women workers participated in additional money-earning activities such as sewing for their private customers and trading after work. The respondents operated these private businesses in order to supplement their factory pay, which they described as poor and insufficient for their needs. Again, for both sexes the single most important activity on Sunday was going to church, since most of them belonged to one Christian religion or another. Both sexes also could not indulge in much visiting of work friends and kinsmen after work, because they tended to live in different parts of the city and the fact the Accra city's public transportation system tended to be irregular did not facilitate this. Moreover, their participation in additional money-earning activities left them with very little time to devote to visiting friends.

Not much dissimilarity was observed between men and women with respect to quality of work, the women were just as capable as the men in sewing the various items manufactured in the factory. It was noted, for example, that there was a small group in the production room known as 'special tailors and seamstresses', who sewed the complexly designed garments which people ordered from the factory, and this group consisted of just as many women as men. These were the people who had been found to be highly skilled and gifted at sewing.

With respect to the quantity of output, not much difference could be observed, because at the time of the study the workload given to each worker was generally low and, thus could be completed well before the end of the working period each day. This implied that one could not easily observe any output differences between the sexes except on occasions when some of the women came to work so late that they could not complete their day's workload.

The main areas where a difference in work behaviour existed between the sexes were absenteeism and lateness. Although the absenteeism rate was not particularly high (7·5 per cent), it was realised that the rate for the women was higher than that for the men workers. The women's absence rate was 9 per cent, while that of the men was only 4 per cent.

This comparatively higher female absenteeism rate seems to be quite a widespread feature. Behrend (1951) also observed a similar phenomenon in the fifty-one factories she studied in Britain. She reported that the absenteeism rate of the British women ranged from 5 to 9 per cent while that for the men was 3·5 per cent. Various explanations have been offered by people to explain the high incidence of women's absences. For example, Argyle, Gardner and Cioffi (1958) offer two possible explanations. One is that absenteeism is higher among unskilled workers and since women tend to have less skilled jobs this explains why they have a high absenteeism rate. According to their second explanation, working women's higher absence rate is due to domestic affairs which impinge on women, especially married women, more than on men. Since almost all the women workers in this Ghanaian garment factory are in skilled jobs, it would appear that Argyle et al.'s first explanation is not applicable to them. Rather relevant is the second reason, since most of the women were married with children and even some of those who were not currently married had children. They therefore absented themselves not only when they themselves were ill but also when their children were ill.

With respect to lateness, although it was found to be less widespread in the factory and to some extent attributable to the poor and irregular transportation system in the city of Accra, it was also observed that the women were more often late than the men. On one occasion during the study period ten seamstresses came to work twenty minutes late. The senior production supervisor stressed the fact that no tailor or male employee was among the latecomers and warned the seamstresses that they would be sent home if they did not refrain from lateness. The next day this supervisor ordered the production room door to be closed five minutes after the start of the shift and three seamstresses who were late were sent home and thus lost their wages for that day.

Like the higher female absenteeism rate, this higher female propensity to be late to work is also explicable in terms of the duties they have to perform at home, such as cooking for the family and cleaning the house before rushing to the bus and lorry stations to queue for long periods for transporation to work. Some even reported sometimes foregoing their breakfast when they realised that they were going to be late to work. This higher female lateness rate would thus seem to be one of the consequences of a woman, or more precisely of a mother or wife, combining her domestic duties with wage employment outside the home.

With regard to turnover, none of the factory's employees, women or men, left their employment either voluntarily or involuntarily during the nine-month period of the study. The employees' intention to remain in the factory or go elsewhere to work was investigated. It was obvious from the responses that while most of the men wanted to leave for higher pay elsewhere, the women, although also discontented with their pay, were generally more inclined to stay. If sticking to one's job is taken as one index of commitment, then these Ghanaian factory women could be described as having a higher commitment to their work than their male colleagues.

With respect to promotions, not much difference was observed between the men and the women. There was no evidence to show that men were favoured in promotion exercises in the factory. The top manager in the factory was a man and his assistant was a women. Next in rank were the production officer and his assistant who were males and who were the longest-serving employees in the factory. The remaining supervisors comprised an equal number of men and women.

As far as supervision is concerned, although according to the formal hierarchical arrangement of the various positions in the factory the female and male supervisory positions should carry with them an equal degree of formal authority, there was a difference between the sexes in their supervisory behaviour. The male supervisors were much more likely than their female counterparts to sanction the workers. The junior male supervisors were often observed reporting subordinates to the senior supervisor. The female junior supervisors, on the other hand, were withdrawn in the performance of their supervisory role and, on the whole, were shadowy figures. For example, no female supervisor was found during the study period to have reprimanded or reported subordinates, while this was a feature of the supervisory style of the male supervisors.

All the supervisors were observed to associate informally with their subordinates, chatting with them during the recess. The female supervisors, more than their male counterparts, however, engaged in this close fraternisation with their female subordinates. The female supervisors in the production room were often in charge of lines one and six where most of the workers were female. Although there were also a few male workers on these lines, the female supervisors did not appear to accept much jurisdiction over them. After allocating the cut materials to be sewn for the day by each worker on these lines, these female supervisors often joined their female subordinates on the lines and were sometimes observed to converse and generally interact informally with them while working.

This non-acceptance of jurisdiction over male subordinates might have stemmed from the fact that occasionally when there were female garments[1] to be sewn the female supervisors supervised only the seamstresses, and the males on these lines joined their other colleagues in sewing male garments. There was no observed evidence to support the contention that the male workers on these lines were reluctant to accept female supervision over them.

What was evident was that through intense interaction, friendship bonds had developed between the female supervisors and their female subordinates, and this friendship imposed a fetter on the female supervisors' exercise of their official sanctioning powers. Thus, because they often chatted during working hours with their female subordinates, they could not ask the latter to refrain from talking when they indulged in too much of it while working. This was usually done by the male production officer or his assistant.

It could be that since this factory's female supervisors had very hard-working male supervisors, like the production officer and his assistant, to do their work for them, they could adopt a lax attitude towards their female subordinates. This meant that they could avoid unpleasant rebukes which might prejudice the friendly relationships between them and their female subordinates. The female supervisory behaviour could not be viewed as a simple reflection of any cultural differences between males and females in the wider Ghanaian society, since there is evidence for and against the view that Ghanaian traditional society is male-dominated. For although in the domestic domain the main figure of authority is the man, marked ambivalence has been noted (Bleek, 1976) and while men hold many traditionally important political positions women also hold important parallel positions (see Arhin, Chapter 5 above, Okonjo, Chapter 14 above). Also the prevalence of the matrilineal system among the Akan group and the vigorous economic roles played by Ghanaian women support female influence and power.

Informal Relations among the Employees

The employees in this garment factory were observed to participate in a number of informal interactions at the workplace such as friendship associations, card-playing and lottery groups and rotating credit associations (*susu*).

In connection with friendship, the workers were asked in the interview who their 'real friends' in the factory were. In spite of the interactions which were observed to occur between most of the workers in the factory during break-time and sometimes during working hours, not all the employees considered the people they interacted with as their friends. Two-fifths of the employees said they did not have any 'real friends' in the factory. Sex, rather than common ethnicity, age and kinship, was the important basis for these work friend-ships. In most cases where the respondents had friends in the factory, the friends belonged to the same sex. Most of their friends from other contexts were also of the same sex as the respondents. Among the activities the friends reported participating in together were conver-sation, sometimes eating together during the lunch/dinner break, providing each other with advice and financial assistance, and in some cases exchange of home visits.

Apart from friendships, some of the other informal associations were cigarette-sharing, card-playing and working on the lottery. The women there did not smoke or show much interest in the lottery. With regard to cigarette-sharing some of the workers who liked smok-ing but could not afford it every day tended to smoke one stick in turns when a member was able to procure one. Those who worked on the lottery were always seen during the break-time checking their staked numbers in the newspapers or discussing which numbers to put their stakes on. Some also engaged in joint-staking.

The *susu* groups among the employees in the factory, were, how-ever, found to be mixed. Men and women belonged to the same group, as did supervisors and ordinary workers. These *susu* groups are primarily economic groups in the sense that they are contributory clubs where members pay fixed sums of money at regular intervals (in this factory, monthly) and the sum realised is given to each member in rotation.

In conclusion, a point can be made regarding the salient difference in life and daily experiences and work behaviour of women and men in the factory. Their daily life patterns appeared to be dissimilar, with the women undergoing an arduous 'double-day' with respect to the factory work and the performance of their household chores and child care duties, which naturally affected their work behaviour. I remarked at the beginning that Ghanaian women often express a preference for work in the 'informal sector', self-employment and cottage industries, which they can more easily combine with domestic and maternal roles. Certainly these women in factory employment were at a disadvantage in comparison to their male counterparts, who were definitely not shouldering their burdens of household responsibilities.

Although it used to be relatively easy for a woman in urban wage-employment to have the services of a less well-off relation or a hired maid in the performance of her domestic chores and child care, it is increasingly being observed that the situation has changed drastically, with rapidly growing numbers of the female population becoming formally educated and shunning domestic employment or demanding higher fees. Thus for the female low-paid wage-earner, combining formal regular employment with domestic and child care duties in the urban area involves great strain and stress, the more so since there are very few crèches and nurseries which could take over some of her child care duties, at least during her working hours, and there are no developed appropriate technologies to lessen the drudgery in her domestic work. Ghana is not likely to experience much increase in its female industrial wage labour force unless, *inter alia*, the above handicaps are considerably reduced; for example, through an increase in the number of crèches in workplaces, husbands assuming some of the domestic duties and responsibilities, and the use of simple appropriate time- and labour-saving technologies in the home.

Note: Chapter 19

1   The factory sewed mainly male garments such as uniforms for the army, border guards and navy.

Chapter 20

Urban Contacts: A Comparison of Women and Men

MARGARET PEIL

The high level of sociability in West African towns cannot fail to impress the observer. The high density of housing, the importance of open markets, the ease in striking up conversations in buses and lorries, the companionship available at workplaces (as, for instance, described by Date-Bah in Chapter 19), provide many opportunities to make friends. Moreover, these are societies in which social contacts provide important economic and political resources. Mutual aid and communal identity are needed in everyday living as well as in emergencies. Prestige is given to people with large numbers of clients or with important patrons, and a low value is put on privacy and isolation. Thus, both men and women have high levels of social involvement. They find these contacts both necessary for daily living and socially rewarding.

Opportunities and Sociability

This chapter investigates the question of the relationships between marriage, employment and friendship contacts, comparing men and women in six towns in Nigeria and The Gambia. Have women narrower circles of friends than men? Does work outside the home expand or constrict the opportunities of urban women to develop friendships and make acquaintances, and to get help in emergencies? Are there differences between the sociability of wage- and self-employed men and women which are independent of education and income? In so far as social contacts add to satisfaction with life in town, greater opportunities for socialising outside the home could encourage more women to enter the labour force, if necessary by overcoming their husbands' resistance. On the whole, the data confirm impressions about the high sociability of urban residents, but they show that structural factors ensure that women have a somewhat narrower range of contacts than men.

The difference between housewives and women in wage- or self-employment is an important one. Wage-employment for African women is still limited, but is expanding with increased educational opportunities. There has been some controversy over the positive and negative effects of these changes. For example, Oppong (1970) showed that Accra women with an income, contributing to domestic expenditure, were more likely to influence conjugal decision-making, to plan their affairs autonomously, or to maintain a relatively egalitarian relationship. Dinan (1977) found that educated Ghanaian professional women often postpone marriage because they hesitate to marry a man who would probably not offer the kind of conjugal relationship they desire. Schuster (1979) found that educated women in Zambia need a career because husbands cannot be depended on for support; the social life of housewives is very limited and divorce, which is common and not followed by alimony, makes a return to employment essential.

Shortage of time is often mentioned as a major problem for working women. Traders work long hours, but women in wage-employment are also expected to fit in shopping, cooking and running the house, even if they are fortunate enough to find someone to look after the children (problems which have been mentioned in Chapters 18 and 19 with regard to factory workers). Pellow (1977) has provided a picture of a very limited social life for both housewives and traders, with little socialising even among co-tenants. However, Dinan, who also studied Accra, found that most women living without husbands she observed had an active social life with friends in their houses and at work (see Chapter 25).

The data came from studies of four towns in Nigeria (Aba in the south-east; Abeokuta in the south-west; Ajegunle, a suburb of Lagos; and Kakuri, a suburb of Kaduna, in the north) and the two largest Gambian towns, Banjul and Serekunda. Censuses of about 100 houses in each town provided the framework for quota samples of about 150 men and 50 women, who were interviewed about their social contacts, among other topics (see Peil, 1979, pp. 483–4). There is considerably more variability in the results for the Nigerian towns, due to differences in size, culture, labour force opportunities and length of stay, than in the Gambian towns. However, because of the small number of women respondents in each, especially in certain age and educational categories, data for each country have been combined here. This hides some important differences, but makes it possible to demonstrate others.

The expected relationships were measured by examining data on the number of friends,[1] a sociability scale[2] and a problem scale.[3] Wage- and self-employment, marital and parental status, age, education, income and length of residence in town were examined for their effects on friendship and acquaintance patterns. In all categories, Nigerian men were more sociable and had more friends than Gambian men, though some categories of Gambians were more likely than Nigerians to seek help beyond their kin-group. Differences between Nigerian and Gambian women were much less consistent.

Background information was less useful for predicting the number of friends than for overall sociability or where an individual would go for help; even in these latter cases it explained only a small proportion of the variance.[4] Income was the best predictor of the number of friends and sources of help; labour force participation told somewhat more about sociability. Length of residence was the best overall predictor when the other variables were taken into account. Marriage is a more important constraint on women than on men. Age had some inhibiting effect on sociability, as network resources do not appear to increase with age as depicted. Education had relatively little independent effect, appearing to be a facilitator rather than a cause of increased sociability.

Employment

The labour force participation of women differed considerably between the two countries, providing far more opportunities for Nigerian than for Gambian women. Most Gambians are Muslim, and women are usually expected to remain at or near home, unless they are well educated. There are some women traders, but these tend to be widows or otherwise needy women who lack male support. The relatively limited access of Gambian girls to education and limited opportunities for female wage-employment mean that those who succeed are mostly more elite in background than is the case in Nigeria. They also have more opportunities for being out and about, interacting with friends, than housewives. Self-employment is far more common among Nigerian women, and housewives are less constrained to remain at home. Thus, there is less difference between the three categories than in The Gambia.

The differences between Gambian men and women in the mean number of friends and mean sociability scores are rather small, but men in all three employment categories were more likely than women to look beyond kinship for problem-solving. Thus, the Muslim ethos appears to have less effect on the scope of women's sociability than on emphasising their essential dependence on husbands and kinsmen. Several women said that they would call on their husbands for help if there were difficulties at work, thus bringing conjugal relations into what should be a universalistic, bureaucratic situation.

Self-employed Nigerian women have a reputation for independence of action and ability to make the most of their opportunities. Housewives also appear to be less constrained to remain at home, at least in the southern towns. It is therefore not surprising to find that position in the labour force has almost no effect on the number of friends Nigerian women reported. Wage-employment does facilitate increased sociability, but the considerable advantage of the wage-employed in solving problems outside the kinship network declines when other variables are taken into account. For these women, it appears to be income (or husband's position), rather than wage-employment *per se*, which enhances access to non-particularistic sources of assistance.

Even more unexpected, given their reputation, is the finding that Nigerian women in all three employment categories had significantly lower means than Nigerian men in numbers of friendships,[5] sociability and problem-solving. In several cases the mean scores were even somewhat below those of the Gambian women. The main difference between the two sets of women is that scores for the Nigerian self-employed are usually much nearer to the wage-employed than to housewives, whereas Gambian self-employed women have scores very close to those of housewives. In Nigeria (at least in the south) it is the housewife who is unusual, less social and more tied to kin than her sisters. In The Gambia the wage-employed are moving toward a new and more 'liberated' norm. Part of the answer seems to be that opportunities given to a few allow them to be deviant in a variety of ways; where a pattern (such as post-primary education and wage-employment for women) becomes fairly common, those taking part are expected to maintain a more conventional life-style. Thus the Gambian woman who takes up wage-employment has usually already been deviant in acquiring an education; this helps to make wage-employment and greater freedom of movement possible.

Other Factors

Women's ability to use contacts outside the family for solving problems appears to be enhanced by a relatively high income; among men, a relatively low income is a constraining factor in problem-solving. The consistent relationship between income and sociability should not be taken to imply indefinite advantages for the rich. Because there were few wealthy people in these samples, the boundary of the open high-income category was set relatively low, at the equivalent of £750 per year.[6]

Peace (1979) has pointed out that the rich men of Agege (another low-income suburb of Lagos) have a position in the community to maintain and develop wide circles of clients to support this position.

On the other hand, poor men often avoid social contacts. At the levels of income common in these samples, the second principle seems to be more important than the first. Thus, although Nigerian men consistently report more friends and greater sociability (at all income levels) than Gambian men, the scores for those in the middle-income category are consistently closer to the high than to the low category. When it comes to seeking help, however, somewhat different factors seem to apply. The differences between The Gambia and Nigeria decline to insignificance and mean scores for middle-income respondents are somewhat closer to low- than high-income scores. Influence can be expensive.

Income makes less difference to friendship among women than among men. The only notable difference by income level between Gambian and Nigerian women is in problem-solving; very few medium- or low-income Gambian women would go beyond the family for help, whereas medium-income Nigerian women are more enterprising and considerably closer to high-income women than is the case in The Gambia. In both countries (and especially in The Gambia) a substantial income appears to give a woman greater autonomy in seeking help beyond the range of kin, which is present regardless of age, marital status or other characteristics, though they may decrease it.

The length of time spent in town is the most important of the other variables studied. As expected, the number of friendships and range of sociability increase with the length of time one lives in a place. The locally born tend to have a small advantage over long-term residents, but this is not always the case.

Respondents were asked whether those who live with a spouse make more or fewer friends than those who live alone. On the whole, they favoured their own marital status: the married thought they had more friends while the single thought they had better opportunities than married people.

Married men are more likely than the single to seek non-kin advice for problems. Married women, on the other hand, are expected and expect to get what help they need from their husbands or kin. In both societies the maintenance of kinship ties is considered very important by both men and women; the majority of people think of kin first when they need help. This help is mainly male; men go to their fathers and brothers – not to their wives, or at least this is not admitted. Women use the same sources if they lack a husband or for some reason he is unable to help. Occasionally they go to their mothers for help in a family dispute. The most common qualification for a helper is that 'he is near to me'.

It is often assumed that education will be a good predictor of the attitudes and behaviour of adults, at least in developing countries.

However, education appears to have relatively little independent effect. It is mainly a facilitator, and individuals do not necessarily make the most of it. If higher education leads to well-paid wage-employment, this may increase sociability and expand helping resources. Without these, education alone may even be a handicap. For example, although the differences are often small, both men and women with primary or Muslim schooling tend to have fewer friends, lower sociability and more reliance on kin than those who never attended school or who had more education. At the opposite extreme are well-educated Gambian women, who are set apart by their achievement and whose life-style differs because of it, and unschooled Gambian men, who were somewhat more prepared to get help from non-kin than men who had formal schooling. Lack of education is not seen as a handicap in seeking help in a society where patron–client relationships are developed through ascribed roles and personal ability.

Conclusion

Most urban residents establish fairly wide social contacts. Thus, as the large numbers of recent migrants settle down, relatively few will find the towns unfriendly places. Newcomers tend to make a few friends fairly quickly; these serve as a basis for an expanding range of contacts, some of which will be useful sources of advice and help in emergencies. Social background is a better predictor of the resources used to handle problems than of the range of social contacts or, especially, the number of close friends. The data show a definite, if small, relationship between the source and level of income of men and women and the social relationships they develop. Housewives are at a considerable disadvantage in this because they are completely dependent on their husbands for money and thus more fully under their authority. They usually appear to make a few close friends, but seem not to expand their contacts beyond household, kin and neighbourhood.

When it comes to solving problems, all women have (or at least are likely to use) more limited resources than men. When help is needed, they seek it from a man, usually their husband or a kinsman. In practice, women are probably more likely to seek advice in minor matters and even financial assistance from other women than their responses indicate, but the norm that males are knowledgeable and influential will lead some to seek male help when another woman might be more efficacious.

When various aspects of their social position are taken into account, the sociability of men and women is quite similar. Thus, the narrower contacts reported by women may be largely due to societal expectations which limit their contacts and resources: lower the education they receive, their access to wage-employment and income; delay their migration to town; and promote their withdrawal from the labour force, at least temporarily, at marriage. The example of the wage-employed Gambian women shows the possibility of change over time, but the Nigerian women's responses suggest that as education and wage-employment become more common, normative ideas about women's position will be reasserted. Thus, while it is clear that women's contacts are broadened by participation in the labour force, more fundamental change of values is necessary if they are to become more nearly equal to men in social opportunities and resources.

Notes: Chapter 20

I am grateful to the Social Science Research Council for financing data collection and to S. Barnes for her comments.

1 Since the word 'friend' can have a derogatory meaning (people one gets into trouble with), respondents were asked to provide information on 'the people you move with/see often'. While a few gave more than five, most mentioned the two or three people they felt closest to. Most of these friends lived in the same town and were seen at least once a week. Mentioning people of different ethnicity and occupation was common.

2 The sociability scale adds together responses to a number of questions on contacts, concentrating on range rather than intensity: the number of friends, of neighbours they know well and of associations they belong to; frequent conversations with co-tenants, neighbours, kin, workmates and others; eating with and visiting the rooms of people outside the household; and whether they have ever given a party. Participation in each 'area' was worth up to 3 points, except 1 for party. Scores ranged from 0 to 19, with a mean of 10·8 in The Gambia and 11·4 in Nigeria.

3 The problem scale is conceptually simpler than the sociability scale. Respondents were asked where they would seek advice or help if they needed money or a job, had trouble at work or with the police, or were involved in a family dispute. Answers received no points if help was sought from family or kin, one point for personal contacts and two for using an impersonal relationship (official, lawyer). Those who had ever actively sought to make their needs known to government officials got an extra two points. Scores ranged from 0 to 12, with a mean of 2·7 in The Gambia and 3·5 in Nigeria. This illustrates the wide reliance on kin for most kinds of assistance.

4 Readers interested in consulting detailed tabulations of statistical data computed from the survey should consult the author at the Centre of West African Studies, University of Birmingham.

5 The one exception is the number of friends reported by self-employed women, where their mean is slightly higher than the mean for self-employed men and significantly higher than that for self-employed Gambian women.

6 Of those who specified how much more than this they earned, the highest was a self-employed electrician who said he made £5,000. Only 13 per cent of the Nigerian women and 30 per cent of the Gambian women earned over £300 per year; 14 per cent of the Nigerian men and 41 per cent of the Gambian men earned

over £500. These differences are partly due to the effects of sampling and inflation. Two of the four Nigerian towns studied were low-income suburbs where few wealthy people lived.

Conclusion to Part Four

Many studies in the past have emphasised the importance of the organisation of work as a major determinant of heterosexual relations, in particular the relative contributions of women and men to subsistence activities. Thus it has been argued that female status is relatively higher in societies in which women make a substantial contribution to agriculture, such as in shifting cultivation (E. Boserup, 1970). It has also been argued that while the female role in production is a necessary condition for the existence of high or equal female status, it is not a sufficient cause (Sanday, 1974). Women might simply form the bulk of the unrenumerated family labour force. Also critical are relative access to and control of important resources, including those basic to production, such as land and labour, as well as control over the end-products – the crops, manufactured goods, or income. Thus a frequently observed fact has been that when a new resource such as training or jobs becomes available and is monopolised for one reason or another by the male half of the population, the women become relatively disadvantaged. For instance, with the introduction of new agricultural techniques and cash cropping, there is a noted worldwide tendency for men to play the dominant role in modernised agricultural production in terms of control of crops and proceeds. This was seen to be the case in the Ghanaian cocoa industry.

Meanwhile one of women's and men's customary valuable resources, children's labour, is diminishing, as increasing numbers of the young attend school, a topic touched upon earlier.

Two of the chapters on work in Part Four have considered specifically urban factory employment and a male bias has been observed especially in the profit-based industries – a bias which is growing.

In the spheres of education, training and high-level employment, we have already noted in Chapter 1 that in West Africa, as in many other parts of the world, there is a marked bias against females. Boys are more frequently sent to school and complete their courses than girls. Young men more often have access to vocational training and are ultimately preferred by employers to fill their vacant jobs. One chapter here, based on a Bauchi case study, indicates the growing dimensions of this problem for young women.

Meanwhile, in the national political arenas the traditional roles which women had have been whittled away and they have become marginal with little manifest power. In the domestic spheres there is also evidence of ideologies of male dominance and among migrants there are indications that women may be more lacking in social contacts and prone to isolation. Meanwhile popular songs are among those communications media which play a tune enhancing the male image and portraying heterosexual relations with a male bias.

In the last set of case studies we turn to a consideration of individualism, autonomy and dependence, and ask whether these are increasing for men and women.

Individualism, Autonomy and Dependence: Migrants and Urban Dwellers

Introduction to Part Five

In Part Five all the five detailed case studies describe the situation and relationships of migrants and urban dwellers based on ethnographic data from three countries, Nigeria, Ghana and Ivory Coast. Three themes recur and are dominant: the increasing individualism and the increased opportunities for social and economic autonomy on the one hand, or the dangers of dependence on the other. During the course of these descriptions we see that a profound reordering of the values associated with different roles of women and men is under way. Attitudes to marriage, child-bearing, the demands and constraints of kin and traditional community leaders are changing. A dominant leitmotiv of several chapters is the search for economic security and admission into the modern world of electrical appliances, travel and entertainments, a far cry from the harsh realities of rural farming with the cutlass and hoe. At least one author sees the basis of these changes in the altered material condition of life. In some cases traditional norms and values regarding sexual equality and autonomy are seen to facilitate women's entry into the urban world.

Independent Women on their Own

In Chapter 21 Renée Pittin has depicted 'houses of women' in Katsina, a Hausa city in northern Nigeria. These accommodate independent women, who differ from the rest of Hausa womankind in that they do not live near or with their kin, they are financially autonomous and their sexuality is not constrained by spouses. They are thus very different from the remainder of the population, in which co-residence of kin, virilocal residence at marriage and wife seclusion are the norms, and economic dependence of women upon men is demanded by the male-dominant ideology. Their status is not necessarily permanent but may alternate with periods of secluded marriage and their income-generation may depend upon sexual services or trade, such as preparation of foodstuffs. Their ultimate aim is to secure their own economic futures through purchase of property. A few manage to establish themselves as contractors. Of these most economically successful women some marry, retaining their independence and living in their own houses unrestricted by seclusion.

Transvestites, homosexuals and bisexuals are the male component of the residents. They earn their living through procuring, cooking and prostitution. They thus inverse customary sex roles by wearing female attire and doing women's work and also act as mediators between women and men in illicit sexual encounters. They are viewed as occupying an intermediate position between men and women.

The Pursuit of Economic Autonomy

The aim of Chapter 22 by Mona Etienne is to examine historical change processes in Ivory Coast, contrasting the situations of women in pre-colonial Baule society and the subsequent transformation of relationships between women and men following the colonial experience. She notes the pervasive concern with achievement of economic autonomy and perceptions of the constraining influence of marriage. For the pre-colonial period, she emphasises the relative equality and interdependence of the sexes and the relative lack of sexual antagonisms or rigid definition of gender attributes. Both sexes entered the competition for political and economic power, a theme which echoes the descriptions by Okonjo and Arhin with reference to Nigerian and Ghanaian cultural areas.

Thus she argues that Baule women's current pursuit of wealth, in the framework of contemporary urban migration, is not merely a response to new opportunities but a traditionally valued pattern, which they recollect their female forebears followed. Furthermore, in the past as in the present, marriage was eschewed by high-status women, in particular political office holders, so as not to prejudice their autonomy. In earlier times this decision was facilitated by the fact that women kept economic rights in their own kin-groups, including rights to the labour of a brother or other kinsman. With him an economic relationship could be established similar to that between spouses – a type of economic co-operation for mutual advantage between female and male kin, which compares with the situations described for fishermen and fishmongers by Vercruijsse and Hagan. From the Baule kinsman's point of view, he could build up a following among uterine kin, such as sisters and sisters' children or other maternal kin, as well as from among his wives' children. Individuals also acquired dependent labour power through fostering and adoption, a pattern widespread in West Africa.

Etienne's description of the division of labour and sharing of control of products between spouses shows great equality and flexibility. Control over surplus production for both women and men is noted to have been largely a function of control over labour of dependants, including domestic slaves, children and junior kin. The critical nature of control over labour power of children and kin is a point also emphasised by Okali in her description of cocoa farmers. In the Baule

case we are told accumulation of capital was facilitated by opportunities for long-distance trade and gold prospecting.

With regard to change, it is important to note Etienne's contention
that what has brought about the transformation is the change in
material conditions through the incorporation of Baule society into
the world economy including the introduction of cash crops. Norms,
values and beliefs are reported to be relatively stable.

During the change processes colonial and post-colonial administrations have consistently prevented or discouraged the holding of traditional political positions by women. Meanwhile women's labour in
cash cropping has not been adequately remunerated, nor have they
had equal access with men to urban-based training and employment.
Consequently many women have not been able to achieve economic
autonomy or an equal exchange of labour with their male counterparts. Some wives have become economically and socially dependent
upon their husbands. And women, we are warned, may even become
'prisoners of their marriages'.

Reluctant Spouses

Chapter 23 by Lynn Brydon focuses upon the several roles played by
the Avatime in the Volta region of Ghana, including occupational,
conjugal, domestic, parental, kin and communal roles. She describes
how formerly these several roles were interlocked within relatively
stable village societies, in which women became adult community
members, then wives, then mothers, and could subsequently appropriate kin roles within their own and their husbands' agnatic descent-
groups. The occupational and domestic roles of women and men were
complementary and inextricably intertwined with marriage. The basic
division of labour was complementary between a wife and husband,
so that the single adult status was inconceivable and economically
unviable. Now social and spatial mobility have made available opportunities for people to acquire means to earn a livelihood outside the
context of marriage, kinship and family farm. The conjugal role is no
longer basic for adult status or motherhood or economic viability or
long-term security, and increasing numbers of men and women are
remaining single into adulthood.

On the other hand, the prestige of marriage according to the introduced Christian rites and European ceremonies remains extremely
high, at least in the village context, but is too costly for most people to
attain.

The index of change upon which she focuses is the female rites of
passage, which were formerly and still are today such an important
indicator of role change for women. The puberty ceremonies socially

recognised in a graphic ritual manner a woman's nubility and reproductive capacity, at the same time as she was recognised as a potential
worker. An inherent part of the rituals was marriage and introduction
to household tasks in the agnatic descent-group of her husband. At
the same time her fecundity was transferred to her husband's agnatic
group.

Living Apart

Roger Sanjek's chapter on female and male domestic cycles is important theoretically and methodologically as well as substantively,
because he presents his materials from a suburb of Accra so as to
challenge the value of earlier models of the developmental cycle of
domestic groups. He shows that it is only valid to use a single model
in social situations in which women and men have identical life-
courses. In the Adabraka case he discusses the life-courses of women
and men are strikingly different, as he demonstrates. He shows that
domestic cycles for women and men must be examined separately.
One important contrast between the sexes is that marriage occurs and
endures through different stages of the life-cycle – much earlier for
women than for men. While most men can look forward to conjugal
residence from their thirties to their old age, and can expect to have a
wife in the house to cook and clean for them and in most cases
supplement their incomes with their wives', on the other hand for
women the probability of living in a conjugal partnership increases
while they are young but after age 35 it decreases. Most women in
their forties and onwards live in households that they head or share
with other adult women.

Sugar and Gold

In the final case study Carmel Dinan describes at length the lives of
twenty-five educated migrant young women in Accra who have or are
seeking employment of a clerical or similar nature in town. Some
head their own households living with junior kin, while some are
themselves junior relatives in households of their parents, uncles and
aunts. They supplement their earnings from employment with government and private bodies by trading and sewing and support from
friends and relatives. Suitable employment in the formal sector with
a wage which can pay a rent, transport, food and other necessities
is scarce or unobtainable for these women. They are therefore
constrained to find other strategies to cater for their needs and to
maintain standards of living to which they aspire including imported

consumer goods and hardware. An important source of such supplementary income and scarce goods is men friends.

Meanwhile they maintain their single status, although some of them have already borne children, and have no intention of marrying unless they meet prospective grooms who fit their somewhat culturally deviant expectations.

Their major life goals focus upon economic autonomy and security for themselves and individual pursuit of comfort, leisure and pleasure. They have put aside the traditional goal of prolific maternity as well as wifehood. They seek their major material advantages in urban employment, entrepreneurial activities and exploitation of heterosexual attachments. They are among the growing minority who value individual advancement and gratification more than traditional goals of high fertility and familism.

Chapter 21

Houses of Women: a Focus on Alternative Life-Styles in Katsina City

RENÉE PITTIN

'Houses of women', as the term is used in Hausa (*gidajen mata*; sing. *gidan mata*), do not necessarily house only women. Nor do most women live in 'houses of women'. Rather, the term is a euphemism for the houses which accommodate women on their own, who support themselves completely or in part by selling their sexual services, and which accommodate also other independent women, and the men who are, economically and socially, an integral part of what may be treated as the sexual *demi-monde* of Hausa society.

This study will centre on these three groups of residents in the *gidan mata*, and on their associated life-styles. An important feature of alternative life-styles in Hausa society, perhaps more particularly for the women, is the strong element of choice inherent in their adoption, and the degree of autonomy maintained by their adherents. This is most clearly apparent through consideration of the organisational structure of the *gidan mata*, and of the process of procurement; both of these are treated below.

The Setting

The city of Katsina, located in the far north of Nigeria about forty miles from the Niger border, is one of the less industrialised northern cities.[1] The basis of Katsina's urban existence at present, as over the past several hundred years, remains agriculture, commerce and administration. The population, numbering around 80,000,[2] is composed predominantly of Muslim Hausa. Designation as Hausa is based on the criteria of common language and key elements of common culture, rather than on distant historical ties.

Unlike most Hausa cities, Katsina has no strangers' quarters out-side the city walls. With the influx of migrants in the 1950s, and the need for additional housing, the emir, Alhaji Sir Usman Nagogo, designated an area within the city where the new community could expand. This area, known as Sabon Layi (New Line), includes not only most of the non-northern strangers, but also many Katsina indi-genes, and the majority of women living on their own.

During the period of research (1971–3) 123 compounds in Katsina were *gidajen mata*, occupied wholely or in part by Hausa women living away from their kin, and available for sexual liaisons. Seventy-three of these houses are located in Sabon Layi, within which are also found the majority of inexpensive hotels, beer parlours and restaur-ants. Katsina's two cinemas are sited on one side of Sabon Layi, and such night-life as there is, is centred in this section of town. Newcom-ers to the city, transients, newly arrived women on their own and men looking for women tend to gravitate to Sabon Layi.

The remaining *gidajen mata* are found in other parts of the city in which accommodation is available, and from which the women can most successfully pursue their trade. An expanding area is in the eastern and south-eastern section of the city, where nineteen *gidajen mata* are located. While not immediately next to any single major source of clientele, the area is not far from the main Katsina lorry park, the Police Barracks, and, at the time of the study, the Army Officers' Mess. Ten *gidajen mata* are near the general hospital, and another seven are on the periphery of the main Katsina city market. While a few *gidajen mata* are located in the older residential areas, most women prefer to live closer to where the action is, where they can conveniently mingle with their prospective partners.

Composition of the *Gidan Mata*: the *Karuwai*

The overwhelming majority of residents in a *gidan mata* are the category of women known in Hausa as *karuwai* (sing. *karuwa*). The term *karuwa*, as noted above, refers to a woman who is living with neither her husband, nor her parents or other kin, and who is depen-dent, totally or in part, upon gifts from one or more men, for whom she provides sexual services.

The spatial criterion is crucial, in that a woman away from her husband and relatives is no longer controlled by them, and has, by her physical removal from their presence, deviated from her socially appropriate place, in spatial and normative terms. In this situation, that she should deviate further is expected and assumed. This attitude must be seen in the context of the tremendous importance accorded to seclusion in Hausa society. Married women of child-bearing age are expected to remain within their husbands' houses except when given express consent to go out for a specified purpose, usually for ceremonial occasions. Non-married women[3] should live with their kin, and should be circumspect and moderate in their movements outside the house, lest these activities be misconstrued.

Hausa women recognise, and resent, this assumption of immorality. Some Hausa women, having fled from home due to insupportable family pressures (a common reason is the imminence, or the existence, of an unwanted marriage), do not initially become *karuwai*. However, economic need and, more important, the absolute certainty that they are believed to be *karuwai*, often tips the balance in favour of this means of sustenance. But the *karuwai* themselves point to other, non-Hausa, Nigerian women living on their own, and are bitter that such women are seen as respectable traders or businesswomen, while Hausa women are assumed to be selling their bodies as soon as they leave the confines of the marital or family home.

Only a handful of the *karuwai* had completed even primary school, so many forms of salaried employment were closed to them. However, Hausa women can be, and often are, economically self-sufficient through commodity production and trade, even from within the walls of the compound. But the dominant ideology demands physical and economic dependence of women upon men; this is extended to, and emphasised, in relation to the woman on her own.

The term *karuwa* has been translated in some studies as 'courtesan' (for example, Bernus, 1969, p. 156 and Barkow, 1971, p. 6), and indeed the *karuwa* is 'courted' rather than being more starkly bought. While 'courtesan' is probably the most appropriate English term, it presents a too-limited portrait of the *karuwa*. In order to mitigate the effects of preconceived value-judgements evoked by any imported expression, whether courtesan, harlot, or hetaira, the Hausa terminology will be used herein. The primary occupation of the *karuwa*, in Hausa, is known as *karuwanci*.

The use of the term *karuwa* also distinguishes the Hausa women from other Nigerian women working in Katsina, whose soliciting techniques are infinitely less subtle, and who generally reside in the larger clubs and hotels. These women, known in Hausa as *Akwato*[4] or 'yan how-much-you-go-pay',[5] sometimes have their minimum rate in writing on the doors of their room. Otherwise the woman and her prospective customer must agree beforehand on an acceptable price – thus the designation, 'how much you go pay'. *Karuwai* consider such behaviour shameful, and have little respect for the women involved.

Among the *karuwai* distinctions are evident in certain aspects of behaviour, dress and orientation. Some of the women, more 'modern' or Westernised than the rest, are known as 'yan good evening'. With a more aggressive soliciting technique than their traditional sisters, they are encountered on the roads frequented by wealthy motorists out for the evening; dialogue is initiated by the woman's greeting of 'good evening'. The 'yan good evening' espouse all things modern, and often wear Western dress. The more conventionally clad *karuwai*, in wrapper and blouse, tend to stay much closer to the *gidan mata*, and may wait for the prospective customer to take the initiative. However, both the 'yan good evening' and the more traditional women share the same cultural background, with the same socialisation and inculcated values. Both types of *karuwai* live together in the *gidan mata*.

During the research period more than five hundred *karuwai* were living in the *gidajen mata*. Like the Nigerian population in general, the majority of the *karuwai* were born and raised in the rural areas. The lure of the city, the bright lights and the easy living are among the many factors which may draw the women to Katsina. The *karuwai* are a young population: more than a quarter of the women were under 20, while more than three-quarters were less than 30 years old.

All of the women had been married at least once before beginning *karuwanci*, and doubtless most would marry again; an important feature of *karuwanci* is its optional nature. Not only do *karuwai* remarry but also they may well marry men who are wealthier, and of higher social status, than the men they left behind in the village. Thus, women may improve their marital prospects through the agency of *karuwanci*. On the other hand, the marriages initiated from *karuwanci* are often more fragile, and shorter-lived, than the marriages of women who have never been *karuwai*. While there are a number of contributory structural reasons for this, also important is the very fact of the alternative options open to the former *karuwa*, including a return to *karuwanci*, and, perhaps, the chance of a better spouse in future.

Other *karuwai* expect, or intend, to continue to support themselves, and plan their economic activities accordingly. About a fifth of the *karuwai* engage in some economic activity besides *karuwanci*. Some of these women, and some of the women who have been made wealthy through the generosity of their lovers, and their own economic foresight, eventually leave the ranks of the *karuwai*, and become, for all intents and purposes, independent women.

Independent Women

The substitution of the term 'independent women' for *karuwai* is significant. Women who have spent much of their adult lives outside their marital or family homes may find it difficult, or undesirable, to readapt to the expectations of submission or subservience inherent in their former roles. For women originally from a village, the harshness of rural life may be an immediate barrier to returning. However, for any woman who has lived long elsewhere, interest in returning to the natal home must be balanced against the network of friends, acquaintances and clients built up during the years of residence in the city. Moreover, greater opportunities for trade and economic independence exist in the city than can be found elsewhere.

Women who enter into *karuwanci* and who do not remarry do not necessarily remain *karuwai*: the change in others' perception of such women is a function of the women's success in their subsidiary, and subsequently primary, occupation other than *karuwanci*. The initial stepping-stone of *karuwanci* becomes no longer socially relevant. The successful independent women may or may not have lovers; the important factor is that they are no longer seen to be economically dependent on these men, and their wealth assures them respect and higher social status. While there is no separate and specific Hausa word for these women (as there is, for example, for a similar category of women in Kampala; see Halpenny, 1975, pp. 282–3), there is no doubt of the change in their status.

The use which the independent women make of their wealth is consistent with their self-reliance. Their aim is to secure their future, and the culturally approved means of so doing is through the acquisition of real estate. This is a strategy employed commonly elsewhere in Africa also. For example, Halpenny (1975, p. 282) and Obbo (1975, p. 291) point out the importance of property-ownership for women in Kampala. Bujra (1975, p. 224) notes that in early Nairobi property provided more security for women than marriage, while a recent Nairobi study (Nelson, 1977, pp. 298 and *passim*) demonstrates that the acquisition of land, houses and businesses is a primary goal for women on their own.

In Katsina 76 of the 123 *gidajen mata*, more than three-fifths of the total number, are owned by women. Almost all these houses were bought or built by the present owners; only five were inherited. The seventy-six houses are owned by seventy-one women; one woman has two houses, and one owns five. The wealthier women own other houses as well; these figures include only the *gidajen mata*.

Once in her own house, the independent woman is in an excellent position to engage in some form of large-scale trade or preparation of foodstuffs. Often this is simply a continuation of the type of work which had helped her to gain sufficient funds to acquire the house initially. All but one of these house-owners had some ongoing economic pursuit, from petty trade to salaried employment. Almost half were engaged in the selling of cooked meals, generally in the entrance room of the house. While profitable, such work is demanding and time-consuming. Assumption of this occupation demands a degree of resolution, a certain amount of wealth to stake in the venture, stability of residence and security of tenure. The independent women are particularly well placed for the task. A few women, at the apex of the economic pyramid, have established themselves as contractors, and are utilising their business acumen and their networks built up within *karuwanci*, to win themselves lucrative government contracts.

These independent women may remarry, and indeed thirteen had remarried. However, they do not depend on their husbands economically, and are certainly not secluded. Six of the thirteen women have remained in their own house, with the husbands either moving in with them or paying conjugal visits. Even with marriage, the women's independent status remains.

'Yan daudu

The third category of residents in the *gidajen mata*, while few in number, make their presence felt in a variety of ways. These are the *'yan daudu* (sing. *dan daudu*): transvestites, homosexuals and bisexuals, who are the male component of the *gidan mata*. The *'yan daudu* are intermediate, and intermediaries, between the men's and women's worlds. The most striking sub group within the category is the transvestites, who adopt not only the women's garb of wrapper and blouse, but also their mannerisms, style of speech and activities: the adaptation is uncanny. Others of the *'yan daudu* dress in men's clothing, and show no overt sign of their homosexuality or bisexuality. Many of the *'yan daudu* participate in the spirit-possession cult of *bori*. This is yet another indicator of their marginality: as in the cults described by I. M. Lewis (1971, ch. 4), adherence offers a means by which the socially deprived may gain ends not otherwise directly attainable, and mitigate or alleviate their low social and political status.

The presence of *'yan daudu* in the *gidajen mata* is predicated on a number of factors. These include their assumption of female roles and their desire to associate mainly with women; their economic activities, which can most conveniently be undertaken within the walls of the *gidan mata*; and the ambivalence of their sexuality, which is as inappropriate as the 'uncontrolled' sexuality of the *karuwai* in this overtly male-dominant society.

The economic enterprises of the *'yan daudu* are centred on three related activities: procuring, cooking and prostitution. The relationship between these activities is in their close linkage with the women's world. Procuring, the mobilisation of women for illicit sexual purposes, clearly demands close ties between the procurer and the women. The *dan daudu*, in his combination of male and female roles, can and does mediate between men and women in this context. According to Mohammed (1980, p. 4), writing of *'yan daudu* in Kano City, this role is especially important in calming prospective clients:

> Because [the *dan daudu*] is essentially a man, he becomes easy to talk to. Secondly, because he exhibits all the social characteristics of women and cherishes the values of prostitution he creates an atmosphere that removes the man's anxiety and thus is relaxed enough to confess his 'love' for the woman to the understanding and sympathetic listening of the *dan daudu*.

Not all *'yan daudu* act as procurers, but the fact that they are expected to do so, and that most of them participate, indicates the social expectations of their role.

As the *gidajen mata* are conveniently located in the strangers' area of town, and as the women in the houses provide an ever-present clientele for the food-sellers, the *gidan mata* is a reasonable site for food preparation. But clearly, the situation is rather more complex than this, in as much as the siting is a conscious choice of the *dan daudu*, who could work from other quarters, equally accessible, without remaining in the 'house of women'. The general location of the *'yan daudu* is influenced both by their desire to remain near the women and by their participation in prostitution. The *gidan mata*, with its preponderance of women, acts as a cover for men seeking homosexual services. The *dan daudu* and his sexual partners can carry out their assignations with greater discretion than would be possible if the *'yan daudu* lived together, or on their own outside the *gidan mata*.

While the *'yan daudu* occupy an intermediate position between men and women, yet their maleness still gives them prerogatives and benefits in Hausa society. This is demonstrated in certain characteristic behaviour patterns of the *'yan daudu* themselves, and of those who associate with them. Thus, for example, there was no female manager or spokesperson in any of the houses in which a *dan daudu* was resident. In all cases, the *dan daudu* or other man (the house-owner or his delegate) acted as manager.

Cooking, along with virtually all other domestic tasks, is the province of women in Hausa society. But the cooking done by the *dan daudu* partakes of the male/female nature of his role. Thus, the food prepared by the *dan daudu* is not everyday fare. Rather, the *'yan daudu* who cook, cook the better, more expensive, more prestigious foods, such as fried chicken. The distinction is rather like that between *haute cuisine* in a fine restaurant, and home cooking, that is, the women's food preparation.[6] So even in adopting women's work, the *'yan daudu* distinguish themselves and their work by the use of costly ingredients, and the production of more expensive dishes. Their choice of foodstuffs is fitting in another respect: the preparation of ready-to-eat beef, either cut into pieces and skewered (*tsire*) or grilled in slabs (*balangu*) over an open fire, is the province of men. The *'yan daudu* have appropriated the smaller animal, and the intermediate cooking process (between the men's open fire and women's pots) for their own.

Some of the *'yan daudu* are quite rich, owning their own houses, some of which they rent out. Their economic activities give them access to considerable wealth, and indeed the bisexuals and heterosexuals among them are considered good marital catches. The marginality of their position as men is often counterbalanced in marriage negotiations by exceptional generosity in the payment of bridewealth and indirect dowry. As is evident among the independent women also, much wealth can nullify or greatly mitigate the effects of other negative status indicators.

Social Organisation in the *Gidan Mata*

Much of the literature concerning *karuwanci* and the houses of women focuses on its hierarchical political structure, dominated by the figure of the head of the *karuwai*, the Magajiyar Karuwai.[7] Appointed by the traditional ruler in the area, the Magajiya acted as liaison between the masculine power structure and the *karuwai*, exercised some control over the *karuwai* in her domain, and was, nominally or actively, leader of the spirit-possession cult. A function of the Magajiya was to protect the *kurawai* from those who sought to mistreat or defraud them. Thus, in *Baba of Karo*: 'if any man took a prostitute to his house and did not give her any money, she was to make a complaint to Magajiya, who would make the man pay the woman her money and also fine him' (M. Smith, 1954, p. 64).

The most striking feature of the organisation of *karuwanci* in Katsina now is the relatively egalitarian nature of the social relations between women, and the lack of structural importance of the former, and formal, female hierarchy. A negative consequence of this is that, with no formal legitimisation or representation, the women are a category ripe for exploitation, and this creates considerable difficulties for them.[8] The women try to avoid confrontation with the authorities, with the threat to their livelihood and well-being which such confrontation entails.

Yet even at the level of the *gidajen mata*, there is a notable absence of formal distribution of authority. In some houses a particular woman may act for the house-owner, collecting rent and overseeing repairs. In this capacity she may be known as the manager (*manaja*) by the other tenants, and she may exercise the limited authority such a post confers. The manager, or an older woman, or the resident living longest in a house, or the most popular woman, may be permitted by the other residents to act as spokesperson for the group, but this is not common.

In houses which are owner-occupied, the senior person is invariably the owner herself. Such authority as she exerts over the residents is directly related to her control over housing and other economic resources. As wealthier members of the community, the houseowners have the resources to supply food, clothing, and/or accommodation on credit to the poorer *karuwai*, who are then under obligation to them.[9] There are a few house-owners in Katsina who are notorious for their attempts to exploit their tenants; turnover of rooms in their houses is high, as the women seek more congenial surroundings. The mobility of the *karuwai*, and the abundance of housing in Katsina, militate against strict constraint or control. A house-owner must be tactful in marshalling the services of her tenants, debts notwithstanding, if she expects to retain them.

Another effect of the wide availability of accommodation for *karuwai*, and of the women's mobility, is that groups of friends, fellow townswomen, older women, or some other category of women, may take over, *en masse*, or over time, an entire compound or compounds. Such houses seem like nothing so much as college sorority houses, each with its particular ambience and interests.

The characteristics which influence the kind of women in a particular house affect also the kind of men who visit the house, and vice versa. There is a quite striking distinction in the clientele of different houses: some houses tend to attract men from certain trades; some have a large percentage of young salaried workers. Women in some houses are better dressed and more sophisticated than their sisters in other houses, and it is the former that the senior civil servants and rich businessmen tend to patronise. Some houses 'specialise' in soldiers, while others, with a preponderance of unsophisticated rural women, provide a more comfortable setting for visiting villagers unaccustomed to city ways. The spatial move from house to house is often accompanied by a mental shift, such as from urban to rural, from generation to generation, or from city to city.

Procurement

The process of procurement demonstrates well the freedom of choice and action which the *karuwai* command. Most women find their own men, usually by frequenting the places in which likely clients will be found. Other than the *gidajen mata* themselves, women may find partners in bars, restaurants, clubs, hotels and cinemas. Any event planned to attract a large number of people – racing, football, dances – draws *karuwai*. The widespread seclusion in Katsina restricts the frequency, duration and direction of married women's movement outside the house; their usual destinations are the houses of other married women. Thus, women seen at these events, or at most forms of mixed entertainment, are assumed to be *karuwai* and available. Men and women can easily approach each other in these situations and arrange to meet.

While men from all levels of Hausa society engage in extra-marital affairs, it is expected that the men of high status in particular should conduct their affairs with some discretion. It is usually in relation to these men that the services of a procurer (m. *kawali*, f. *kawaliya*) are, at least initially, required. There are significant differences in the rights, and roles, of the Hausa procurer, in comparison with his Western counterpart. The Hausa procurer has exclusive control over no women. The *karuwai* are free agents; they may use the services of a number of procurers, or of one, or none. There is no long-term commitment on either side, although *karuwai* living in the house of a procurer, whether the resident house-owner or a *dan daudu*, are more likely to arrange their assignations through the resident middle-person than are others. Some of the procurers in Katsina are men who provide these services as a part-time occupation; these men are not resident in the *gidan mata*.

The procedure of procurement is the same in most cases. A man or his representative approaches a procurer, who undertakes to introduce the man to a woman, or women, he would like. Women who receive work from the procurer show their appreciation of his assistance by giving him some of the money they receive. This amount will depend on the amount the woman has received, and on her interest in maintaining contact with the procurer for future work. The procurer will of course favour the more open-handed women, and their own generosity is increased by greater access to free-spending men. The procurer profits also from the men who have sought his help, who either at the time or subsequently send him some money in payment. These transactions are not standardised at a fixed percentage, or at a flat rate. Each of the participants gives the amount consonant with his or her benefits, status and future expectations. The success of the procurer depends not upon control of a group of women, but rather upon his or her tact and finesse, and access to a good information network in order to learn of and act upon the whims and desires of his or her clients.

Conclusion

The *gidajen mata*, or houses of women, are the locus of activities for *karuwai*, independent women and marginal Hausa men. The *'yan daudu* tend to maximise upon the ambivalence of their sexuality, living with and, for the transvestites in particular, as women. And yet, through their maleness, they gain authority within the compound, and are accepted as intermediaries between prospective clients and the women they seek.

Women in the *gidajen mata*, from the young *karuwai* to the independent women, have availed themselves of one career option which is open to Hausa women. While the male-dominant ideology tends to suggest passivity on the part of women, the fact that women move back and forth between marriage, non-marriage and *karuwanci* demonstrates a more active involvement than can be explained through reference to the dominant belief-system.

The egalitarian nature of the *gidan mata* and the lack of a formal political hierarchy within *karuwanci* give considerable room for the development of individual initiative and entrepreneurial skills. The more capable, industrious and far-sighted woman may use her earnings gained through *karuwanci* and other economic endeavours as the foundation for a secure, independent and comfortable future. Ironically, both for women who do remarry, and for women who become independent, the practice of *karuwanci* may ultimately result in a higher achieved social status than may have been possible through remaining in the respectable, and far more common, confines of marriage.

Notes: Chapter 21

1 Plans are under way to build a steel-rolling mill in Katsina, which, with its allied industries, may well change the nature of the urban economy.
2 Based on the 1971 tax assessment figure of 76,060.
3 'Non-married women' refers to women who have been, but are no longer, married, and is distinct from 'unmarried women', women who have not yet married.
4 Akwato is the Hausa name for the Idoma. In Katsina, however, the 'Akwato' population is composed mainly of Tiv and Ibo women.
5 *'Yan*, meaning 'children of. . .', is a term commonly used to signify 'the people associated with, or who practise (some specific activity or thing)'.
6 This situation is the obverse of the depressing, yet seemingly accurate, picture painted by Jules Feiffer: 'Whatever ground woman manages to establish for herself, man abandons, denying its importance' (Morgan, 1970, p. 565).
7 See especially, M. Smith, 1954, pp. 63–4, 136, 229–30; also A. Cohen, 1969, p. 63; and Bovin and Holtedahl, n.d., pp. 21–2. An exception is the *karuwanci* practised in rural Zaria described by Barkow, 1971, pp. 7–8, which also shows a limited degree of authoritarianism.

8   The methods and effects of the exploitation of Hausa marginal women is a major theme in Pittin, 1979b, ch. 6.
9   In his Sokoto study Mohammed suggests that up to 40 per cent of the *karuwai* are 'at the mercy of their "matrons". . .' (1975, p. 13).

Chapter 22

Gender Relations and Conjugality among the Baule

MONA ETIENNE

Baule women of Ivory Coast are famous for their independence and the ease with which they adapt to the urban environment. In the capital city of Abidjan they represent an important fraction both of the female population and of the Baule population. This is not a recent phenomenon, but rather a long-established pattern.[1] Some of these women are, of course, wives, married either to Baule men or to men of other ethnic groups. Many, however, among the middle-aged and elderly, as well as among the young, are unmarried. Most of the older women who have remained in town – as opposed to those who ultimately returned to their villages – have, through hard work and careful investment, achieved prosperity and 'success' within the limits of possibilities accessible to non elite women: the only group with which I am concerned here. They are owners of their own compounds and a pole of attraction for various dependants, especially visitors and new migrants from their home villages. They also have sufficient income to sustain these dependants and to maintain important complex social networks, both of which in turn contribute to their income by contributing to their productivity and to their opportunities for trade. They may have educated adult children or foster children in well-paid salaried positions, who supplement their incomes, ensure their well-being in old age, and will finance a prestigious funeral when they die – an important concern for all Baule. The younger women hope to follow in their footsteps. Some see marriage as incompatible with this goal. Others consider it with ambivalence or as a means to an end: a 'generous' husband may help them attain wealth and success. Very few envisage marriage as an end in itself.

This type of situation is not unusual in Africa, especially in West Africa, and has been the object of many studies, the earlier ones, often superficial, with undue emphasis on 'prostitution' as a source of revenues and on 'freedom from constraints' as a decisive factor in attracting women to towns. More recent studies have gone beyond this view, particularly in their attention to the complexities of women's adaptive strategies in the urban environment.[2] Few, however, have studied, for women, the meaning of urban migration in relationship to the society of origin, that is, the structural factors and concrete conditions which may facilitate or motivate it, as well as the profound reasons for resistance to marriage on the part of many non-elite urban women. Even more rare are references to historical factors which may have contributed to present attitudes and behaviours. It is the purpose of this chapter to examine some of the structural and historical factors which clarify the meaning of urban migration for Baule women, as well as their reluctance to marry. I shall focus on the situation of women in pre-colonial Baule society and on the transformation of the relationship between women and men – and especially between wives and husbands – subsequent to colonisation. I am here concerned with urbanisation only as an end-product, so to speak: one aspect among others of the socio-historical processes to be analysed; and so will not go beyond the brief description of the urban scene given above, except for details that are relevant to this analysis.

The resistance to marriage observed in town is, in fact, not limited to the urban context. Rural women express similar attitudes. If many do not want to marry because they want to go to the city, others want to go to the city because they do not want to marry. Underlying this superficial expression of motivation, however, is deep concern with achieving economic autonomy and avoiding a situation in which it may be undermined. Today, as in the past, Baule society is characterised by great respect for personal autonomy and individual freedom of choice, for women as well as men. General social constraints are therefore not the issue. Pressure to marry is perhaps greater in the village than in town, but women can and do remain unmarried without migrating. Single life in the village is, however, more difficult than in town, if only because of limited economic opportunities. Opportunities to acquire wealth are now concentrated in the cities, for women even more than for men, or at least so it appears to village women. Men have their cash crops, often lucrative, and women's share in the profits is disproportionate to the considerable labour they contribute. Why this is so will be explained below. The important point, for the moment, is that women perceive marriage, at best, as a constraint that prevents them from realising their full potential, economically and socially, and at worst, as outright exploitation. There are two key questions evoked by this observation. (1) Was this always so, that is, have Baule women always considered marriage a constraint, in this sense, or can their attitude be considered the result of colonial and post-colonial transformations of conjugal relations – and perhaps of relations between the sexes in general? (2) What is their frame of reference, that is, how and on what basis do they define their goals and especially to what extent do they refer to the con- temporary context and the opportunities it presents or rather to a vision of themselves and their rights rooted in the history of their society? It is these questions I shall attempt to answer. It is necessary first to present an overview of Baule society, with reference to those structural and historical aspects which appear relevant.

The Baule are believed to have emerged as a cultural entity only in the late seventeenth or early eighteenth centuries, as a result of the conquest and/or assimilation of Mande-Dyula, Kru and Voltaic peoples by successive waves of Akan, notably from Denkyera and Ashanti. Political organisation remained kin-based and was rarely operative beyond the village unit. In correlation with their history, characterised by discontinuous migration and the merging of cultur- ally different populations – some patrilineal, some matrilineal – the Baule developed a kinship-system based on cognatic descent, although succession and inheritance were generally matrilineal.[3] The cognatic principle, because it gave people potential membership in more than one kin-group, favoured competition between kin-groups to retain or increase their constituency. The structural and historical factors determining mobility were compounded by economic factors, especially during the late pre-colonial period (the late nineteenth century), when gold-prospecting, trade and the acquisition of domes- tic slaves[4] were pursued with renewed intensity.

In this context, individual autonomy was the counterpart of generalised competition for wealth and power. From the point of view of an elder, to increase one's wealth was to attract dependants and to attract dependants was to increase one's wealth. From the point of view of a junior person, because kin-group membership was not rigidly ascribed, an elder whose prosperity offered opportunities for entrepreneurial undertakings, and whose generosity offered his dependants a share in the profits, was a pole of attraction. Gerontoc- racy – and autocracy in general – were incompatible with such a system. Although elders commanded respect and had some degree of authority founded in their spiritual powers and in the powers of ancestors,[5] the heavy-handed exercise of such authority could result in the departure of dependants, and even in the dying out of a kin- group for lack of members.

The absence of relations of domination–subordination between husband and wife was one aspect of the generalised absence of such relations in Baule society. Before examining the position of Baule women as wives, however, it is necessary to examine their position in the society at large, an important distinction, notwithstanding the persistent tendency, where women are concerned, to extend the attributes of a specific role, especially that of wife, to gender identity as a whole.[6]

Early observers are unanimous in noting the high position of Baule women. As individual members of the village community, they participated freely in the decision-making process in affairs concerning the village. As members of the village-based society of all adult women, whose rituals could not be seen by men, they acted collectively to defend the interests of the community against outside threats, such as illness or warfare, or to defend the interests of women against men. The former function seems to have been the more important and, in a sense, it implied the latter. Women's rituals were so vital to the survival of all that it was believed that men who went to war without their support would surely meet defeat and death. Men too were organised in a society which could be dangerous to women. Yet, beyond this ritual dichotomy, there does not seem to have been a high level of antagonism or even separation between the sexes, nor were gender attributes rigidly defined.[7] The division of labour, assigning different tasks to women and men, was an organising principle of production, but no more than that. It was not rigidly enforced by either supernatural or civil sanctions. Deviations were considered acceptable in case of convenience or necessity and were not ridiculed. At best they were admired; at worst they were pitied, but only in so far as the individual must be so isolated socially that he or she could not find a partner of the opposite sex – wife or husband, sister or brother – whose labour could be called upon. Only the few tasks that required a long apprenticeship, such as spinning for women and weaving for men, were not the object of at least occasional deviations from the norm. Most of the various types of healers or diviners could be either women or men.

These examples suggest that gender was not the primary focus of the principles which served to define social identity. This suggestion is supported by the position of women in the competition for political and economic power. As members of their kin-group, women had equal rights of inheritance and succession to the position of elder or chief – on the level of the localised kin-group, the village, or the confederation of villages. The importance of women chiefs during the pre-colonial period and at the time of colonisation is well documented, although, as we shall see, they were no doubt less numerous than men. Nor were women excluded from the entrepreneurial pursuit of wealth described above. They participated in trading and gold-prospecting expeditions and acquired domestic slaves in their own right. Junior women, like junior men, might trade and prospect for gold as delegates of an elder. The elder who mandated their expedition might well be a woman. The accounts of contemporary women are rich with anecdotes about enterprising grandmothers and great-grandmothers who, perhaps mandated by their own mothers, sought and found fortune in the trading centres and goldfields of southern Baule country towards the end of the nineteenth century. This, then, appears to answer one of the questions formulated above. Baule women's pursuit of wealth in the framework of contemporary urban migration is not simply a response to new and unprecedented opportunities. It is deeply rooted in history and in the traditional models that govern their sense of identity and their goals.

The answer to our other question, as to whether marriage traditionally imposed constraints on the freedom women otherwise enjoyed, is less categorical and more complex. Baule marriage is the locus of a contradiction. On the one hand, the mutual rights and obligations of spouses are defined in such a way as to make it appear an egalitarian relationship, and to a great extent this seems to have been the case. On the other hand, in a society where residence was a crucial determinant of status, and, on its most basic level, authority was vested in the elder of the localised kin-group, the principle of virilocality that governed marriage necessarily imposed constraints on wives. Whereas spouses as such owed one another mutual respect, a wife, not because she was a wife, but because she was a resident of her husband's compound, owed him special deference, as did other persons residing with him. Although the effects of simple deference behaviour were minimal, the political implications were not. Virilocal residence was incompatible with a woman's effective access to political office, whether as elder of her localised kin-group or on a higher level, and an obstacle to her inheritance of the sacred treasures corresponding to these positions, which materialised the identity of the group and could under no circumstances be moved from their place of residence. This contradiction was sometimes resolved by hypogamy combined with uxorilocal residence, by divorce, or by separation.[8] But uxorilocal or duolocal residence were exceptions, probably more so than divorce. While the early stages of marriage were marked by long periods of duolocality, when the wife continued to reside with her kin, a marriage normally was not complete until the wife had definitively taken up residence with her husband. For this reason, it is said that 'noble' (*agwa*) women, that is, women belonging to families who traditionally held high political office, 'did not marry'. Even today, although traditional political office does not have the same importance it had in pre-colonial Baule society, one encounters cases of women who refuse marriage – or whose families oppose their marriage – because they are presumptive heirs. Such cases must nevertheless be less frequent than in the past, if only because the colonial and post-colonial administrations have consistently prevented or discouraged the holding of traditional political positions by women.

It is clear, then, that in the political domain marriage represented a constraint, and that in the past, as today, ambitious women were not anxious to marry, or, if they did so, to remain married. Their choice was, and still is, facilitated by the fact that women retain economic rights in their own kin-group, including rights to the labour of a brother or other kinsman, with whom they could establish an economic partnership on the same model as that which prevailed between spouses, and which will be described below. Dissolution of marriage was further simplified by the absence of bridewealth properly speaking and because individuals had considerable freedom in their choice of marriage partners.[9] The elders, therefore, even though their consent was required, generally had no vested interest in maintaining a marriage. This was especially true of the woman's kin, who, in case of divorce, were likely to acquire any children born of the union. As for the man's kin, they might well lose the children even if the marriage remained intact, since, under pressure from their mother or on their own initiative, the children might at any time decide to take up residence among their maternal kin.

By restricting her access to political office, virilocal marriage inevitably affected a woman's economic opportunities. Elders and chiefs were in the most favourable position to command dependants, and prosperity was, to a great extent, a function of the number of dependants who contributed to one's revenues. However, as suggested above, neither elders nor chiefs could entirely co-opt the labour or the revenue of their dependants (except perhaps those of a newly acquired slave, as opposed to the slave-born, who also had rights). What they did receive for the most part served to increase the sacred treasure. But much wealth circulated outside this sphere, as personal property of those who had acquired it by their labour or their enterprise, and also in the form of estates transmitted matrilineally among individuals who were not in line for succession to office. Further, relationships of dependency were relative and flexible, based more on active and immediate ties between a senior and a junior person than on hierarchical allegiance to a kin-group elder or chief. This gave all adults, as they grew older, the possibility of building a constituency of personal dependants. Thus, for example, a son who remained with his father's kin-group had the status of 'child of a male' (*yaswa ba*) and normally could not inherit there, nor could his children (unless the marriage was more or less endogamous and his wife belonged to the same kin-group). An heir had to be the 'child of a female' (*bla ba*). For this reason, a man might eventually rejoin his maternal kin, especially after the death of his father. He could, however, build his own personal constituency of uterine kin, not only by retaining sisters and sisters' children, but also by attracting maternal kin other than siblings and therefore unrelated to the father, such as mother's sisters' children. These individuals would owe only minimal allegiance to the elder of the wider kin-group. Their primary allegiance went to their uterine kinsman, with whom they would form a quasi-autonomous unit, contributing their labour to his enterprises and at the same time receiving some benefit for themselves.[10]

A woman residing virilocally enjoyed similar opportunities. She shared with her husband rights in the labour of her children and, of course, especially benefited by the contribution of her unmarried or returned daughters. But she could also have dependants unrelated to her husband – her own domestic slaves and junior members of her own kin-group. Fosterage and adoption were vital institutional mechanisms for providing a married woman with her own dependants (see Etienne, 1979a, 1979b). It was, in fact, an established custom that when a woman took up residence with her husband she should be accompanied by a child, usually a girl, given in adoption, most often a younger sister or a sister's child, or perhaps a slave child given by her mother or her maternal uncle. In the course of her lifetime a woman could receive other adoptees and, if she had a reputation for wealth and generosity, could also attract junior dependants who would join her on their own initiative. A woman's constituency of dependants owed respect, but no real allegiance, to her husband. At the same time as they guaranteed her economic and personal autonomy, they maintained and consolidated her relationship to her own kin-group by reinforcing the personal ties which are essential to kin-group status in this system.[11]

The ability to attract and maintain personal dependants was, however, contingent on a woman's economic status and on a definition of the conjugal relationship which made it possible for her to control the products of her own labour, and especially the surplus production which was at the origin of new wealth. In spite of the formal deference a woman might owe her husband, marriage was perceived as the association of a woman and a man for purposes of reproduction and production, with shared rights in both children and products. The working out of rights in children was complex and cannot be described in detail here, but, as suggested above, mothers tended to have the advantage over fathers. In exchange for procreation and nurturing, children owed labour and allegiance to fathers as well as mothers, but this tie was individual and circumstantial, whereas rights of – and in – maternal kin were inalienable and generally determined a greater ascendancy of the mother over her children.

As for the productive relationship, it was founded on principles of reciprocity and complementarity, with an intricately defined balance of rights and obligations giving women control over certain products and men control over others. This worked out in such a way that, of the two products most essential to subsistence in pre-colonial Baule society, yams and cloth, men controlled the former and women the latter, although the division of labour was such that both women and men substantially contributed to the production of both yams and cloth.

The underlying principle that determined control of surplus, once family needs were met, was that 'ownership' of a product was vested in the person who had taken initial and primary responsibility for production. The labour of the other, even if it was indispensable and quantitatively important, was a service rendered, for which he or she might receive a share of the surplus, more or less at the discretion of the primary producer, who otherwise disposed of it to his or her own ends. A man prepared at least one yam plot 'for' a wife, at least as many separate plots as he had wives – and perhaps others for sisters and other kinswomen residing with him. Although each plot was assigned to a specific adult woman, the man, because he cleared the ground and initiated production, as well as taking responsibility for other vital tasks such as the building of mounds and fences, controlled distribution of surplus. The woman had usufructuary rights in the plot, using it for intercropping and secondary crops, such as cotton, condiments and cassava. These 'belonged' to her. Particularly important is the case of cotton, which eventually became cloth. Because the raw material belonged to the woman, the end-product also belonged to her, even though weaving, a man's task, was an essential phase of the production process (see Etienne, 1980). An industrious weaver, in exchange for his services to his wife, certainly received a fair share of the finished cloth; and there was a form of semi-specialisation which made it possible for men to control cloth they wove outside the sphere of strictly domestic relations of production. But, the definition of 'ownership' on the level of domestic cloth production, that is, within the family unit, was a key factor in permitting women to acquire personal wealth, as was their control of food products such as cassava. Cloth was the principal product used to acquire trade goods, and so could also finance gold-prospecting expeditions, which were often combined with trade. In the last years of the nineteenth century, in the war-ravaged regions of northern Ivory Coast, cassava and other food products could purchase domestic slaves.

For both women and men control over surplus production was largely a function of control over the labour of dependants – domestic slaves, but also children and junior kin. The number and size of yam plots allotted to a woman by her husband would be determined both by her capacity to exploit them and by her needs. These in turn were determined by the number of children and junior women (or domestic slaves) under her dependency. These dependants worked alongside their elder and contributed to her productivity. Young adults would receive a share of the surplus they produced, but it would partially benefit the elder. Thus, the more a woman could produce, the more dependants she could maintain, and, the more productive dependants she could maintain, the more she could produce. Her productive capacity was, to some extent, contingent on her husband's capacity to furnish male labour for the men's tasks, both his own labour and that of his dependants. She did, however, have other options. If her kin resided in the same or a nearby village, she could ask a brother or other kinsman to work a yam plot for her. A male domestic slave, even though adult and married, could be expected to work for his mistress as well as for his own family. Although land belonged to the village and was generally allotted to individuals through their kin-group elder, its availability was not generally a problem. Therefore, even an outsider, perhaps a wife's junior kinsman adopted in childhood, who had remained in the village but had no other ties with it than through his kinswoman, could be given land which he might work with her as a partner. An enterprising woman, even though married, could thus expand her productive capacity, both within the conjugal relationship and through other relationships, and use her surplus production as a basis for participation in the broader economic sphere of long-distance trade and gold-prospecting.

I have so far used the past tense in order to give an integral picture of things as they were in pre-colonial Baule society, without indicating at each step what has changed and what has not. In fact, the representations and fundamental principles defining relations between the sexes, as well as the rules governing marriage, remain for the most part intact or have only begun to change. What have been transformed radically are the material conditions which made these rules and principles effective, guaranteeing the autonomy of women in spite of the constraints which marked their position as wives. This transformation corresponds to the incorporation of Baule society in the world capitalist economy and the resulting impact on production relations, affecting all women, but reflected with special clarity in the conjugal relationship.

At the core of changed production relations are cash crops, introduced in the earliest days of colonisation, both by outright force and by persuasion – the latter in the form of new needs for cash, at first to pay taxes and then to acquire goods no longer available by any other means. This process was self-perpetuating in that cash crop production mobilised time and labour formerly used to produce goods which then had to be replaced by imported products purchased with cash. The effects on indigenous cloth production and especially on women's control of the product were particularly devastating (see

Etienne, 1980). Cotton as a cash crop was an early focus of the colonial administration and coincided with the wide-scale introduction of factory-made thread, making men's weaving independent of women's cotton. Subsequently, factory-made cloth progressively replaced indigenous cloth for everyday use, completing the breakdown of pre-existing production relations. Women still control intercropped cotton on the yam plots, but whether they sell it at the market place or give it to husbands to weave, this cotton is quantitatively and economically of little importance. Produced as a cash crop requiring monetary investment (e.g. for insecticides) and the surveillance of male-oriented technical experts, cotton has become the province of men, as have other cash crops such as coffee.

The rules of co-operative labour between spouses continue to prevail, but are played out more and more to the disadvantage of women. They contribute their labour to the cash crops of husbands and receive remuneration when the crop is sold, but their share in the profits is arbitrary and generally disproportionate to their contribution. They maintain usufructuary rights in yam plots, at least for intercropping and often for secondary crops, but the land on which they can exercise these rights tends to be restricted to what is necessary for strict subsistence needs – unless yams too are cultivated for sale. (Then, if the woman sells them at the market place she will receive a share of the profits, but if they are sold wholesale she is likely to receive nothing.) In either case, the opportunity a woman has to grow her own products is diminished by time devoted to cash crops, as is the availability of male labour that she may use for her own ends. In so far as cash crops are more lucrative than condiments, cassava and other women's products, it is in the overall interest of the family that more labour time be devoted to them. It is therefore not only a sense of conjugal obligation, but also sound economic logic, that motivate women to sacrifice their own production to men's cash crops. The result, however, is that the equitable exchange of labour which previously characterised the wife–husband productive relationship has become a form of unequal exchange. Above all, whatever may be their actual income, because they depend on a husband's 'generosity' rather than on their own industry and control of distribution, women do not enjoy the economic autonomy they had in the past. In especially prosperous regions some women may have sufficient revenues to regain their autonomy by employing labourers – or husbands may sometimes pay labourers to work for their wives.[12] But these exceptions are all the more rare in that the opportunity for a woman to grow her own crops also depends on the availability of land, and cash crops have often made land, as well as labour, less available.

Concurrently with loss of control over production, women are losing control over dependents. As I have shown, the two are indissoluble, and change in either direction tends to be self-perpetuating. Just as a woman could in the past increase her productivity by attracting dependants and attract dependants by increasing her productivity, her diminished productivity – in the realm of products she herself controls – diminishes her ability to attract dependants, and fewer dependants further diminish her productive capacity.

This loss is compounded by urban migration, now considered the only means to acquire real wealth, especially for women. The city drains the countryside of the young women – and the children – who might otherwise choose to work alongside their elder kinswoman or be given to her for adoption. While the custom of giving a married woman a child who will accompany her when she goes to reside with her husband has not disappeared, a candidate may not be available. Further, although in principle one gives children out of generosity and in the interest of the recipient, the child's interests – and indirectly the parents' – are taken into account. The gift of a child is generally made with an eye to future prosperity, whatever the present situation may be. Even a schoolgirl, because her future is promising, may be given a younger sister or sister's child, while her older uneducated sister must go unaccompanied to her husband's home.[13]

Other children are given by their parents in adoption or fosterage to urban kinswomen, or even strangers, who, although uneducated, are believed to offer them opportunities for prosperity, perhaps because they themselves have prospered, perhaps simply because they are in the city. The hopes of such parents are more and more likely to be illusions, but they remain for the moment a decisive factor in transforming both Baule society and the condition of rural married women.

Another tendency is for men to play a more important part in adoption relations than they did in the past. Although adoption has never been restricted to females – as donors, recipients, or adoptees – they were, and no doubt still are, in the majority in all three roles. Because child-rearing is a woman's task, a very young child – and adoptees, as opposed to foster children, are given as babies – would not normally be given to a man. This would mean that the child would be raised by the man's wife, with whom the donor might have no relationship. If she did, she would give the child to the wife herself.[14] But, because children go where the wealth is, and it is most often with men, and also because prosperous urban men are considered to have control over their wives – and their children – such men may today receive even infants. As for the recipient, she or he may prefer to receive a child from a kinsman rather than a kinswoman, because the parent who is the active donor (the other giving only consent to the transaction) is primarily responsible for maintaining the adoptive relationship, eventually persuading a reluctant child to remain with the foster parent. And, once again, men are now considered to have more influence than women over their children, perhaps directly, perhaps through the influence they have over their wives. In receiving a child from a woman, one runs the risk that the father, even though he consents, may not really desire the transaction. In this case, he will not use his authority to maintain it. As for the adoptees themselves, where schooling rather than the apprenticeship of gender-specialised tasks is the reason for giving children to urban kin, they are more frequently boys. This is not because of any stereotype concerning differential aptitudes of girls and boys, but because schooling is an important investment. Parents and foster parents see that, in a male-dominated society, boys are more likely to benefit from their education by attaining well-paid positions and to be able to make the investment profitable by future contributions to the well-being of their elders.[15]

These changes that affect the participation of females and males in adoption relations, besides having a direct effect on the position of women, reflect broader changes in the relations between the sexes. They also suggest why marriage is hardly more attractive to urban women than it is to their rural sisters. Some non-elite women, especially among the middle-aged and elderly, appear to have maintained both durable marriages and their economic autonomy. They have substantial revenue from trade and other sources, and their own constituency of dependants, both living with them and supported by them, in the village and elsewhere. They may, for example, own coffee farms worked by junior dependants. Although they reside in their husband's house, they may themselves own urban real estate which provides them with both revenues and a place to go if their marriage should break up. They usually have built a house in their home village, where they may eventually return, no matter how long they have lived in town.

Younger women, on the other hand, appear to be more dependent on husbands. This could be simply a phase in early marriage, but case histories show that successful older women began their economic undertakings very young, and some of these younger women have been married for ten years or more with no prospect of establishing their economic autonomy. What they have, they receive from husbands, their only personal income being small amounts – 'pin money', so to speak – from petty trade. Junior dependants residing in their home tend to be the husband's kin rather than theirs. If these dependants are schoolboys or unemployed young men, as is frequently the case, they represent a burden rather than a productive contribution. The woman's own small income is likely to be absorbed by household needs, since it is ultimately her responsibility to feed everyone, what-

ever the amount she receives from her husband. It is difficult to
determine how much this difference between older and younger married women is due to changes in attitudes and values among younger
non-elite couples and how much it is due to the broader economic
context. Both these factors appear to operate in such a way as to
reinforce each other.

The husbands of all these women are for the most part salaried
workers, illiterate or barely literate, or with just enough education to
hold positions as lower-level civil servants and clerks (if they obtained
these positions before there were so many educated men available).[16]
Although the older men seem to respect a wife's right to economic
autonomy, the younger ones tend more to perceive the role of wife in
terms of the European model, expecting her to be constantly atten-
tive to her husband's needs, serving him, his children and frequent
visitors to the home. Such a husband may also be oriented towards
the model of the nuclear family, perhaps conceding to tradition and
his own long-term interests by maintaining one or two children of his
own kin, but unwilling to maintain a wife's junior kin. The couple's
own children may all be in school, depriving the wife of their help
precisely at an age when children become useful. In these marriages,
the relative isolation of the young wife has both short-term and long-
term consequences. Working alone, she cannot both take care of her
family and engage in economic enterprises on her own account. She is
therefore economically dependent on her husband. But, by confining
herself to the conjugal relationship, she also becomes socially dependent. As we have seen, the ability to maintain personal dependants
reinforces a woman's social networks, especially through ties with her
own kin. Conversely, reliance on the nuclear family weakens these
networks. This process may in time make a woman a prisoner of her
marriage. Kin ties are rarely so weak that she would have no place to
go; but, in her village or among urban relatives, her status as a
returned kinswoman might be somewhat that of a 'poor relative', if
she had not built up her status as 'mother' or 'sister' by nurturing and
supporting junior kin or giving in adoption or fosterage her own children. As for the latter, although they would always owe their mother
some support, they might find it in their interest to remain with the
father and/or invest more heavily in their allegiance to him. Even
small children are remarkably sensitive to their prospects for a prosperous future and, on the occasion of a divorce, may elect to remain
with the father because 'he can pay for their schooling'. (They also
enjoy enough autonomy to be able to make a choice.) In these circumstances a woman is more likely than she would otherwise be to
maintain an unsatisfactory marriage.

But changes in attitudes and values are, at best, a partial explanation. The process whereby wives become dependent on husbands is

promoted by the urban economy, even more than by the economy of the village. Among the non-elite, salaried positions are almost entirely the prerogative of men.[17] Even if their income is not supplemented by other sources, such as coffee farms worked by kinsmen, it is regular, and life in town requires regular income to meet daily cash expenses and more important periodic expenses such as the payment of rent. With progressive replacement of old 'spontaneous' housing by rental units, this need has become more pressing and widespread than ever, giving non-elite men a substantial advantage over non-elite women. The new housing itself, by offering cramped and unexpandable living quarters, tends both to curtail many of the home-based and space-consuming economic activities of women and to support the nuclear family model by making room unavailable for dependants. Women might perhaps better defend their interests – and some do – by demanding the opportunity to pursue their own economic activities, perhaps even receiving seed money from husbands, but they are in a bad bargaining position. In town, where all needs are mediated by cash, a wife is not as indispensable as she is in the countryside. Besides, 'there are too many women in Abidjan', as goes the refrain of a popular song (Vidal, 1977). A man can easily replace a refractory wife, either by paying for the services she provides or by contracting a temporary union with one of the many available women.

Major developments in the broader economic context further contribute to the growing dependence of wives on husbands. The deterioration of the world economy in the past ten years has profoundly affected the Third World, and Ivory Coast is no exception, although its economic situation may be better than that of other countries. In Abidjan, precisely because the opportunities there are better than elsewhere, the effects of inflation and recession are compounded by migration from other parts of West Africa, as well as from rural Ivory Coast. At the same time, advances in education disadvantage the non-elite by making it possible for employers to demand qualifications which exlude them from jobs or from promotions which were accessible to them ten or twenty years ago. By and large, whatever the relative advantages and disadvantages of women and men, the economic crunch makes money generally less available in this sector of the population. Where a man's salary barely covers the expenses necessary to support his family, he is unlikely to make concessions to his wife's need to establish her economic autonomy, and she cannot demand it. Although a tight budget may sometimes favour a wife's economic participation, such as preparation of food for sale and petty trade, it is almost certain that her income will in this case be absorbed by day-to-day family needs, especially since other tight budgets limit her profits.

Low salaries and high prices have in turn affected the 'informal sector' and the revenues an urban woman can hope to obtain through her labour. This sector is important in sustaining the urban economy precisely because it can survive pressures that would bankrupt a formal business. Having no other choice, women devote more and more time and effort to undertakings which bring them lower and lower profits. With their income and the savings it represents – if they do manage to accumulate savings – being further eroded by a rapid rate of inflation, the disappearance of the prosperous and successful non-elite woman may be just a question of time. She will nevertheless remain a model for future generations, both among the uneducated and among the young women who hope to enhance their opportunities for future success by obtaining a formal education. Schooled and unschooled, married and unmarried, Baule women are unlikely to forget their great-grandmothers, grandmothers and mothers, who, from pre-colonial times to the present, from the southern goldfields and trading posts to the newly created cities, established durable reputations as enterprising and prosperous women.

Marriage itself can follow models other than those described above. Many young women, especially if they have received some schooling, are less reluctant to marry if the husband agrees to finance the continuance of their education, and such commitments are not infrequent. In such cases, it is the understanding of both partners that the wife will thus be equipped to pursue her own career. In this and other ways many Baule men demonstrate their continued respect for a woman's right to personal and economic autonomy. They do so in response to the demands of women, but also because they themselves have not rejected traditional models. Both the struggle of women to assert their rights and the persistence of values that legitimise their goals are forces that must be taken into consideration. They are likely to modify the direction of transformations which, examined too abstractly, suggest the inevitable breakdown of the social and economic power women had in pre-colonial Baule society.

Notes: Chapter 22

I am grateful to the Ivory Coast government and the Wenner-Gren Foundation for Anthropological Research, who made possible the research on which this chapter is based. The source of my data is fieldwork in 1962–3 among rural Baule of the Bouaké region, sponsored by the Ivory Coast Ministère du plan, and in 1974–5 among urban Baule of Abidjan (neighbourhood of Port-Bouet), supported by grant no. 3067 from the Wenner-Gren Foundation and authorised by the Ivory Coast Ministère de la recherche scientifique and the University of Abidjan Institut d'éthnologie.

I also thank my field assistants, Kouamé Kodjoua Christine and Kouassi Affoué Yvonne, for their tireless collaboration, my many Baule informants for their patient and intelligent responses to endless questions, and Chantal Collard, Christine Gailey and Betty Potash for their comments on an early draft of this chapter, which is a slightly modified version of an article that first appeared in *Culture*, Journal of Canadian Ethnological Society, vol. 1, no. 1, 1981, pp. 21–30.

1   According to a 1965 study, the Baule population of Abidjan was 55 per cent female. This corresponds to an exceptional inversion of the overall ratio of 45 per cent females to 55 per cent males for the total African population of Abidjan, among whom the Baule represent approximately 11·5 per cent (Côte d'Ivoire, 1965a; see also Côte d'Ivoire, 1965b).

2   For examples of the former, see Little, 1973, and many of the works cited in his bibliography. For examples of the latter, with reference to Abidjan, see Lewis, 1976 and 1977. Dinan (1977) presents an excellent overview and critique of views on African women with reference to urbanisation and modernisation.

3   Dole (1972) makes a convincing argument for the correlation between cognatic kinship and the historical traits described here. For further information on the Baule kinship system, and especially on the nomenclature, which is 'Hawaiian' or 'generational', see P. and M. Etienne, 1967.

4   Domestic slaves did not constitute a separate caste or class and, through intermarriage, they were eventually assimilated. They nevertheless made an important contribution to the wealth of their masters – and mistresses – especially in the first generation. They could own property, but did not control it, particularly where inheritance was concerned. Their property reverted to their owner. Rights in slaves, as in other forms of wealth, were transmitted matrilineally. See Etienne, 1976, for the importance of slaves to the status of women.

5   It was considered that the rancour of a parent could cause the death of a child. The power of the ancestors was operative mainly in the matriline, but the ghost of a father was powerful, and connections with various spiritual forces were transmitted patrilineally.

6   As Sanjek demonstrates in Chapter 24 in his examination of the female and male domestic cycles, marriage is by no means a permanent condition of all adult women. Nor does the position of 'wife' entirely determine a woman's social identity in many African societies, where they retain their status as 'sisters', as Bisilliat points out in Chapter 6.

7   It is interesting that among the Baule menstrual taboos are not defined strictly in terms of gender identity.

8   For a comparable case, see E. N. Goody (1962) on the Gonja, where women may dissolve their marriage in order to take office and 'terminal separation' is a generalised practice for older women. It is less systematic among the Baule, but nevertheless frequent.

9   Child betrothal existed, along with other forms of marriage, but even in this case the marriage could not be concluded without the girl's consent. Women could – and did – refuse to conclude the marriage because they 'did not love the man'. One exception to the general rule was a patrilineal form of marriage with bridewealth, but it was practised only by some wealthy and noble families and disappeared even before colonisation.

10   Among these uterine kin might be the eventual heir of the *yaswa ba*, whose wealth could not be inherited by his paternal kin any more than he could inherit theirs. If the group maintained its residence and expanded, it would in time become a new kin-group, considered *yaswa ba* in relationship to the founder of the village, as was its founder, but completely autonomous *vis-à-vis* his paternal kin.

11   She might also, with the consent of her husband – who would hesitate to refuse, if he wanted to maintain good relations with his affines – give her own children in adoption or fosterage. In this case she would sacrifice her short-term economic interest to long-term social and economic advantages. Besides the general advantage of reinforcing her social networks, if, as a widow or a divorcee, she returned

among her kin, she would benefit by having children of her own definitively integrated in her own kin-group. Again, E. N. Goody (1962) presents comparable data for the Gonja. For a more detailed account of Baule adoption and fosterage, see Etienne, 1979a and 1979b.

12 If they themselves pay labourers, they may be returned migrants who prospered in the city but tired of city life. Some enterprising townswomen maintain labourers in their home village, thus supplying their own trade in food products and perhaps contributing to the support of village kin. They may eventually return, and even marry in the village, without losing all their economic advantages.

13 The child will be raised by its mother or grandmother until her adoptive mother is grown and sends for the adoptee, but is considered hers from the day the promise is made.

14 Just as a child is given *by* one parent, although the consent of the other is required, it is always given *to* one person, never to a couple. A child *can* be given to an affine, if the personal relationship is a good one and the marriage appears solid, but, considering the general fragility of marriage, the donor would normally not want to given an affine rights in a child given to a relative.

15 Parents also hesitate to invest in the education of girls either because pregnancy may result in their being expelled from school, or because avoidance of pregnancy may deprive them of descendants. This inequality is to some extent mitigated by customary law: the boy responsible for the pregnancy, or his parents, must refund the amount of the investment, or he must marry the girl and finance her continued schooling after childbirth. The effectiveness of this law depends on social pressure and on circumstances. In practice, it does not always work.

16 I am referring here to cases studied in low-income rental and spontaneous housing in the Port Bouet neighbourhood. My data, besides excluding the elite, do not include non-elite women married to elite men. I have left aside some cases of unemployed men largely supported by their wives, these among the older couples. Younger unemployed men, even when married, were generally dependants of elders.

17 The case of the Gonfreville textile factory in the city of Bouaké, which employs many Baule women, is I believe still an exception. I know of no comparable cases in Abidjan, where even positions as salaried domestic servants for Europeans and well-to-do Africans are almost entirely monopolised by men.

Chapter 23

Avatime Women and Men, 1900–80

LYNNE BRYDON

The early years of this century brought enormous changes to Avatime. These changes, economic, political and ideological, although initiated by colonial powers, have gained a momentum of their own. This chapter looks at Avatime society today, almost a century since it became a German colony, but first it traces out a pattern of what Avatime women and men were and did in the early years of colonial influence.

The Avatime traditional area lies in the hills of the Volta region of Ghana and consists of seven villages with their farmlands. It is one of the larger 'Togo remnant' groups, having a population of over 7,000 in the 1960 census. Descent in Avatime is agnatic; the widest descent-group may be termed a clan. The members of the minimal descent-group (*oku*, pl. *ikune*) are responsible for settling disputes within the group and for land-holding and distribution. In the past, residence in the villages was completely localised with respect to these minimal descent-groups and clans.

Female Rites of Passage

An Avatime female must pass through a series of formal statuses during her life. Although children in Avatime are socialised into sex-specific roles, it is only when a girl approaches puberty that any formal recognition is given to her fecundity. At this time she is referred to by a term that means 'small woman' rather than by the asexual term for 'child'. On reaching puberty a girl should have ceremonies performed for her which mean that she is formally recognised as a 'woman', an adult Avatime female, *kedamidze*. In the earlier period these ceremonies included marriage: a woman was not a woman in Avatime unless she was also a wife. Becoming *kedamidze* meant that social recognition was given to a woman's reproductive capacity; she was encouraged to bear children. Recognition was also given to a woman's productive capacity: women should work in the farm and in the compound for their immediate family of husband and children. As an adult a woman could take part in decision-making procedures (to the extent that women ever did). Becoming *kedamidze* legitimated a woman's social, economic and jural potentialities.

The status change from child to *kedamidze* was the most dramatic for Avatime women. Once a girl began to menstruate she had to have a long series of ceremonies performed for her. The cycle can be divided into two for analytical purposes but in practice it was a continuous set of rituals. The first parts of the rituals recognised the transition to adulthood – the girl's nubility ceremony. This culminated in a girl being stripped of her childhood clothes and having a new cloth wrapped around her by her father's sister. The second phase of the ritual was concerned with marriage. During this phase a girl spent some time in seclusion, after which she was gradually introduced to household tasks in the *oku* (minimal agnatic descent-group) area of her husband. Marriage is patri-virilocal. Following immediately from the cloth putting-on, however, was a ritual which both signalled the attainment of a married status for the girl and her new husband and served to legitimate the fecundity of both. This ritual consisted of the girl and her future spouse being annointed with the sap of a particular bush. It was done at the girl's father's house every day for a week. Later in the cycle, once the girl had begun to work again, she was annointed with the sap, together with palm oil, at her husband's house. The first annointing legitimated the fecundity of both the girl and the man and also served to give notice of their attainment of a married status. The second annointing, at the man's house, can be seen as the appropriation of the girl's fecundity by the man's *oku*.[1]

Throughout her life an Avatime woman accumulates statuses: adulthood, wifehood, eldership – and these are irremovable.[2] After the menopause a woman loses some of the ritually polluting quality associated with menstrual blood. The fact of association with menstruation debars females of all ages from holding ritual positions within Avatime. After the menopause they may take some part in rituals and can take a prominent part in matters affecting the *oku*.[3]

In the earlier period a man's first marriage marked the transition from 'child' to 'adult' and conferred a formal 'married' status which could not be lost. The sap-smearing parts of the marriage ceremony served to legitimate a man's fecundity. But a man could be regarded as an adult even if he was not married. A man could fulfil his expected economic and political roles whether married or unmarried. He did not *have* to be recognised formally as an adult; a woman did.

The old form of marriage ceremonies ensured that a couple had somewhere to live after their marriage; ideally this was a house close to but separate from that of the man's parents. It was the responsibility of a girl's family to provide her with domestic equipment and cloths with which to begin her adult life. A man, by virtue of the tacit recognition of his adulthood – his marriage, his proved ability to farm, his *oku* membership – had access to land. A couple therefore entered marriage with a means of subsistence, a house, tools and cloths.

Whereas in the cultivation of yams, maize and cassava division of labour was a matter of convenience and physical strength, hill rice, which was (and is) the most important crop for ritual purposes, was cultivated according to a strict sexual division of labour. Planting, harvesting and first eating of rice were strictly controlled by rituals. Rice cultivation was also an activity which required organisation of labour. For rice planting, only men were allowed on the farms and the labour groups consisted of male *oku* members together with sisters' sons. After two weeks women were allowed on to the farms to weed around the rice. Women were not allowed to harvest rice, nor could they take part in threshing. Harvesting and threshing of rice was done entirely by men and involved a long series of rituals. Women were not allowed even to see the rice grain until it had been brought safely within the confines of the village.

Men hunted, wove cotton, carried out house repairs and provided such items as sleeping mats and baskets. Women cooked, fetched water and span, in addition to keeping the house clean and swept. They were also responsible for making soap and oil for lamps. A man and his wife were an efficient production unit.[4] Within the domestic unit a man and his wife were expected to discuss their affairs and plans. Outside the domestic sphere women had very little power with respect to decision-making. It was men who had effective political power and who were responsible for settling disputes and maintaining order. In the ritual sphere, too, men held the power.

Bearing children is one of the most important attributes of an Avatime woman. The only socially approved framework into which children can be born is marriage. It is from their father that children inherit their name and place in the society and the right to land. The status 'single adult female' was anomalous in Avatime, since the nubility and marriage ceremonies were mandatory and remarriage after divorce or widowhood was expected to take place within a short time. Some old widows did return to their natal *oku* areas, where they were supported by younger members of the *oku* and by their adult children, if they had borne any. For women as well as men the funeral was carried out by their *oku* members. Thus there was no sense in which a woman was 'incorporated' into the *oku* of her husband. The status of 'unmarried adult Avatime', whether male or female, was anomalous: it was anti-social. A woman who left her husband and refused to remarry lived with her brothers in her natal *oku* area. She farmed for herself and any children on *Oku* land but she had to rely on kin to help clear the land for her and to help with house repairs or thatching. A single adult male had to do such unmanly things as cooking regularly and he had no descendants. Even if he impregnated women, social paternity of any children born was claimed by the woman's husband (if she was married) or by her natal *oku* members.

Change

After Avatime became part of the German colony of Togoland in 1884, mission influence expanded rapidly. One of the most visible effects of missions in Avatime was with respect to residence. Missions tended to build on land a little apart from the villages and encouraged their converts to move out of the villages proper to live nearer to the mission station. Sons no longer necessarily built houses near to their fathers. Christian sons moved away. Christian children went to school, an act which further distanced them from their village con-temporaries. Not only did they learn to read and write, but the Ger-mans also taught craft skills: masonry, carpentry and smithing. Although it was mainly boys who went to school in the early years of the century, some girls did go. For those girls who did not go to school, the missionaries' wives taught cooking, sewing and European housecraft.

The area to the east of the Volta contained important trading centres before the Europeans moved in. With the European influx Avatime not only took their own produce to market but were also employed as carriers by the Germans. Carrying was one of the earl-iest ways in which Avatime earned the cash needed for newly imposed taxes and to buy imported goods. By the beginning of the twentieth century Avatime were already working away from the vil-lages on a regular basis as catechists and craftsmen and, from 1911, as pastors. Cocoa began to be grown on a large scale in an area about fifty miles north of Avatime in the first decade of this century. By 1920 Avatime men were leaving the villages to go to these areas to work on cocoa farms and to try to establish farms of their own.

Missionary activity was not the only source of change. Teutonic zeal was also a characteristic of administrators and businessmen. Taxes were imposed, law and order enforced and the cultivation of already introduced cash crops was systematically investigated. These changes affected Christians and villagers alike. I have suggested a pattern of occupational and social roles concomitant with the statuses of Avatime 'women' and 'men' for the early colonial period. Nubility/marriage ceremonies were mandatory for women to be regarded as women, but not for men. In looking at what is happening to Avatime women and men now, I shall concentrate on what has happened to the nubility/marriage ceremonies and discuss the significance for Avatime women and men.

When I first visited Avatime in 1973 the old form of nubility and marriage ceremonies was defunct. In the old form the two phases, nubility and marriage, were parts of the same cycle. Now, although a version of the nubility ceremonies is mandatory for all Avatime women, ceremonies connected with marriage are arbitrary and the whole cycle is condensed into, at most, five days. In full, the cycle used to take up to two months to complete.

The nubility ceremonies now consist of a shortened version of the cloth putting-on ritual, which takes no more than two days. The ceremonies usually end with attendance at church the following Sunday. If a girl is getting married at the same time then the ceremonies are more elaborate, but now there is no accepted form that 'marriage' takes. What follows from the nubility rites, although variable in detail, broadly takes one of three forms. Some girls having the nubility ceremonies performed for them have no prospective husband. When this is the case then the nubility ceremonies end with the church service on Sunday. Now the girl may be married; before the ceremonies, she may not. If the girl wants to be married some time after the performance of the ceremonies, then her prospective husband will give drinks to the elders of the girl's *oku*. This is an essential preliminary to all the forms of marriage, whatever the subsequent ceremonies. A girl wanting the highest accolade of prestige in the village will have a church wedding, which follows immediately from the nubility ceremonies. Such ceremonies with the formal European dress and refreshments are very expensive. But there is a less expensive alternative to the wedding in customary marriage. The man's family cooks and distributes food on the day of the girl's nubility rites and the couple and both of their families move in procession around the village together. Such couples may also have a church blessing said for them.

Women and Men in the Villages

Within the villages I have defined marriage as a co-residential and commensal union. Ideally now in the villages a married woman should bear children and should work on her husband's and her own farms, keep the compound tidy, cook, and help train her children (who should be brought up to respect their elders and kin and to work hard for their families). In fact what women should do, their occupational and social roles, differs little from the earlier pattern. Many village women now trade in addition to farming, but the villages are still their base. The village, the family and the farms are the pivot around which life is structured.

In addition to mixed cash crops/subsistence farming, men and women in Amedzofe can also find work in the Training College (as labourers or in the kitchen) or as labourers in an experimental tea plantation. None of these occupations means that a person's occupational or domestic roles are significantly different from those of men and women in the earlier period. At the politico-jural level, although the national legal system has reduced the scope of customary law, the scope of male and female power has not changed much. Men are recognised as village chiefs and preside over the settlement of disputes. Women have a voice as a collectivity as the group of *kedamidzeba*.

But there are changes. In the earlier pattern the status of 'single woman' was anomalous: this implies that women could not be on their own as heads of residential groups. However, in 1973/4 over 30 per cent ($\frac{64}{212}$) of residential groups in Amedzofe were headed by women. Female heads of residential groups are generally either widows, divorcees, or unmarried. Only in a very few cases is a woman head of a residential group because her husband is working away. Within the formal politico-jural system Avatime women cannot be recognised as the *de jure* heads but for all practical and everyday purposes they are effectively the heads of residential units. Such women may be economically independent or else rely on financial support from migrant children and/or help from relatives with the heavier tasks of farming, if they cannot afford to hire labour. Apart from the heavy tasks of burning and clearing the ground for new farms, women are as viable as men as farmers.

A residential group headed by a woman usually contains her children and/or grandchildren. These latter are usually the children of Avatime women who are working away. Sending a child to the village to be reared is one of the Avatime solutions to child care problems faced everywhere by working women. Women's occupational roles in the villages have changed to some extent but what village women do now is not incompatible with the earlier period or with statuses formally tenable by an Avatime woman. Only when Avatime women are migrants are their roles and formal statuses incompatible.

Migrant Roles and Statuses

Many Avatime women and men now live and work away from the villages for most of their working lives and women migrate independently of men. Migrants maintain links with home villages. Most send money and provisions and agricultural produce is also sent to them from the villages. Most migrants try to visit home at least once a year. Fostering children in rural areas provides a means for strengthening links between migrant Avatime and those at home. Moreover, it is cheaper to bring children up in the rural areas than it is in the cities. From an early age children can contribute to the rural agricultural economy and the villages are self-sufficient in staple foodstuffs.

Not only do urban occupations involve activities different from farming and subsistence crafts, but the basis for the work is different. Only in the towns do people have to use cash to provide wholly for shelter and food. In the villages the domestic group functions as a production and consumption unit. Work is focused around the house and farms and the members of the domestic group. In the urban areas men's and women's total dependence on the cash-based economy precludes this.

In the villages a woman may not live with a man unless she has had the nubility rites performed for her. Away from the villages many Avatime girls who have not had the nubility rites performed for them live with men. These unions may persist and become formal marriages after the nubility rites, but they are just as likely to break up. Sometimes such unions are encouraged. A girl living with an Avatime man away from the village is unlikely to 'roam around', to become a prostitute. Some recognition is given to the union to the extent that the man will give a small amount of drink to the elders of the girl's *oku*.

Simple paternity is established by giving drinks to the elders of a mother's *oku*. A father is supposed to contribute regularly to the children's upbringing. Should the genitor refuse to acknowledge paternity then an elder of the *oku*, usually the girl's father, will claim formal paternity of the child. In this way all children can have a place in Avatime society. Many children now are not born within a framework of formal marriage and children are often born to couples who have no long-term liaison, but they are recognised through formal acknowledgement of paternity.

In traditional Avatime society Avatime women were recognised as such because they had a series of rituals performed for them. Becoming *kedamidze*, that is, becoming an Avatime woman, is still mandatory for Avatime females in the sense that the title *kedamidze* still carries the implications that a woman may have children, is married and an adult, and has a formal standing in her natal descent-group. The problem is that what the title implies no longer encompasses what women do. Now a woman may be an independent adult economically and socially. Wifehood in the traditional sense and its economic implications are less viable options away from Avatime.

Most women now become mothers before their nubility rites are performed. In all the sixteen nubility ceremonies I have seen, the women had had children prior to the ceremony. The chiefs and elders of Avatime (men and older *kedamidzeba*), concerned about what ought to be and what is, have on at least two occasions issued decrees stating that women who have had children must have the nubility rites performed for them by a fixed date, on pain of fines. The dates have passed and nothing has happened. The rationalisation given is that there are too many girls to have all the ceremonies performed in the specified time. Formerly it was a mother's responsibility to provide her daughter with what she needed for the nubility/marriage ceremonies. A mother provided sets of cloths and headties, beads, pots and brooms, all essentially women's property and distributed and inherited by women. Now mothers usually live in the villages and cannot afford to buy cloth and other goods necessary for the nubility rites. The money must be provided by the girl herself, if she can find a job, or by her siblings. The importance of the ceremonies is seen from the fact that rather than abandoning them in the face of vastly increasing cost, families will save and prepare for years, and hence the time-lag. The chiefs have tried to restrict the scale of the ceremonies, but this has failed: prestige must be upheld in the villages. At Easter in 1979 the alternative of holding a mass ceremony was tried. Seven Amedzofe girls had the ceremonies performed for them simultaneously. Cooking was shared out among the families of all of the girls and palm wine was obtained jointly. When there are seven foci of activity on the same day, the amount of goods that each girl has becomes less important and the scale of food distribution for each family, less lavish. The lengths to which families go to ensure the performance of the ceremonies (conferring on them formal adult, *kedamidze* status) is an indication of their importance.

It might be supposed that with the decline in importance of a traditional politico-jural system, along with the increasing influence of a national legal system, that the importance of women's roles as *kedamidzeba* would decline. Becoming *kedamidze* entitled a woman to represent her natal *oku* or village as a woman in intra- or inter-village affairs. It also entitled her to have some say in discussions in her natal lineage. Becoming *kedamidze* is still important in these respects. But the vital point is that a woman as *kedamidze* is an adult member of her natal group. Now, when a woman does not *have* to use her reproductive, economic and domestic assets for the benefit of other descent-groups, the status of adult female of one's natal group, *kedamidze*, assumes a different relevance. This raises not only questions about the importance of women and men in patrilineal societies but also more fundamental questions about the nature of patriliny.

Conclusion

With the political and economic changes that have taken place in the last century Avatime is now part of the wider political and economic structure of Ghana. Avatime men and women are enmeshed in this wider economy and this has had its effects on the formal social ideology.

Avatime men never had to be confirmed in their status of 'men'. In general how men are thought of has changed with changes in what men do. Avatime women had and still have to be confirmed in their status as 'women'. Any female Avatime who has once menstruated must have nubility ceremonies performed for her before she dies.[5] But now what a 'woman', that is, *kedamidze*, is, is ambiguous. Motherhood is culturally valued and the *kedamidze* status still legitimates a woman's standing in the politico-jural sphere. It is the status of 'wife', formerly inseparable from the mother and adult statuses, around which there is ambiguity.

It is not just the cost of becoming a wife that has changed its significance. Only if a girl wants the prestige of a wedding is the cost enormous. We must therefore question the persistence of the formal status recognition of women as mothers and adults and the separability of these from the status of wife. Women still see wifehood ideally as part of the *kedamidze* status but being a wife is not essential in practice. Wifely roles are identified with the occupational, agricultural and domestic roles in the earlier period, and it is because a woman's occupational and domestic roles have changed so much that the 'wife' part of the *kedamidze* package has become separated. Women can be economically independent from men.

Women want to become mothers: they see the maternal role as an essential part of being a woman, and their children will provide support in their old age. Now women in Avatime can have children who are recognised as legitimate without the presence of a husband. Becoming an adult, in the sense of 'potential female elder', has relevance, since most older Avatime women live in the villages. Those who have worked away tend to return to the villages on retirement. Only a woman of *kedamidze* status commands respect and authority in the villages. The 'mother' and 'potential female elder' components of the *kedamidze* package are relatively little affected by Avatime's incorporation into a wider socio-economic system. The 'wife' component, with its identification with economic roles, is. It is the involvement with a wider system that has meant the separability of the wifely component from the *kedamidze* package. And there is evidence of further change. Outside Avatime, women can live with men as wives before they have nubility ceremonies performed for them. Within the villages they cannot: being a 'wife' can only come with the achievement of adulthood.

Notes: Chapter 23

I have done fieldwork in Avatime on three occasions: 1973–4, 1976–7 and in the summer of 1979. During the first period I held the Wyse Studentship in Social Anthropology from Trinity College, Cambridge. The second field trip was financed jointly by the SSRC and the Smuts Fund and the third, again jointly, by the British Academy and the University of Liverpool.

1 See Brydon, 1976, ch. IV, for a fuller discussion of this.
2 Even if a woman becomes a widow she still maintains a formal 'married' status.
3 There is a special term for a post-menopausal woman: *kekusidze*.
4 Polygyny did occur in Avatime but was not frequent in the period I am concerned with.
5 If a woman dies before she has the ceremonies performed for her then a version of the nubility rites is performed for the corpse in the coffin.

Chapter 24

Female and Male Domestic Cycles in Urban Africa: the Adabraka Case

ROGER SANJEK

The concept of 'the development cycle in domestic groups' (J. Goody, ed., 1958) has become widely accepted in studies of social organisation. In essence, variation in household structure at one point in time is analysed in terms of longer-term processes affecting each household as its members age.

> Families go through development cycles as the individuals who compose them go through their life-cycles. A census taken at a given point in time takes a cross-section and gives a static picture of households and families that the historian or sociologist can sort into types... But rather than being types these may simply be phases in the development cycle of a single family organisation. (Berkner, 1972, p. 405)

As Fortes puts it, 'Residence patterns are the crystallisation, at a given time, of the development process' (1958, p. 3).

The concept was introduced by Fortes in his analysis of Tallensi social structure (1949a, pp. 63–77), and has been used subsequently by many others (Fortes, 1949b; R. T. Smith, 1956; Berkner, 1972; J. Goody, 1973). While accepting the usefulness of this form of analysis, Lamphere (1974, pp. 97–8) has criticised previous work for focusing too closely upon men in domestic development processes, and for not paying enough attention to women's roles and strategies.

I side with Lamphere in detecting male bias in uses of the development cycle concept, but for an additional reason to the ones she discusses – the absence of a clear separation between female and male domestic cycles. In the earlier principal analyses a single development cycle is presented where separate analysis by sex would be more illuminating. In societies where all women and men marry, where age of marriage for each sex is the same, where divorce is rare, where polygamy is absent, where conjugal marital residence is the rule, where widows and widowers have equal chances for remarriage, and where female and male life expectancy is identical, then male and female development cycles will be isomorphic. In societies where these conditions are not met, women and men will experience diverging domestic cycles. Few of these conditions characterise Adabraka, the urban Ghanaian neighbourhood I shall discuss. Here strikingly different female and male domestic cycles are evident, and female socialisation prepares girls for adult life accordingly (Sanjek and Sanjek, 1976, pp. 10–13).

Before turning to the Adabraka case, however, I shall briefly review the treatment of women and men in the major development cycle analyses.

A Brief History of the Development Cycle Concept

Fortes's analysis of 'the development cycle of the joint family' among the Tallensi (1949a, pp. 63–77) is an account of the male life-cycle in terms of residence. He shows how a Tallensi male,

> starts his career as a family man with only one wife, his aim and ideal . . . is to have as many wives as he can afford . . . as the younger males grow up, marry and have children of their own . . . a tendency to split appears. . . The oldest son of the family head 'goes out on his own' or 'cuts his own gateway' in the family homestead. (Fortes, 1949a, pp. 65–7)

The analysis is anchored in Fortes's account of male–male relations within the hierarchy of patrilineal descent-group segments.

Although Fortes speaks of the male development cycle as '*the* development cycle', in fact most women's domestic careers appear to coincide with those of their husbands. Following her first, or first few 'experimental' marriages (ibid. pp. 84–5), a Tallensi woman rarely divorces (ibid. p. 87; cf. Goody and Goody, 1969). If widowed, she will remarry in her husband's agnatic group, or live there with her eldest son (Fortes, 1949a, p. 219). (The question does arise, however, to what degree second and succeeding young wives who marry older men may have substantially different residence histories from first wives.)

Berkner's study of household development processes in eighteenth-century Austria, though more complicated than Fortes's Tallensi case, is similar in its male orientation: 'The phases of *the* individual's cycle are: *son*, and heir; head of household; retired parent. The critical events in *his* life cycle are *his* marriage and the transfer of authority through retirement or inheritance' (Berkner, 1972, p. 418, emphasis added). Presumably divorce here too was infrequent, and women once married remained in their husband's household until death or widowhood. But with only the male development cycle presented, and presented as *the* development cycle, it is impossible to tell whether women's domestic cycles paralleled men's or not.

In his analysis of Ashanti residence Fortes does not explicitly use the development cycle concept, but speaks rather of 'the time factor' (1949b). He presents residence patterns by age-cohort for all women in two Ashanti towns (ibid., pp. 76–8; see Figure 24.1). In Asokore rates of conjugal residence peak at 47 per cent in the 26–30 age-group, and drop thereafter, accounting for only 32 per cent of women over 50. In Agogo lower rates of female conjugal residence obtain, peaking at only 26 per cent in the 41–50 cohort, and dropping to 11 per cent among women over 50. Since virtually every Ashanti marries (Fortes, 1954, p. 269), Ashanti wives obviously can expect to live apart from their husbands for some or all of their marital career. Divorce is also frequent (ibid. p. 263), and 57 per cent and 63 per cent respectively of the women over 50 in the two towns are divorced or widowed, many heading their own households (Fortes, 1949b, pp. 77, 67).

While Fortes's data give a clear picture of the female domestic cycle, due to the exigencies of the Ashanti social survey and its focus upon demography and fertility, similar data for men were not collected (Fortes, 1954, p. 263). Whether the male domestic cycle parallels the female in terms of conjugal residence, or whether older men remarry, and co-reside with younger wives, cannot be determined with the data at hand.

Smith (1956) presents residence data similar to Fortes's for Ashanti women on both women and men in three rural Guyana villages. But rather than separating female and male domestic cycles, he discusses a single 'developmental sequence of the household group' (Smith, 1956, pp. 112–22). He does, however, discuss the high rates of non-conjugal residence among women after the menopause, and emphasises that not all individual life careers can be fitted into the domestic cycle he presents.

Smith's data for August Town (ibid, pp. 116–17), the largest of the villages studied, show very different cycles by sex. For men, conjugal residence climbs to 50 per cent in the 31–35 age-group and 67 per cent in the 36–40 cohort, and varies between 71 and 89 per cent through the rest of the male life-cycle.[1] Among August Town women conjugal residence rises to 70 per cent in the 31–35 age-group, stays

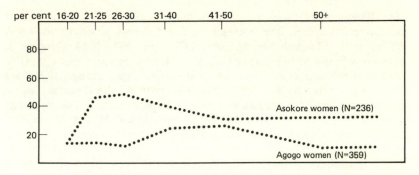

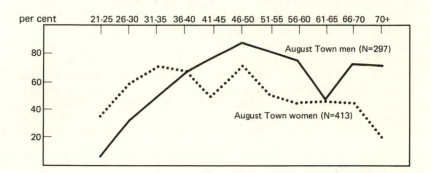

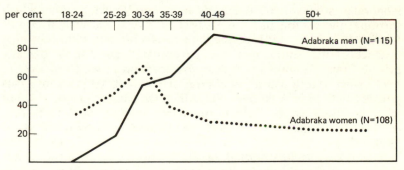

Figure 24.1   Conjugal residence in selected towns.

at roughly that level throughout the child-bearing years, and then drops to 52 per cent in the 51–55 cohort and averages only 45 per cent in the 56–70 age-groups. Most older men can expect to reside with a spouse; most older women cannot.

E. N. Goody (1973, p. 280) contrasts 'individual maturation' with 'the developmental pattern of domestic groups', yet her discussion of development cycles, like Fortes's for the Tallensi, is strictly in terms of the male life-cycle (E. Goody, 1973, pp. 281–301). Divorce is relatively frequent in Gonja (ibid., p. 134; Goody and Goody, 1967), and it is women who move upon divorce. Even though the male pattern is treated as *'the* developmental pattern', the residence cycle for women is well covered earlier, in the chapter entitled 'The termination of marriage' (E. Goody, 1973, pp. 131–70). As in Smith's Guyana case, Goody's data show different domestic cycles for women and men.

As Lamphere writes of the development cycle literature: 'Most discussions, though not ignoring the position of women, have treated processes within the family from a male ego's point of view. Authors such as Fortes and [J.] Goody [we may add Berkner, Smith and E. Goody] emphasise the continuity of domestic groups and the transmission of property and authority roles. Since both are in the hands of males, the focus is on men rather than on women' (Lamphere, 1974, pp. 97–8). There is certainly no argument against analysing these topics, but it would be more appropriate to speak in such circumstances of a *male* development cycle, rather than *the* development cycle.

A Neighbourhood in Adabraka

Adabraka is one of the dozen or more residential sections which surround the central business district of Accra, the capital city of Ghana. Lying just north of the hub of Accra, and within walking distance of the central markets, government ministries and many private firms, Adabraka is a desirable location in which to live. In 1960, when Accra had a population of 388,000, 10 per cent of its population lived in Adabraka. Since then the city has grown outward in all directions. By 1977 Accra numbered 840,000 inhabitants, or 8 per cent of Ghana's 10·6 million population (Department of State, 1978, p. 1).

Adabraka was first settled in the early 1900s. A 1916 Lands Department map shows the streets laid out rectangularly as they are today. Since the late 1940s, as the population of Accra has increased by a factor of six, the dominant housing pattern in Adabraka, as in much of urban Ghana, has been the privately owned, multihousehold building, containing from four to forty rooms, most of them rented by the landlord to tenants.

The many large two-storey concrete buildings, the paved streets, the tall palm trees, and the numerous schools, churches, shops and bars give Adabraka a settled rather than a raw or unfinished character. It is a quiet area in the daytime, when most people are at work and children are in school. By late afternoon as people are coming home, the streets become livelier – friends and neighbours greet each other, stop to chat, or walk along together as one 'sees the other off'. In the evening knots of people in conversation may be seen in the building courtyards, in front of the houses on the street, or around the kerosene lamp-lit tables of women selling prepared food and provisions until as late as 10 or 11 p.m.

Fieldwork in 1970–1 and 1974 focused on eleven buildings all in the same neighbourhood of Adabraka. The buildings range in size from thirteen to sixty-one residents. Households of landlords and their kin account for 34 per cent of the neighbourhood population; tenant households account for 66 per cent. In all, 423 persons live in these eleven buildings. Typical of Adabraka, the residents are predominantly literate Christian southern Ghanaians.

Half the adults work in the formal economic sector – in government employment and private firms. The other half, including 79 per cent of the working women, earn their livelihood in small-scale distribution and production. One-fifth of the Adabraka people form part of the Ghanaian middle bourgeoisie: petty businessmen and women, professionals, middle managers and higher clerical workers. Most, some 63 per cent, are petty bourgeois lower clerks, small and middle traders, craftswomen and men, and skilled and semi-skilled manual workers. Another fifth are urban proletarians: unskilled manual workers, washermen, hawkers, houseworkers and prepared food producers (Sanjek, 1979).

Twenty-two ethnic identities are represented in the eleven buildings (Sanjek, 1977, p. 605), with only three amounting to more than 6 per cent of the population: Kwawu, 25 per cent; Ga, the indigenous group in Accra, 18 per cent; and Ewe, 16 per cent. Inter-ethnic relations are harmonious and common (Sanjek, 1977, 1978), and ethnic categories are well distributed in the neighbourhood, not clumped in ethnic enclaves. Some 80 per cent of the tenants are of ethnic identities different from that of their landlord.

Almost one-quarter of the adults, tenants and landlords, Ga and non-Ga, were born in Accra, and have no intention of ever living anywhere else in Ghana. Most of the migrants, some of whom came to Accra as children, feel the same way, and expect to live out their lives, raise families and earn their livelihood in Accra. Some migrants have little or no interest in their home towns, making only rare visits, characteristically when a relative is sick or has died. Others visit more frequently, and have plans to retire to their home towns. But all expect their children to remain in urban employment, in Accra or in other Ghanaian towns, or overseas.

Domestic Cycles in Adabraka

In marking out the phases or stages through which individual life-cycles may pass, both household types (Berkner, 1972) and marital status (Smith, 1956) have been used. For the Adabraka data a series of seven *household residence roles* is employed: child, employee, independent co-member, solitary adult, conjugal partner, single parent, grandparent. These roles take both marital status and intra-household social relationships into account. Household residence roles vary independently of household type. For example, when a *simple family household* (see Hammel and Laslett, 1974) of husband, wife and children adds a schoolboy nephew or a maidservant female relative, the household type changes to *extended family household* (ibid.). The conjugal partner household residence role, however, does not change.[2] The following case illustrates this more fully.

Figure 24.2 depicts two tenant households in one of the Adabraka buildings. Ages are indicated above each person, and occupations

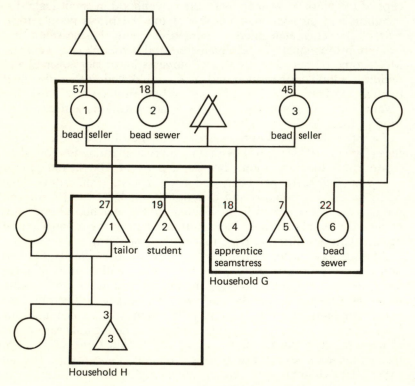

Figure 24.2   Two tenant households in Ababraka

below. All five women in household G are members of an extended family household, but within it they play very different roles.

Child

G4, an apprentice seamstress (now working for H1), illustrates the first role: an adult residing in her or his household of rearing. Most persons in the child household role in Adabraka live with their parents, but a few reside with other relatives who have reared them as foster children.

Employee

This role is played by persons whose presence in a household is based upon the work they do for their employer. G2 and G6 are both petty commodity workers: they sew strings of beads for G1 and G3, who each separately sell beads in the market. Though G2 and G6 have lived in this household since they were young girls, I consider them employees rather than children of the household because their residence depends upon their work relationship to their mistresses, and not solely (as with G4) upon kinship. Most Adabraka women in the employee household role are maidservants.

Independent Co-Member

This role subsumes those household members who live with one or more other adults, but who do not have a spouse or any dependent children of their own living with them, and who are not children or employees of other household members. Most independent co-members reside in the 'no family' category of households (Hammel and Laslett, 1974), but as G1 and H2 illustrate, they are found in extended families as well.

Solitary Adult

These individuals live alone, or with a child in a servant or foster child role. There are no examples of this role in households G and H.

Conjugal Partner

Co-resident husbands and wives, with or without children, are conjugal partners. Again, no examples of this role are present in Figure 24.1. G1 and G3, however, did play this role when their husband was alive and living in this household. Similarly, by 1974, H1 moved into a household as conjugal partner with his wife, who in 1970–1 was living in her mother's house with her and H1's daughter.

Single Parent

H1 and G3 both illustrate the single parent role: residing without a spouse, and with at least one of their own children as a dependant. (I classify mothers with adult but childless co-resident daughters as independent co-members, and the daughters as playing the child household residence role. If the adult daughter does have a dependent child, she is a single parent, but her mother's household role remains independent co-member. I realise this classification might be approached differently.)

Grandparent

This role is played when a woman (or man) resides with one or more grandchildren, who are dependent upon her, and with none of her own children. It is not present in households G and H. (When a grandparent lives with a grandchild, but is also a conjugal partner or single parent, these roles over-ride grandparent for purposes of classification.)

Using this approach, it is apparent that the five women in household G are more than equivalent members of an extended family household. Four household roles are present here: independent co-member (G1), employee (G2, G6), single parent (G3) and child (G4).

Table 24.1 extends this analysis of household residence roles in Adabraka to all adult women and men, grouped by age-cohorts in columns. This shows in dynamic form the proportions of men and women in each household role through the life-cycle. I have used the convention of a rectangle for calling attention to the *dominant* household role in each age-cohort (0·45 or greater) and a diamond for *subdominant* household residence roles (0·25 to 0·44). As in August Town and Gonja, the patterns in Adabraka for men and women are different.

For men, the picture is relatively simple. Most men in their twenties live as independent co-members, usually in households of siblings, cousins and unrelated men. They move into conjugal partner roles in their early thirties. Through the rest of the male life-cycle conjugal partnership is the dominant household residence role. Solitary residence is an important transitional pattern for some men in their late twenties and their thirties, leading to conjugal partnership.

A few men in their late teens and early twenties live with parents in the child role. (The one case in the 25–29 cohort is a mentally retarded man living with his grandmother). Few adult men in Adabraka reside in the employee role. The single parent role is rare among men, and the grandparent role is absent.

Table 24.1 Household Roles and Life-cycle position in Adabraka.

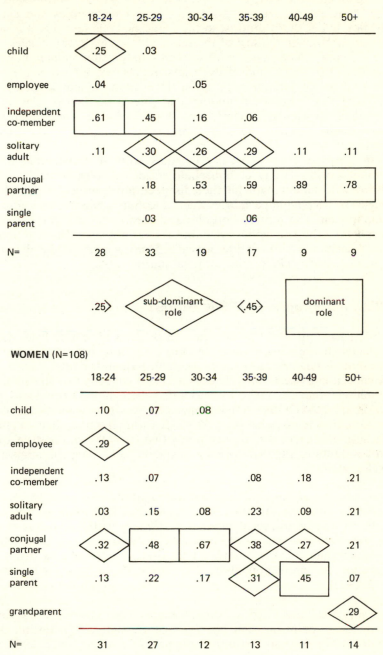

MEN (N=115)

	18-24	25-29	30-34	35-39	40-49	50+
child	.25	.03				
employee	.04		.05			
independent co-member	.61	.45	.16	.06		
solitary adult	.11	.30	.26	.29	.11	.11
conjugal partner		.18	.53	.59	.89	.78
single parent		.03		.06		
N=	28	33	19	17	9	9

.25⟩ ⟨ sub-dominant role ⟩ ⟨.45⟩   dominant role

WOMEN (N=108)

	18-24	25-29	30-34	35-39	40-49	50+
child	.10	.07	.08			
employee	.29					
independent co-member	.13	.07		.08	.18	.21
solitary adult	.03	.15	.08	.23	.09	.21
conjugal partner	.32	.48	.67	.38	.27	.21
single parent	.13	.22	.17	.31	.45	.07
grandparent						.29
N=	31	27	12	13	11	14

For women the situation is less clear-cut. Conjugal partnership is the dominant pattern for women in their late twenties and early thirties, but in sharp contrast to the domestic cycle for men, it is not dominant through the rest of the female life-cycle. Between ages 35 and 50 conjugal partnership for women is only a subdominant household residence role, and of even less importance for women older than 50. Single parenthood, present throughout the female life-cycle in Adabraka, becomes a subdominant role in the late thirties, and dominant for women in their forties. After 50 female household roles vary widely, with only the grandparent role becoming a subdominant pattern.

In their late teens and early twenties, women in Adabraka also exhibit a wide variety of household residence roles, with the employee role subdominant, but then disappearing. Conjugal partnership begins to become important in this age-cohort while it is still absent among men. The solitary household residence role remains present throughout the female life-cycle, but it does not have the subdominant, transitional nature it does for men. Many women, unlike all but a few men, never take on the conjugal partner role.

Still Photographs or Movie Strips?

Laslett has criticised the construction of domestic cycles from data collected at one point in time. 'In most cases only somewhat insecure inference is possible as to . . . its probable past and possible future. . . A collection of such individual listings is a collection of still photographs and they cannot be used as if they were movie strips' (Laslett, 1972, pp. 33–4). Gluckman defends analyses of domestic cycles; not because they tell us what the past was, or what the future will be, but because they order data in such a way that testable hypotheses about past and future, and therefore about stability and change in domestic cycles, result:

> an analysis of this kind does not state that the institution has operated in that way in reality in the past, or will continue to operate thus in the future; the analysis is not dealing with the institution of real, historical time. . . Whether the institution is in actual stable equilibrium . . . is a matter of historical record over a denoted period, or prediction about the future. (Gluckman, 1968, pp. 221–2)

Smith was very aware of this problem in his Guyana work, and hastened to point out that his case histories tended to confirm the reality of the domestic cycle over the past fifty years (Smith, 1956, p.

Table 24.2   *Changes in Household Residence Roles, 1970/1–4*

	18–24	25–29	30–34	35–39	40–49	50+
MEN	Ch. – IC Ch. – IC IC – SA IC – SA IC – SA	Ch. – IC IC – CP SA – CP SP – CP	IC – SA	SA – CP	SA – CP	
WOMEN	Ch. – SP IC – SP IC – CP SP – CP Emp. – Ch.	Ch. – CP IC – SA SA – CP SP – CP		CP – SP CP – SP SP – CP		GP – CP

Key:

Ch. = child	CP = conjugal partner
Emp. = employee	SP = single parent
IC = independent co-member	GP = grandparent
SA = solitary adult	

112). A more rigorous confirmation could consist of 'actually observing a developmental sequence over a period of years' (loc. cit.).

In Adabraka it is possible to examine some residence changes between 1970–1 and 1974. Data are available for twelve men and thirteen women who changed their household residence role during this period. (In several other cases people moved out but I was not able to determine their new household residence role.)

These twenty-five household role changes are listed in Table 24.2 (ages are for 1970–1). All male role shifts conform to the domestic cycle constructed in the previous section. Three female cases, underscored in Table 24.2, do not conform.

(1)   A 21-year-old maidservant left her employer, and returned to her natal household in the child role. According to the domestic cycle model, and the experience of other women who left the employee role, one would predict a shift to a solitary adult, single parent, or conjugal partner role.

(2)   A 38-year-old woman in the single parent role shifted to conjugal partner household residence role. From the domestic cycle model, one would not expect this relationship to endure.

(3)   A 52-year-old woman living with her grandson shifted to the conjugal partner role when her man friend moved in and her grandson moved out. In this age-cohort, also, conjugal partnership is diminishing numerically. Solitary adult or independent co-member would be the forecasted residence change.

These three cases, though not predicted by the model, do confirm that female household residence roles are more variable than male household residence roles. We may conclude that the proposed male domestic cycle in Adabraka is strengthened by these limited time-series data, and that the variability in the female domestic cycle is slightly increased.

Conclusion

Domestic cycles in Adabraka are different for men and women. Most men can look forward to conjugal residence, from their thirties into their old age. A man can expect to have a wife in the house to cook and clean, and in most cases supplement his income with her own. For a woman the probability of living in a conjugal partnership increases while she is young, but after age 35 it decreases. Most women from their forties onwards live in households they head or share with other adult women.

The domestic cycles in Adabraka are similar to those in August Town and, for women at least, in Asokore. In each case cultural alternatives for older women who must support themselves are found. August Town women inherit houses as husbands die, and receive economic support from their children (Smith, 1956, pp. 65–6, 119, 121). And during their forties they also 'quite often begin to embark on economic enterprises of their own', to their husbands' dismay (ibid. p. 115; for a case of similar strategies among elite Ghanaian women, see Oppong, 1982 [1974], discussed in Sanjek, 1976). Asokore women too are able to survive alone economically, through open access to farm land, and with the support of children and matrikin (Fortes, 1949b, 1954; see also Okali in Chapter 11 above).

Adabraka women begin independent economic activities by the time they leave their natal household, if not before. All girls are trained in trade, and all Adabraka girls living with one or both parents are also sent to school, giving them skills for both formal and informal sector employment (Sanjek and Sanjek, 1976, pp. 10–13). In the eleven buildings, 82 per cent of the adult women work full-time as cash income producers. Many of the others are caring for infants; they conduct part-time housetrades, and expect to return to full-time work as soon as child care arrangements (with female kin, a maidservant, or day nursery) are practicable. Older women are accustomed to earning an income.

Conjugal partnership has its economic (and of course other) rewards: a husband helps support a woman's children, and pays the rent, freeing her income for other purposes. But non-conjugal residence, which most women can expect, does not present Adabraka women with economic catastrophe. They are already working, and their former conjugal partner may continue to provide money to support children. Rent becomes the major financial liability. Those women whose trade or wage-employment is not sufficient to ease the new burden of rent alternatively receive financial help from children, live as independent co-members with kinswomen, or secure a room in the building of a relative.

The search for *the* domestic cycle in Adabraka would be fruitless. Domestic cycles for women and men must be examined separately. Meaningful analysis of male and female social life, from the enculturation of children to support in old age, must begin from this premise. The same may be said for domestic cycles elsewhere. With this in mind, Fortes's concept of 'the development cycle in domestic groups' will continue to be a powerful tool in understanding how women and men – old, middle-aged and young – daily re-create human societies.

Notes: Chapter 24

Research in Accra for eighteen months in 1969–71 was supported by a Foreign Area Fellowship and a New York State Lehman Fellowship; research for two more months in 1974 was funded by a Faculty Research Award from the University Committee on Research of the City University of New York. Lani Sanjek and I worked together in Adabraka; the data presented in this chapter are a product of our common efforts. The present tense used here refers to the early 1970s. More information on the Adabraka research is found in Sanjek, 1977, 1978, 1979, and Sanjek and Sanjek, 1976.

1 Except in the 61–65 cohort, where it drops to 47 per cent, perhaps as a statistical anomaly. The percentages here were computed by me from Smith's table.
2 A full analysis of Adabraka households is found in Sanjek, 1979.

Chapter 25

Sugar Daddies and Gold-Diggers: the White-Collar Single Women in Accra

CARMEL DINAN

The normal pattern for Ghanaian women in traditional and contemporary rural and urban contexts is to marry and have children.[1] This definition of the proper female adult role is so intensely held that attempts are even made to enforce compliance when women do not appear to desire marriage.[2] Considerable informal pressure is also placed on women to marry and the popular press frequently carries stories which highlight this process.[3] Ghanaian woman journalists are especially vocal on this question.[4] Even when women attain economic independence and self-sufficiency, they are still expected to have husbands. In one large-scale social survey subjects were asked for their opinions on successful career-women in interesting jobs who chose to remain single and childless: the responses were overwhelmingly against such a life-style. The writer (Caldwell, 1969, p. 66) records: 'Disapproval of spinsterhood was expressed almost always in terms of Ghanaian values. Unmarried women were suspected by men of being hard and selfish and by women of being immoral and a lure to husbands.'

Clearly, therefore, Ghanaian normative standards require marriage and motherhood: the cultural ideology on the 'proper' female role is so strongly held that considerable moral and, failing that, legal pressure is exerted on women to find husbands. As a corollary, a strong negative stereotype attaches to the status of single women. Yet despite the fact that the status of being single is likely to earn them social disapproval, there is emerging in urban Ghana an increasingly large number of women, who have decided to break with the traditionally defined roles of wife and mother, and are attempting to maintain their economic and social independence of husbands. Some of these women have never married; others have been widowed, divorced, or deserted by their husbands; still others have themselves divorced or deserted their husbands. Their existence is confirmed by many sources: sociological and anthropological monographs on married couples frequently refer to the threat the large numbers of single women in the towns pose for the married women (Caldwell, 1968a; Oppong, 1982). Other writers, sociologists in particular, when studying particular female occupational categories, for example, traders or white-collar workers, note in passing the marital status of these workers and surprisingly large numbers are recorded as being single (McCall, 1961; Kumekpor, 1974). Journalists in the Ghanaian daily and weekly newspapers, letters to the papers, women's magazines – all keep the issue of the single woman in the minds of the reading public, often in highly charged moralistic tones.

In this chapter I shall try to discover – against the background of the anomalous position of single women in traditional Ghanaian society and the fact that, even today, marriage remains culturally prescribed and women themselves agree that this is the correct status for women – why single women figure as such a prominent category in the urban environment. This will involve some discussion of the relationship perceived by single women to exist between men and women in marriage. Consideration will then be given to the types of relationships that they can enjoy as single women. The particular category of single women with whom I shall be concerned are those pursuing white-collar occupations. Such women form a minute percentage of the total female population of the country. They do, however, constitute an important and salient reference group and model of modern life-styles and behaviour for other women.

Extended interviews and observation of twenty-five single women engaged in or interested in white-collar occupations from a random sample survey carried out in an Accra suburb form the basis of my material for discussion.[5] These women included clerical workers, receptionists and salesgirls, and came from a range of socio-economic and educational backgrounds. Most were in the age-group 21–25 with a few in their late twenties and early thirties. They nearly all belonged to various Christian churches and were immigrants into Accra from several regions, mainly from small towns of less than 20,000 inhabitants. The majority were Akan and Ewe and from polygynous family backgrounds. Most of them had had some technical, vocational, or secondary schooling after finishing middle school. Nearly all had lived in Accra for over two years. Thirteen were heading their own independent households, mainly sharing with kin (cousins, sisters, nephews and nieces), three lived alone, one with a girlfriend and one with her own child. The remaining twelve were staying with kin as dependants, with parents, uncles and aunts and one with an older sister. Most had worked continuously since their first employment in their late teens or early twenties, in government ministries, semi-state bodies and private industrial and financial concerns. There were substantial salary differences among them ranging from ₵32 to ₵140.[6] To augment their earnings five women were also engaged in some form of part-time entrepreneurial activity such as 'petty' trading or dressmaking. Such spare-time work earned on average an additional ₵40 monthly.[7] Seven of the women had no permanent work at the time of the study and were anxiously looking for work. Two women had been married and declared they had left their husbands because of other women and the fact that their husbands were not providing adequate maintenance for them or their children.[8] The rest had never married but had had many men friends. Most of them had had three or more regular relationships with men in the past. The general pattern was to start as young, teenage schoolgirls forming friendships with boys met, typically, in their own co-educational schools or at interschool sports events. In some instances these affairs involved covert sexual relations; in other instances relations were maintained on a non-sexual basis.

A number of the women mentioned that they had also had affairs – while still schoolgirls – with 'sugar daddies', men considerably older than themselves. With these men no emotional attachment was involved: they were cultivated in a calculated fashion by the girls.

> This 'sugar daddy' used to come to the school to pick me. He wasn't really my boyfriend – he was 'old man bogey', about forty or forty-five. But how he looked me,

> This man flirted with me but I wasn't serious with him. I didn't mind him because, by then, I didn't want to secure boyfriend. Whenever I meet him I tell him: 'I need something – shoes, bag, dress, buy it for me' and he would.

More often than not, however, the women's first serious romantic attachments were with young university students, when they themselves were engaged in vocational training. Most of these attachments ended, however, when the women realised that they were not alone in competing for their boyfriends' affections. Later liaisons – often formed when the women were already in employment – were also typically terminated as a result of the men's 'womanising'.

Nine of the twenty-three unmarried women had had a child in the course of these relationships. These births testified to the women's ignorance about contraception rather than any desire for motherhood. In all instances they reported that their pregnancies were unwelcome. They tended to conceive at a very young age – a number as young as 14 – and pregnancy was the predictable outcome of their early sexual experimentation and their unsophisticated use or ignorance of contraceptives. Abortion had been contemplated, in fact, in many instances – with the women typically urging for termination and the men refusing. Martina, an unemployed Asante, found herself pregnant at 14 years of age:

> I saw this boy when I was in Form 2 elementary school. He also was a schoolboy. We became friends. The first day I was afraid but later the boy told me not to be afraid because he was using something – this apiolestil, a tablet.[9] But he wanted me to be pregnant so he didn't take his. Later on he told me this. So I conceived. I told my mother and she said I shouldn't abort; my father too asked me not to abort. At first they were angry and abusing me but later on they cooled off.

Helena, an Akuapim salesgirl working for the Ghana National Trading Company, got pregnant when she was 15 years of age. She described how unwelcome the pregnancy was at that point in her life, involving, as it did, a disruption of her schooling:

> I was in Form 4 and would have sat my middle school certificate that year but I got pregnant. I wanted to perform abortion but the man said no. I was even afraid to tell my parents but later on they saw signs so they asked me and I had to confess. They said I should allow it to stay but they forced me to leave school. I was just accompanying my mother to farm. I delivered the child with my mother in the house.

In other cases the women were persuaded to keep their pregnancies by promises of marriage from the fathers which never materialised. Not all fathers were willing, initially, to acknowledge paternity: In some cases after delivery, the men merely named their children and presented customary gifts to the women and their infants.[10]

The twenty-five women had had a total of thirteen children – four born within marriage and nine outside. Most of these children were living with the women's mothers (five) or mothers' sisters (three), back in their home-town villages. In only two instances were they living with their fathers. In one further case – that of a divorcee – two children were living with her ex-husband's sister. Only one woman had her child with her. The women and their kin were the ones largely responsible for the children's maintenance.

Typically, however, the women were not prepared to let pressures from their boyfriends or families push them prematurely into motherhood and a majority of the women had in fact terminated at least one pregnancy at some time or other in their lives.[11] Altogether thirty-two abortions were accounted for by these women. Termination of pregnancy was undertaken naturally and guiltlessly by the women. A number administered their own local 'folk' abortifacients. When such remedies failed, or they feared that prolonged use might be injurious, some resorted to other methods. A number successfully aborted by means of saline injections. If this method failed and if the woman or her boyfriend could afford it, they underwent D and C operations. These were generally performed by qualified doctors in either hospitals or private clinics and cost between 25 and 60 cedis. When the women could not afford either saline injections or such medical intervention they were forced to resort to crude instrument abortions. These operations were performed by medically unqualified persons and the women received neither local nor general anaesthetics.[12]

Most of the conceptions terminated in this way took place when the women were considerably younger. They were adamant that they were not prepared for motherhood at that stage. For some it would have involved an interruption of their schooling or of their career plans. Others felt that they were too young. Still others were concerned that they were not in a position to maintain a child. Some abortions were accounted for on the grounds of the genitor's general unsuitability, such as being impecunious or already married. In some cases the boyfriends urged them to terminate the pregnancy.

The relationships with the men who impregnated them broke up for the same reason, by and large, as for other boyfriends – the men were 'flirting' with other girlfriends, or not providing financially for them in an adequate manner.

This boy – even if you want some money from him you have to go to his office all the time. And I used to feel embarrassed at going to his office. (Martina, unemployed)

This boyfriend wasn't providing for me. Anytime I would go to his place he would only give me my transport to my house. He would be saying that he would give me money 'moondie'[13] but when the time came he would have some other excuses. So I thought, wearing myself out like that, going up and down, I thought I was wasting my time and that I should look for another boyfriend. (Helena, salesgirl)

All of the women were asked whether they would like to get married and if yes, when they would like the marriage to take place. All of the employed women below the age of 28 dismissed an immediate intention to marry.

Why are these women – despite the ideological importance of

marriage in their society – so anxious to maintain their single state? Why are they so reluctant to convert their relationships with men into marriage? The discussion which follows will focus on the sets of expectations and behavioural patterns within which the women operate, to see how the decisions being made at the level of individual choices are interconnected with the wider system of constraints and incentives present in their environment.

Prevailing Norms

As I have already emphasised, the basic normative prescriptions defining the cultural framework of these women's actions was that they should marry and have children. All of the women noted that they were under considerable pressure to marry, referring to the persuasion, criticism and insults to which they were subjected by their relatives. They also emphasised that considerable pressure is put upon women, especially older ones, to have a child – with or without marriage:

> My mother keeps talking, talking, talking. She say I've wasted all my time and now I'm old and have no child; nobody to give me what I want. Later on, too, my brother joined in. I am always trying to defend myself. I tell my mother, later. (Beatrice, 33-year-old Asante receptionist/telephonist)

> Even recently my own uncle was insulting me that because I've been having so many abortions, that's why I haven't any child. He feels I'm useless for not having a child. (Georgina, 30-year-old Ewe clerical worker)

But despite familial disapproval and societal displeasure, the women were determined to maintain their single statuses for a number of years yet. This decision was undoubtedly influenced by the highly inequitable marriage bargain[14] which they considered was on offer to them from their menfolk. The women had very strong ideas as to what marriage should entail but found nothing remotely likely to meet these expectations in the marriages they saw around them. 'Actually I don't think I know of any happy marriage,' 'As far as I can see about ten per cent of marriages in Ghana are successful but ninety per cent are not,' 'Marriage in Ghana? Oh, it's terrible. It's just absolutely terrible.'

It was evident that the women were ideologically committed to the idea of romantic love as being the basis for a successful marital union. They were convinced, however, that the Ghanaian males' conception of marriage precluded such aspirations, even where they were opting for monogamous church or Ordinance marriage. They were confident that men did not choose their partners on the basis of romantic love and that they did not intend to sustain romantic, emotional relationships with their wives once married.

They felt, in the first place, that the main reason men married was to have women who would bear them children. Another consideration was the economic status of the woman.

> These men marry girls because of their money. Some girls are rich and maybe they are in love with the man but the man doesn't love the girl but because of the money he will marry her. You see, these graduates always feel the high cost of living, so if they meet somebody with money they will marry them. I know of so many such cases. (Rosina, 21-year-old unemployed)

A further benefit for the man was the acquisition of a housekeeper.

> At times, too, they just want somebody to keep the house for them. And, you know, sometimes, too, as bachelors they go home without any food ready for them. Also, they need a woman in the house, not only there to cook but somebody just to keep up the prestige of the man. If he has a wife in the house, anytime he brings somebody to the house, there is a woman there to receive them and he feels big, that sort of thing. (Lorraine, 25-year-old receptionist/ telephonist)

The woman's ideal of the marital relationship, however, was that it should be of an egalitarian, intimate, companionable nature, involving trust, affection and shared intimacies. They were convinced that such aspirations were unrealistic and that Ghanaian men adopt an authoritarian role in a marital relationship and expect a considerable degree of subordination from their wives.

> I think the best marriage is where you and your husband are like a brother and a sister – to have common interests, outings and where we could discuss everything. I think nobody should control the other. But to find such a man in Ghana – I think it's impossible. He will still want his position as man in the house, to order the wife, to expect to be obeyed in everything he says. You see our Ghanaian men are by nature bossy. (Beatrice, 33-year-old receptionist/ telephonist)

The women also believed that marriage should be an institution for the containment of sexual relationships, but they knew they had little chance of realising this in their own marriages. In fact, they were convinced that there was less of a place for sexual love in marriage than there was outside; they seemed to think that men regarded sexual relations with wives as being functional and obligatory and that romantic sexuality tended to be associated with 'outside' girl-friends.

> Our Ghanaian men, they don't feel fine having sex with the wife all the time. They like to go and try having it somewhere else. They say, you know, that you can't eat palmnut soup through unless you eat light soup or groundnut soup in addition.[15] They say if you always take palmnut soup you will become fed up so they go around and around for their light soup. They are like small boys – they just need to feel big. (Ursula, 22-year-old unemployed)

The women were of the opinion that much of this sexual activity was prompted by a kind of *macho*[16] game-play acted out among males.

> These our Ghanaian men have to restrain themselves from just jumping on any nice girl that they see because they want to make a name for themselves. They are so funny. They try to look big before their own men friends, to be able to say; 'Ah, this girl, she has been my girlfriend before' – this sort of thing. They think enjoyment is when you've got money, a 'myself',[17] and you are not really tied to one girl. Ghanaian men, even though they have their minds on one girl, they will go about with four. I don't know what they get from it – I don't know. (Naomi, 24-year-old clerical worker)

The women, it was obvious, accepted that it was hopeless to expect husbands to be faithful; at the same time they were highly critical and resentful of this adulterous behaviour, especially as absolute fidelity was required of them as wives. Their conception of a marital relationship also entailed leading a joint social life with their husbands. They were convinced, however, that Ghanaian husbands were reluctant to mix socially with their wives.[18]
They also perceived few economic advantages for themselves in marriage, knowing that the husband's financial input into the marriage would be dependent on how much of his resources could be diverted, in the first instance, from getting into the hands of girl-friends.[19] In the second place, they anticipated that, even after marriage, the husband would remain financially obligated to his own kin and that such obligations would remain more important than those of marriage.[20]

The extent of family relationships in Ghana is also a problem – so many relatives. The man must still look backwards – grandmothers, mothers, uncles – so many. Because the mother or the uncle will say: 'Well, we have contributed in looking after you whilst you were going to school so now that you are finished you can look after my son or whoever as well.' So the man has to spend his money in that way as well. So its entirely left to the woman to be giving out money for her own children. (Rosario, 24-year-old counter assistant)

They therefore anticipated being in competition with both girl-friends and their husband's kin for his resources. Such competing forces were imagined likely to undercut any hopes they might have of conjugal solidarity in financial or budgeting matters or of joint investment in their children's future. They foresaw that considerable responsibilities for the maintenance of their children and the purchase of clothing would fall to them as mothers.[21] They were also aware that prevailing ideologies and laws did not support the solidarity of the elementary family in matters of financial support and inheritance. Although recent legislative reforms in Ghana entitled women to minimal maintenance for their children and as widows to $\frac{2}{9}$ of the self-acquired property of their husbands, the problem remained of translating even these statutory reforms into a reality, given the ingrained reluctance on the part of Ghanaian women to initiate action against their children's fathers or their families. They were widely sceptical that such action, in any event, was likely to lead to any positive results for themselves and their children, given the male-dominated legal system.[22]

In summary, the attitudes of these white-collar workers revealed deep disillusionment and cynicism about the whole institution of marriage. They were consistent in their denunciations of Ghanaian men as husbands: sexually and financially they felt that they were totally irresponsible. As marriage was understood by their menfolk, it did not meet any of the women's emotional, sexual, social, or economic desires. In their minds marriage as an institution in Ghana was a totally inequitable arrangement: the constraints from their point of view were numerous and the rewards minimal.

Supports for Singles within the System

In addition to the constraints involved in the actual marriage bargain, a number of incentives or facilitating features were present in the wider social environment, which appeared to be exerting some influence on the women's behaviour and on their decision to remain single. The first such facilitating feature appeared to be the general ideological emphasis on women playing a positive and active economic role – a point which has been emphasised in several previous chapters, and which has facilitated a positive view by women of their work roles. It probably influenced the women's own self-images and introduced a sense of themselves as being active agents in the shaping of their own economic environment. In the urban context the same expectations that women should play an active economic role still existed, but with even greater opportunities for realising them. The more complex urban economy offered a much greater variety of economic roles and a more propitious environment for the opportunist than anything that prevailed in the traditional order.

Another positive feature appeared to be the cultural interpretation placed on female sexuality. Traditionally, it would seem that the sexual act was regarded as a service and sexual ethics seem to have operated according to the same ethical principles that regulated other services: they were based on reciprocity. In the traditional courtship system a man exchanged valued gifts in return for sexual services. In marriage the reciprocity involved the exchange of the women's sexual/procreative services in return for maintenance. Sexuality never became bound up with religious belief-systems which implied any notions of sinfulness; nor was it ever bound up, as in Europe, with the refinements of romanticism. Sex, therefore, could legitimately be viewed rather more objectively and instrumentally.

The urban environment provided women with many opportunities for using their sexuality in just this instrumental manner. In Accra the trend away from polygynous marriage forms in the direction of monogamous unions has been noted by many writers (Omari, 1962; Tetteh, 1967; Caldwell, 1968; Oppong, 1982, *passim*.) But this trend appeared to be more an economic adaptation to conditions in the cities than an ideological one. Thus certain ambiguities, resulting from a lack of normative commitment to these relatively recent marriage forms, were apparent. A pattern has emerged whereby monogamously married men tended to pursue a more informal type of polygyny or polycoity outside their formal marriages, in an institutionalised system of 'girlfriend' relationships (Omari, 1960, *passim*; Little, 1973, 1975, 1977, *passim*; Dinan, 1977, pp. 164–5). This pattern was sustained by the strong element of *machismo* which attached to the masculine role in Ghanaian society. In Accra this *machismo* was given expression or articulated by men's ability to attract and maintain attractive 'girlfriends'. Such a situation provided a very fertile area for female manipulation, especially because women have managed to preserve continuity with the traditional pattern: in return for their sexual services, the men had to assume responsibility for their main financial outlays – rent, food and clothing. Their sexual roles were, consequently, of considerable economic potential.

The third very general facilitating factor on the ideological level appeared to be the particularistic-ascriptive quality of Ghanaian life. Traditional Ghanaian social organisation was not characterised by the operation of legal-rational principles: particularistic considerations were given precedence over universalistic ones and the ascriptive status of sex was also important. This relative absence of rationality in human relationships has had important consequences with the advent of a modern economy. Recruitment or selection in the modern sectors of the economy continued to be dependent on task-irrelevent factors such as kinship, friendship, or erotic associations, rather than on specialised skills, knowledge, or other similar aspects of task performance. Such features of social organisation were potentially highly advantageous to a determined, ambitious individual willing to manipulate personal ties.

In summary, on the ideological level, the strong emphasis on women playing a positive economic role, the cultural interpretation of female sexuality and the particularistic-ascriptive quality of Ghanaian life, all seem to be supportive or facilitating factors which encourage or at least make possible the maximisation of single female interests. The actual structural provisions also support female attempts for occupational and economic attainment (Dinan, 1977, pp. 160–1). In the modern sectors of society no overt sex discrimination exists against women. They are free to avail themselves of any type of vocational, professional, or academic training (Bannerman, 1975, pp. 1–2). No legal barriers prevent women from entering whatever occupations that they wish to and no jobs are specifically reserved for men (North, 1975, p. 3, quoting Ghanaian Appeals Court Judge Annie Jiagge). Women are eligible for all posts in both national and local government service and for all public appointments. There are no differential remuneration schemes for men and women (Greenstreet, 1972, p. 353). In addition, women are entitled to three months' maternity leave with full pay (ibid.).

Marriage or Spinsterhood? The Decision-Making Process

It is within this ideological and structural environment that these women have to make their choice whether to marry or to remain single.

The first alternative – to get married – enables a woman to comply with the normative expectations of her culture; she appeases her kin, and she can enjoy considerable prestige from her child-bearing role;[23] she stands to gain considerably, therefore, in general social esteem.

On the other hand, a woman on marriage takes on a whole range of domestic, familial and financial responsibilities; she submits to the control of a husband; she experiences considerable curtailment of her own social life: above all, she loses control of her own sexuality which as a single woman is a highly valuable asset. The second alternative – to remain single – enables a woman to devote all her efforts to her own self-advancement; she can improve her existing vocational skills and accumulate her own economic assets. She also enhances, by so doing, her own matrimonial prospects: on the women's own testimony, a high earning capacity allows a woman greater choice in husband selection and, consequently, a better chance of making a 'good' match. Women also exercise more control over decisions within the conjugal home when they contribute financially and are more likely to enjoy an egalitarian relationship with their husbands if the educational levels of the partners are similar (Oppong, 1970, 1982, *passim*). Economic self-sufficiency also places a woman in a realistic position when it comes to handling an unsuccessful marriage. If her husband is not providing adequate maintenance or if she is divorced, her own financial earnings will at least enable her to support herself and her children.

For the white-collar workers it was the latter alternative – to remain single – which, in their opinion, offered the highest long-term payoffs. They were convinced that their future status as wives and the long-term security of themselves and their children could best be served by postponing marriage and concentrating, in the meantime, on the development of their own careers and economic resources. The statements of the women themselves made it clear that this was the reasoning behind their decisions to remain single for the time being.

> I feel I must get what I want before I marry. I want to get this higher grade in my job and to do these extra courses. Also, I would like to have all my household furnitures – wardrobe, gas cooker, fridge, cooking utensils together. I feel I must get these things for myself especially, as, if you go to a man's house without anything, when you leave, you have to leave the things and go out without anything. Maybe by that time, too, you will have the responsibility of your children so you must be able to look after them. At that time too you may not be able to buy these household things to set up your home afterwards. (Grace, 22-year-old secretary)

Relationships with Men

Given that men still monopolised most positions of power and influence in Ghana and that they were also the main controllers of financial resources, they still had a very crucial role to play in the women's lives – first, as 'patrons' to enable them to advance their occupational careers and, secondly, as cash-paying boyfriends. In pursuit of their goal of career advancement, all channels for improving their occupational statuses were being explored by the women. None of them was satisfied with her existing occupational status and the majority were in the process of adding to their existing vocational skills. Those employed as clerks were enrolled in commercial institutions learning to type; typists were enrolled for instruction in shorthand; and even those employed as secretaries were busy improving their speeds or were enrolled for language courses in the long-term hope of becoming bilingual shorthand-typists. But advancing their own occupational careers required more than the task-relevant skills as far as these women were concerned, given the essentially non-bureaucratic functioning of organisations in Ghana: it required a patron. Even entry into government employment or one of the state corporations, where eligibility was dependent on objective criteria such as GCE results, required, in the opinion of the women, a patron to secure being actually appointed. At a number of points in their lives the manipulation of their sexual or socio-sexual roles[24] in the cultivation of patrons had been the crucial factor leading to their employment.

This manipulation of their sexual role in the cultivation of patrons was obviously paying occupational dividends. Considerable upward mobility could be detected in their relatively short working lives. Where they had remained in one particular organisation they were not, generally speaking, at the time of interview in the grade at which they had started. In instances where they changed organisations, the moves all resulted in an improvement in status.

Their long-range career objectives did not involve remaining as salaried white-collar workers. Most of the women had ambitions to open their own private businesses and had already devised well-planned schemes for realising these goals, such as opening boutiques and stores. Cloth-trading, at the time of the study a highly lucrative business in Ghana, was another business outlet desired by a number of the women. The majority had worked out precisely how they planned to operate. Many aimed at wholesale trading in textiles and planned to distribute to areas outside Accra. A further minority of the women had already gone, or planned to go, into some form of contracting business, such as carting sand and stones.

The second main way that men were being used to further the women's own interests was as boyfriends. The cultivation of financially rewarding relationships with men, whether as steady boyfriends or as casual 'friends', was a major tactic of these women. Some had regular bachelor boyfriends, who were mainly professional and clerical workers and who all made regular money gifts to them, which were often quite substantial and formed an important subsidiary source of income for the women – between 50 and 60 cedis monthly. They said marriage was not then under consideration.

The rest were exploiting what is known in Accra as the 'sugar daddy' and 'gold-digger' relationship. These relationships were with older married men and were, especially from the financial point of view, highly rewarding. The women were quite frank about these affairs and quick to explain the advantages of such associations over those they could hope to enjoy with younger, single men.

> You see, the married men – they are the ones who will give you everything. The young boy, they wouldn't do that. They will just take you out and that is all. But for the married men, they will do everything – pay your rent, give you pocket money – everything. So that is why we girls prefer the older married men. This is why you have been seeing us moving with these 'sugar daddies'. (Grace, 22-year-old Ewe secretary)

The type of arrangement involved in such relationships was typified by the following account given by Salina who was involved with one such 'sugar daddy'.

> This man is paying my rent for me – thirty cedis a month. He also gives me a monthly payment of about one hundred cedis for my shopping and my food. This man even wanted me to stop my work but I was thinking: 'These sorts of men, they look for girls who are always up to date and very often when you're working, you are abreast of the times.' So I thought the best thing for me to do was to continue working – even with my own few cedis a month. And I don't necessarily have to stop at my rent and 'chop money'; I can go in and take more than that. I occasionally ring him and tell him 'Oh, I've seen this dress, I've seen these shoes', and he will buy them for me. This man, too, has got so many cars so I never have need to take a taxi. He sends one of the cars to pick me from my office every day. Or, I can just lift the phone and I ring and he just sends the car to collect me. You know, when it comes to this sort of man, I don't know; he just goes on giving the money. (Salina, 26-year-old Ewe pay clerk)

Not all assistance was on such a lavish scale; usually, however, the men did undertake to pay the women's rent, supply them with their 'chop money' and give them the occasional gift of dresses and shoes.[25]

It was apparent from the fieldwork observation that many of the women played the field quite vigorously and kept a number of such affairs going simultaneously. They were reticent to volunteer that they personally had more than one 'sugar daddy' and tended to discuss the issue with reference to other women:

> Me like this, I don't like to be going around so much but you will see many single women who have got at least three 'sugar daddies'. Some won't admit but they have. One is going to buy her furniture; another is going to buy her a fridge; another one is going to buy her something else. You will see these girls swinging here and swinging there and it is these married men who will be grooving with them. (Juliana, 22-year-old Kwawu receptionist/telephonist)

These 'sugar daddy'/'gold-digger' relationships were essentially exploitive – on both sides. For the women's part, they offered straightforward economic reasons to account for their involvement in them.

> The fact is – for most of us who are working, the pay we get is not sufficient for us to live as we want to live. We also want to dress nicely and, at the same time, to make life secure for ourselves so that, in future, we know we will be all right. So we have to go to get a few cedis from going out with this or that man. (Lorraine, 25-year-old Ewe receptionist/telephonist)

> I flirt not because of sex but because I feel I cannot be satisfied with my own pay. These our salaries are meagre and I, too, like to wear the best. These my wages are seventy-two cedis in a month but when I go to buy these 'guarantee'[26] shoes which is thirty cedis, and the 'ready made'[27] dress which is thirty-five cedis, what is left? And I like to be changing too. So unless I'm flirting like this with these married men and they help me – I could not manage. (Mary, 22-year-old Fante wages clerk)

The women saw themselves, from the men's point of view, in the first instance as a means of meeting their *macho* needs. They knew that having girlfriends was an important criterion determining status within male peer-groups – not only as evidence of female conquest but, as the women had to be maintained and 'fashioned up', as a means of expressing differentials of wealth amongst men. The women were under no illusions that the men were in love with them: they knew that for such men women were interchangeable once they possessed the minimal qualifications of education, sophistication and physical attractiveness or, as Juliana stated, 'an English-speaking vagina'.

In the second instance, the women felt that they played an important supportive role for the men, as became clear when they contrasted their own behaviour with the men and the behaviour of their wives.

I know it's different the way I receive him and it's different the way the wife receives him because she's always rebelling. Because she knows what he is doing and she knows her rights. So she is always insisting on her rights and he doesn't like that. So when he comes to my place I'm there, submissive, doing everything to please him, looking after his comforts. But from the wife when he gets back he will only get a cool reception and always argument. This is what our men can't take. Like a small boy he will want to come and the woman receive him fully in the arms, plant kisses on his cheek and saying, 'oh, darling, here is your food', despite everything he does, you see? But the wife knows the foolish man he is, so how can she? (Beatrice, 33-year-old Asante receptionist/telephonist)

These insights into their own and the men's behaviour revealed that the women were under no illusions. But they were quite happy to continue boosting the men's ego-strength for as long as they could continue sapping their monetary one. And their own savings served as active testimony to this. For, despite their low wages, the majority of the women were saving money regularly – either in banks or post offices, or putting their money into capital goods or property of one sort or another. The amounts that the women were saving were very high when their incomes were considered. Thus for instance, Grace, a 22-year-old Ewe secretary who earned 140 cedis monthly managed to save over half her income.

Of course I save. I try to put down seventy cedis every month. At the moment I'm trying to buy these household things so that I can have them with me when I go into my marriage home. I'm buying my furniture step by step now. I've already bought all my cooking utensils, my chairs, a centre-table and all these sorts of things. I'm getting a wardrobe now so every month I'm putting some money by for the wardrobe. This month I may pay about forty cedis so maybe it will leave very small for me to put in the bank – maybe only about thirty cedis.

Naomi, a 24-year-old Dagomba clerical assistant, who earned 110 cedis monthly, saved 60 cedis with her bank in addition to paying off the hire purchase payments on some items of household furniture.

I put sixty cedis into the bank every month. Also I'm now buying a bed on hire purchase so that is another expense. The bed costs forty cedis but the 'vono' mattress is about seventy cedis or seventy-five so I'm paying twenty cedis every month to buy the two. Then after I've finished paying for it I will start on something else. The same way I bought my wardrobe – paying for it bit by bit.

I have now all my cooking utensils, cooker, cupboards, chairs and all that.

Other women, already in possession of such essential items of furniture, were saving for refrigerators, electric cookers, fans and other luxuries. Apart from such household items, the women were also investing their money in other ways. Lorraine, a 25-year-old Ewe receptionist/telephonist who earned 140 cedis monthly, explained how she was investing her surplus income.

For the last two years now I have been planning to buy a piece of land. I know the place in Accra where I can get this land for nine hundred cedis. So every month I have been putting down fifty cedis in the bank. My savings now have almost reached and I know by all means I will get it by the end of this year. Then I will build a wall around it for the meanwhile until I can start building on it.

Others were busy investing in trading items or getting their capital together for the time when they planned to become full-time business women. All appeared concerned generally about 'security' and had some little nest-egg put by, in case anything unexpected happened either to themselves or to their families, which they could draw upon. And they obviously had not squandered their money in the past. Two of the women – Anastasia, a 27-year-old secretary, and Alphonsina, a 34-year-old receptionist/telephonist – had already placed deposits of 700 cedis and upwards to purchase their own flats in one of the new government housing estates, which they hoped to occupy in the near future. The furniture and household luxuries in their own homes also bore witness to their own or their boyfriends' past investment – modern dining-room suites, bedroom furniture and an array of kitchen items from electric cookers to refrigerators; in addition, many of the homes were equipped with cassette tape-recorders, record-players, televisions, radios and electric cookers and fans.

Life-Styles

The women also enjoyed a comfortable current standard of living, although considerable differences in level of expenditure could be observed between them. Room accommodation varied considerably. The thirteen women heading their own independent households had all rented either apartments or single rooms in large compound buildings. Rentals varied from the 70 cedis paid monthly by Lorraine, the receptionist in the car assembly plant, for her two large rooms and kitchen which she shared with a younger sister, to the 5 cedis paid by Caroline, one of the unemployed women, for her single room which she shared with a cousin (mother's sister's daughter) and a young schoolgirl friend. The average rental paid for room accommodation was 20 cedis. In the twelve instances where the woman stayed with relatives, no rent was contributed or expected; the convention was to contribute towards the household food.[28] The flats themselves, whether the larger units or single rooms either hired or provided by kin, were invariably well furnished and attractively and neatly maintained.

The women were very fashion-conscious and spent a lot of money on keeping up to date with the latest styles. They tended to wear the most expensive dresses available – the imported 'ready-made' dresses and imported shoes and wigs and wiglets. The styling of these hair pieces required frequent visits to hair-stylists. All the women had quite extensive travelling experience. They tended to shop on a fairly regular basis in neighbouring Togoland, where the stores and range of European goods were more to their tastes than similar shops and goods in import-restricted Ghana. A number of the women had also travelled to Europe on holidays usually sponsored by boyfriends. Weekends spent outside Accra with boyfriends were also quite common – 'going for "time" ', as they termed it. This 'time' was usually spent staying in luxury state hotels in either the coastal towns of Cape Coast or Sekondi/Takoradi, or inland at Akosombo on the Volta Dam.

In Accra the women disliked travelling on the overcrowded municipal buses or the even more undignified, privately run 'tro tros' or 'Mammy wagons':[29] they travelled mainly by taxi. The more fortunate women, however, either had a regular arrangement with boyfriends to be collected to and from their workplaces or were collected from set pick-up points to and from their workplaces in transport provided by their employers.

Around Accra the women led a very active social life although this tended to be concentrated at weekends. They were particularly fond of the discothèques held in the many fashionable air-conditioned night-clubs of Accra. These clubs tended to be favoured by their young professional boyfriends and also by their older married ones who found the darkened, intimate environment of these clubs ideal for entertaining the women. They also attended the 'afternoon jumps' at the state hotels. And they were very keen cinema-goers. Their preferences tended to be for films of a light romantic nature – 'love films, ones that will give you advice' – or for crime-detection ones. Nights spent at home were usually devoted to listening to their record-players or to watching television. Few of them expressed a liking for reading: those who did tended to read 'romantic books' or magazines 'in order to look at the girls'. Newspapers were read for their horoscopes or fashion pages.

Only nine of the women were regular church-goers. The women had no interest in joining any benevolent, ethnic, or town development associations, although they were all aware of the existence of such associations, where and when they met, and their functions. Even staff associations in their places of work did not engage the active participation of these women; they deemed that they did not 'have time for such things'.

Conclusions

This account of the biographies, loves and plans of 'white-collar' women workers in Accra has placed the emphasis on the women as decision-makers, influenced by incentives and constraints present in their environment. These constraints and incentives, particularly those relating to the current marriage bargain offered to women, appear decisive in determining the actual choices of the women to remain single. The underlying thinking behind their choices involved consideration of their own long-term goals; these emerged as being the maximisation of their own economic assets to ensure their own future, long-term security. To further these ends the women attempted to evade the normative code for 'proper' female behaviour – namely, marriage and motherhood – and chose to hold on to their 'single' status. One could conclude that, on any criterion, the women's drives to promote their own careers and to gain control over certain basic economic resources were succeeding.

Men remained, however, vital to their plans, not for the moment as husbands, but as patrons and boyfriends. They themselves were fully aware that they were acting in a calculating and exploitative way and that men were merely instrumental in promoting their own long-term financial interests. But if 'sugar daddies' required attestation of their virility or wealth, they were quite willing to play along as sexual objects or to act out whatever expressive or supportive role was required of them. After all, while 'sugar daddies' needed the socio-sexual services that the women could offer, they, the 'gold-diggers', needed the goodies which the men could provide. The transaction was viewed by them as a straightforward exchange of services.

But this pragmatic adaptation which the women had made in response to the constraints and incentives present in their social environment did not go unchecked. The normative themes of marriage and motherhood were raised periodically in newspapers and among their own families to discredit them and oblige them to marry. They were from time to time branded as selfish, worldly, irresponsible, sexually promiscuous and grasping. Such attempts to restate and reinforce the norms did not, however, divert the women from their chosen pragmatic courses. They were single but, viewed pragmatically, their status in terms of wealth and potential mobility was high. They realised that they could not simultaneously attain their own economic ambitions and comply with the normative expectations of their culture. For the present they had chosen to content themselves with the steady improvement of their economic resources and with the enhancement of their bargaining positions. The social esteem following from the roles of wife and mother could wait

Notes: Chapter 25

Survey data on which this paper was based were gathered in the period January 1974–February 1975. The material formed part of a wider study on single women of various occupational categories in a residential area of Accra. The research was sponsored by a grant from the British Social Science Research Council.

1   See for example, Fortes, 1949, p. 69, and 1950, p. 262, regarding the universality of marriage in Ashanti and the 'outcast' role of the barren woman.
2   One such example is an order (*Mirror*, 1975) which emanated from a local traditional council as recently as March 1975, which stipulated that 'all unmarried girls should get married within six months and submit particulars of their husbands to the council'. A customary fine of 'one live sheep, ten cedis, two bottles of schnapps and a pot of palm wine' would be levied on all girls who disobeyed this ruling.
3   One columnist (*Mirror*, 1974c) represents this pressure in the following terms.

> If your mother is alive, you would discover that the talk of grandchildren will be recurring in her conversation every now and again, and you know (she will say) these days it is quite respectable to have a baby without a golden band . . . and of course you can only gasp at your very proper mother who used to tell you that you had to play it tough with men.

4   One woman writing in the Ghanaian *Daily Graphic* (Akuffo, 1975) outlines the contemporary thinking on the issue of marriage and motherhood for women.

> The traditionally narrow definition of the role of women in society . . . is seen broadly as that of wives and mothers. Thus every girl is expected to have two aims in life, first to become somebody's wife, and then somebody's mother; in our modern age if not the first then definitely the latter. A woman may gain the whole world . . . but she would have lost her soul . . . if she doesn't become a male's extension, or somebody's mother.

Another woman, in an article in a popular Ghanaian women's magazine (*Ideal Woman*, November 1974, p. 30), makes the important point that the norms requiring marriage are not only supported by public opinion in general but by Ghanaian women themselves. She notes:

> Our society and the women themselves look upon marriage as very essential. Even where there is the rare individual who does not wish to get married, the

society frowns upon her as an abnormal person. Women who love their careers and therefore don't get married are considered 'an unpleasant class apart'.

5   The study on which this chapter is based was carried out in a mixed residential area of 18,695 persons in Accra. The methodology involved a systematic random sample of every fifteenth house in the area. This yielded a total number of sixty-five large, mixed-dwelling houses and brief, demographic-type data were collected on the 1,581 occupants of these houses. The questionnaires were then scrutinised for single women between the ages of 21 and 45. Single was taken to include all women unmarried at the time of the survey, regardless of any former marital or quasi-marital status; no more rigorous definition of single was demanded beyond self-definition as such by the women. Ninety-four women (32·4 per cent of the total population of 290 women in the sample houses who were between the ages of 21 and 45) emerged as being single. Eighty-seven of these women agreed to co-operate in the research. Two women refused to co-operate; a further two were unobtainable after twelve visits and three women had actually moved out of the area by the time they were contacted for the long, in-depth interview. Of this number twenty-five were engaged or interested in white-collar occupations and are the group to be considered. The method of study combined prolonged first-hand observational and participatory techniques together with a quite intense relationship with the women over a fifteen-month period, in addition to focused, tape-recorded interviews with them. The other broad occupational categories found in the survey included professional and sub-professional women (doctors, lawyers, teachers, nurses and others of similar professional status), self-employed traders and service workers (for example, wholesale businesswomen, women running a variety of retail establishments and dressmakers) and prostitutes.

Fictitious names of informants have been used throughout in order to honour the promise of confidentiality and anonymity which was given to all respondents. Data on ethnic background and place-names have also in some instances been altered by transposing details; in all cases where such changes have been made, however, care has been taken that no significant facts were lost.

6   At the time of fieldwork 1 pound sterling exchanged for 2·4 cedis.

7   The minimum basic wage was 2 cedis a day at the time of fieldwork. Estimating on the basis of a twenty-seven-day working month, this would work out at 54 cedis monthly.

8   As was noted in Chapter 9 there are three different marriage forms in Ghana: marriage under the various systems of customary law which were all potentially polygynous; marriage according to Islamic law which was also polygynous; and marriage under the Ordinance which could be either by religious rites in church or by civil rites before a registrar. This last was the form most closely related to the conjugal, Western form of marriage in that a man could lawfully marry only one wife, certain property rights were guaranteed to the wife, and the marriage could only be terminated by legal divorce in the courts (Tetteh, 1967, pp. 205–9).

9   There was a widespread belief amongst the women that there was an effective oral male contraceptive. A variety of pills were also used by the women. Taken soon after intercourse they were assumed to affect the lining of the uterus so that a fertilised egg could not implant.

10   Traditionally among the Akan once a child had been publicly named by the acknowledged father on the eighth day after birth – with or without the customary marriage exchanges or rites – the child was considered fully legitimate, as far as his or her status in the lineage system was concerned; the child was absorbed as a full member with full legal rights and privileges (Amoo, 1946, p. 228; Antubam, 1963, p. 48; Danquah, 1928, pp. 148, 185; Fortes, 1949b, p. 76, 1950, p. 266; Manoukian, 1950, p. 89; Rattray, 1929, p. 25). Writers are, however, divided as to whether any *social* stigma attached to 'illegitimate' offspring.

11   Although illegal, both 'backstreet' abortions and dilation and curettage (D and C) operations performed by qualified gynaecologists were widely available in Accra. They provided a highly lucrative form of income for doctors and para-medical personnel employed in both the public and private sectors of medicine in the city.

12   Many of these 'backstreet' abortionists performed these operations without properly sterilised instruments. High mortality rates were reported for young women undergoing these operations resulting from acute peritonitis, tetanus and other septic causes. A whole ward in Korle Bu, the large teaching hospital in Accra, catered for these casualties.

13   'Moondie' was the local Ghanaian expression for payday – coming as it did at the end of the month. The related term 'moondie-ers' referred to money-loving women who were said to appear at this time of the month when money was plentiful.

14   Some of the disadvantages involved in Ghanaian marriage have already been discussed in relation to professional women in Dinan, 1977, pp. 164–6.

15   Palmnut soup, light soup and groundnut soup are three of the most popular Ghanaian main-meal dishes.

16   *Macho* – a Spanish word meaning exaggerated masculinity. *Machismo* involves lusty displays of virility through daring – often accompanied by violence – and especially through prodigious feats of sexual conquest.

17   A 'myself' – a popular Ghanaian expression for a self-driven car; the term implied ownership of a car.

18   Caldwell (1968a, pp. 61–3) found in his survey of elites that 32 per cent of his female respondents claimed that they never or rarely had joint outings with their husbands. Of those who did, one-third specified that these joint outings involved attending church or memorial services together.

19   This theme of girlfriends coming before wives when it came to finance occurred frequently in the newspapers. It featured many times in the fieldwork period in the popular column 'Chat with Grandma' in the Ghanaian weekly newspaper, the *Mirror*.

20   This would appear to be an accurate reading of the situation. Oppong (1982, p. 215) found among her population of married elites that financial responsibility for kin was almost universal. Such assistance took the form of 'help, either with maintenance, education or trading and building projects or medical and other expenses' in addition to monthly remittances, occasional gifts, money to cover funeral expenses and 'the rearing and education of relatives' children'.

21   Oppong (1982, pp. 85–94) noted the marked economic autonomy of husbands and wives. She found that less than one in ten couples had joint savings accounts; only a few jointly owned property; and the usual practice was for wives to assume full responsibility for their own and their children's clothing and partial responsibility for the provision of the household food and the payment of domestic servants.

22   This issue has been discussed by a number of prominent Ghanaian legal practitioners. In particular, see Bentsi-Enchill, 1975; Jiagge, 1974.

23   Fortes (1950, p. 262) recorded: 'Prolific child-bearing is honoured. A mother of ten boasts of her achievement and is given a public ceremony of congratulation.' Manoukian (1950, p. 52) also noted: 'In general parents of large families are held in special esteem, not only during life but after death also.'

24   Being older and wiser, the majority (fifteen) of the women were, at the time of fieldwork, using some regular form of contraception: seven were taking recognised oral contraceptive, three were using foam suppositories, two were on the 'morning-after pill', two were using the 'natural rhythm' method and one woman had had an intra-uterine device (IUD) inserted. Ten women, however, continued to take no precautions against conception or persevered with their purgatives or quinine tablets when they suspected conception had occurred.

25   'Chop' was the local West African term for food; hence 'chop money' – money for
      food.
26   'Guarantee' shoes – the local Accra term for the high platform shoes in fashion at
      the time of the fieldwork.
27   'Ready-mades' – the local Accra expression for imported Crimplene dresses.
28   Despite these financial advantages most of those currently staying with relatives
      were not happy with the arrangement and looked forward to the time when they
      could set up their own independent establishments. They were hampered from
      doing so because of the very acute shortage of accommodation in Accra.
29   'Tro tro' or 'mammy wagon' were the local Accra terms for the converted lorries
      used to convey passengers. The backs of the lorries were built up with wooden
      frames, and planks were strung across to serve as benches for the passengers. The
      average 'tro tro' would accommodate approximately thirty-six passengers.

Conclusion to Part Five

The case studies in Parts Two and Three emphasised the theme of the interlocking complementarity of female and male roles, showing how this interconnectedness pervaded every sphere of political, economic, ritual, aesthetic and sexual life. The southern Ghanaian essays in Part Three portrayed relations which were tension and conflict prone, in situations of legal, political and economic change, and in which women and men were involved in the cash nexus of crop and fish production and processing and marketing. But still co-operation was a hallmark of heterosexual relations and when one particular conjugal relationship was broken, often for economic reasons, one or two others tended to take its place. Men and women were portrayed as being involved in mutually rewarding webs of relationships with spouses and kin, in which needed goods and services were exchanged.

The cases in Part Four gave indications of radical change: of increasing inequality of men and women, through the whittling away of female political roles; the unequal access to training and employment and meanwhile the persistence of ideologies of male dominance; and the unequal division of domestic labour and parental responsibilities. Two further critical changes portrayed were the disintegration of the co-operative labour bond between spouses and kin, in situations in which income generation and financial maintenance increasingly depend upon individually earned incomes in impersonal work settings; and also the scattering of kin, consequent upon migration and urbanisation and the resultant dwindling of exchanges of goods and services and solidarity among them. Indeed, relative social isolation for women and men in towns and the dwindling of needed social supports has become a possibility, women being potentially more vulnerable than men through the tasks and responsibilities associated with their maternal roles.

Several of the studies indicated that marriage and all that it entails for women may have a constraining effect upon their training and employment opportunities, their ability to devote their maximum time and energy to a demanding job outside the home, or to be as mobile and sociable as their male counterparts. Not only do husbands have a tendency in some cultures to restrict their wives' range of action but a problem which arises with the increasing spatial separation of income-generating activities and the home – where infants are cared for and cooking and other domestic tasks are carried out – is role conflict, at least for those who are expected, or who attempt, to be active in both spheres. And since few men as yet assume an equal share of domestic and child care responsibilities, women tend to face double or treble burdens which affect their efficiency and concentration in one or more spheres. Women who can get no help whatsoever for the care of their infants may be compelled to give up formal sector employment.

Meanwhile, unequal access to scarce opportunities for education, vocational training and employment may lead to increasing economic and social dependence of women upon men.

In Part Five we have considered some of the possible outcomes of these radical changes: what happens when conjugal bonding and economic co-operation break down; how scattered members of kin-groups behave in increasingly individualistic ways, ignoring the traditional norms and dictates of elders, and how those women and men who succeed financially in the contemporary cash economies allocate their resources and organise their domestic relations – or on the other hand are constrained by material necessity to appear to neglect traditional values.

They gave evidence of increasing economic autonomy and individualism, and of growing opportunities for the pursuit of financial security and personal gratification by single men and women with access to needed resources in urban settings. Among them a radical reordering of the values traditionally associated with different roles is obviously taking place; with devaluation of the maternal and conjugal roles by women who increasingly perceive their constraining effects, and growing emphasis upon occupations outside the home to generate cash incomes which provide avenues to social status, high levels of living in the present, and future material security.

On the other hand, for those who have lost traditional sources of status, security and support – such as land, and labour of children and kin – and who have not managed to obtain access to valued resources in the new urban world – such as training and higher levels of employment – the picture is grim: increased dependence upon other individuals in exploitive, often sexual, relationships.

An important change over the past decades which several of these studies highlight is that regarding conjugal roles. Whereas formerly the unmarried status referred only to a brief period after puberty or to short interludes between marriages or perhaps a period of widowhood, divorce, or terminal conjugal separation in old age, there is ample evidence that now increasing numbers of young people as well as the more mature are living as unmarried singles. Increasingly women and men are occupied or employed as adult individuals and do not depend upon a complementary division of labour with a spouse in order to gain a livelihood. At the same time sanctions following the birth of children outside any recognised wedlock are breaking down; and increasingly adult status, sexual relations, parenthood and headship of domestic groups occur without the addition of the conjugal role.

Several of the studies in Part Five illustrate this phenomenon. They also indicate the weight of social pressures brought to bear on women to compel them to marry and to live more traditional life-styles. Renée Pittin described houses of autonomous women in Katsina; Mona Etienne portrayed the autonomy or dependence of Baule women; Lynne Bryden demonstrated the reluctance to marry of migrants from the Avatime region of Ghana; Roger Sanjek showed the incidence of independent singlehood among young men and mature women in an Accra suburb; and Carmel Dinan illustrated graphically the situations of single educated women in Accra. The changing orientation towards the conjugal role appears related to several factors and is facilitated by the economic and social individualism made possible by migration and employment.

Individuals who earn their own incomes in rural or urban settings, and particularly those who migrate, are less subject to traditional prescriptions regarding domestic and sexual behaviour. At the same time they are constrained by the lack of resources traditionally available, such as houses for the married pair to move into or an immediate source of livelihood which can support a growing family and several offspring, as the family farm was expected to do. Again, new values have been introduced, including monogamous, companionate, egalitarian marriage, symbolised by Christian rituals, which are proving too expensive for the majority to attain, although for a deviant few, in particular educated women, they appear to be the ideal.

We noted at the beginning of this book the great value attached to high fertility and parenthood and the general tendency for women and men to reproduce throughout the fertile span of life. We now see that not only are some people remaining unmarried during their nubile years, they are also not bearing and begetting children in such prolific numbers. Economic autonomy for some is being achieved at the expense of marriage and parenthood. In some instances this autonomy may be viewed as a perpetuation of a traditional pattern in a modern setting, as we gather for the cases in Baule and Ga contexts. In other cases the pattern is viewed as deviant and pressure is brought to bear on occasion, through the edicts of chiefs, community sanctions, or kin pressures.

Postscript

Change and Development

The West African region is currently an arena of massive demographic, economic and political change reaching, in some spheres and areas, revolutionary proportions. The economic conditions of the several countries in which the case studies reported have been carried out are very diverse – in terms of the speed and directions of economic growth, the levels of exploitation of natural resources and the current propensity to economic stagnation and inflation and the growth and types of labour markets. Furthermore the resources, colonial experiences and governmental policies of the various countries are also quite diverse.

Economic development, whether the government is socialist or capitalist, egalitarian or elitist, centrally controlled or *laissez-faire*, unavoidably entails the disintegration of the division of labour between the two sexes traditionally established in the village. With modernisation of agriculture and with migration to the towns, as E. Boserup (1970, p. 5) contended ten years ago, 'a new sex pattern of productive work must emerge for better or worse'. Indeed, a major feature of economic development has been defined as the progress towards more and more complex and sophisticated patterns of labour specialisation. The earliest stage is typified by production and consumption of goods and services within the domestic group. All cultures have their characteristic ways of dividing the tasks and rewards associated with such production and consumption between females and males, old and young, and we have seen examples in this collection. We looked briefly at the Limba division of labour and Hausa households.

In this volume the most detailed description of the division of farm labour is that of the Akan cocoa farmers, in which the traditional division of tasks and resources (in an area of 'female farming'; E. Boserup, 1970, p. 16) has already been affected by cash and capital accumulation, the availability of wage labour and migration. Women are noted to be at a relative disadvantage in this process.

Meanwhile the catching, processing and marketing of fish by non-mechanised methods, though still based on networks of co-operative exchanges of labour, credit and goods between affines and kin, is probably increasingly subject to the potential control of big dealers among boat-owners and traders and likely to be transformed in the process of mechanisation, involving a radical reordering of relations between the catchers, processors and sellers of fish.

With regard to the emergence of urban populations of would-be wage-earners and the disparities in the opportunities and resources of men and women, we have seen several examples from Ibadan, Bauchi and Accra, including the development of sex-segregated labour markets.

Changing Roles: the Domestic Domain

Anthropologists and other social scientists have long pointed out and demonstrated that several of the altering aspects of behaviour associated with economic and demographic change, such as rural–urban migration, school attendance and wage labour in farm and town, are likely to be associated with significant changes in traditional cultural norms, values and beliefs associated with sex roles and the relinquishment of customary behaviours associated with the roles of parent, spouse, household member, relative and community member. Studies of behavioural changes with reference to the procreative aspect of the parental role – to childbirth and fertility and its regulation – have tended to be more common, and to have more resources and research money and time lavished upon them, than studies examining changes in conjugal relations, domestic organisation and kinship and community roles. More research and documentation in these latter areas has been called for (e.g. by E. Boserup, 1977, p. xiii). Indeed, the latter kind of studies are increasingly recognised as vital to the pursuit of the former.

But understanding of the effects upon women's and men's roles of traditional norms, values and perceptions and practices on the one hand, and of economic and demographic change on the other, cannot grow without a firm basis in the relevant ethnographic facts – in detailed descriptive studies by social scientists of several disciplines. Such a documentation process needs to be followed up by cross-national and cross-cultural dissemination and comparison of findings. This book is one more attempt to fulfil such an aim, for it has been our task in this volume to call attention to some aspects of the processes of continuity and change in the relations and comparative positions of women and men in divergent cultural contexts, and especially in the domestic domain, consequent upon macro changes in the economic and demographic spheres. In the course of these descriptions particular situations have been highlighted in some detail. A major and recurrent theme has been the changing interactions between men and women in the process of earning a living and organising domestic life.

Models of Change

It has frequently been argued that while both men and women may become victims in the process of economic development, it is more difficult for women to adapt to new conditions. Family obligations make them less mobile. Their choice of jobs outside the home is more narrowly limited by custom. They often have fewer opportunities for education and training than their male counterparts. And in addition they often face sex discrimination in recruitment (E. Boserup, 1977). These are themes which reappear with supportive evidence in both the comparative overviews and the case studies in this book, together with another frequently noted phenomenon in the development process: that more women than men remain in the traditional occupations which are currently being replaced by modern enterprises.

Alternative models of the changing economic roles of the sexes have portrayed the relationships between the politico-economic status of women and men and the processes of modernisation in very different ways. In extreme versions they have even stated the opposite regarding the changing relative positions of women and men in pre-industrial and industrial societies. Thus in some accounts women in pre-industrial societies are viewed as bound by traditions and patriarchal power. In contrast, women are considered to be rapidly achieving sexual equality with men in industrialised societies, with changes in norms and attitudes and especially as new role opportunities become available to women.

In contrast researchers working within an historical dialectical frame of reference have rather argued that whereas women had relatively high status in many pre-industrial (and pre-colonial) societies, their positions have declined as a result of colonialism and capitalist based modernisation. They often note the effects of their dependent status in economically isolated nuclear families as a primary factor in this process (e.g. Oppong et al., 1975). There is certainly a growing mass of evidence that changes in the sexual and class division of labour through the advent of plough agriculture, tractors, cash cropping, wage labour, migration and the spatial separation of the home and productive and income-generating activities have had penetrating and pervasive influences upon sex roles in other spheres than production (E. Boserup, 1970; Hamilton, 1978).

Meanwhile, feminists of the industrial world have emphasised the effects of women's burdens associated with maternity and domesticity as hindering their equal participation in other spheres, including occupations outside the home.

Our studies here could be used to illustrate all three hypothesised models; for some chapters have indicated the opening-up of opportunities for women with urban living and chances for urban employment; the dwindling of kin constraints; and the increasing possibilities for autonomy and potentials for choice. Other contributions, however, have demonstrated the dwindling of women's opportunities relative to men and their increased tendencies to depend instead of co-operating. Still others have emphasised the fundamental dilemma of women who attempt to work outside the home while bearing unequal burdens of domestic responsibilities.

One theme is constant, however, and that is the declining need of one sex for the other to play conjugal and co-parental roles for the achievement of economic and social status. Growing numbers of men and women no longer need spouses as they used to in order to survive in economic terms. Both men and women have increasing scope for independent adult status, economically or socially, and this is a profound change in itself. Individual financial attainment is an avenue to urban success. Marriage and parenthood are no longer the *sine qua non* for adult social status.

Meanwhile, the varying themes in the studies presented here have emphasised the complexity, the diversity, the multifaceted nature and the multidirectionality of change and the need for more sophisticated observations and measures, if we are meaningfully to equate and compare the roles and relationships of women and men (Oppong, 1980).

Previous scholars have pointed to the dangers of considering women only as a special category, of segregating them for special treatment because of the view that women are somehow fundamentally different from men. In this volume we have rather tried to look at men's and women's behaviour symetrically, recognising that women and men are people with similar potential abilities and patterns of responses to incentives, but whose life opportunities and constraints may differ to varying degrees and in many ways in diverse cultures. Thus we have eschewed a narrow focus upon women apart from men, an all-too-common feature of many works on sex roles in the past decade, and have sought rather to depict female and male interrelationships at different stages of their lives, in different roles, and among different social classes.

Our topics are of current widespread popular concern; for they are relevant to debates and studies not only about changing sex roles, in particular women's roles, but also to population issues – migration, both internal and international, and differential fertility, as well as to processes of economic, legal and political change and potentials for development and modernisation.

References

Abloh, F. A. (1969), *Some Urban Social and Demographic Trends in Ghana* (Kumasi: Faculty of Architecture, University of Science and Technology).

Addo, N. O. (1975a), 'Internal migration differentials and their effects on socio-demographic change', in Caldwell *et al.* (eds) (1975), pp. 383–407.

Addo, N. O. (1975b), 'Immigration and socio-economic change', in Caldwell *et al.* (eds) (1975), pp. 367–82.

Adegbola, O. (1977), 'New estimates of fertility and child mortality in Africa south of the Sahara', *Population Studies* vol. 31, no. 3, pp. 467–86.

Adeokun, L. A. (1979), 'Lactation abstinence in family building among the Ekitis of south-west Nigeria', paper presented at the National Workshop on Population and Economic Development in Nigeria in the 1980s, Human Resource Unit, University of Lagos, 12–14 September.

Adepoju, A. (1975), 'Urbanisation and migration in West Africa', unpublished MS, University of Ife.

Adepoju, A. (1977), 'Rationality and fertility in the traditional Yoruba society, south-west Nigeria', in J. C. Caldwell (ed.), *The Persistence of High Fertility*, Pt I (Canberra: Australian National University), pp. 123–51.

Adepoju, A. (1980a), 'Rural migration and development in Nigeria', project report, Population and Development Policy Research on Migration in Developing Countries, to the Ford Foundation, New York.

Adepoju, A. (1980b), *Migration and Development: The Case of Medium-Sized Towns in Nigeria,* project report, Research Programme on Socio-Demographic Studies on Population Trends in Relation to Development, to UNESCO (Population Division), Paris.

Afigbo, A. E. (1972), *The Warrant Chiefs: Indirect Rule in South Eastern Nigeria 1891–1929* (London: Longman).

Afigbo, A. E. (1974), 'Women in Nigerian history', mimeo., University of Nigeria, Nsukka.

Akintoye, S. A. (1971), *Revolution and Power Politics in Yorubaland 1840–1893* (London: Longman).

Akuffo, Sophia (1975), 'International women's year', *Daily Graphic*, 7 January.

Amin, S. (ed. (1974), *Modern Migrations in Western Africa* (London: Oxford University Press).

Amoo, J. W. A. (1946), 'The effect of Western influence on Akan marriage', *Africa,* vol. XVI, no. 4, pp. 228–37.

Anderson, J. N. D. (1970), *Islamic Law in Africa* (London: Frank Cass).

Anaza, J. A. (1975), 'The labour market implications of the UPE', paper presented to the NISER Conference on Economic Development and Employment Generation in Nigeria, University of Ibadan, November.

Andreski, I. (1970), *Old Wives' Tales: Life-Stories from Ibibioland* (New York: Schocken Books).

Antubam, K. (1947), 'Cultural contributions of the queen mothers of Bono Manso Tackyiman to the reigns of Bono kings from the middle of the sixteenth century onwards', unpublished ts., Institute of African Studies, University of Ghana, Legon.

Antubam, K. (1963), *Ghana's Heritage of Culture* (Leipzig: Koehler & Amelang).

Ardener, E. (1975a), 'Belief and the problem of women', in S. Ardener (ed.) (1975).

Ardener, E. (1975b), 'The problem revisited', in S. Ardener (ed.) (1975).

Ardener, S. (ed.) (1975), *Perceiving Women* (London: Dent).

Argyle, M., Gardner, G., and Cioffi, F. (1958), 'Supervisory methods related to productivity, absenteeism and labour turnover', *Human Relations,* vol. II, pp. 23–40.

Arhin, K. (1967), 'The structure of greater Ashanti 1700–1824', *The Journal of African History,* vol. VIII, no. 1, pp. 65–85.

Arhin, K. (1982), *Traditional Rule in Ghana: Past and Present* (Sedco, Accra).

Arinola, O. A. N. (1978), 'The implications of female labour force participation on the family: a case study of some factory workers', B.Sc dissertation, Department of Sociology, University of Ibadan.

Arnaldi, J. (1975), 'La médecine au Niger en 1975', *Revue de pédiatrie,* vol. 11, no. 8, pp. 413–20.

Aronson, D. R. (1978), *The City is Our Farm: Seven Migrant Ijebu Yoruba Families* (Boston, Mass.: Hall).

Asante-Darko, N., and Van der Geest, S. (n.d.), 'The political meaning of highlife songs in Ghana', mimeo., Amsterdam.

Ascadi, G. T., Igun, A. A., and Johnson, G. Z. (1972), *Survey of Fertility, Family and Family Planning in Nigeria,* Institute of Population and Manpower Studies (IPMS) Publication No. 2 (Ile-Ife: University of Ife).

Ashley-Montagu, M. (1937), *Coming into Being Among the Australian Aborigines* (London: George Routledge).

Awe, B. (1977), 'The Yalode in the traditional Yoruba political system; in A. Schlegel (ed.), *Sexual Stratification: A Cross-Cultural View* (New York: Columbia University Press), pp. 144–60.

Bame, K. N. (1969), 'Contemporary comic plays in Ghana: a study of innovation and diffusion and the social functions of an art-form', MA thesis University of London.

Bame, K. N. (1975), 'Des origines et du developpement du "concert-party" au Ghana', *Revue d'histoire de théâtre,* no. 1, pp. 10–20.

Bannerman, C. V. L. (1975), 'What education for women and girls in Ghana?', unpublished MS, Accra.

Banton, M. (1957), *West African City: A Study of Tribal Life in Freetown* (London: Oxford University Press).

Bargery, G. P. (1934), A *Hausa–English Dictionary and English–Hausa Vocabulary* (London: Oxford University Press).

Barkow, J. (1971), 'The institution of courtesanship in the northern states of Nigeria', *Genève-Afrique,* vol. X, no. 1, pp. 1–16.

Barkow, Jerome H. (1972), 'Hausa women and Islam', *Canadian Journal of African Studies,* vol. 6, no. 2, pp. 317–28.

Bartle, P. F. W. (1978), 'Urban migration and rural identity, an ethnography of a Kwawu community, Obo, Ghana', PhD thesis, University of Ghana.

Bashir, M. K. (1972), 'The economic activities of secluded married women in Kurawa and Lallokin Lemu, Kano City', B.Sc thesis, Ahmadu Bello University, Zaria.

Beckett, W. H. (1947), *Akokoaso: A Survey of a Gold Coast Village*, Monographs on Social Anthropology No. 10 (London: Percy Lund Humphries for the London School of Economics and Political Science).

Behrend, H. (1951), *Absence under Full Employment,* Monograph A3 (Birmingham: University of Birmingham).

Bentsi-Enchill, K. (1975), 'Some implications of our laws of marriage and succession', in Oppong (ed.) (1975), pp. 125–8.

Berkner, L. K. (1972), 'The stem family and the developmental cycle of the peasant household, an eighteenth-century Austrian example', *American Historical Review,* vol. 77, no. 2, pp. 398–418.

Bernus, S. (1969), 'Particularismes ethniques en milieu urbain: l'exemple de Niamey', Université de Paris, *Mémoires de l'Institut d'ethnologie – I,* Institut d'ethnologie, Musée de l'homme, Paris.

Blauner, R. (1964), *Alienation and Freedom* (Chicago: Chicago University Press).

Blécourt, W. de (1979), 'Een antropoloog in faërie', in Van Bremen *et al.* (eds) (1979), pp. 130–8.

Bleek, W. (1975), *Marriage, Inheritance and Witchcraft: A Case Study of a Rural Ghanaian Family* (Leiden: Afrika-Studiecentrum).

Bleek, W. (1976), *Birth Control and Sexual Relationships in Ghana: A Case Study of a Rural Town* (Amsterdam: Antropologisch-Sociologisch Centrum).

Blood, R. O., and Wolfe, D. M. (1960), *Husbands and Wives, the Dynamics of Married Living* (New York: The Free Press).

'Blueprint for the future of education', (1979), *West Africa,* no. 3253, 19 November.

Boelman, W. J., and Van Holthoorn, F. L. (1973), 'African dress in Ghana', *Kroniek van Afrika,* no. 13, pp. 236–56.

Bohannan, P., and Curtin, P. (1971), *Africa and Africans* (New York: Natural History Press).

Boserup, E. (1970), *Women's Role in Economic Development* (London: Allen & Unwin).

Boserup, E. (1977), preface to Wellesley Editorial Committee, *Women and National Development: The Complexities of Change* (Chicago: Chicago University Press).

Brass, W., et al. (1968), *The Demography of Tropical Africa* (Princeton, New Jersey: Princeton University Press).

Bray, T. M. (1977), 'Universal primary education in Kano state: the first year', *Savanna*, vol. 6, no. 1, pp. 3–14.

Bray, T. M. (1978), 'Universal primary education in Kano state: the second year', *Savanna,* vol. 7, no. 2, pp. 176–8.

Bremen, J. van, Van der Geest, S., and Verrips, J. (eds) (1979), *Romantropologie: Essays over Antropologie en Literatuur* (Amsterdam: Antropologisch-Sociologisch Centrum).

Brooks, G. E., Jr (1976), 'The *signares* of Saint-Louis and Gorée: women entrepreneurs in eighteenth-century Senegal', in Hafkin and Bay (eds) (1976), pp. 19–44.

Brydon, L. (1976), 'Status ambiguity in Amedzofe-Avatime: women and men in a changing patrilineal society', Ph.D thesis, University of Cambridge.

Brydon, L. (1979), 'Women at work: some changes in family structure in Amedzofe-Avatime, Ghana', *Africa,* vol. 49, no. 2, pp. 97–111.

Bujra, J. (1975), 'Women "entrepreneurs" of early Nairobi', *Canadian Journal of African Studies,* vol. IX, no. 2.

Busia, K. A. (1951), *The Position of the Chief in the Modern Political System of Ashanti* (London: Oxford University Press).

Busia, K. A. (1954), 'The Ashanti of the Gold Coast', in D. Forde (ed.), *African Worlds* (Oxford University Press).

Caldwell, J. C. (1967), 'Population: general characteristics', in *A Study of Contemporary Ghana,* vol. 2: Some Aspects of Social Structure. W. Birmingham, I. Neustadt and E. N. Omaboe (eds.) pp. 17–177 (Evanston: Northwestern University Press).

Caldwell, J. C. (1968a), *Population Growth and Family Change in Africa: The New Urban Elite in Ghana* (Canberra: Australian National University Press).

Caldwell, J. C. (1968b), 'Determinants of rural–urban migration in Ghana', *Population Studies,* vol. 22, no. 3, November.

Caldwell, J. C. (1969), *African Rural–Urban Migration: The Movement to Ghana's Towns* (Canberra: Australian National University Press).

Caldwell, J. C., Addo, N. O., Gaisie, S. K., Igun, A., and Olusanya, P. O. (eds) (1975), *Population Growth and Socio-Economic Change in West Africa* (New York: Population Council).

Caldwell, J., and Caldwell, P. (1977), 'The role of marital sexual abstinence in determining fertility: a study of the Yoruba in Nigeria', *Population Studies,* vol. 31, no. 2, pp. 193–217.

Campbell, E. K. (1978), 'City-ward migration in Sierra Leone: determinants, consequences and policy implications', paper presented at the International Seminar on Integration of Theory and Policy in Population Studies, University of Ghana, Legon.

Cantrelle, P. (1965), 'Mortalité: facteurs', Part 5 of *Délégation générale à la recherche scientifique et technique, demographic comparée,* Afrique Noire, Madagascar, et Comores, Paris.

Cantrelle, P. (1975), 'Mortality: levels, patterns and trends', in Caldwell *et al.* (eds) (1975), pp. 98–118.

Case, F. I. (1977), 'The socio-cultural functions of women in the Senegalese novel', *Cultures et Développement,* no. 9, pp. 601–29.

Central Bureau of Statistics (1967–8), *Statistical Year Book* (Accra: Central Bureau of Statistics).

Changing African Family Project, Nigeria 2 (1974), *The Value of Children* (Canberra: Demography Department, Australian National University).

Church, K. V. (1978), 'Women and Family life in an Ashanti town', MA thesis, University of Ghana, Legon.

Clarke, R. (1843), *Sierra Leone* (London: James Ridgeway).

Clignet, R. (1970), *Many Wives, Many Powers: Authority and Power in Polygynous Families* (Evanston, Ill.: Northwestern University Press).

Cohen, A. (1969), *Custom and Politics in Urban Africa: A Study of Hausa Migrants in Yoruba Towns* (Calif.: University of California Press).

Cohen, A. (1971), 'Cultural strategies in the organisation of trading dia-sporas', in Meillassoux (ed.) (1971).

Cohen, R. (1967), *The Kanuri of Bornu* (New York: Holt, Rinehart & Winston).

Collins, E. J. (1976a), 'Comic opera in Ghana', *African Arts,* vol. 9, no. 2, pp. 50–7.

Collins, E. J. (1976b), 'Ghanaian highlife', *African Arts,* vol. 10, no. 1, pp. 62–8, 100.

Condé, J. (1980), 'Migration in Upper Volta', in 'Demographic aspects of migration in West Africa, vol. 2: French-speaking countries', World Bank Staff Working Paper, Washington, DC.

Côte d'Ivoire (République de) (1965a), *Etude socio-économique de la zone urbaine d'Abidjan, Rapport no 3: Etat de la population d'Abidjan en 1965, Tome I – Tableaux statistiques* (Abidjan: Société d'économie et de mathématiques appliquées).

Côte d'Ivoire (République de) (1965b), *Etude régionale de Bouaké, 1962–63, Tome I – Le Peuplement* (Abidjan: Ministère du plan).

Dahrendorf, F. (1957), *Class and Class Conflict in Industrial Society* (London: Routledge & Kegan Paul).

Danquah, J. B. (1922), *Cases in Akan Law* (London: George Routledge).

Danquah, J. B. (1928), *Akan Laws and Customs and the Akim Abuakwa Constitution* (London: George Routledge).

Darkwa, A. (1974), 'The new musical traditions in Ghana', Ph.D thesis, Wesleyan University, Middletown.

Date-Bah, E. (1972), 'Informal relations among the employees of a Ghanaian factory', *Ghana Social Science Journal,* vol. 2, no. 1, pp. 86–97.

Date-Bah, E. (1974), 'Societal influences on work behaviour and interaction of Ghanaian workers: a case study', Ph.D thesis, University of Birmingham.

Dawood, N. J. (1959), translation of *The Koran* (Harmondsworth, Middx: Penguin).

de Graft Johnson, K. T. (1978), 'Factors affecting labour force participation rates in Ghana, 1970', in G. Standing and G. Sheehan (eds), *Labour Force Participation in Low Income Countries* (Geneva: ILO), pp. 123–8.

Department of State (1978), *Background Notes: Ghana* (Washington, US: Government Printing Office).

Di Domenico, C. M. (1973), 'Nigerian industrial recruits: a case study of new workers at the Nigerian Tobacco Company factory at Ibadan', Ph.D thesis, Ibadan.

Dinan, C. (1977), 'Pragmatists or feminists? The professional single women in Accra, Ghana', *Cahiers d'études africaines,* vol. 17, no. 1, pp. 155–76.

Dobkin, M. (1968), 'Colonialism and the legal status of women in fran-cophone Africa', *Cahiers d'études africaines,* vol. 2, no. 8, pp. 390–405.

Doctor, K., and Gilles, H. (1966), 'Size and characteristics of wage employ-ment in Africa: some statistical estimates', *International Labour Review,* vol. 93, no. 1 (January), pp. 149–73.

Dole, G. (1972), 'Developmental sequences of kinship patterns', in Priscilla Reining (ed.), *Kinship Studies in the Morgan Centennial Year* (Washing-ton, DC: Anthropological Society of Washington), pp. 134–66.

Doornbos, M., and Cook, P. (n.d.), 'Rwenzuru protest songs', unpublished MS, Leiden.

Dow, T. (1977), 'Breastfeeding and abstinence among the Yoruba', *Studies in Family Planning*, vol. 8, no. 8, pp. 208–14.

Dwyer, D. H. (1978), *Images and Self-Images: Male and Female in Morocco* (New York: Columbia University Press).

Ebrahim, G. J. (1978), *Practical Mother and Child Health in Developing Countries* (London: English Language Book Society/Macmillan).

Economic Commission for Africa (1972), 'Women: the neglected human resource for African development', *Canadian Journal of African Studies*, vol. 6, no. 2, pp. 359–70.

Educational Statistics for Kano State 1975–76 (Kano: Government Printer).

Ejiogu, C. N. (1975), 'Metropolitanisation: the growth of Lagos', in Caldwell *et al.* (eds) (1975), pp. 308–20.

Elkan, W. (1955), *An African Labour Force*, East African Studies No. 7 (Kampala: East African Institute of Social Research).

Essomba, R. Abada (1974), *La Femme vue par Sembène Ousmane dans ses cinq premiers romans* (Yaoundé: Université de Yaoundé).

Etienne, M. (1976), *Women and Slaves: Stratification in an African Society: The Baule, Ivory Coast*, paper presented at the Seventy-fifth Annual Meeting of the American Anthropological Association, Washington, DC.

Etienne, M. (1979a), 'The case for social maternity: adoption of children by urban Baule women', *Dialectical Anthropology*, vol. 4, no. 3, pp. 237–41.

Etienne, M. (1979b), 'Maternité sociale, rapports d'adoption et pouvoir des femmes chez les Baoule (Côte d'Ivoire)', *L'Homme*, vol. 19, nos 3–4, pp. 63–107.

Etienne, M. (1980), 'Women and men, cloth and colonisation: the transformation of production-distribution relations among the Baule', in M. Etienne and E. Leacock (eds), *Women and Colonisation: Anthropological Perspectives* (New York: J. F. Bergin/Praeger), pp. 214–38.

Etienne, P., and Etienne, M. (1967), 'Terminologie de la parenté et de l'alliance chez les Baoule', *L'Homme*, vol. 7, no. 4, pp. 50–76.

Etienne, M., and Leacock, E. (1980), 'Women and anthropology: conceptual problems', introduction to Etienne and Leacock (eds), pp. 1–24.

Etienne, M., and Leacock, E. (1980) (eds), *Women and colonization: Anthropological Perspectives* (New York: J. F. Bergin/Praeger).

Evans-Pritchard, E. E. (1940), *The Nuer* (London: Oxford University Press).

Evans-Pritchard, E. E. (1965), *The Position of Women in Primitive Societies* (London: Faber).

Fabian, J. (1978), 'Popular culture in Africa: findings and conjectures', *Africa*, vol. 4, no. 48, pp. 315–34.

Fadipe, N. (1978), *The Sociology of the Yoruba* (1939) (Ibadan: University of Ibadan Press).

Fafunwa, A. B. (1974), *History of Education in Nigeria* (London: Allen & Unwin).

Fagbemi, S. O. (1978), 'Occupational and familial role conflicts of working women: a case study of the Lafia canning factory, Ibadan', B.Sc dissertation, Department of Sociology, University of Ibadan.

Fajana, A. (1978), *Education in Nigeria 1842–1939: An Historical Analysis* (Ikeja: Longman Nigeria).

Fapohunda, E. R. (1978), 'Women at work in Nigeria: factors affecting modern sector employment', in U. G. Damachi and V. P. Diejomaoh (eds), *Human Resources and African Development* (New York: Praeger), pp. 225–38.

Fapohunda, E. R. (1979), 'Population, labour utilisation and manpower development', in Olaloku *et al.* (eds) (1979).

Fikry, M. (1977), *Traditional Maternal and Child Health Care and Related Problems in the Sahel: A Bibliographic Study* (Ann Arbor, Mich.: United States Agency for International Development).

Finnegan, R. H. (1965), *Survey of the Limba People of Northern Sierra Leone,* Overseas Research Publication No. 8 (London: HMSO).

Finnegan, R. H. (1967), *Limba Stories and Story Telling* (Oxford: Clarendon Press).

Fortes, M. (1949a), *The Web of Kinship Among the Tallensi* (London: Oxford University Press).

Fortes, M. (1949b), 'Time and social structure: an Ashanti case study', in M. Fortes (ed.), *Social Structure Studies presented to A. R. Radcliffe-Brown* (Oxford: Clarendon Press), pp. 54–84.

Fortes, M. (1950), 'Kinship and marriage among the Ashanti', in A. Radcliffe-Brown and D. Forde (eds), *African Systems of Kinship and Marriage* (London: Oxford University Press).

Fortes, M. (1954), 'A demographic field study in Ashanti', in Lorimer, F. (ed.), *Culture and Human Fertility,* pp. 253–95 (Unesco: Paris).

Fortes, M. (1958), Introduction, in Goody J. (ed.) (Cambridge: Cambridge University Press).

Fortes, M. (1969), *Kinship and the Social Order: The Legacy of Lewis Henry Morgan* (Chicago: Aldine).

Fortes, M. (1970), *Time and Social Structure and Other Essays* (London: Athlone Press).

Fortes, M. (1980), 'Informants', *L'Uomo,* vol. IV, no. 2, p. 363.

François, M. (1975), 'Gabon', in Caldwell *et al.* (eds) (1975), pp. 630–56.

Gluckman, M. (1950), 'Kinship and marriage among the Lozi of northern Rhodesia and Zulu of Natal', in A. Radcliffe-Brown and D. Forde (eds), *African Systems of Kinship and Marriage* (London: Oxford University Press).

Gluckman, M. (1968), 'The utility of the equilibrium model in the study of social change', *American Anthropologist,* 70, pp. 219–37.

Goody, E. N. (1962), 'Conjugal separation and divorce among the Gonja of northern Ghana', in Fortes (ed.) (1962), *Marriage in Tribal Societies* (Cambridge: Cambridge University Press), pp. 14–54.

Goody, E. N. (1969), 'Kinship fostering in Gonja', in P. Mayer (ed.), *Socialisation: The Approach from Social Anthropology,* ASA Monograph No. 8 (London: Tavistock), pp. 51–74.

Goody, E. N. (1971), 'Forms of pro-parenthood: the sharing and substitution of parental roles', in J. Goody (ed.), *Kinship* (Harmondsworth, Middx: Penguin), pp. 331–45.

Goody, E. N. (1973), *Contexts of Kinship* (Cambridge: Cambridge University Press).

Goody, E. N. (1978), 'Some theoretical and empirical aspects of parenthood in West Africa' in Oppong *et al.* (eds) (1978), pp. 227–73.

Goody, J. (1971), 'Class and marriage in Africa and Eurasia', *American Journal of Sociology,* No. LXXVI, 4 January, pp. 585–603.

Goody, J. (1973), 'Bridewealth and dowry in Africa and Eurasia', in J. Goody and S. J. Tambiah (eds), *Bridewealth and Dowry* (Cambridge: Cambridge University Press), pp. 1–58.

Goody, J. (ed.) (1958), *The Developmental Cycle in Domestic Groups* (Cambridge: Cambridge University Press).

Goody, J. (ed.) (1969), *Comparative Studies in Kinship* (London: Routledge & Kegan Paul).

Goody, J. (ed.) (1975), *Changing Social Structure in Ghana: Essays in the Comparative Sociology of a New State and an Old Tradition* (London: International African Institute).

Goody, J., and Goody, E. (1969), 'The circulation of women and children in northern Ghana', in J. Goody (ed.) (1969), pp. 184–215.

Gough, K. (1975), 'The origin of the family', in Reiter (ed.) (1975), pp. 51–76.

Green, M. (1964), *Igbo Village Affairs* (London: Frank Cass).

Greenstreet, M. (1972), 'Social change and Ghanaian women', *Canadian Journal of African Studies,* vol. VI, no. 2, pp. 351–5.

Gugler, J., and Flanagan, G. W. (1978), *Urbanisation and Social Change in West Africa* (Cambridge: Cambridge University Press).

Hafkin, N. J., and Bay, E. G. (eds) (1976), *Women in Africa: Studies in Social and Economic Change* (Stanford, Calif.: Stanford University Press).

Halpenny, P. (1975), 'Three styles of ethnic migration in Kisenyi, Kampala', in David Parkin (ed.), *Town and Country in Central and Eastern Africa* (London: International African Institute/Oxford University Press), pp. 276–87.

Hamilton, R. (1978), *The Liberation of Women: A Study of Patriarchy and Capitalism* (London: Allen & Unwin).

Hammel, E. A., and Laslett, P. (1974), 'Comparing household structure over time and between cultures', *Comparative Studies in Society and History,* vol. 16, pp. 73–109.

Hammond, T. N. (1976), 'The image of women in Senegalese fiction', Ph.D thesis, University of New York, Buffalo.

Hance, W. A. (1970), *Population, Migration and Urbanisation in Africa* (New York: Columbia University Press).

Handwerker, W. P. (1973), 'Kinship, friendship and business failure among market sellers in Monrovia, Liberia, 1970', *Africa,* vol. XLIII, no. 4, pp. 288–301.

Harrell-Bond, B. (1975), *Modern Marriage in Sierra Leone: A Study of the Professional Group* (The Hague: Mouton).

Harrington, J. (1978), 'Some micro-socioeconomics of female status in Nigeria', paper presented at a conference, 'Women in Poverty: What Do We Know?', International Centre for Research on Women (Washington).

Hauser, P. (ed.) (1979), *World Population and Development: Challenges and Prospects* (Syracuse: Syracuse University Press).

Hill, P. (1969), 'Hidden trade in Hausaland', *Man,* vol. 4, no. 3, pp. 392–409.

Hill, P. (1971), 'The types of West African house trade', in Meillassoux (ed.) (1971), pp. 303–18.

Hill, P. (1972), *Rural Hausa: A Village and a Setting* (Cambridge: Cambridge University Press).

Hill, P. (1977), *Population, Prosperity and Poverty: Rural Kano 1900 and 1970* (Cambridge: Cambridge University Press).

Hiskett, M. (1975), 'Islamic education in the traditional and state systems in northern Nigeria', in G. N. Brown and M. Hiskett (eds), *Conflict and Harmony in Education in Tropical Africa* (London: Allen & Unwin), pp. 134–51.

Hodder, B. W., and Ukwu, U. I. (1969), *Markets in West Africa: Studies of Markets and Trade Among the Yoruba and Ibo* (Ibadan: University of Ibadan Press).

Hoffer, C. P. (1972), 'Mende and Sherbo women in high office', *Canadian Journal of African Studies,* vol. 6, no. 2, pp. 151–64.

Hogben, S. J., and Kirke Greene, A. H. M. (1966), *The Emirates of Northern Nigeria: A Preliminary Survey of Their Historical Traditions* (Oxford: Oxford University Press).

Hubbard, J. P. (1975), 'Government and Islamic education in northern Nigeria (1900–1940)', in G. N. Brown and M. Hiskett (eds), *Conflict and Harmony in Education in Tropical Africa* (London: Allen & Unwin), pp. 152–67.

Imoagene, O. (1976), *Social Mobility in Emergent Society: A Study of the New Elite in Western Nigeria,* The Changing African Family Project Series, Monograph No. 2 (Canberra: Demography Department, Australian National University).

International Labour Organisation (1975), *ILO Tripartite Regional Seminar on the Situation of Migrant Workers in West Africa.* Report of the Seminar, Geneva.

International Labour Organisation (various years), *Year-book of Labour Statistics* (Geneva: ILO).

Jiagge, A. (1974), 'Necessary new social legislation', paper presented at a seminar, 'The Demographic Implications of Women's Participation in Society' (sponsored by the United Nations Fund for Population Activities), Accra.

Johnson, S. (1966), *The History of the Yorubas from Earliest Times to the Beginning of the British Protectorate* (London: Routledge).

Joshi, H., Lubell, H., and Mouly, J. (1976), *Abidjan: Urban Development and Employment in the Ivory Coast* (Geneva: ILO).

Kaberry, P. M. (1952), *Women of the Grassfields: A Study of the Economic Position of Women in Bamenda, British Cameroons,* Colonial Office, Research Publication No. 14 (London : Colonial Office).

Karanja-Diejomaoh, W., and Scott, J. (1976), 'Social structure, economic independence and the status of Nigerian women: the dialectics of power', paper presented at a conference on Women in Development, Ibadan University, Nigeria.

Katcha, A. (1978), *An Exploratory Demographic Study of the Nupe of Nigeria* (Canberra: Australian National University Press).

Kilson, M. (1977), 'Women and African literature', *Journal of African Studies,* no. 4, pp. 161–6.

King, K. (1977), *The African Artisan: Education and the Informal Sector in Kenya* (New York: Teachers College Press).

Kleinkowski, H. (1976), 'Women's organisations and their contribution to development in Ghana: with special reference to the Christian Mothers' Association', MA thesis, Reading University.

Koll, M. (1969), *Crafts and Cooperation in Western Nigeria: A Sociological Contribution to Indigenous Economics* (Groiburg: Arnold-Bergstraesser-Institut).

Kumekpor, T. K. (1974), 'Mothers and wage labour employment: some aspects of problems of the working mother in Accra', *Ghana Journal of Sociology,* vol. 7, no. 2, pp. 68–91.

Lamphere, L. (1974), 'Strategies of cooperation and conflict among women in domestic groups', in Rosaldo and Lamphere (eds), pp. 79–112.

Laslett, P. (1972), 'Introduction: The history of the family, in *Household and Family in Past Time,* pp. 1–89, P. Laslett and R. Wall (eds) (Cambridge: Cambridge University Press).

Laws, J. L. (1976), 'Work aspirations of women: false leads and new starts', *Signs,* vol. 1, no. 3, pt 2, pp. 33–49.

Lawson, R. M. (1968), 'The transition of Ghana's fishing', *Transactions of the Historical Society of Ghana,* vol. IX.

Lawson, R. M. (1972), *The Changing Economy of the Lower Volta 1954–67* (London: Oxford University Press).

Lawson, R. M., and Kwei, E. A. (1974), *African Entrepreneurship and Economic Growth. A Case Study of the Fishing Industry of Ghana* (Accra: Ghana Universities Press).

Lebeuf, A. (1963), 'Women in political organisation', in Paulme (ed.), pp. 93–120.

Lee, S. M. (1974), 'L'image de la femme dans le roman francophone de l'Afrique occidentale', in Ph.D thesis, University of Massachusetts.

Leith-Ross, S. (1965), *African Women* (London: Routledge & Kegan Paul).

Lele, U. (1975), *The Design of Rural Development: Lessons from Africa* (Baltimore, Md: Johns Hopkins University Press).

Lesthaeghe, R., *et al.* (1979), 'Anthropological references', paper presented at African Traditional Birth Spacing Workshop, Brussels.

Lewis, B. (1976), 'The limitations of group action among entrepreneurs: the market women of Abidjan, Ivory Coast', in Hafkin and Bay (eds), (1976) pp. 135–56.

Lewis, B. (1977), 'Economic activity and marriage among Ivoirian urban women', in A. Schlegel (ed.), *Sexual Stratification: A Cross Cultural View* (New York: Columbia University Press).

Lewis, I. M. (1971), *Ecstatic Religion* (Harmondsworth, Mddx: Penguin).

Lippert, A. (1972), 'The changing role of women as viewed in the literature of English- and French-speaking West Africa', Ph.D thesis, University of Indiana.

Little, K. (1970), *West African Urbanisation: A Study of Voluntary Associations in Social Change* (Cambridge: Cambridge University Press).

Little, K. (1973), African Women in Towns: An Aspect of Africa's Social Revolution (Cambridge: Cambridge University Press).

Little, K. (1975), 'Some methodological considerations in the study of

African women's urban roles', *Urban Anthropology*, vol. 4, no 2 (Summer), pp. 107–21.

Little, K. (1977), 'Women's strategies in modern marriage in anglophone West Africa: an ideological and sociological appraisal', *Journal of Comparative Family Studies,* vol. VIII, no. 3 (Autumn), pp. 341–56.

Locoh, T. (1978), 'Conséquences de la baisse de la mortalité sur l'évolution des structures familiales africaines', in Oppong *et al.* (eds) (1978).

Lowy, M. J. (1977), 'Establishing paternity and demanding child support in a Ghanaian town', in Roberts (ed.), *Law and the Family in Africa* (The Hague: Mouton).

Mabogunje, A. L. (1975), 'Migration and urbanisation', in Caldwell *et al.* (eds) (1975), pp. 153–68.

Malinowski, B. (1913), *The Family Among the Australian Aborigines* (London: London University Press).

Manoukian, M. (1950), 'Akan and Ga-Adangme peoples', in D. Forde (ed.), *Ethnographic Survey of Africa: Western Africa,* Part 1 (London: International African Institute).

Marris, P. (1961), *Family and Social Change in an African City: A Study of Rehousing in Lagos* (London: Routledge & Kegan Paul).

Marx, K. (1965), *Pre-Capitalist Economic Formations,* with an introduction by E. J. Hobsbawn (New York: International Publishers).

McCall, D. (1961), 'Trade and the role of wife in a modern West African town', in Southall (ed.) (1961), pp. 286–99.

Meek, C. K. (1937), *Law and Authority in a Nigerian Tribe: A Study in Indirect Rule* (London: Oxford University Press).

Meillassoux, C. (ed.) (1971), *The Development of Indigenous Trade and Markets in West Africa* (London: Oxford University Press).

Mensah, E. (1977), 'A note on the distribution of beggars in Zaria', *Savanna,* vol. 6, no. 1, pp. 73–6.

Mernissi, F. (1975), *Beyond the Veil: Male–Female Dynamics in a Modern Muslim Society* (Cambridge, Mass.: Schenkman).

Mohammed, A. (1980), 'Home outside the home (a sociological conception of prostitution among the Hausa)', Seminar paper. Department of Sociology, Bayero University, Kano.

Morgan, R. (1970), *Sisterhood Is Powerful* (New York: Vintage Books).

Mullings, L. (1976), 'Women and economic change in Africa', in Hafkin and Bay (eds) (1976), pp. 239–64.

Murdock, G. (1967), *Ethnographic Atlas* (Pittsburg, Pa: University of Pittsburg Press).

Mutiso, G. C. M. (1971), 'Women in African literature', *East African Journal,* no. 8, pp. 4–14.

Nelson, N. (1977), 'Dependence and independence: female household heads in Mathare valley, a squatter community', Ph.D thesis, University of London.

North, J. (1975), 'The sociological, economic and legal status of women in Ghana', in US Agency for International Development Ghana (ed.), *Women in National Development in Ghana,* mimeo., Accra, pp. 2–12.

Obbo, C. (1975), 'Women's careers in low income areas as indicators of country and town dynamics', in David Parkin (ed.), *Town and Country in*

Central and Eastern Africa (London: Oxford University Press International African Institute), pp. 288–93.

Ogunbiyi, I.A. (1969), 'The position of Muslim women as stated by Uthman b. Fudi', *Odu,* no. 2, pp. 43–61.

Ogunsola, A. F. (1974), *Legislation and Education in Northern Nigeria* (Ibadan: Oxford University Press).

Okali, C. (1975), *Dominase: A Mobile Cocoa Farming Community in Brong Ahafo,* Technical Publication Series No. 35 (Legon: Institute for Social Statistical and Economic Research).

Okali, C. (1976), 'The importance of non-economic variables in the development of the Ghana cocoa-industry: a field study of cocoa-farming amongst the Akan', Ph.D thesis, University of Ghana.

Okali, C., and Kotey, R. A. (1971), *Akokoaso: A Resurvey,* Technical Publication Series No. 15 (Legon: ISSER).

Okali, C., and Mabey, S. (1975), 'Women in agriculture in southern Ghana', *Manpower and Unemployment Research in Africa,* vol. 8, no. 2 (November), pp. 13–41.

Oloko, B. A. (1979), 'Socio-cultural correlates of school achievement in Nigeria', Ph.D thesis, Harvard University.

Omari, P. (1960), 'Changing attitudes of students in West African society towards marriage and family relationships', *British Journal of Sociology,* 11 September.

Omari, P. (1962), *Marriage Guidance for Young Ghanaians* (Edinburgh: Nelson).

Omolulu, O. (1974), 'L'importance de l'allaitement maternel', *Afrique médicale,* no. 120, pp. 485–7.

Oppong, C. (1970), 'Conjugal power and resources: an urban African example', *Journal of Marriage and the Family,* vol. 32, no. 4, pp. 676–80.

Oppong, C. (1972), 'A note on matriliny and marriage in Accra', *Journal of Asian and African Studies,* vol. VII, nos 3–4, pp. 211–18.

Oppong, C. (1973), *Growing up in Dagbon* (Accra: Ghana Publishing Corporation).

Oppong, C. (1980), *A Synopsis of Seven Roles and Status of Women,* WEP Research Working Paper No. 94 (Geneva: ILO).

Oppong, C. (1982), *Middle Class African Marriage* (London: Allen & Unwin): first published as *Marriage among a Matrilineal Elite,* Cambridge Studies in Social Anthropology No. 8 (Cambridge: Cambridge University Press, 1974).

Oppong, C. (ed.) (1974), *Domestic Rights and Duties in Southern Ghana,* Legon Family Research Papers No. 1 (Legon: Institute of African Studies).

Oppong, C. (ed.) (1975), *Changing Family Studies,* Legon Family Research Papers No. 3 (Legon: Institute of African Studies).

Oppong, C., with C. Okali and B. Houghton (1975), 'Woman power: retrograde steps in Ghana', *African Studies Review,* vol. XVIII, no. 3.

Oppong, C., and G. Adaba, M. Bekombo-Priso and J. Mogey (eds) (1978), *Marriage, Parenthood and Fertility in West Africa* (Canberra: Australian National University Press).

Oppong, C., with E. Haavio Mannila (1979), 'Women, population and development', in Hauser (ed.) (1979), pp. 440–85.

Orubuloye, I. O., and Caldwell, J. C. (1975), 'The impact of public health services on mortality: a study of mortality differentials in rural area of Nigeria', *Population Studies*, vol. 29, no. 2, pp. 259–72.

Otite, O. (1979), 'Rural migrants as catalysts in rural development: the Urhobo in Ondo State, Nigeria', *Africa*, vol. 49, no. 3, pp. 226–34.

Ottenberg, S., and Ottenberg, P. (eds) (1969), *Cultures and Societies of Africa* (New York: Random House).

Paden, J. (1973), *Religion and Political Culture in Kano* (Berkeley, Calif.: University of California Press).

Page, H. J., and Lesthaeghe, R. (1981), *Child Spacing in Tropical Africa* (London: Academic Press).

Paulme, D. (ed.) (1963), *Women of Tropical Africa* (translated) (Berkeley, Calif.: University of California Press).

Peace, A. (1979), *Choice, Class and Conflict: A Study of Southern Nigerian Factory Workers* (Brighton, Sussex: Harvester Press).

Peil, M. (1966), *The Ghanaian Factory Worker: Industrial Man in Africa* (Cambridge: Cambridge University Press).

Peil, M. (1975), 'Female roles in West African towns', in J. Goody (ed.) pp. 73–90.

Peil, M. (1979), 'Urban women in the labour force', *Sociology of Work and Occupations*, no. 6, pp. 482–501.

Pellow, D. (1977). *Women in Accra: Options for Autonomy* (Algonac, Mich.: Reference Publications).

Pittin, R. (1979), 'Marriage and alternative strategies: career patterns of Hausa women in Katsina City', Ph.D thesis, University of London.

Pogucki, R. J. H. (1955), *Gold Coast Land Tenure, Vol. IV: Land Tenure in Ga Customary Law*. Map supplement Accra 1836–1954 (Accra Gold Coast Lands Department).

Population Census of Nigeria, Northern Region Vol. II. (1963) (Lagos: Federal Office of Statistics).

Post, K. W. J. (1963), *The Nigerian Federal Election of 1959: Politics and Administration in a Developing Political System* (London: Oxford University Press).

Priestly, M. (1969), *West African Trade and Coast Society: A Family Study* (London: Oxford University Press).

Rattray, R. S. (1913), *Hausa Folk-Lore*, Vol. I (London: Oxford University Press).

Rattray, R. S. (1923), *Ashanti* (London: Oxford University Press).

Rattray, R. S. (1927), *Religion and Art in Ashanti* (London: Oxford University Press).

Rattray, R. S. (1929), *Ashanti Law and Constitution* (Oxford: Clarendon Press: 2nd edn, 1969).

Raulin, J. (1967), 'Commentaire socio-ethnologique', *Démographie comparée* (Paris: INSEE. INED).

Raynaut, C. (1968), 'Aspects socio-economiques de la preparation et la circulation de la nourriture dans un village Hausa (Niger)', *Cahiers d'etudes africaines*, vol. 17, no. 4, pp. 569–97.

Reiter, R. R. (ed.) (1975), *Toward an Anthropology of Women* (New York: Monthly Review Press).

Remy, D. (1975), 'Underdevelopment and the experience of women: a Nigerian case study', in Reiter (ed.) (1975), pp. 358–71.

Retel-Laurentin, A. (1974), *Infécondité en Afrique noire: maladies et conséquences sociales* (Paris: Masson).

Robertson, C. (1974), 'Economic women in Africa: profit-making techniques of Accra market women', *Journal of Modern African Studies*, no. 12, pp. 657–64.

Robertson, C. (1976), 'Ga women and socioeconomic change in Accra, Ghana', in Hafkin and Bay (eds) (1976), pp. 111–33.

Rogers, Susan C. (1975), 'Female forms of power and the myth of male dominance: a model of female/male interaction in peasant society', *American Ethnologist*, no. 2, pp. 727–57.

Rosaldo, M. Z., and Lamphere, L. (eds) (1974), *Women Culture and Society* (Stanford, California: Stanford University Press).

Rosen, L. (1978). 'The negotiation of reality: male–female relations in Sefrou, Morocco', in L. Beck and N. Keddie (eds), *Women in the Muslim World* (Cambridge, Mass.: Harvard University Press), pp. 561–84.

Rourke, B. E. (1974), 'Profitability of cocoa and alternative crops in Eastern Region, Ghana', in R. A. Kotey, C. Okali and B. E. Rourke (eds), *The Economics of Cocoa Production and Marketing* (Legon: Institute for Social Statistical and Economic Research), pp. 20–46.

Sanday, P. R. (1974), 'Female Status in the Public Domain', in Rosaldo and Lamphere (eds).

Sanjek, R. (1976), 'New perspectives on West African women', *Reviews in Anthropology*, vol. 3, no. 2 (March/April).

Sanjek, R. (1977), 'Cognitive maps of the ethnic domain in urban Ghana: reflections on variability and change', *American Ethnologist*, no. 4, pp. 603–22.

Sanjek, R. (1978), 'A network method and its uses in urban ethnography', *Human Organization*, no. 37, pp. 257–68.

Sanjek, R. (1979), 'The organization of households in Adabraka, Ghana: towards a wider comparative perspective', paper presented at the National Council on Family Relations Conference, Boston, August.

Sanjek, R., and Sanjek, L. (1976), 'Notes on women and work in Adabraka', *African Urban Notes*, vol. 2, no. 2, pp. 1–27.

Sankale, M. (1969), *Médecins et action sanitaire en Afrique noire* (Paris: Présence africaine).

Sarbah, J. M. (1897), *Fante Customary Laws* (London: Cloves & Sons).

Schildkrout, E. (1973), 'The fostering of children in urban Ghana: problems of ethnographic analysis in a multi-cultural context', *Urban Anthropology*, vol. 2, no. 1, pp. 48–73.

Schildkrout, E. (1978a), 'Age and gender in Hausa society: socio-economic roles of children in urban Kano', in J. S. LaFontaine (ed.), *Sex and Age as Principals of Social Differentiation* (New York: Academic Press), pp. 109–37.

Schildkrout, E. (1978b), *People of the Zongo: the transformation of ethnic identities in Ghana* (Cambridge: Cambridge University Press).

Schildkrout, E. (1979), 'Women's work and children's work: variations among Moslems in Kano', in S. Wallman (ed.), *Social Anthropology of Work*, ASA Monograph No. 19 (London: Academic Press), pp. 69–85.

Schildkrout, E. (1981), 'The employment of children in Kano, Nigeria, in G. Rodgers and G. Standing (eds), *Participation or Exploitation? The Economic Roles of Children in Low-Income Countries* (Geneva: ILO), pp. 81–112.

Schlegel, A. (ed.) (1977), *Sexual Stratification: A Cross-Cultural View* (New York: Columbia University Press).

Schuster, I. M. G. (1979), *New Women of Lusaka* (Palo Alto, Calif.: Mayfield).

Sethauraman, S. V. (1977), 'The urban informal sector in Africa', *International Labour Review*, vol. 116, no. 3 (November–December), pp. 343–52.

Simmons, N. (1972), 'Croyances badyaranké concernant certains animaux', *Objets et mondes*, vol. 12, no. 4, pp. 409–10.

Simms, R., and Dumor, E. (1976–7), 'Women in the urban economy of Ghana: associational activity and the enclave economy', *African Urban Notes*, vol. II, no. 3, pt 2 (Fall–Winter), pp. 43–52.

Skinner, N. (1969), *Hausa Tales and Traditions*, Vol. I (London: Frank Cass).

Sklar, L. R. (1963), *Nigerian Political Parties* (Princeton, NJ: Princeton University Press).

Smedley, A. (1974), 'Women of Udu: survival in a harsh land', in C. Mattiasson (ed.), *Many Sisters: Women in a Cross-Cultural Perspective* (New York: The Free Press).

Smith, M. F. (1954), *Baba of Karo: A Woman of the Muslim Hausa* (London: Faber).

Smith, M. G. (1952), 'A study of Hausa domestic economy in northern Zaria', *Africa*, no. 22, pp. 333–47.

Smith, M. G. (1954), introduction in M. F. Smith, *Baba of Karo: A Woman of the Muslim Hausa* (London: Faber).

Smith, M. G. (1955), *The Economy of the Hausa Communities of Zaria*, Colonial Research Studies No. 16 (London: HMSO).

Smith, M. G. (1959), 'The Hausa system of social status', *Africa*, vol. 29, no. 3, pp. 239–52.

Smith, M. G. (1962), 'Exchange and marketing among the Hausa', in P. Bohannan and G. Dalton (eds), *Markets in Africa* (Evanston, Ill.: Northwestern University Press), pp. 299–334.

Smith, R. T. (1956), *The Negro Family in British Guiana* (London: Routledge and Kegan Paul).

Songre, A. (1973), 'Mass emigration from Upper Volta: the facts and implications', in *Employment in Africa: Some Critical Issues* (Geneva: ILO).

Southall, A. W. (ed.) (1961), *Social Change in Modern Africa* (London: Oxford University Press).

Standing, G. (1976), 'Education and female participation in the labour force', *International Labour Review*, vol. 114, no. 3 (November–December).

Standing, G., and Sheehan, G. (eds) (1978), 'Economic activity of women in Nigeria', in G. Standing and G. Sheehan (eds), *Labour Force Participation in Low Income Countries* (Geneva: ILO), pp. 129–36.

Steel, William F. (1977), 'The small-scale sector's role in growth, income distribution and employment of women', paper presented at the African Studies Association Twentieth Annual Meeting, Houston, Texas, 2–5 November.

Sudarkasa, N. (1973), *Where Women Work: A Study of Yoruba Women in the Marketplace and in the Home*, Museum of Anthropology, Anthropological Papers No. 53 (Ann Arbor, Mich: University of Michigan).

Sudarkasa, N. (1974), 'From stranger to alien: a case study of the Nigerian Yoruba in Ghana 1900–1970', mimeo., University of Michigan, Ann Arbor.

Sweeney, J., and Clignet, R. (1978), 'Female matrimonial roles and fertility in Africa', in Oppong *et al*. (eds) (1978).

Tait, D. (1961), *The Konkomba of Northern Ghana* (London: Oxford University Press).

Talbot, P. (1915), *Woman's Mysteries of a Primitive People: The Ibibios of Southern Nigeria* (London: Cassell).

Talbot, P. (1932), *Tribes of the Niger Delta: Their Religions and Customs* (London: Sheldon Press).

Tetteh, P. A. (1967), 'Marriage, family and household', in W. Birmingham, I. Neustadt and E. N. Omaboe (eds), *A Study of Contemporary Ghana*, Vol. 2 (London: Allen & Unwin), pp. 201–16.

Trevitt, L. (1973), 'Attitudes and customs in child birth amongst Hausa women in Zaria City, Nigeria', *Savanna*, vol. 2, no. 2.

Trevor, J. (1975). 'Family change in Sokoto: a traditional Moslem Fulani/Hausa city', in Caldwell *et al*. (eds) (1975), pp. 236–53.

Trimingham, J. S. (1959), *Islam in West Africa* (Oxford: Clarendon Press).

Unesco Statistical Yearbook (Various years) (Paris: Unesco).

United Nations Demographic Yearbook (various years) (New York: UN).

United Nations Economic Commission for Africa (1963), *Women in the Traditional African Societies* (Addis Ababa: Workshop on Urban Problems).

United Nations Economic Commission for Africa (1971), 'Spatial redistribution of population in Africa (colonisation, resettlement and urbanisation)', paper presented at African Population Conference, Accra, December.

United Nations Economic Commission for Africa (1973), *Nigeria Country Report on Vocational Training Opportunities for Girls and Women* (Addis Ababa: UN Economic Commission for Africa, Women's Programme Unit).

United Nations Economic Commission for Africa (1977), *The New International Economic Order: What Roles for Women*, Addis Ababa, August.

Van Allen, J. (1972), ' "Sitting on a man" colonialism and the lost political institutions of Igbo women', *Canadian Journal of African Studies*, vol. 6, no. 2, pp. 165–82.

Van der Geest, S. (1974), 'Family dynamics in a changing society. A case of a rural Ghanaian community', M.Sc thesis, University of Ghana, Legon.

Van der Geest, S. (1975), 'Appearance and reality, the ambiguous position of women in Kwahu', in P. Kloos and K. W. van der Voen (eds), *Rule and Reality: Essays in Honour of André J. F. Kobben* (Amsterdam: University of Amsterdam).

Van der Geest, S. (1980), 'The image of death in Akan high life songs of Ghana', *Research in African Literature*, ii (2), 145–74.

Van Ginneken, J. K. (1977), 'The chance of conception during lactation', in *Fertility Regulation During Human Lactation, Journal of Biosocial Science* Supplement No. 4, pp. 41–54.

Vellenga, D. D. (1974), 'Changing sex roles and social tensions in Ghana: the law as measure and mediator of family conflict', Ph.D thesis, Columbia University.

Vellenga, D. D. (1977), 'Attempts to change the marriage laws in Ghana and the Ivory Coast', in P. Foster and A. Zolberg (eds), *Ghana and the Ivory Coast: Perspectives on Modernisation* (Chicago: Chicago University Press).

Vercruijsse, E. (1972), *The Dynamics of Fanti Domestic Organisation, A Comparison with Fanti Ashanti*, Survey Research Report Series No. 12, Social Studies Project, University of Cape Coast.

Vercruijsse, E. (1974), 'Composition of households in some Fanti communities: a study of the framework of social integration', in Oppong (ed.) (1974), pp. 35–56.

Vidal, C. (1977), 'Guerre des sexes à Abidjan. Masculin, féminin, CFA', *Cahiers d'études africaines*, vol. 17, no. 1, pp. 121–53.

Wallace, C. C. (1978), 'The concept of *Gandu*: how useful is it in understanding labour relations in rural Hausa society?', *Savanna*, vol. 7, no. 2, pp. 137–50.

Ware, H. (1977), 'Women's work and fertility in Africa', in S. Kupinsky (eds), *The Fertility of Working Women: A Synthesis of International Research* (New York: Praeger), pp. 1–34.

Ware, H. (1979), 'Polygyny: women's views in a transitional society, Nigeria 1975', *Journal of Marriage and the Family*, vol. 41, no. 1, pp. 185–95.

West Africa (1979a), 'Nigeria: blueprint for education', 19 November, pp. 2127–8.

West Africa (1979b), Nigerian education blueprint – II', 26 November, pp. 2178–9.

West Africa (1979c), 'Education blueprint for Nigeria – III', 3 December, pp. 2234–7.

Wilks, I. (1975), *Asante in the Nineteenth Century: the Structure and Evolution of a Political Order* (Cambridge: Cambridge University Press).

Williamson, N. (1976), *Sons or Daughters: A Cross-Cultural Survey of Parental Preferences* (Beverly Hills, Calif.: Sage).

World Health Organisation (1979), *WHO Collaborative Study on Breastfeeding: Methods and Main Results of the First Phase of the Study, Preliminary Report*, MCH/79/3 (Geneva: ILO).

Wright Mills, C. (1959), *The Sociological Imagination* (London: Oxford University Press).

Zachariah, K. C. (1980a), 'Migration in the Gambia', in 'Demographic aspects of migration in West Africa, vol. 1: English-speaking countries', World Bank Staff Working Paper, Washington, DC.

Zachariah, K. C. (1980b), 'Migration in the Ivory Coast', in 'Demographic aspects of migration in West Africa, vol. 2: French-speaking countries', World Bank Staff Working Paper, Washington, DC.

Zachariah, K. C., and Condé, J. (1978), 'International migration in West

Africa – demographic and economic aspects', in International Union for the Scientific Study of Population, *Economic and Demographic Change: Issues for the 1980s*, Proceedings of the Conference, Helsinki, Vol. 3, Liège.

Zachariah, K. C., and Condé, J. (1980), *Migration in West Africa: The Demographic Aspects* (London: Oxford University Press).

Zachariah, K. C., and Nair, N. K. (1980a), 'Demographic aspects of recent international and internal migration in Ghana', in 'Demographic aspects of migration in West Africa, vol. 1: English-speaking countries', World Bank Staff Working Paper, Washington, DC.

Zachariah, K. C., and Nair, N. K. (1980b), 'Senegal: patterns of internal international migration in recent years', in 'Demographic aspects of migration in West Africa, vol. 2: French-speaking countries', World Bank Staff Working Paper, Washington, DC.

Zachariah, K. C., and Nair, N. K. (1980c), 'Togo: external and internal migration', in 'Demographic aspects of migration in West Africa, vol. 2: French-speaking countries', World Bank Staff Working Paper, Washington, DC.

Zerbe, E. A. (1974), 'Veil of shame: role of women in the modern fiction of North Africa and the Arab world', Ph.D thesis, University of Indiana.

Index